Shojo Beat

kimi ni todoke
From Me to You

Vol. 10

Story & Art by
Karuho Shiina

Volume 10

Contents

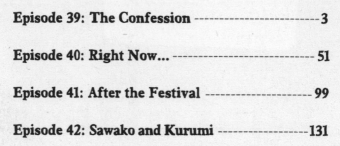

Story Thus Far

Sawako Kuronuma has always been a loner. Though not by choice, this optimistic girl can't seem to make any friends. Stuck with the unfortunate nickname "Sadako" after the haunting movie character, rumors about her summoning spirits have been greatly exaggerated. With her shy personality and scary looks, most of her classmates will barely talk to her, much less look into her eyes for more than three seconds lest they be cursed. Thanks to Kazehaya, who always treats her nicely, Sawako makes her first friends at school, Ayane and Chizu. Since Sawako is not used to people being nice to her, she is confused about Kazehaya's feelings toward her and is unable to bring herself to give him chocolate on Valentine's Day.

Sawako turns 16. Kento, a new classmate, is very friendly toward her. Kazehaya feels the need to tell Sawako about his feelings for her and does it in front of everyone. Sawako misunderstands and thinks Kazehaya is just being nice and tells everyone not to take it the wrong way. Kazehaya takes her reply as a rejection and begins keeping his distance from her. Sawako is dejected, but with some support from Ayane and Chizu, she decides to tell Kazehaya about her feelings and runs to him...

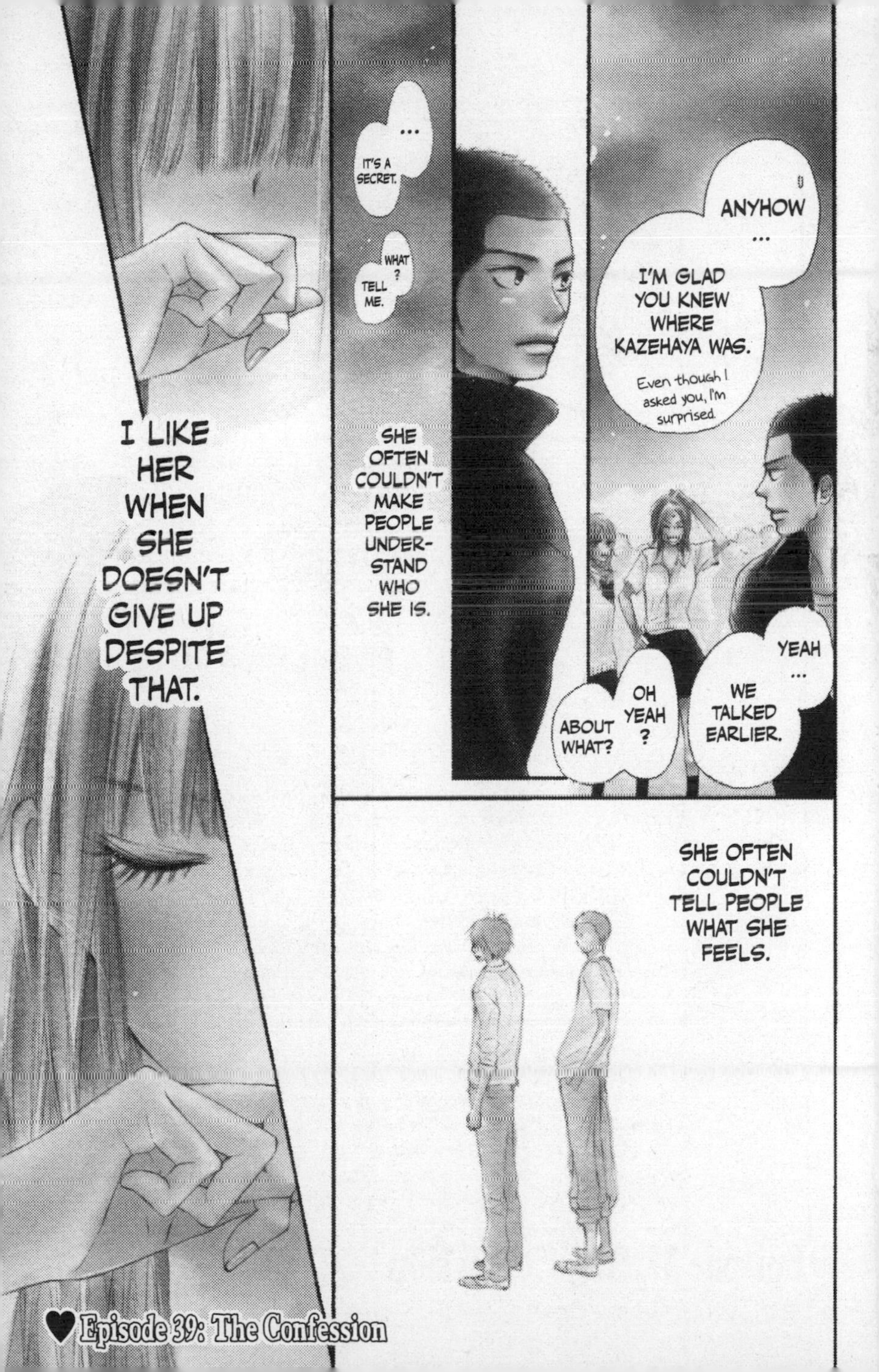
ANYHOW ...
I'M GLAD YOU KNEW WHERE KAZEHAYA WAS.
Even though I asked you, I'm surprised.
YEAH ... WE TALKED EARLIER.
OH YEAH ?
ABOUT WHAT?
...
IT'S A SECRET.
WHAT ?
TELL ME.
SHE OFTEN COULDN'T MAKE PEOPLE UNDER-STAND WHO SHE IS.
SHE OFTEN COULDN'T TELL PEOPLE WHAT SHE FEELS.
I LIKE HER WHEN SHE DOESN'T GIVE UP DESPITE THAT.
Episode 39: The Confession

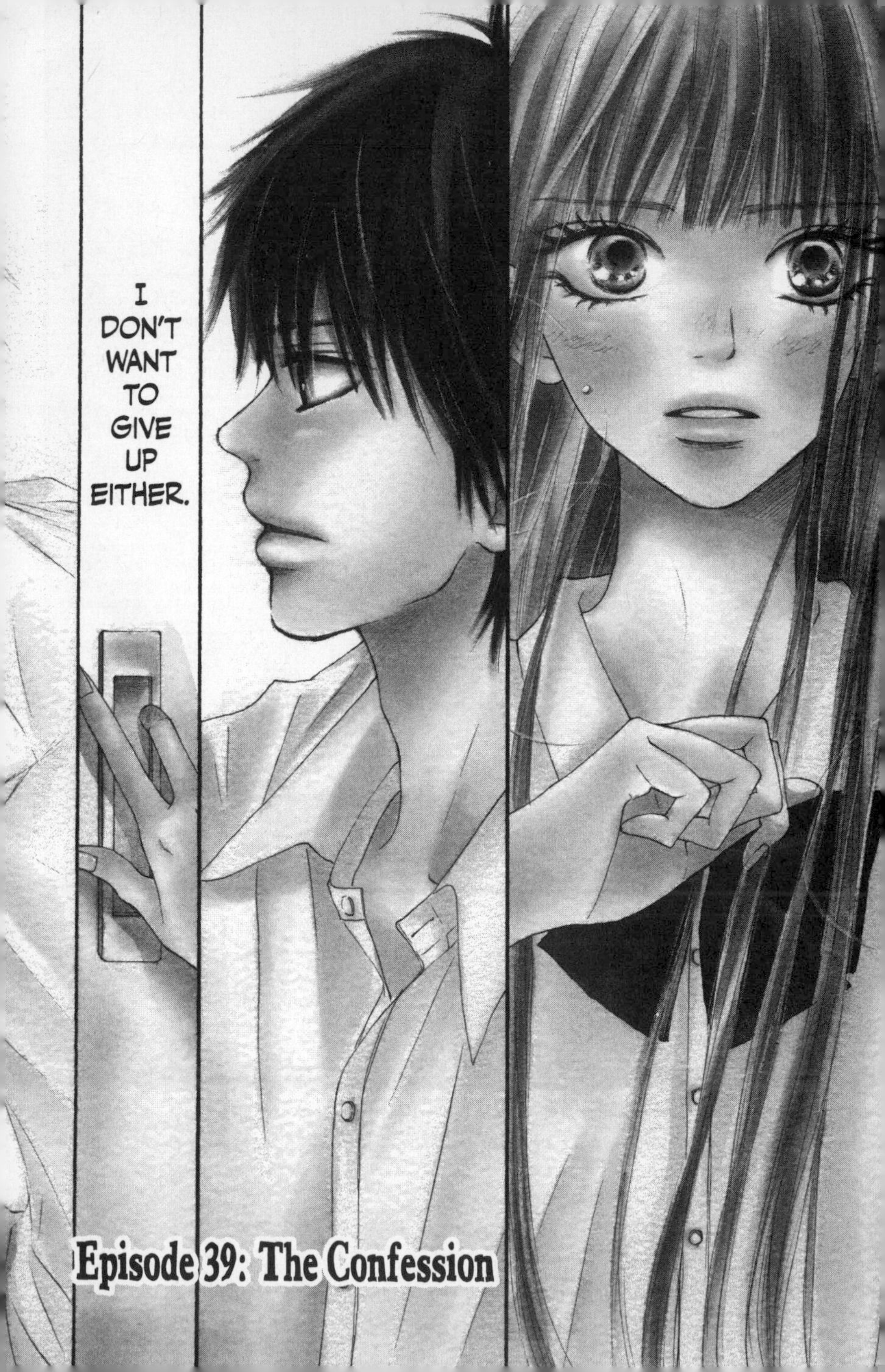
I DON'T WANT TO GIVE UP EITHER.

Episode 39: The Confession

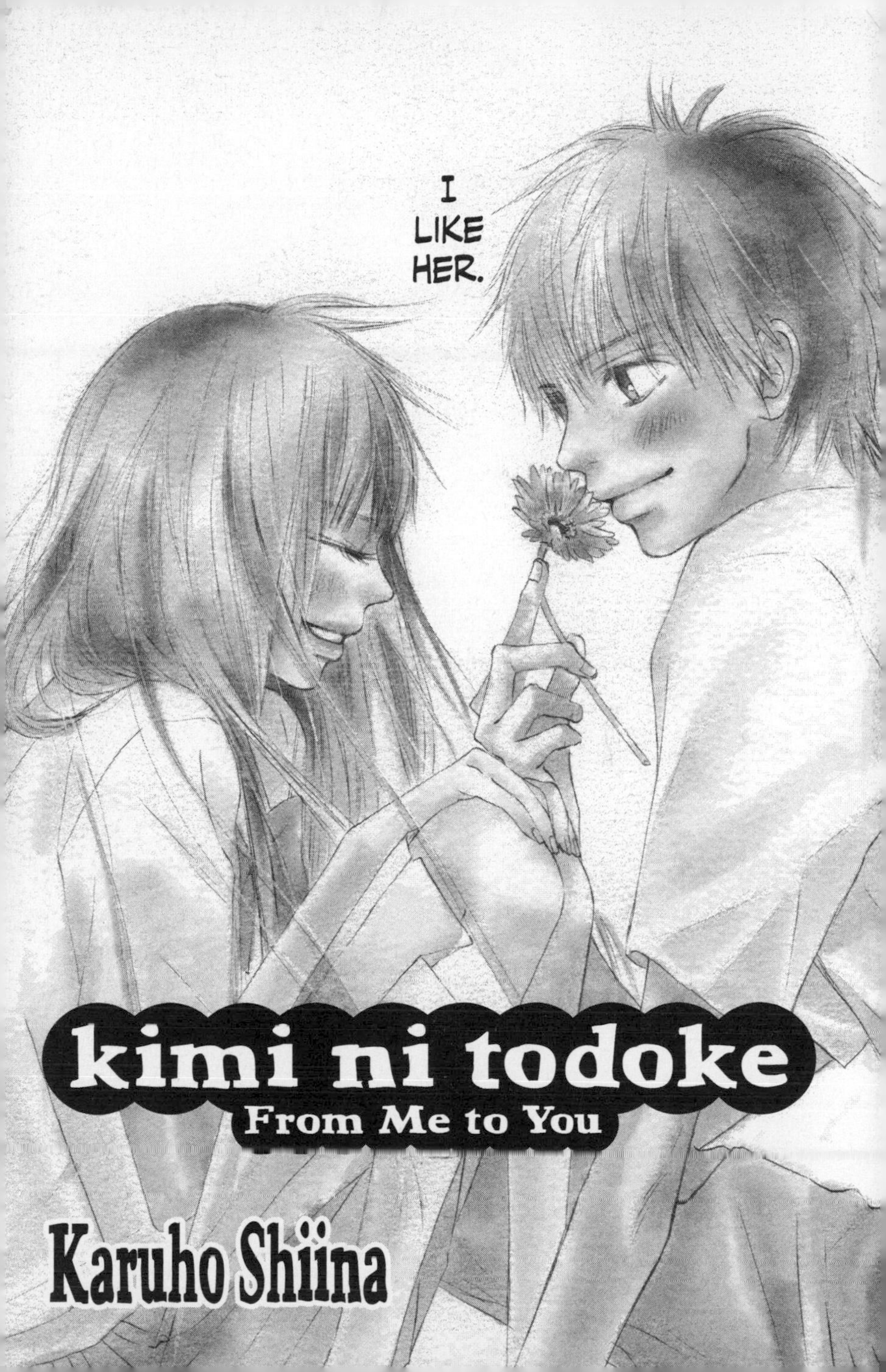
I LIKE HER.
kimi ni todoke
From Me to You
Karuho Shiina

Surprise!

You may be reading the wrong way!

It's true: In keeping with the original Japanese comic format, this book reads from right to left—so action, sound effects, and word balloons are completely reversed. This preserves the orientation of the original artwork—plus, it's fun! Check out the diagram shown here to get the hang of things, and then turn to the other side of the book to get started!

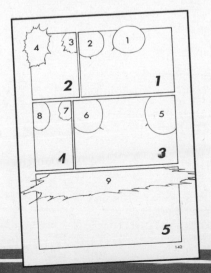

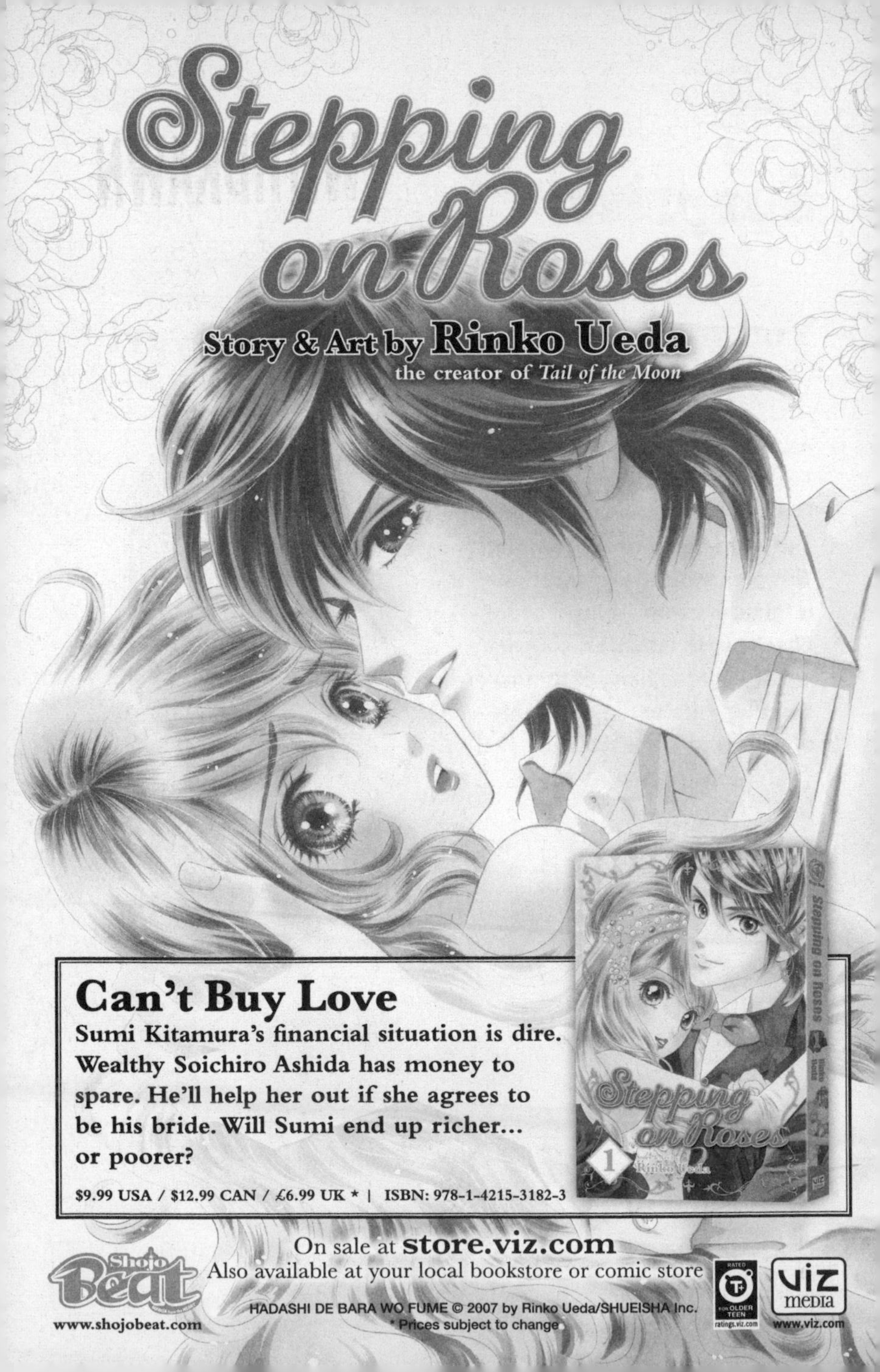
Stepping on Roses
Story & Art by Rinko Ueda
the creator of *Tail of the Moon*
Can't Buy Love
Sumi Kitamura's financial situation is dire. Wealthy Soichiro Ashida has money to spare. He'll help her out if she agrees to be his bride. Will Sumi end up richer... or poorer?
$9.99 USA / $12.99 CAN / £6.99 UK * | ISBN: 978-1-4215-3182-3
Stepping on Roses
1
Rinko Ueda
On sale at store.viz.com
Also available at your local bookstore or comic store
Shojo Beat
www.shojobeat.com
HADASHI DE BARA WO FUME © 2007 by Rinko Ueda/SHUEISHA Inc.
* Prices subject to change
RATED T+ FOR OLDER TEEN
ratings.viz.com
VIZ media
www.viz.com

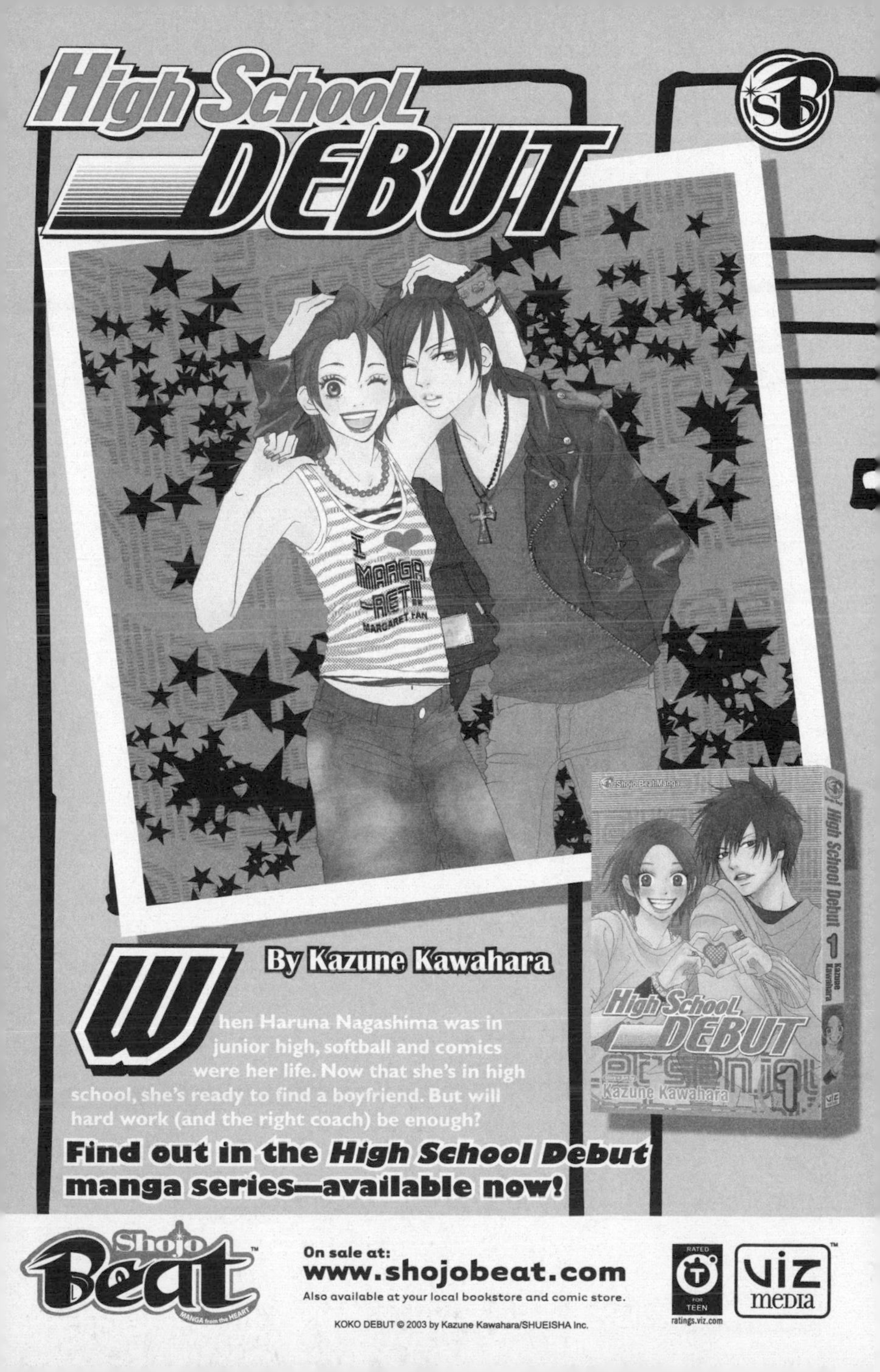
High School DEBUT
By Kazune Kawahara
When Haruna Nagashima was in junior high, softball and comics were her life. Now that she's in high school, she's ready to find a boyfriend. But will hard work (and the right coach) be enough?
Find out in the *High School Debut* manga series—available now!
Shojo Beat Manga
High School Debut 1
Kazune Kawahara
Shojo Beat
MANGA from the HEART
On sale at:
www.shojobeat.com
Also available at your local bookstore and comic store.
KOKO DEBUT © 2003 by Kazune Kawahara/SHUEISHA Inc.
RATED T FOR TEEN
ratings.viz.com
VIZ media

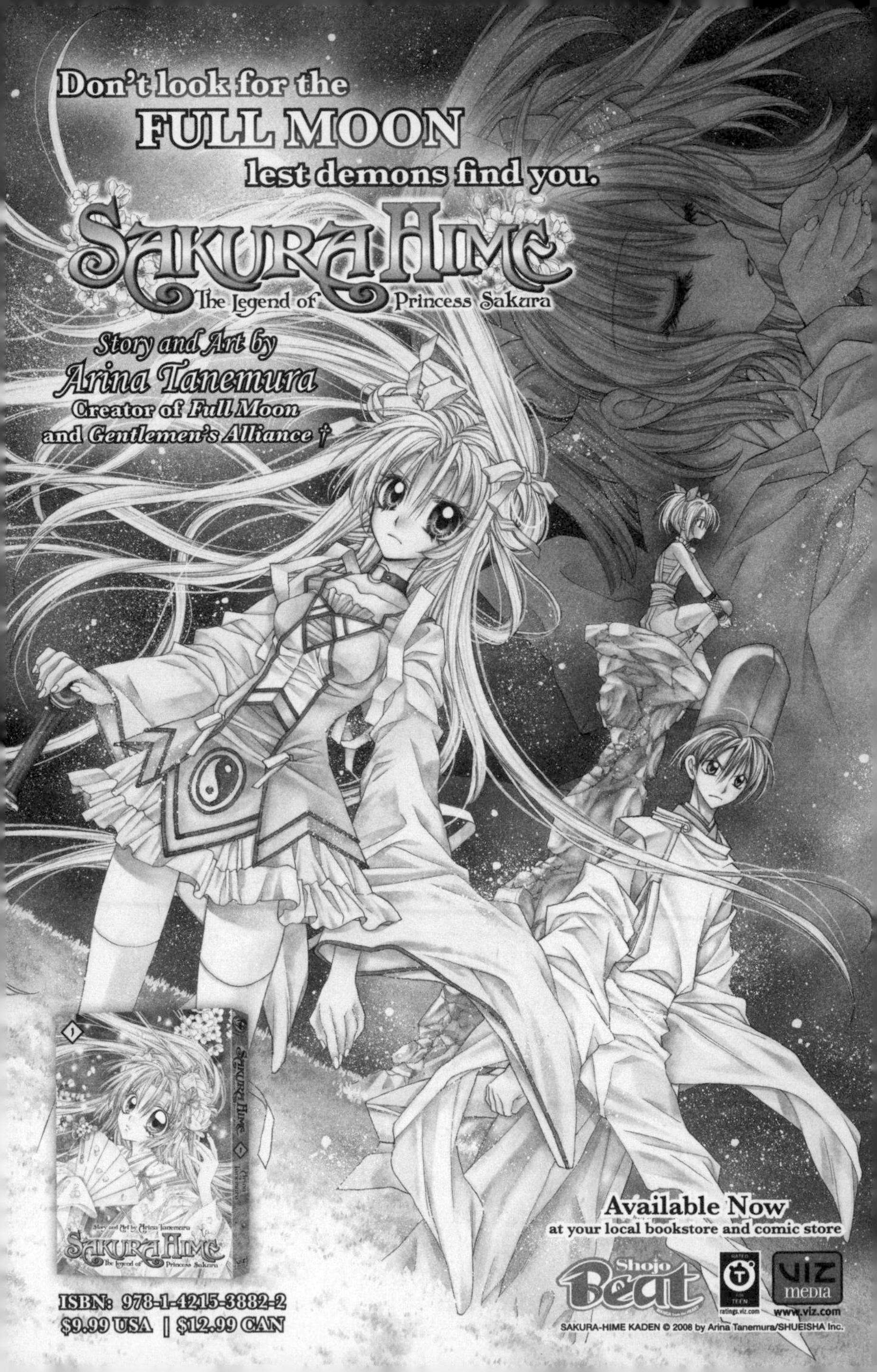
Don't look for the
FULL MOON
lest demons find you.
SAKURA HIME
The Legend of Princess Sakura
Story and Art by
Arina Tanemura
Creator of Full Moon
and Gentlemen's Alliance †
Available Now
at your local bookstore and comic store
Shojo Beat
RATED T FOR TEEN
ratings.viz.com
VIZ media
www.viz.com
SAKURA-HIME KADEN © 2008 by Arina Tanemura/SHUEISHA Inc.
ISBN: 978-1-4215-3882-2
$9.99 USA | $12.99 CAN

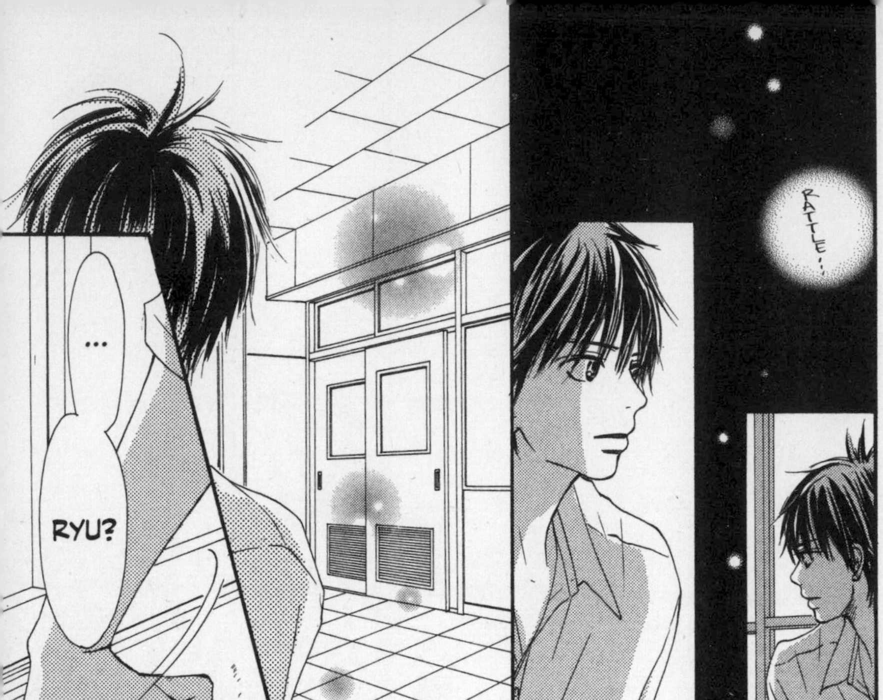
RATTLE...
...
RYU?
CHAK

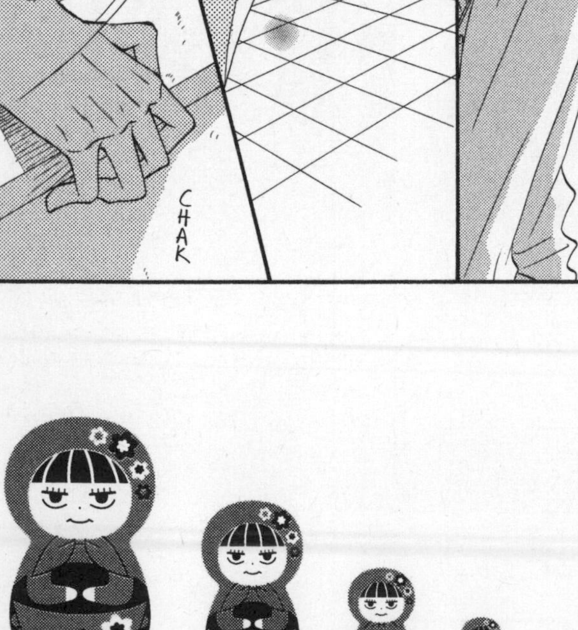

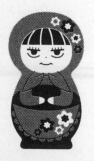

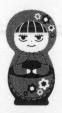

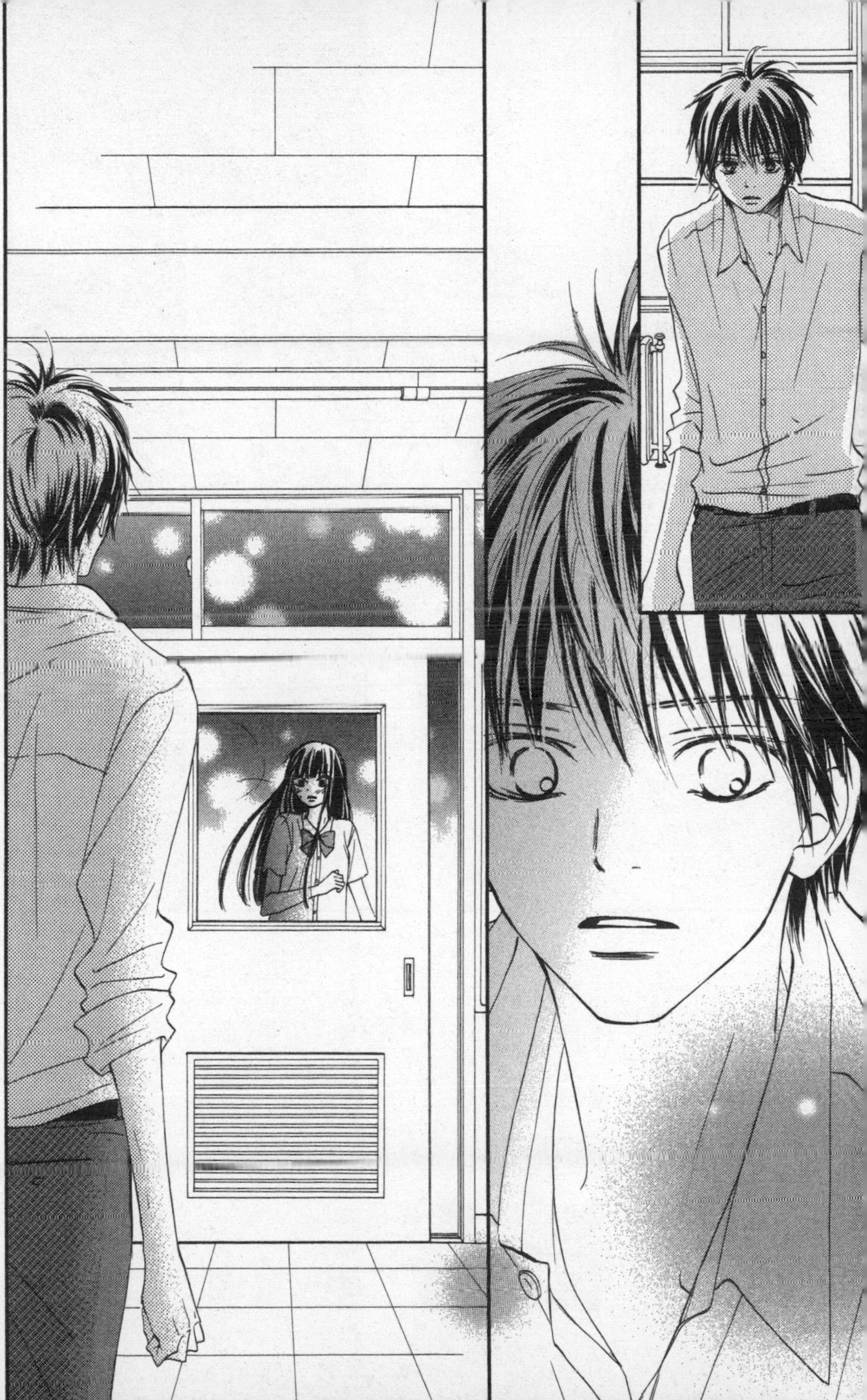

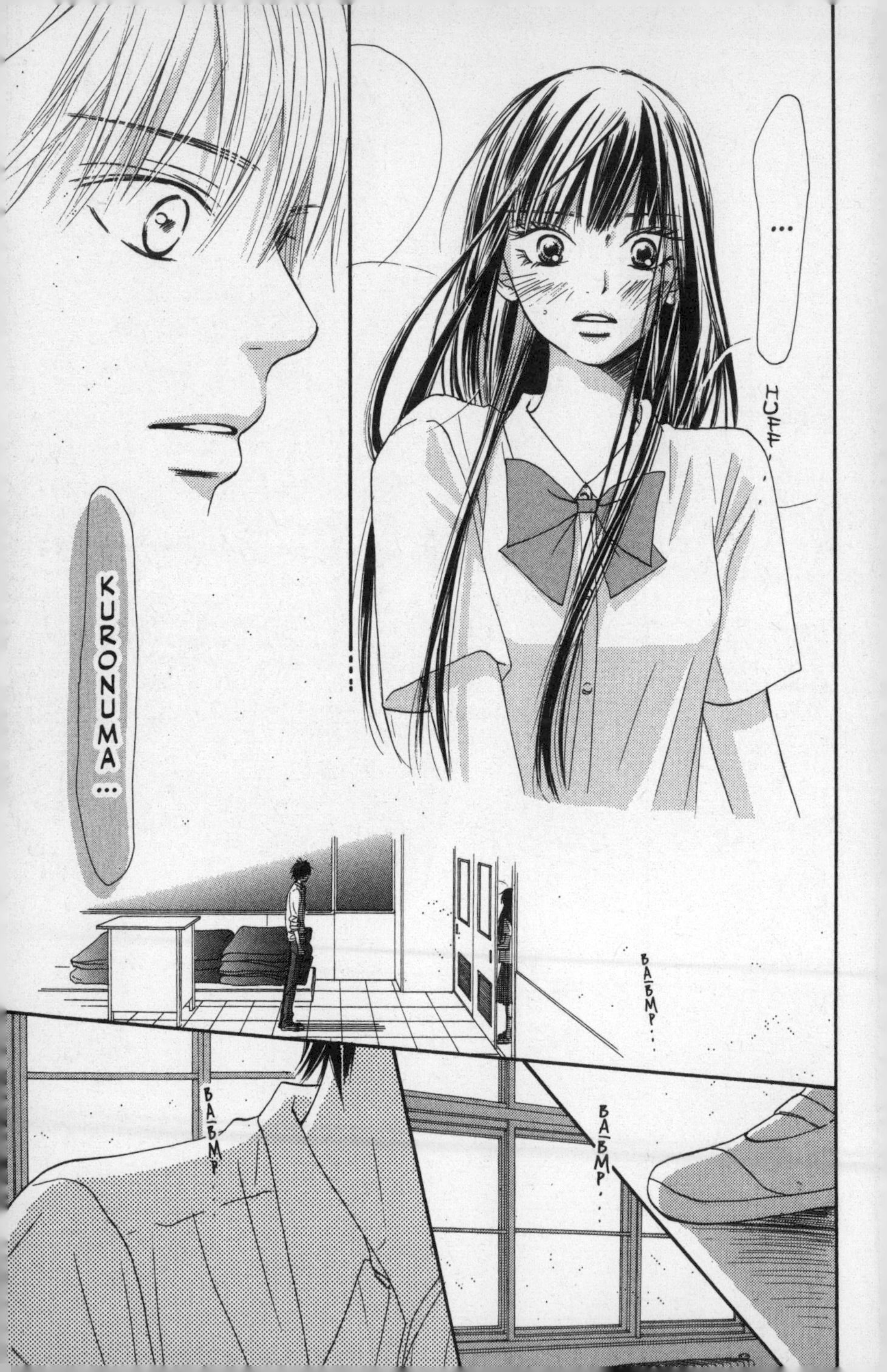
...
HUFF...
...
KURONUMA...
BA-BMP...
BA-BMP...
BA-BMP

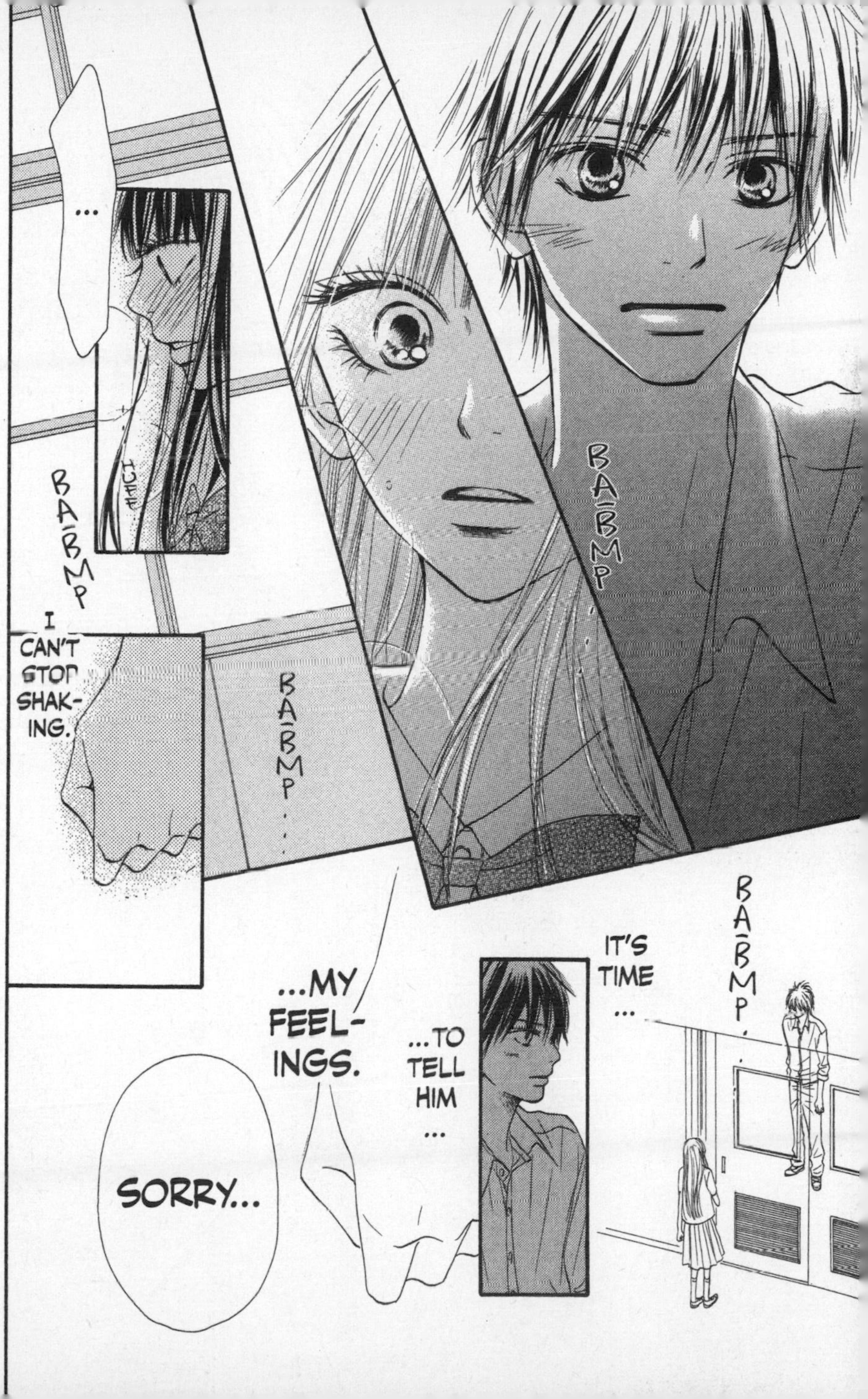
BA-BMP...
BA-BMP...
...
HUFF
BA-BMP
I CAN'T STOP SHAKING.
BA-BMP.
IT'S TIME ...
...TO TELL HIM ...
...MY FEELINGS.
SORRY...

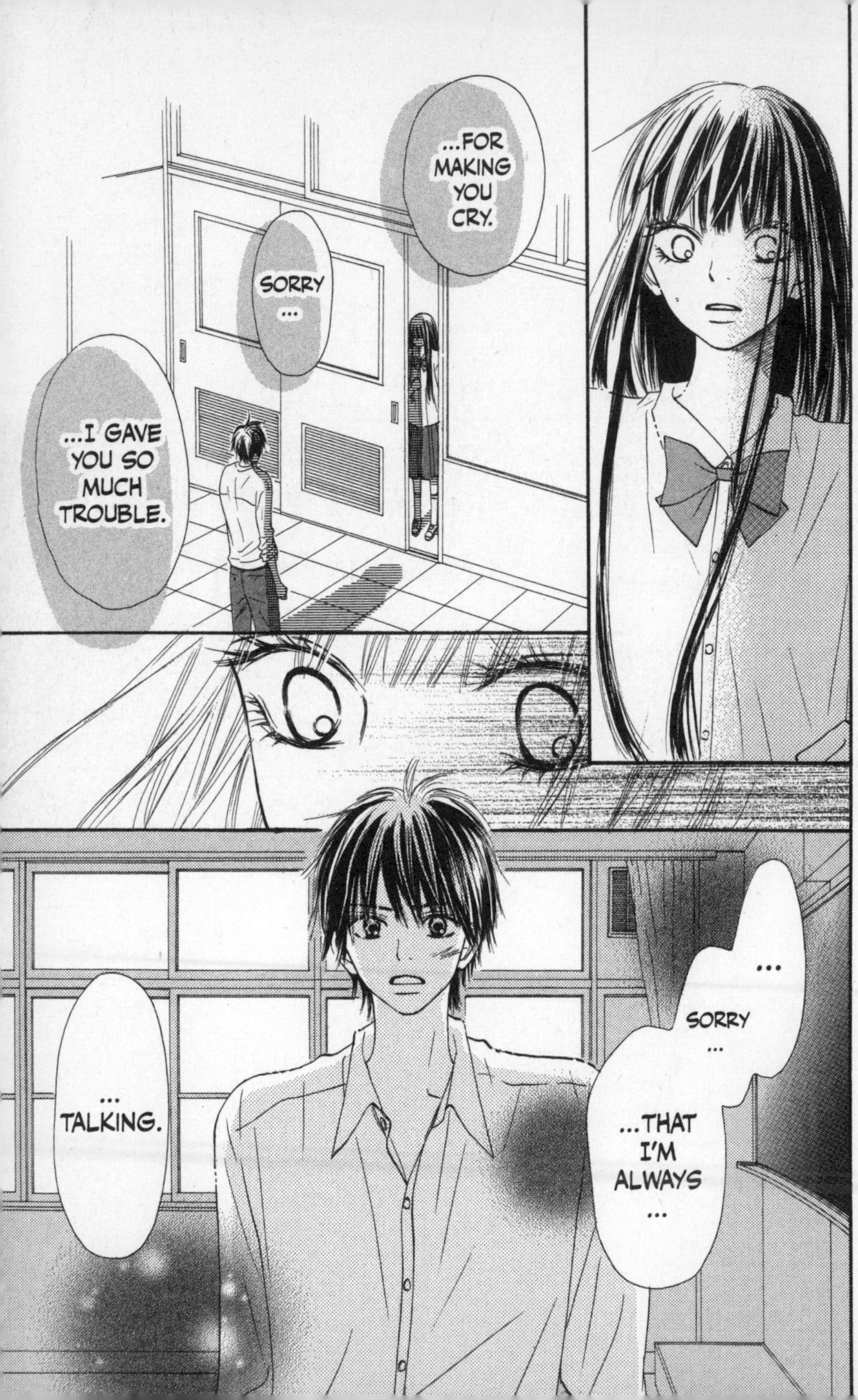
...FOR MAKING YOU CRY.
SORRY ...
...I GAVE YOU SO MUCH TROUBLE.
... SORRY ...
...THAT I'M ALWAYS ...
... TALKING.

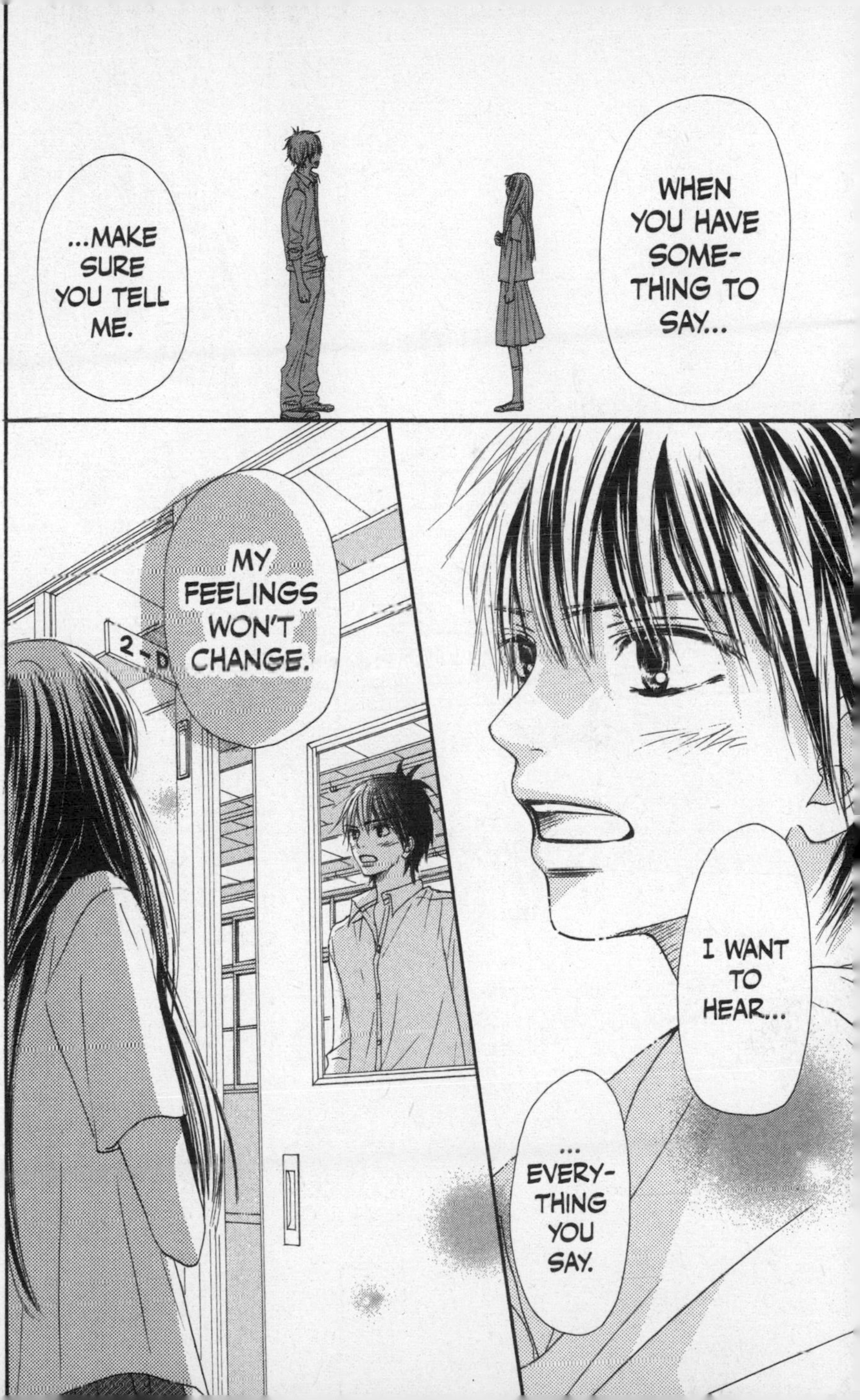
WHEN YOU HAVE SOME-THING TO SAY...
...MAKE SURE YOU TELL ME.
I WANT TO HEAR...
...EVERY-THING YOU SAY.
MY FEELINGS WON'T CHANGE.
2-D

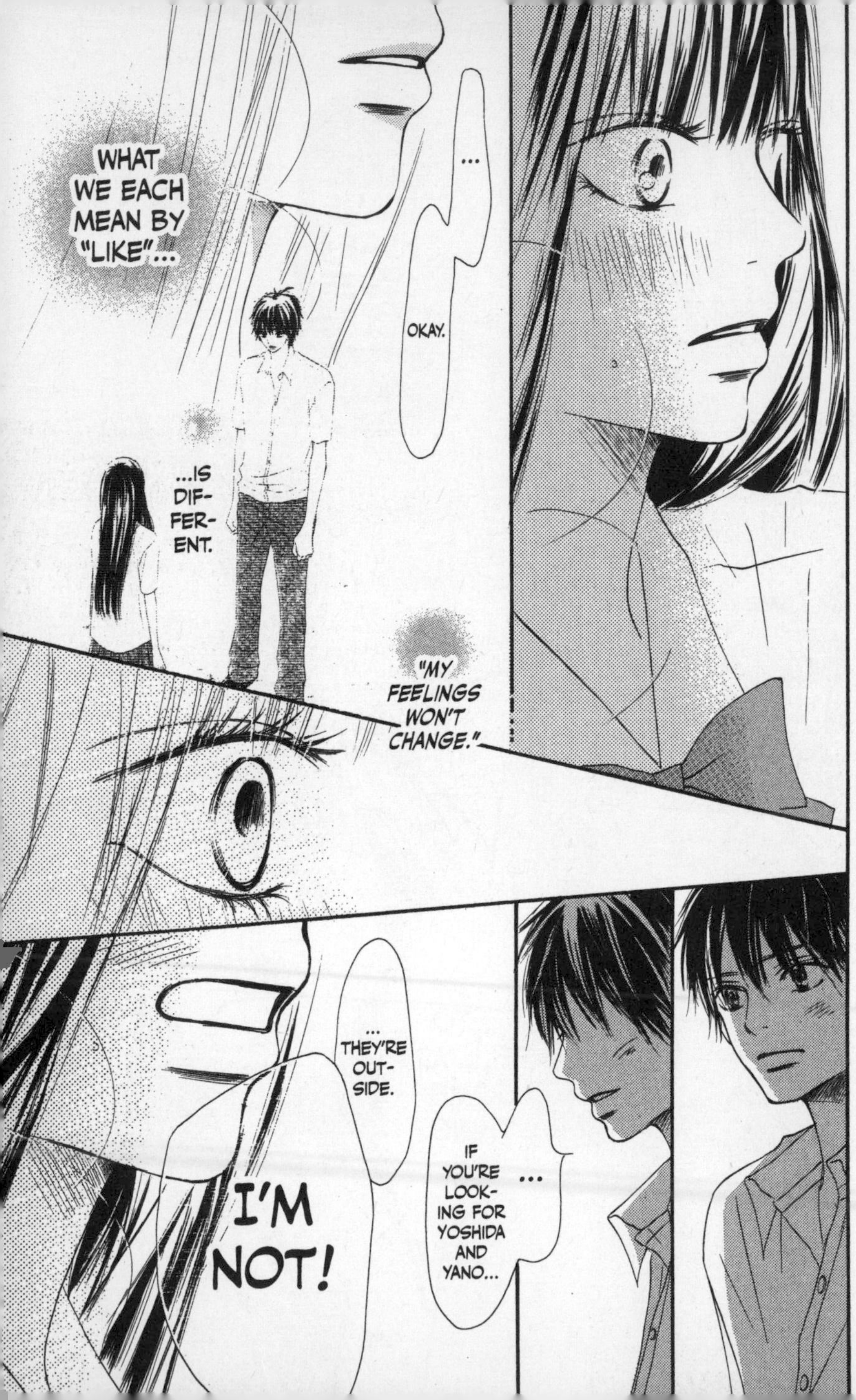
...
OKAY.
WHAT WE EACH MEAN BY "LIKE"...
...IS DIFFERENT.
"MY FEELINGS WON'T CHANGE."
...
IF YOU'RE LOOKING FOR YOSHIDA AND YANO...
...THEY'RE OUTSIDE.
I'M NOT!

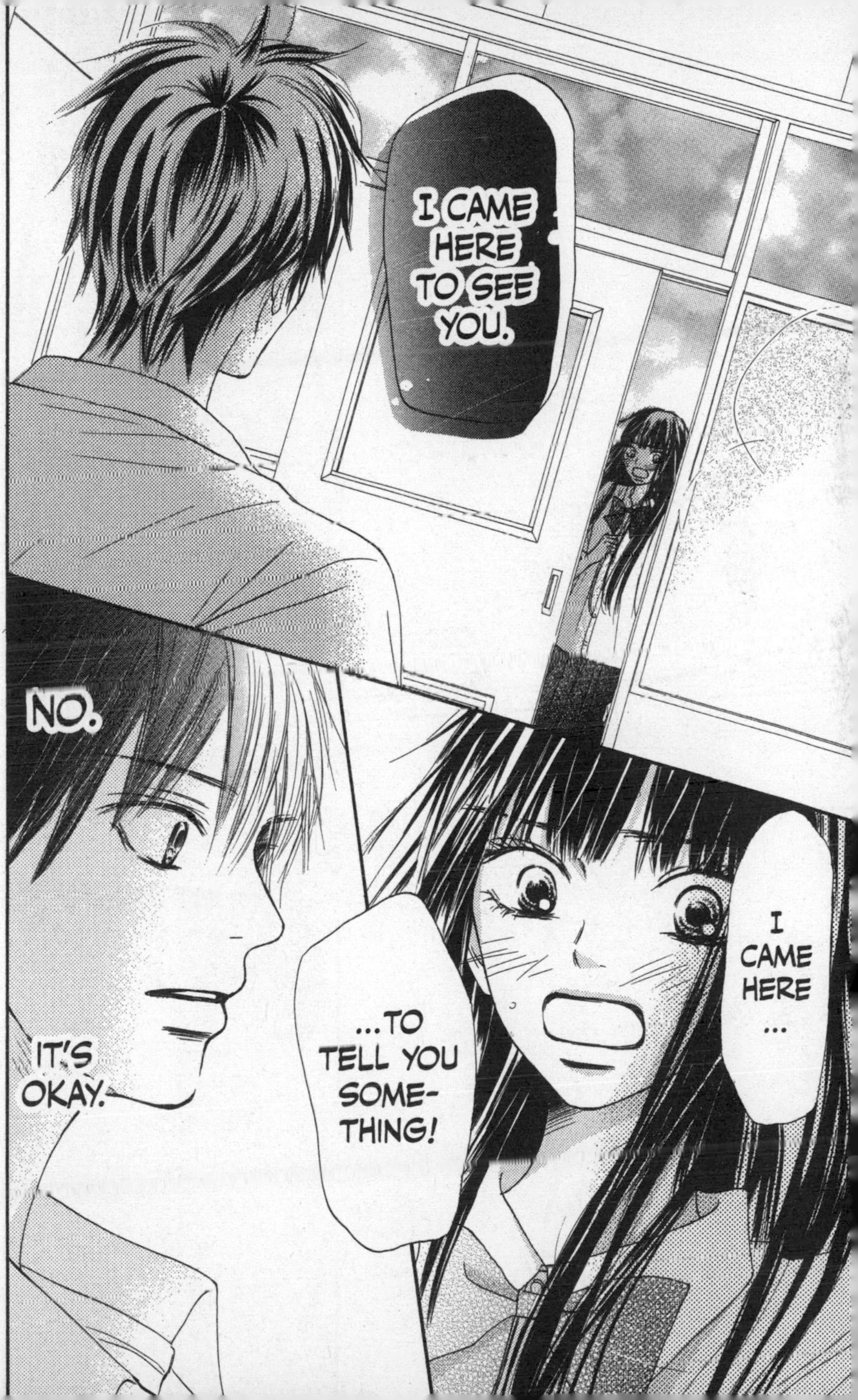
I CAME HERE TO SEE YOU.
I CAME HERE ...
...TO TELL YOU SOME-THING!
NO.
IT'S OKAY.

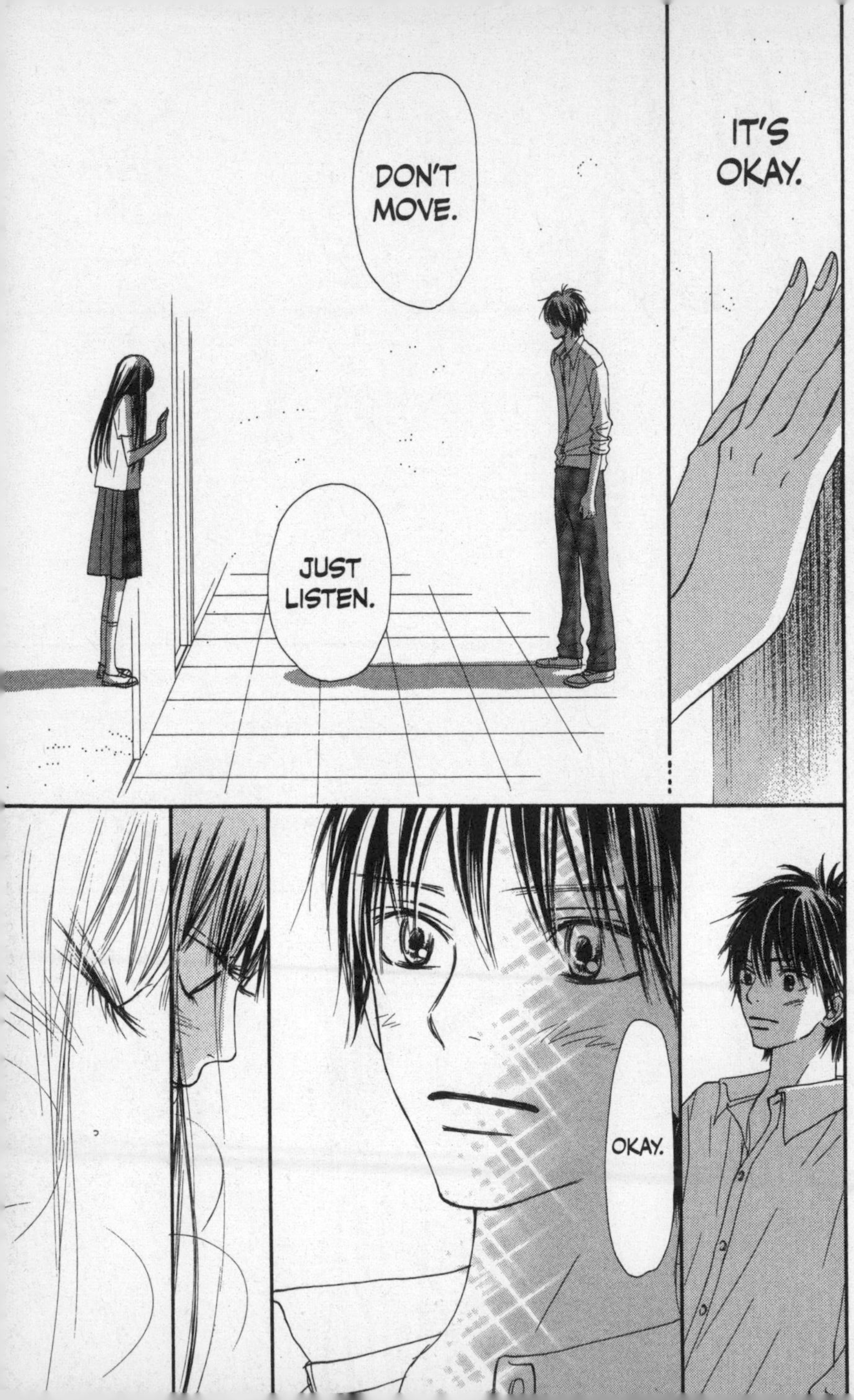
IT'S OKAY.
DON'T MOVE.
JUST LISTEN.
OKAY.

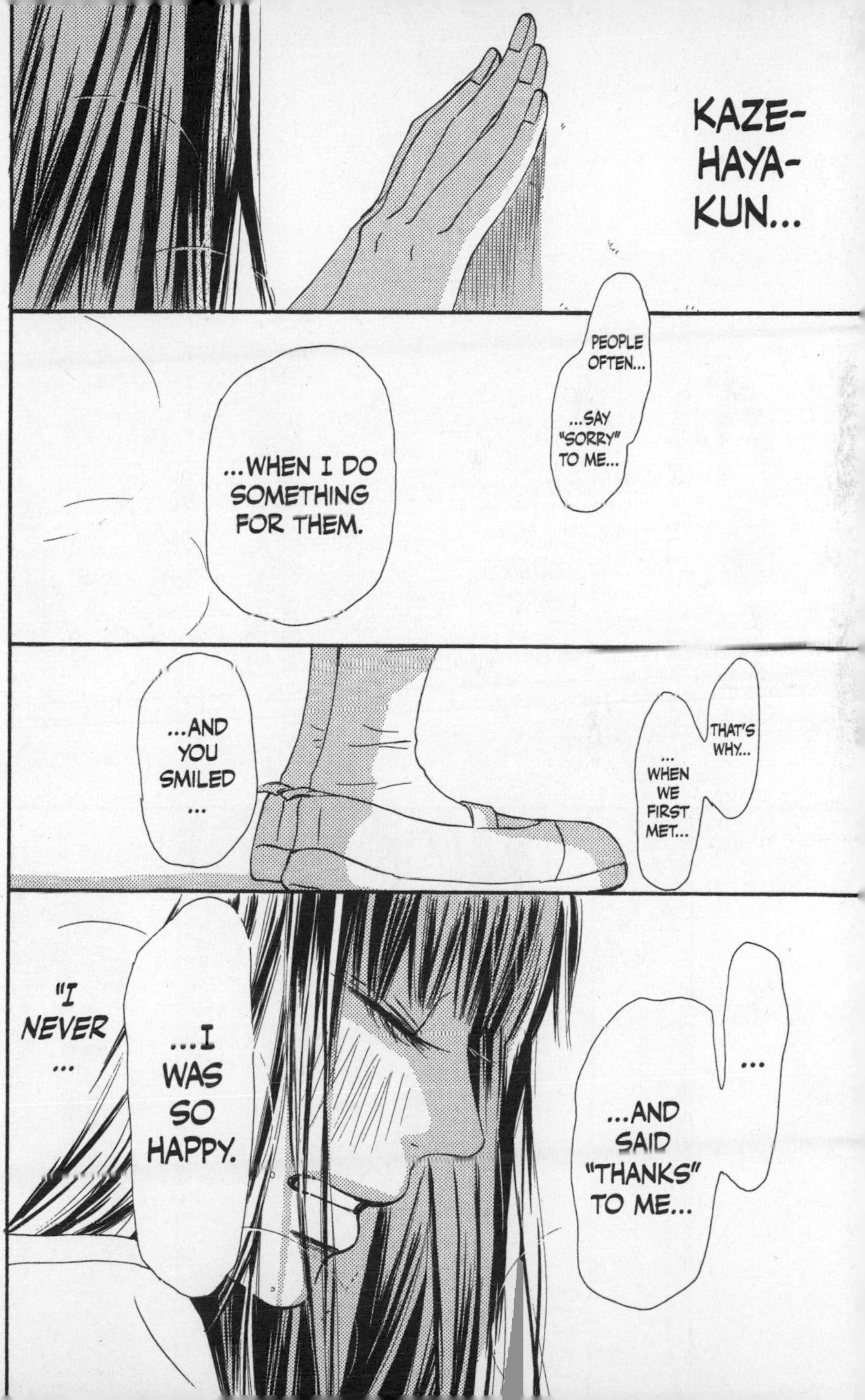
KAZE-HAYA-KUN...
PEOPLE OFTEN...
...SAY "SORRY" TO ME...
...WHEN I DO SOMETHING FOR THEM.
THAT'S WHY...
...WHEN WE FIRST MET...
...AND YOU SMILED ...
...
...AND SAID "THANKS" TO ME...
...I WAS SO HAPPY.
"I NEVER ...

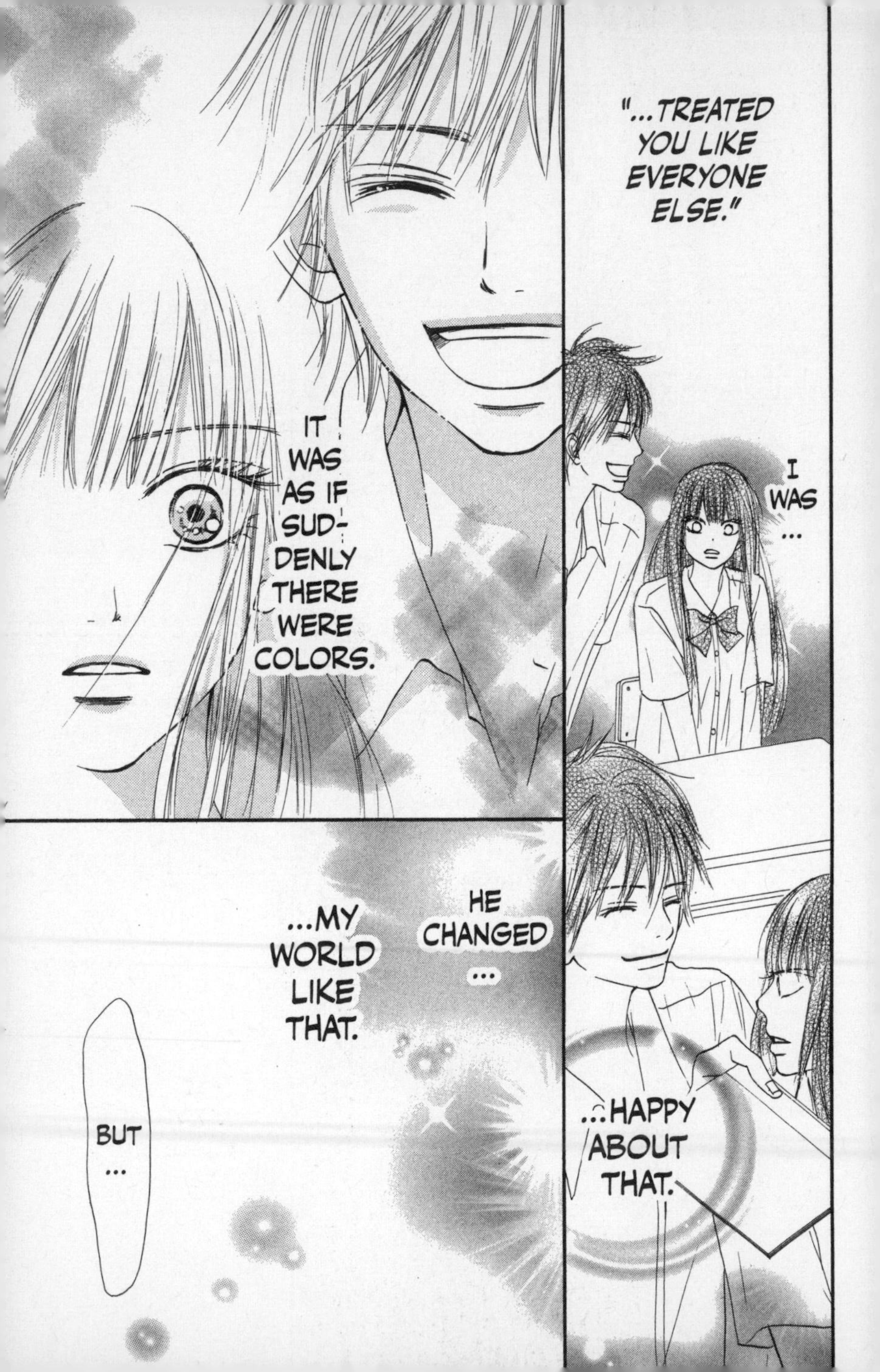
"...TREATED YOU LIKE EVERYONE ELSE."
I WAS ...
...HAPPY ABOUT THAT.
IT WAS AS IF SUD-DENLY THERE WERE COLORS.
HE CHANGED ...
...MY WORLD LIKE THAT.
BUT ...

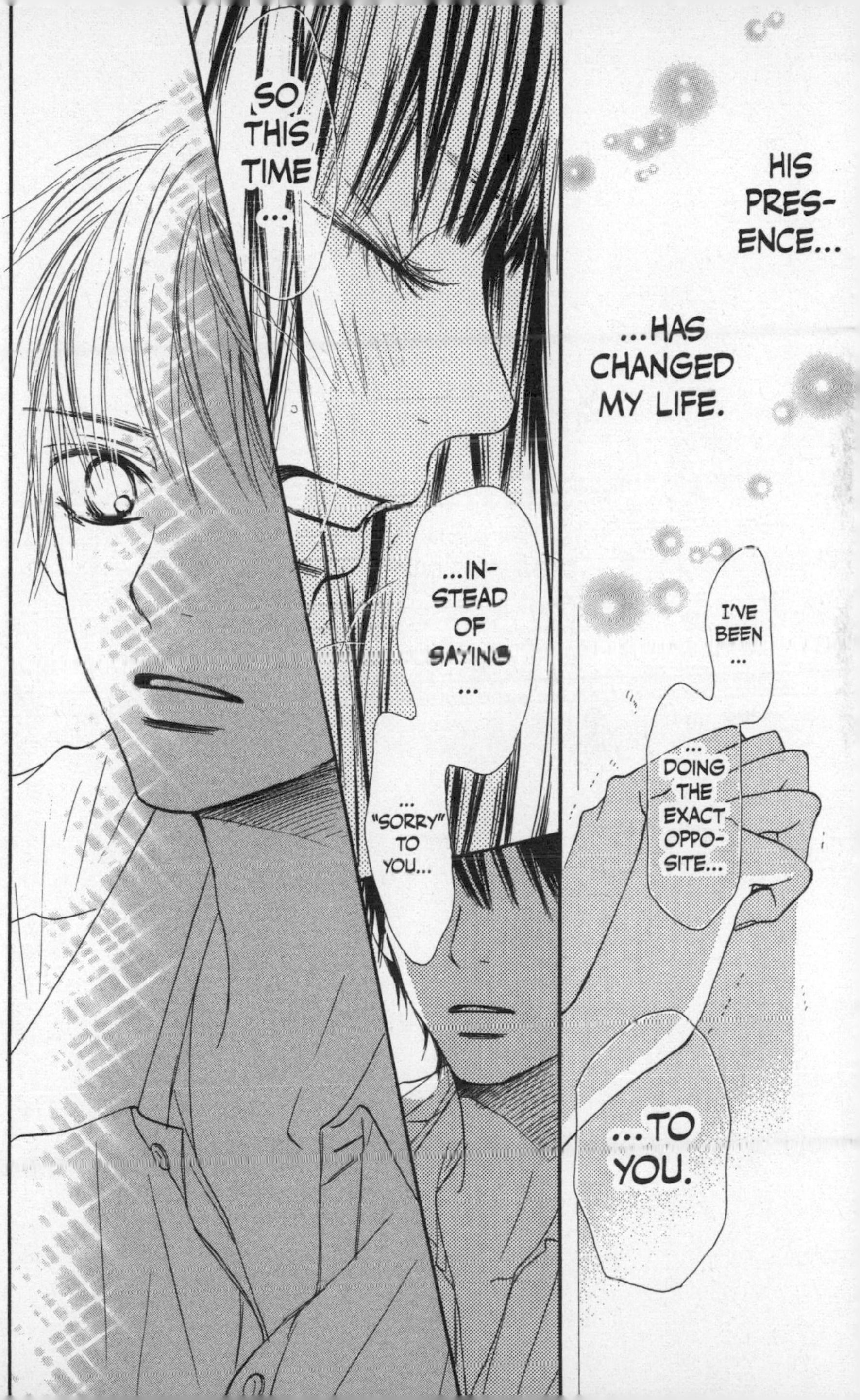
HIS PRESENCE...
...HAS CHANGED MY LIFE.
I'VE BEEN...
...DOING THE EXACT OPPOSITE...
...TO YOU.
SO THIS TIME...
...INSTEAD OF SAYING...
..."SORRY" TO YOU...

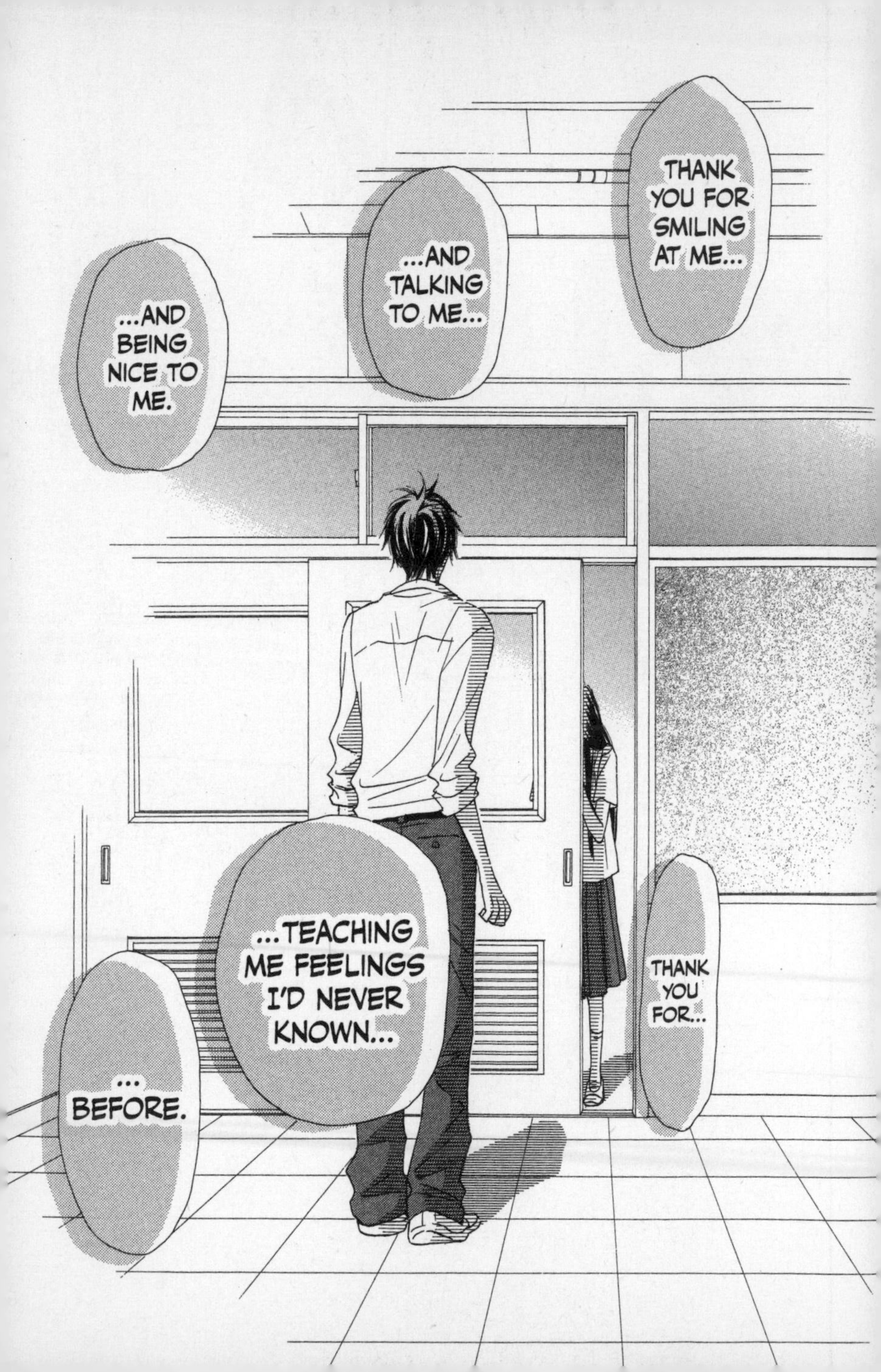
THANK YOU FOR SMILING AT ME...
...AND TALKING TO ME...
...AND BEING NICE TO ME.
THANK YOU FOR...
...TEACHING ME FEELINGS I'D NEVER KNOWN...
... BEFORE.

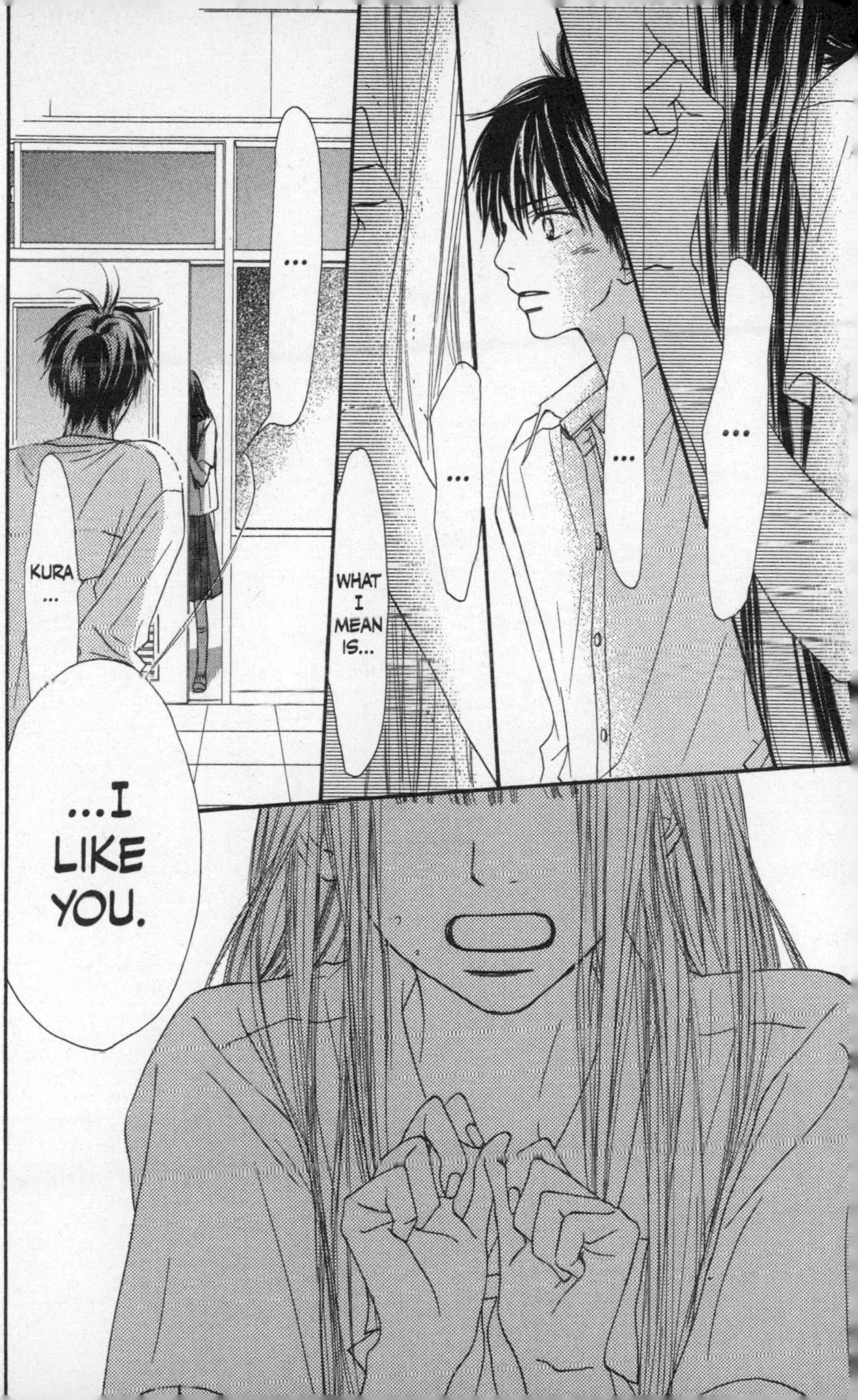
...
...
...
WHAT I MEAN IS...
...
KURA ...
...I LIKE YOU.

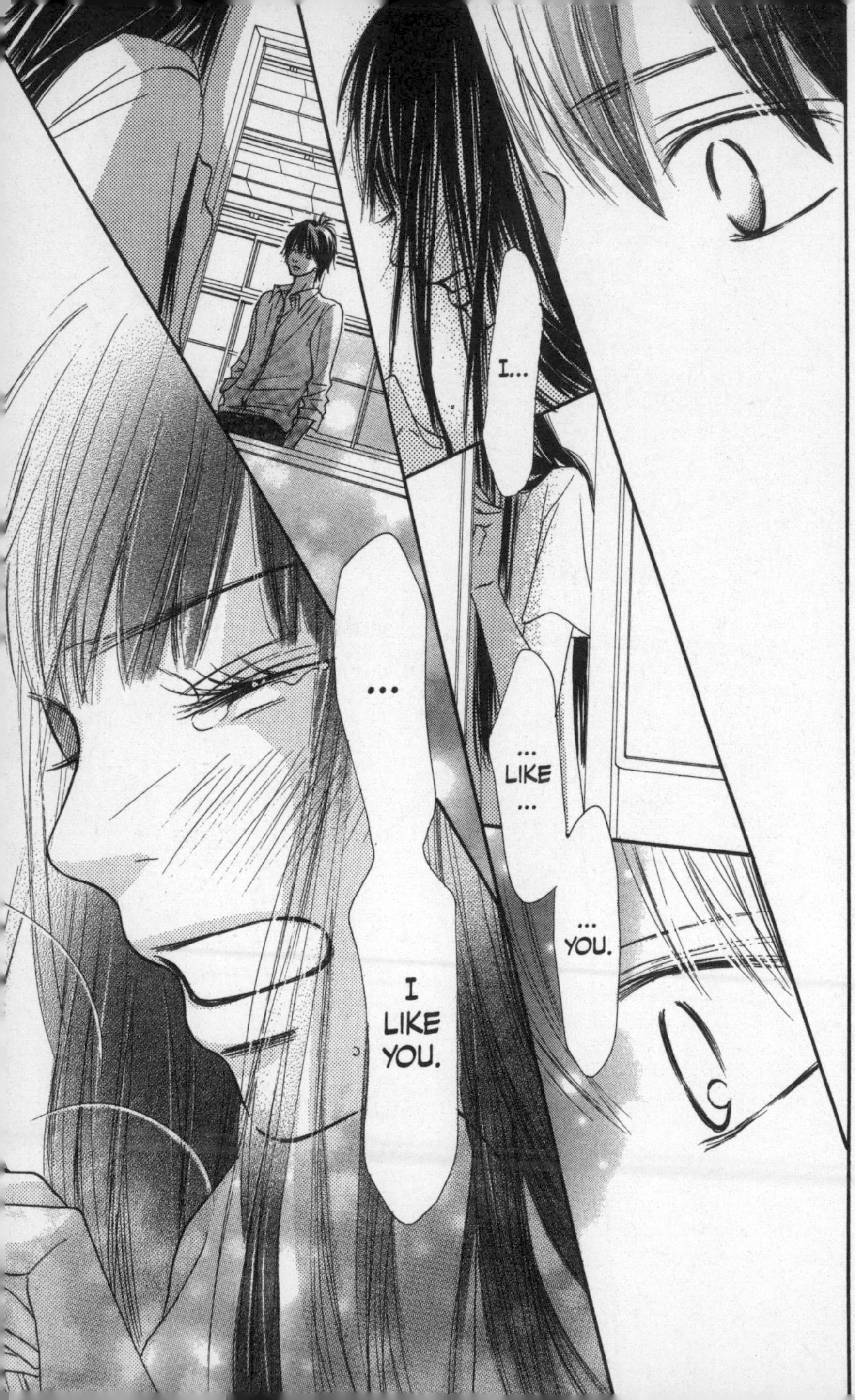
I...
...LIKE...
...YOU.
...
I LIKE YOU.

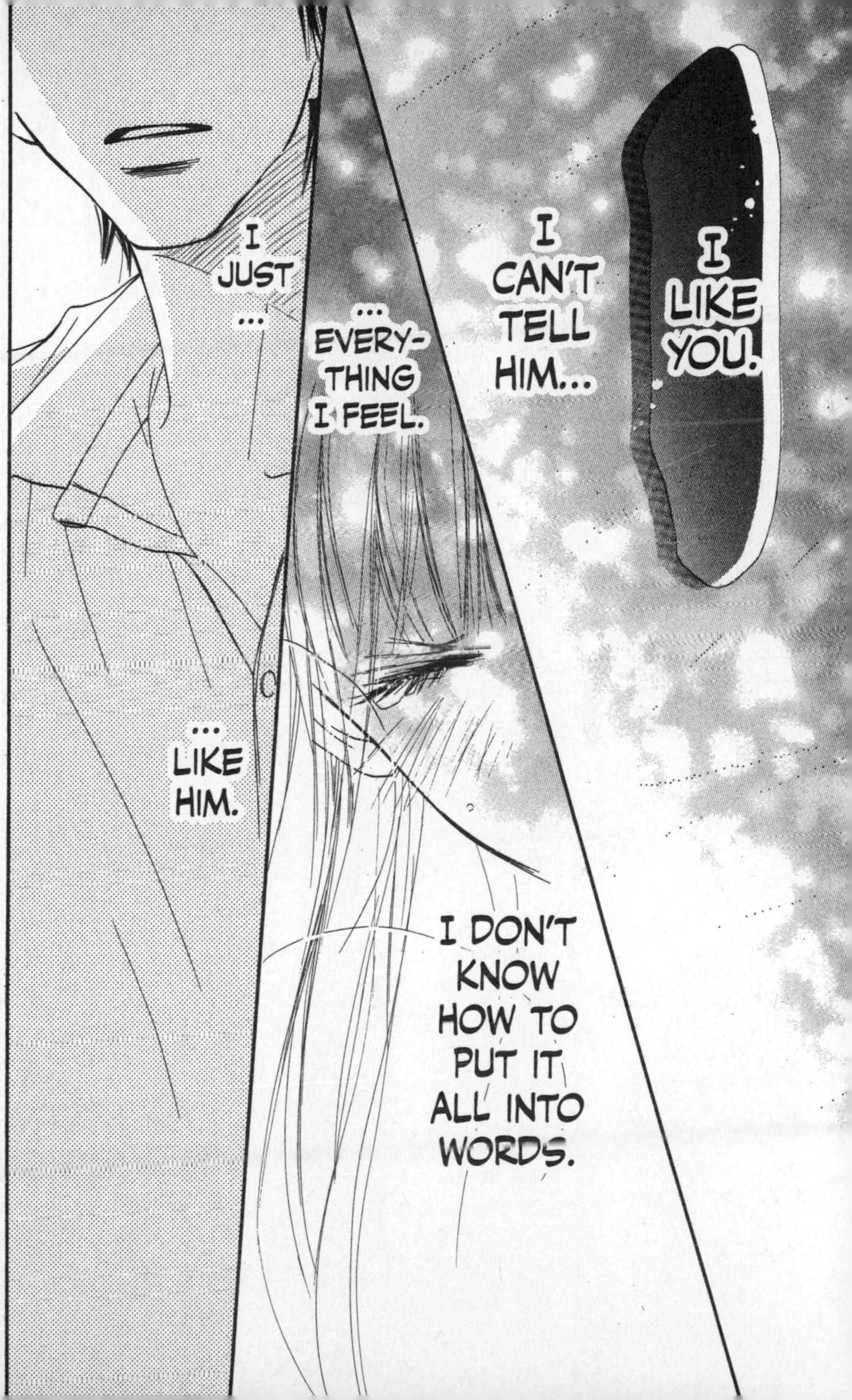
I LIKE YOU.
I CAN'T TELL HIM...
... EVERY-THING I FEEL.
I JUST ...
... LIKE HIM.
I DON'T KNOW HOW TO PUT IT ALL INTO WORDS.

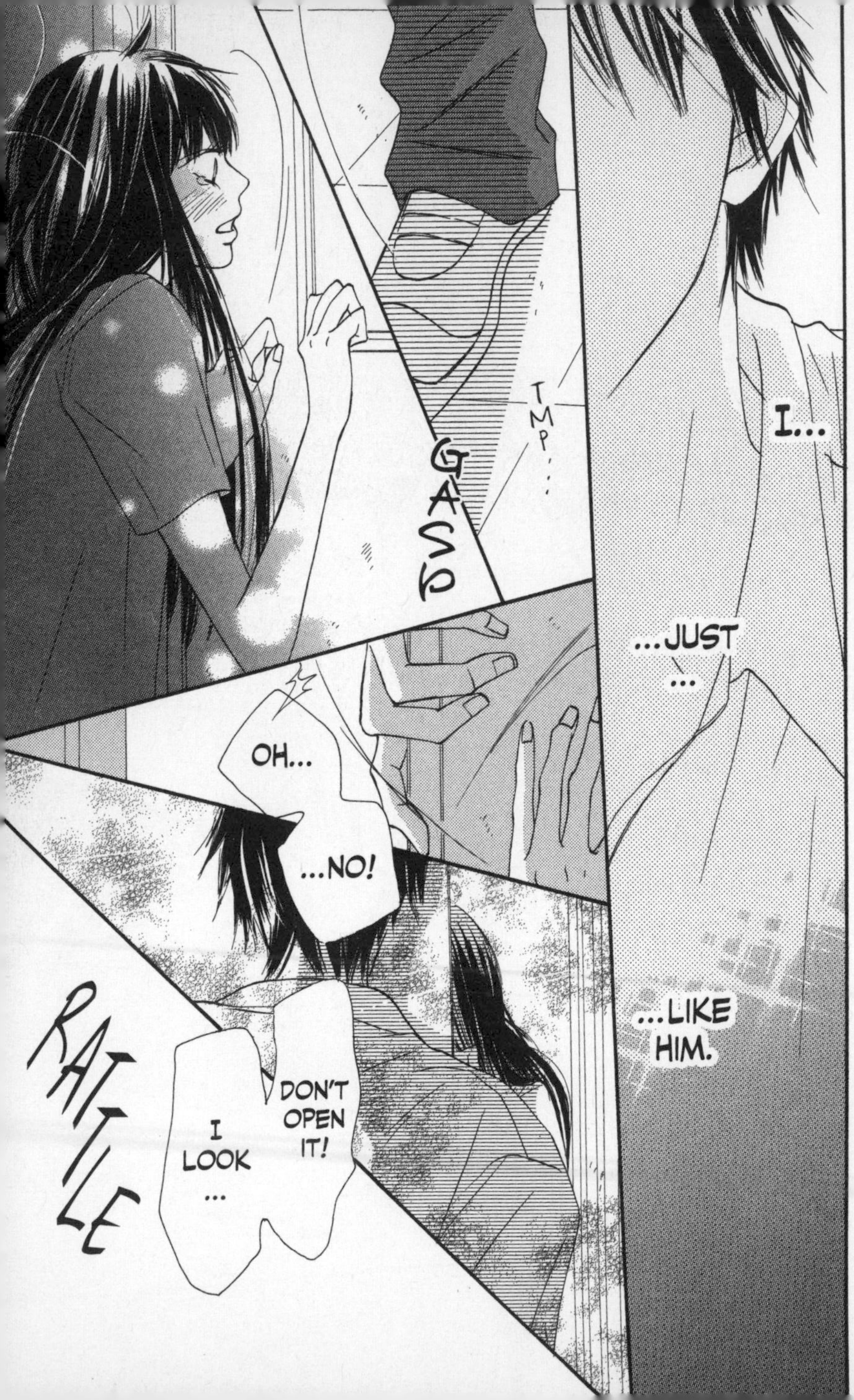
I...
...JUST ...
...LIKE HIM.
TMP...
GASP
OH...
...NO!
DON'T OPEN IT!
I LOOK ...
RATTLE

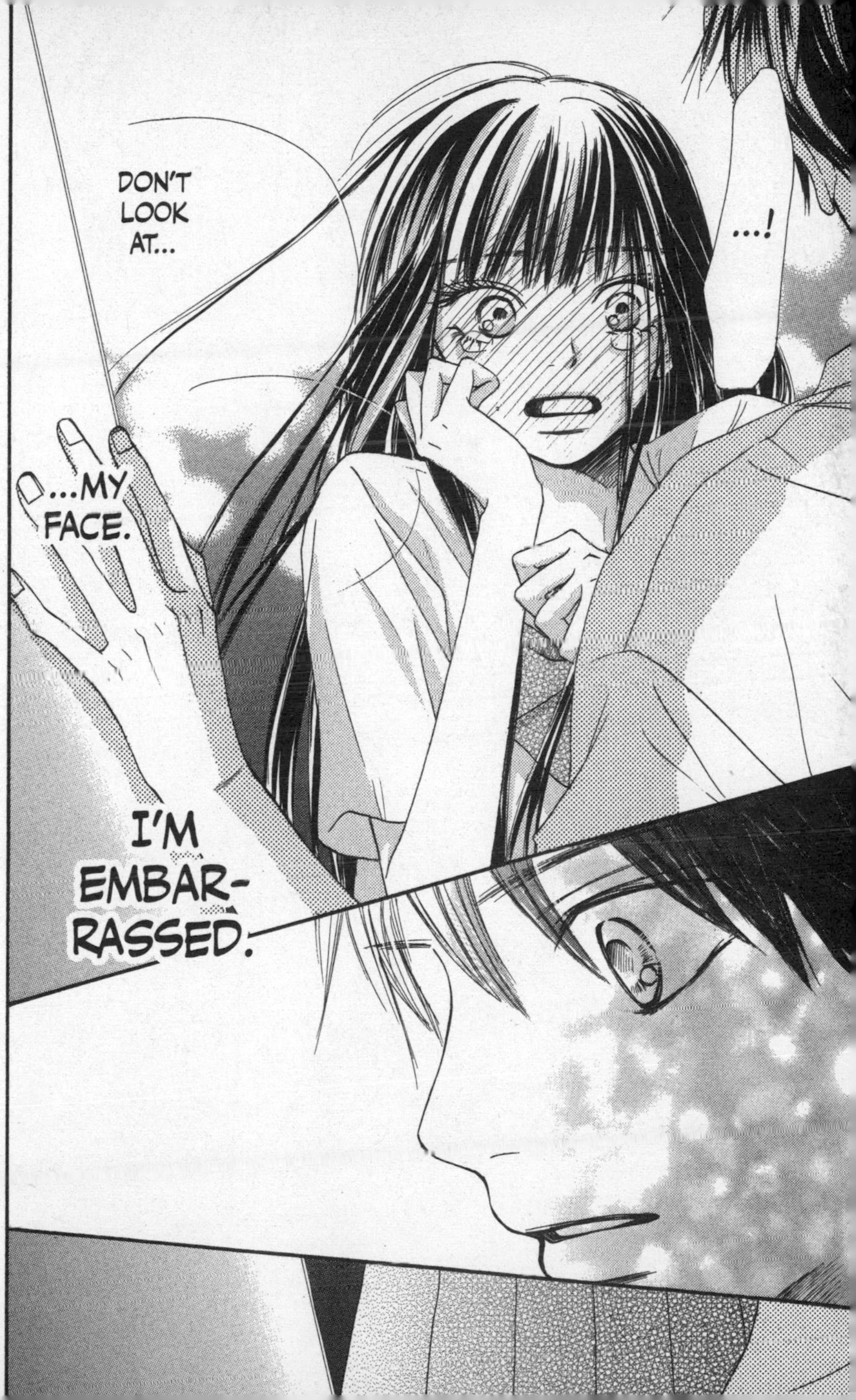
...!
DON'T LOOK AT...
...MY FACE.
I'M EMBAR-RASSED.

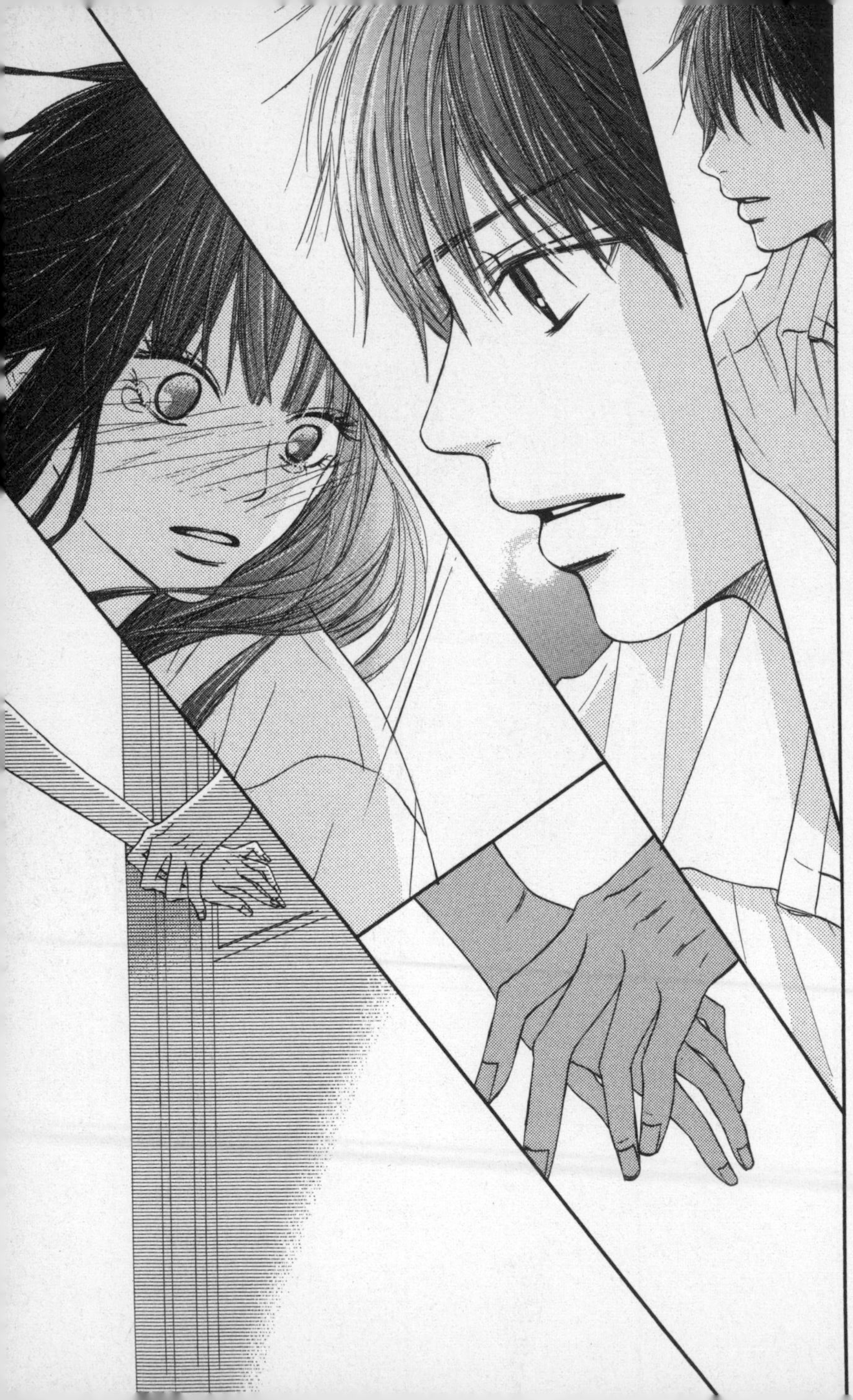

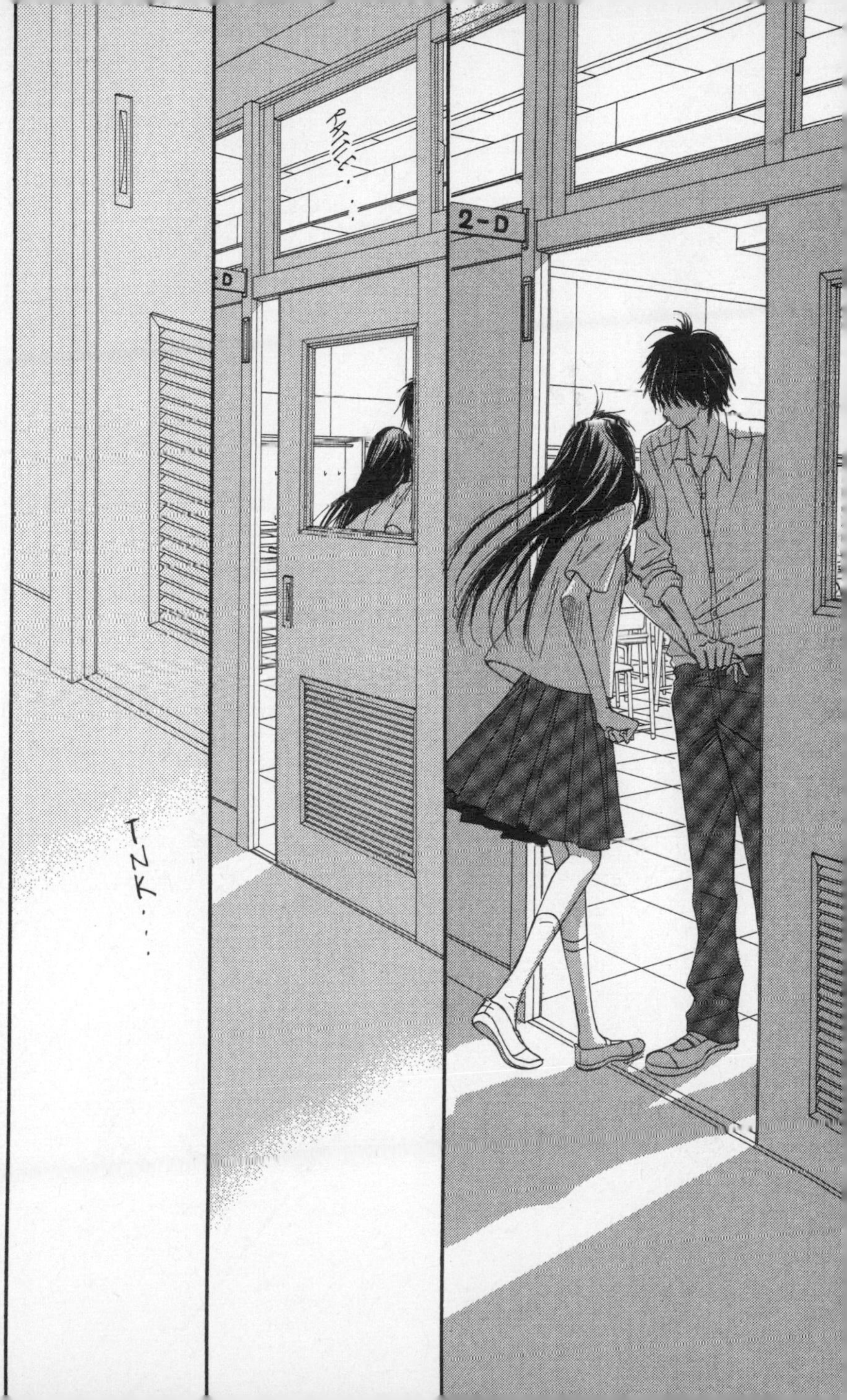
2-D
RATTLE...
TNK...

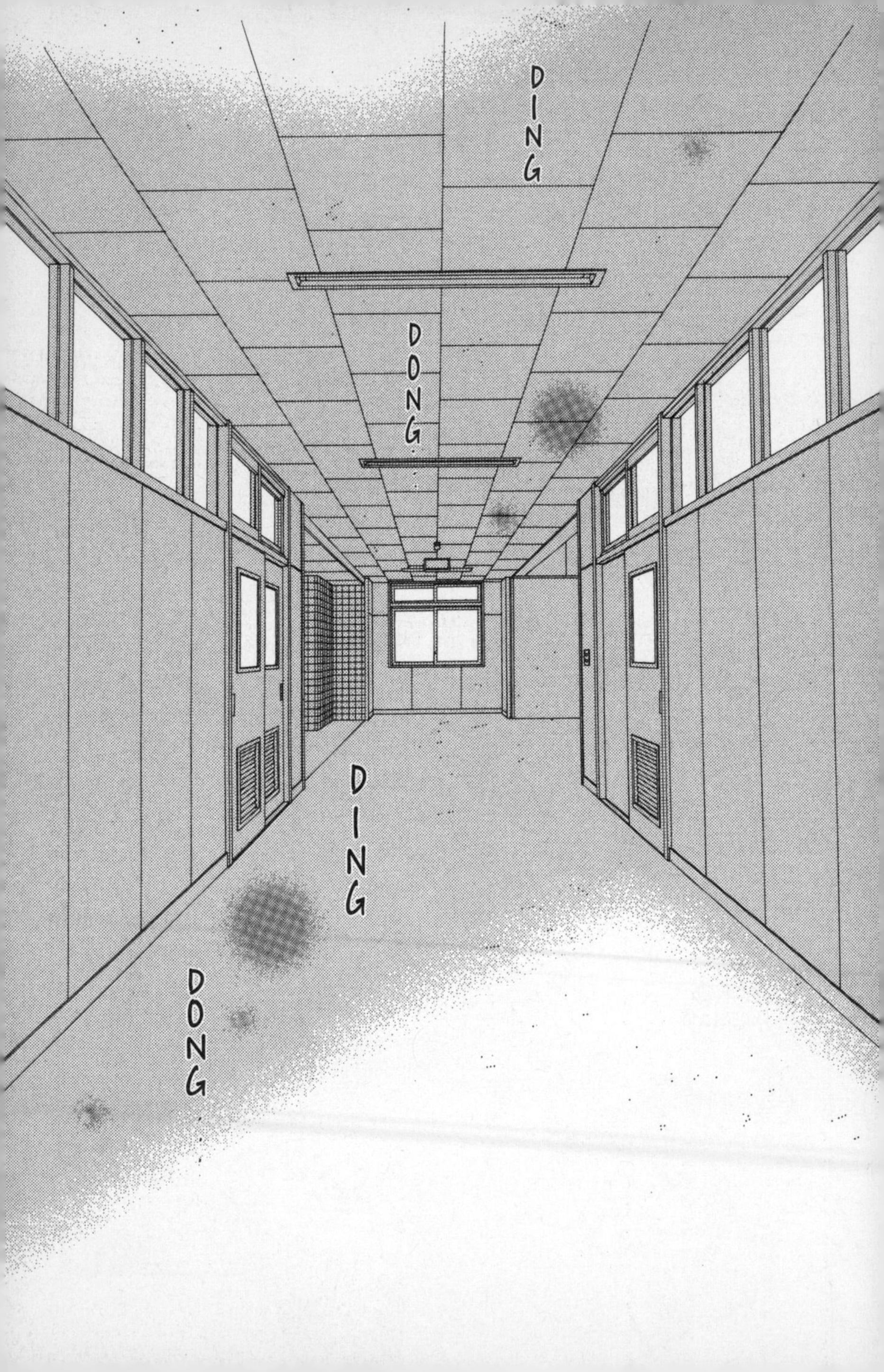
DING
DONG
DING
DONG

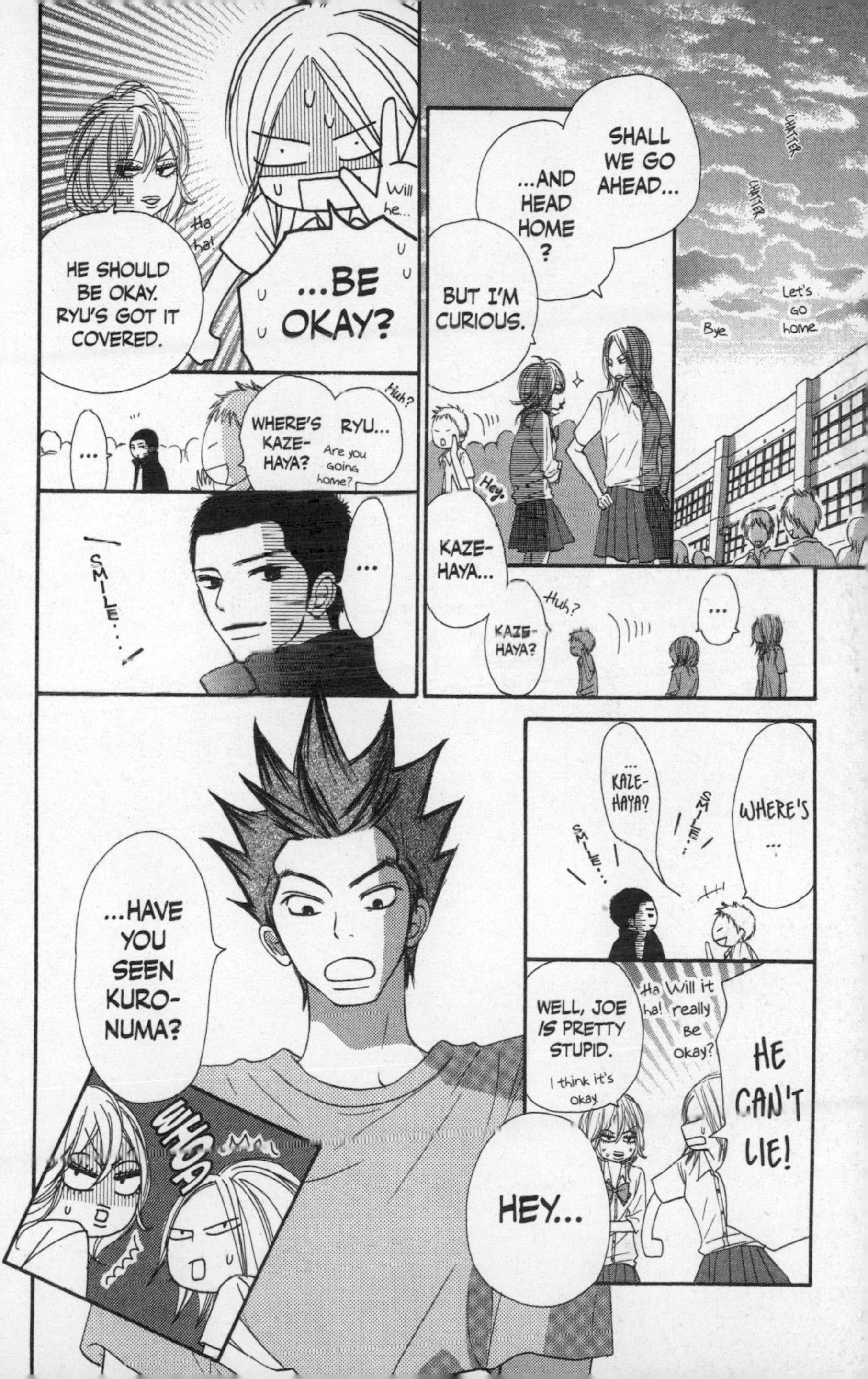
CHATTER
CHATTER
Let's GO home
Bye
SHALL WE GO AHEAD...
...AND HEAD HOME?
BUT I'M CURIOUS.
Hey.
KAZE-HAYA...
Huh?
KAZE-HAYA?
...
Will he...
Ha ha!
...BE OKAY?
HE SHOULD BE OKAY. RYU'S GOT IT COVERED.
Huh?
RYU...
Are you going home?
WHERE'S KAZE-HAYA?
...
...
SMILE...
WHERE'S ...
...KAZE-HAYA?
SMILE...
SMILE...
HE CAN'T LIE!
Will it really be okay?
Ha ha!
WELL, JOE IS PRETTY STUPID.
I think it's okay.
HEY...
...HAVE YOU SEEN KURO-NUMA?
WHOA!

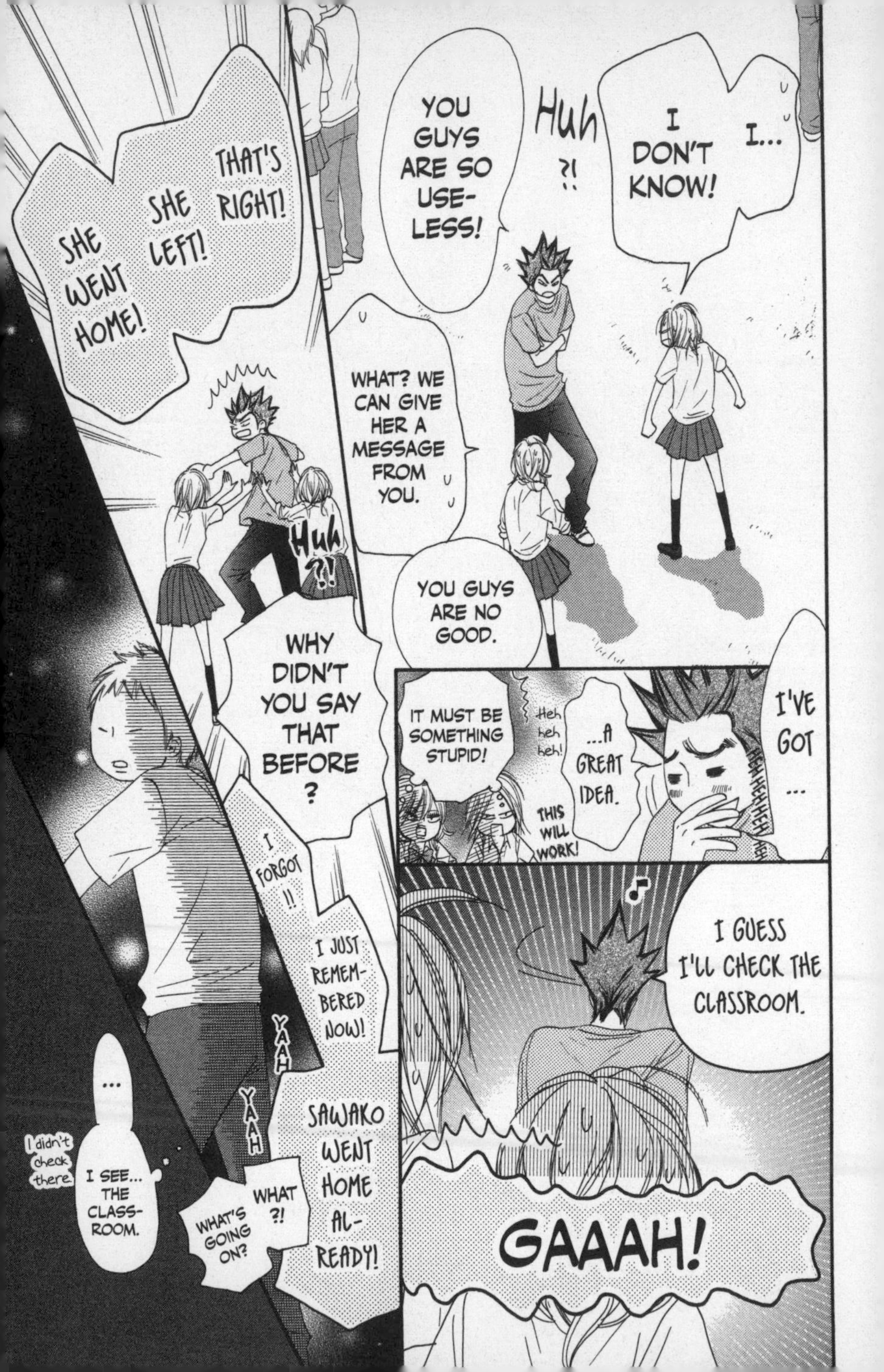
I...
I DON'T KNOW!
Huh ?!
YOU GUYS ARE SO USE-LESS!
WHAT? WE CAN GIVE HER A MESSAGE FROM YOU.
YOU GUYS ARE NO GOOD.
THAT'S RIGHT!
SHE LEFT!
SHE WENT HOME!
Huh ?!
WHY DIDN'T YOU SAY THAT BEFORE?
I FORGOT!!
I JUST REMEM-BERED NOW!
I'VE GOT...
HEH HEH HEH HEH
...A GREAT IDEA.
THIS WILL WORK!
Heh heh heh!
IT MUST BE SOMETHING STUPID!
I GUESS I'LL CHECK THE CLASSROOM.
GAAAH!
YAAH
YAAH
SAWAKO WENT HOME AL-READY!
WHAT?!
WHAT'S GOING ON?
...
I SEE... THE CLASS-ROOM.
I didn't check there.

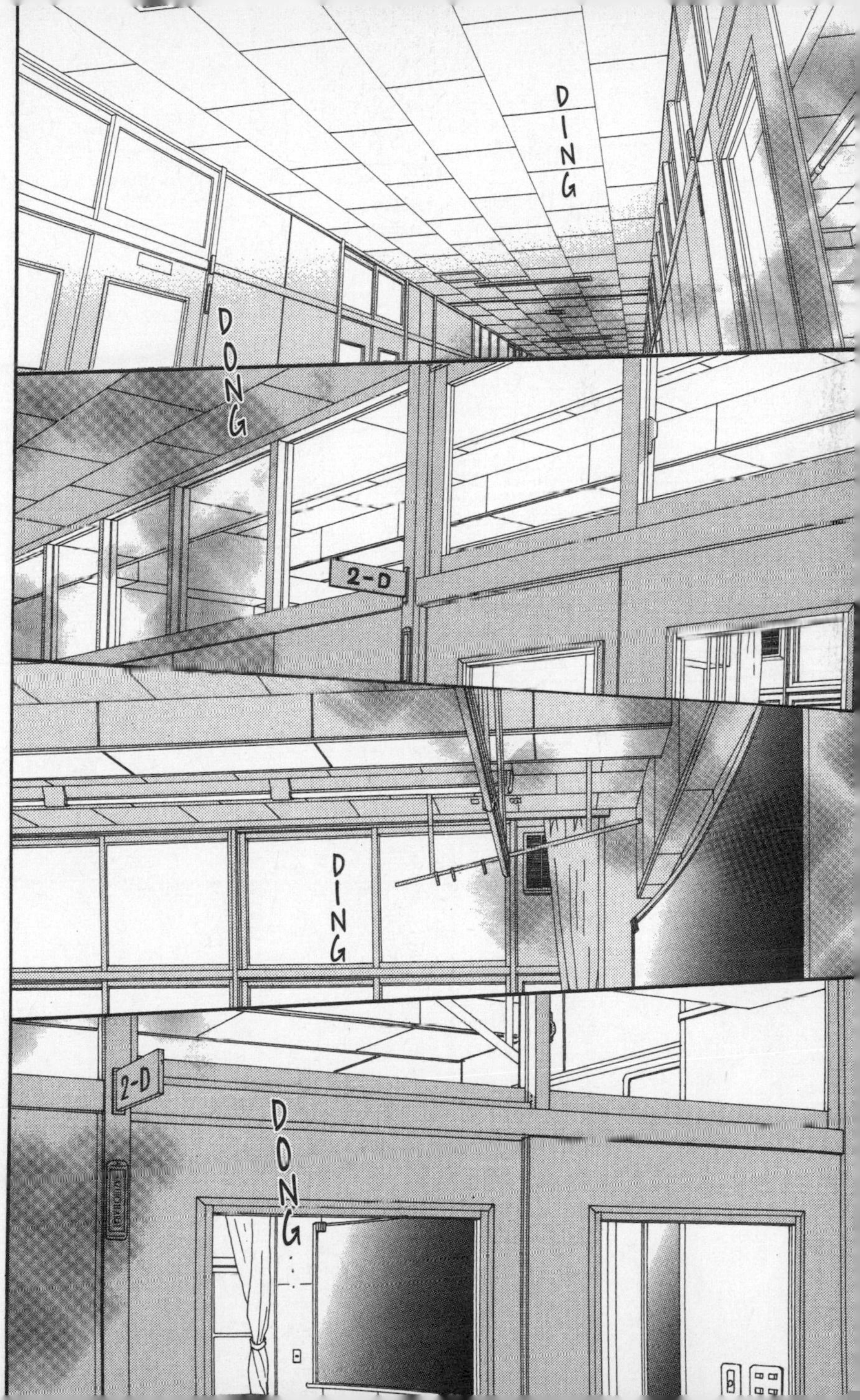
DING
DONG
2-D
DING
2-D
DONG...

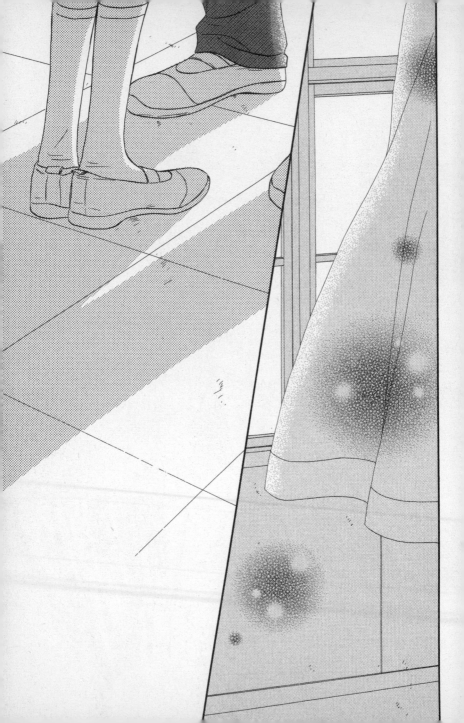

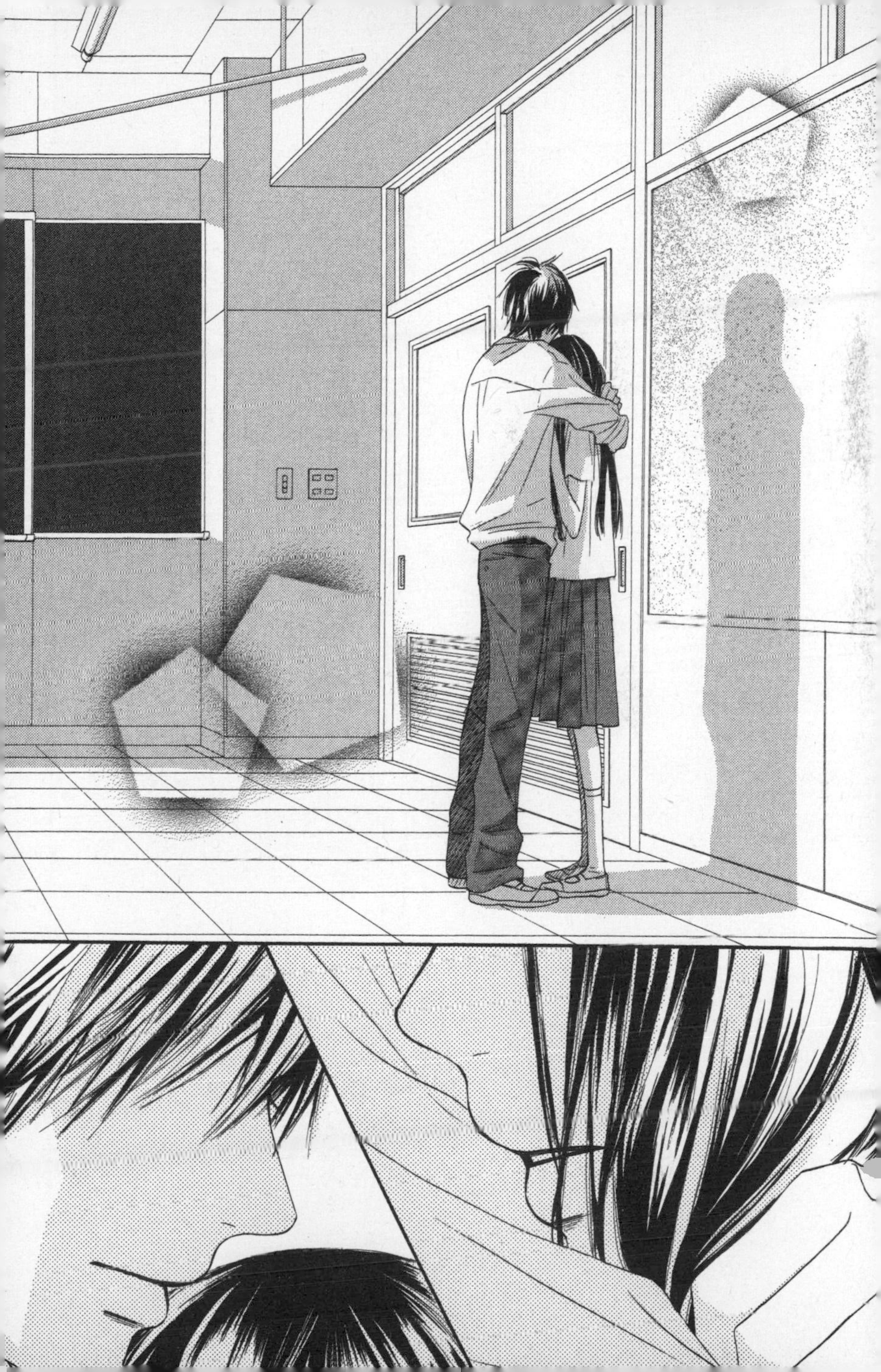

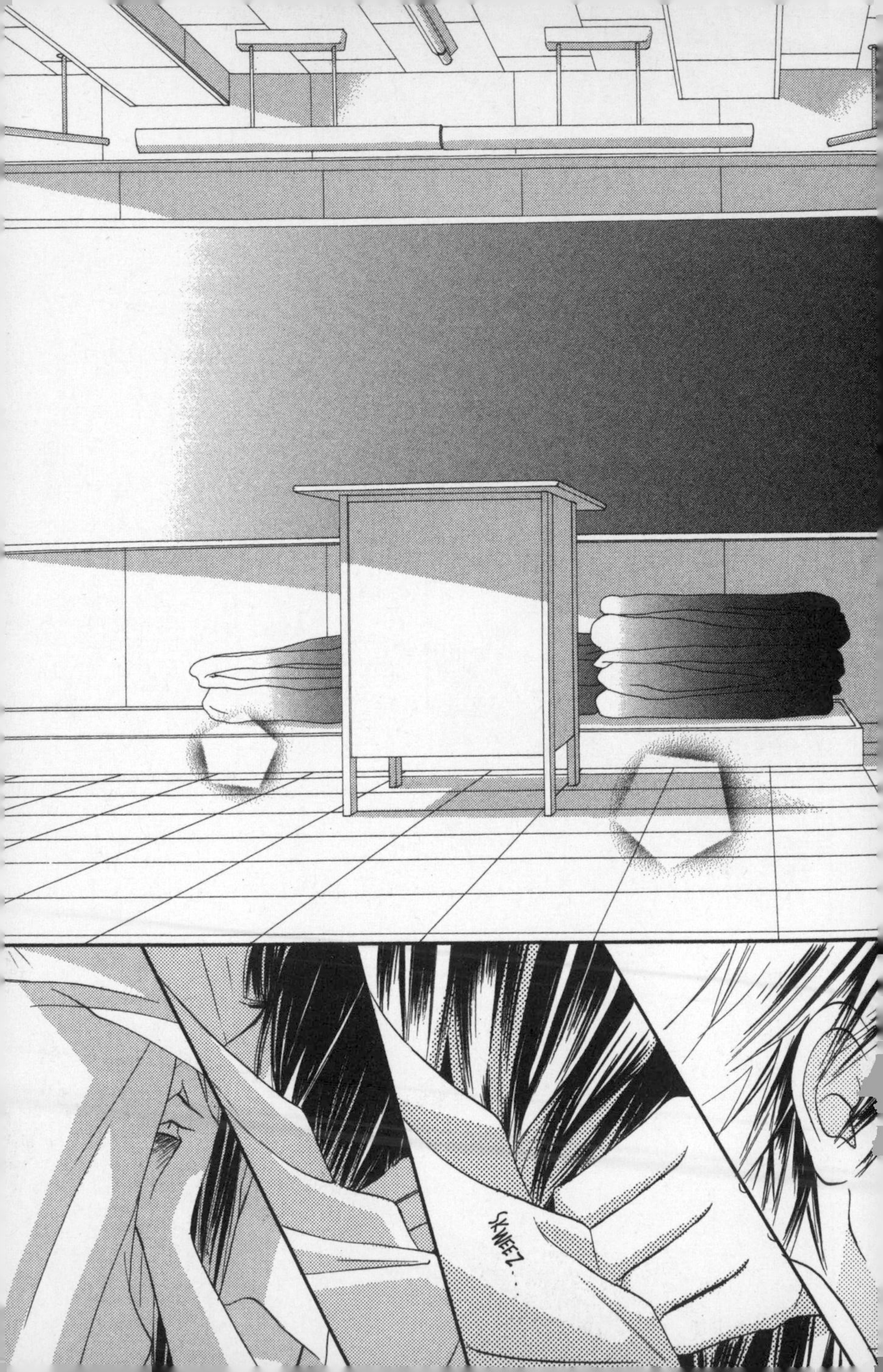
SKWEEZ...

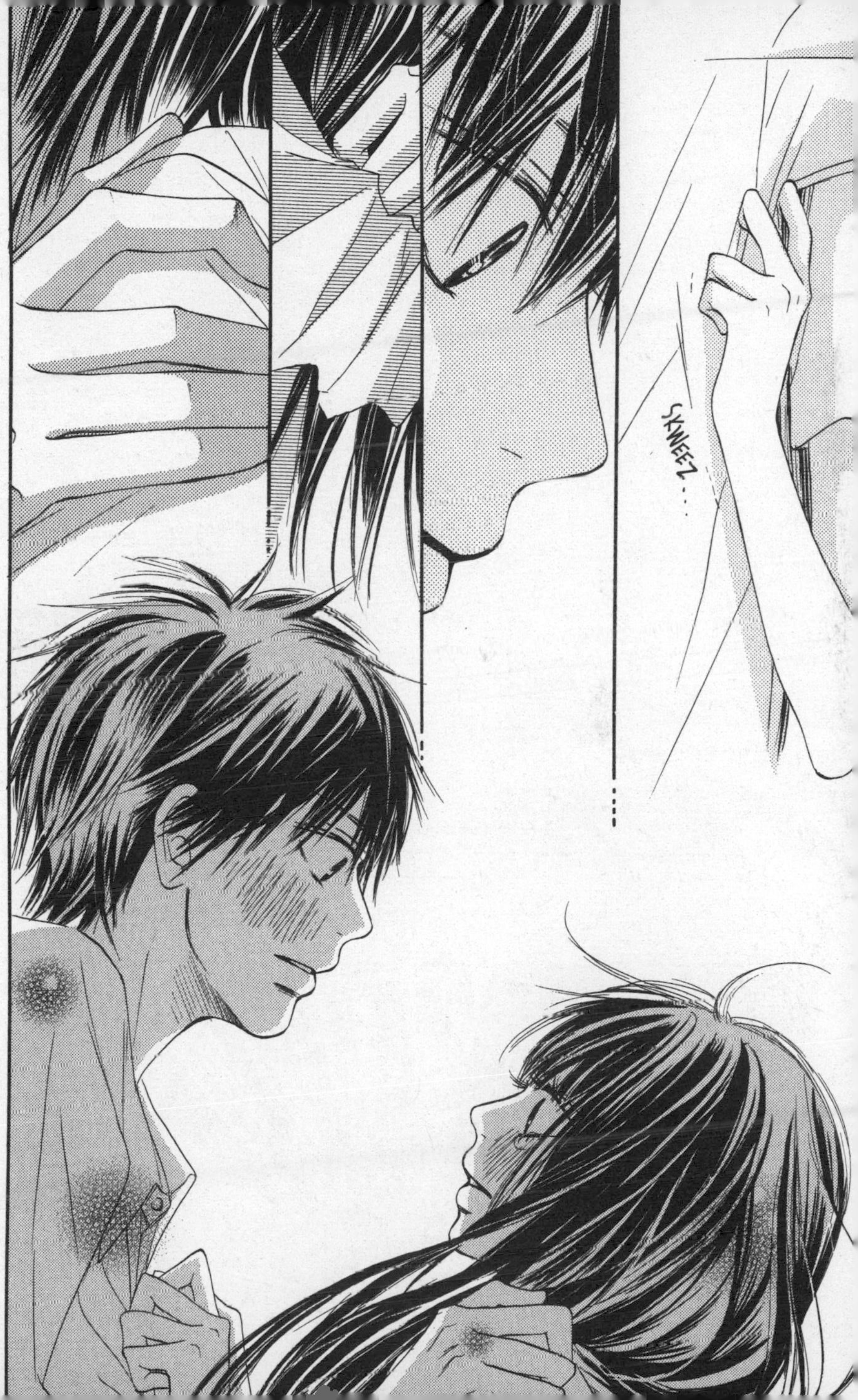
SKWEEZ...

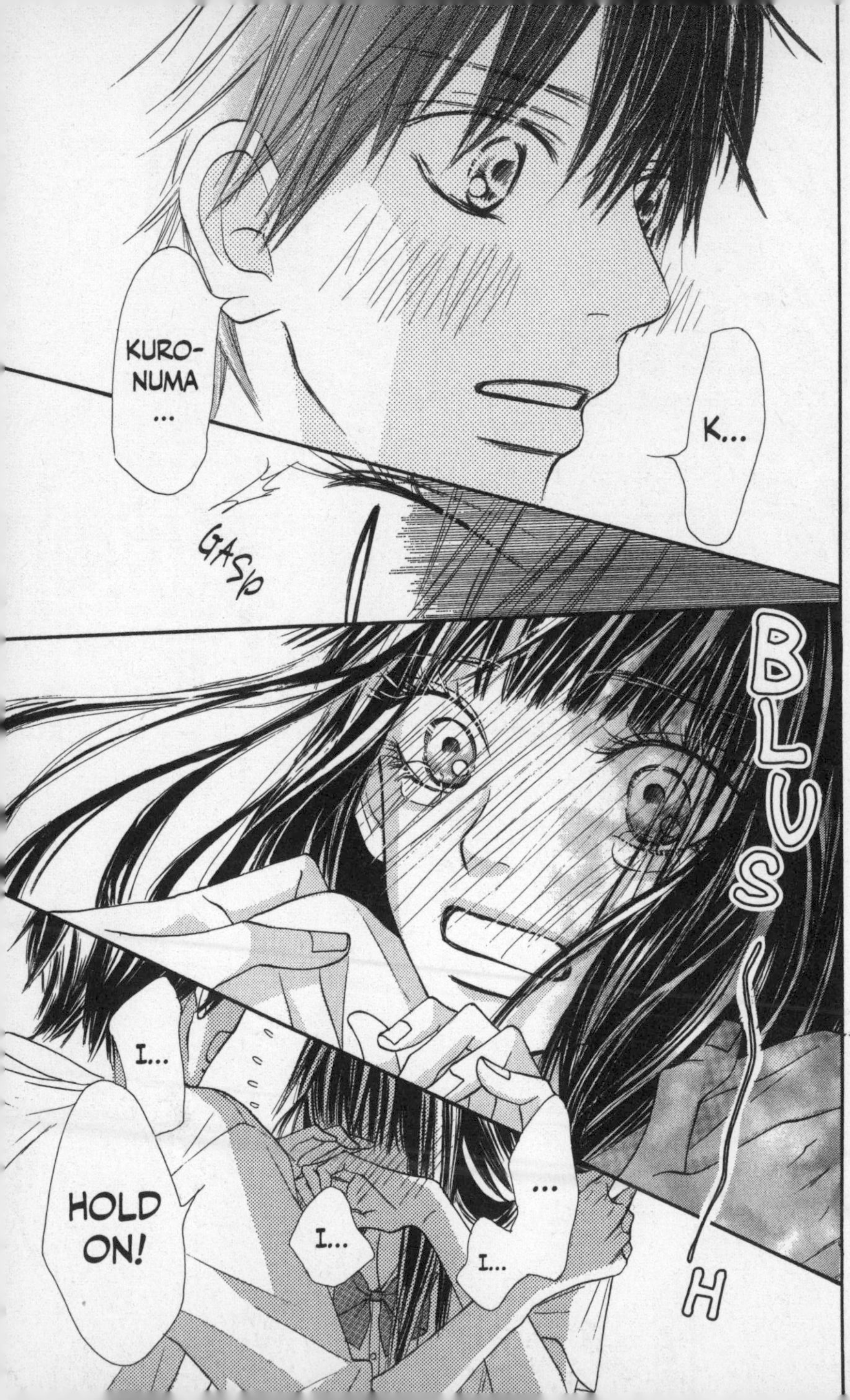
K...
KURO-NUMA...
GASP
BLUSH
... I...
I...
I...
HOLD ON!

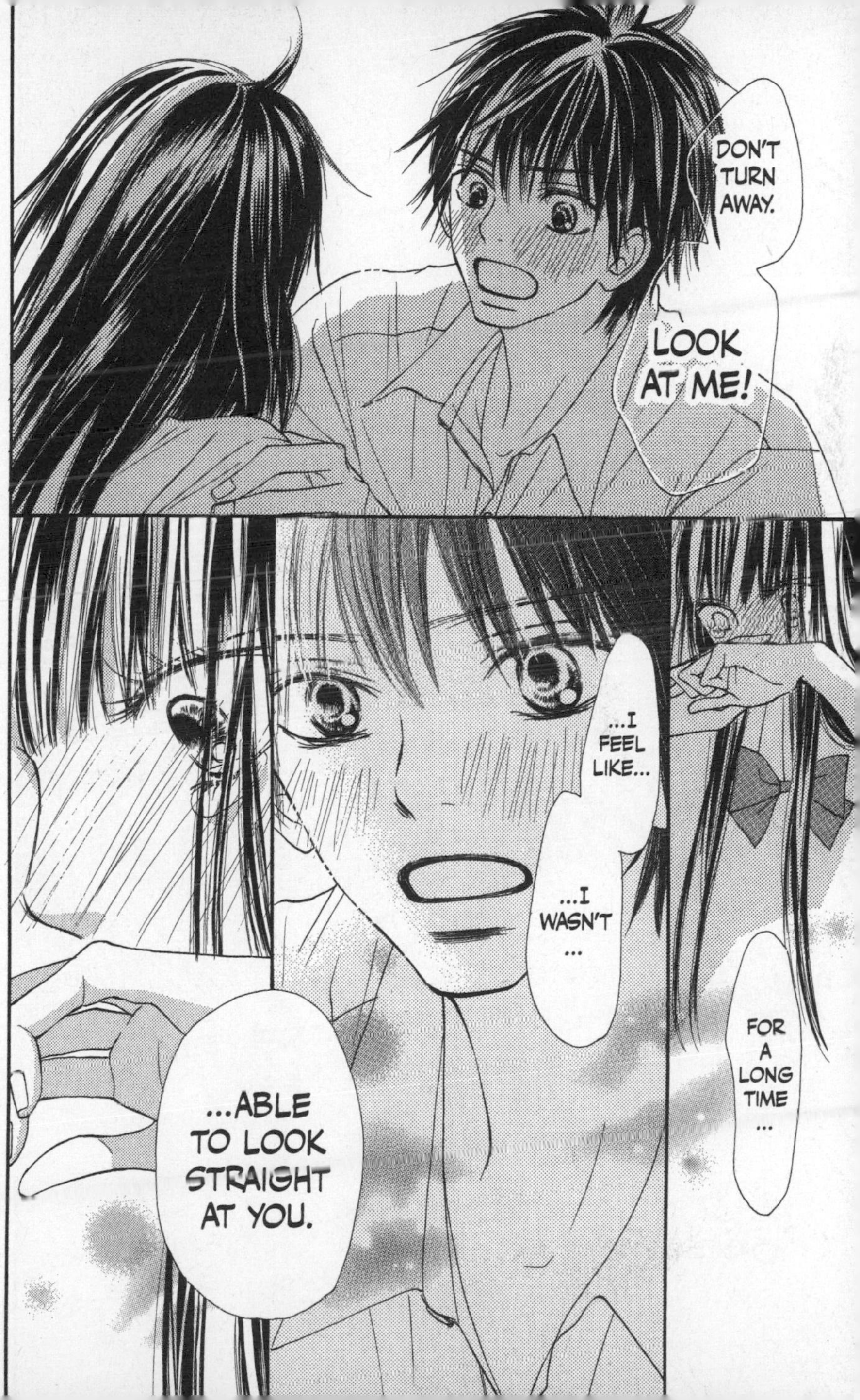
DON'T TURN AWAY.
LOOK AT ME!
...I FEEL LIKE...
FOR A LONG TIME ...
...I WASN'T ...
...ABLE TO LOOK STRAIGHT AT YOU.

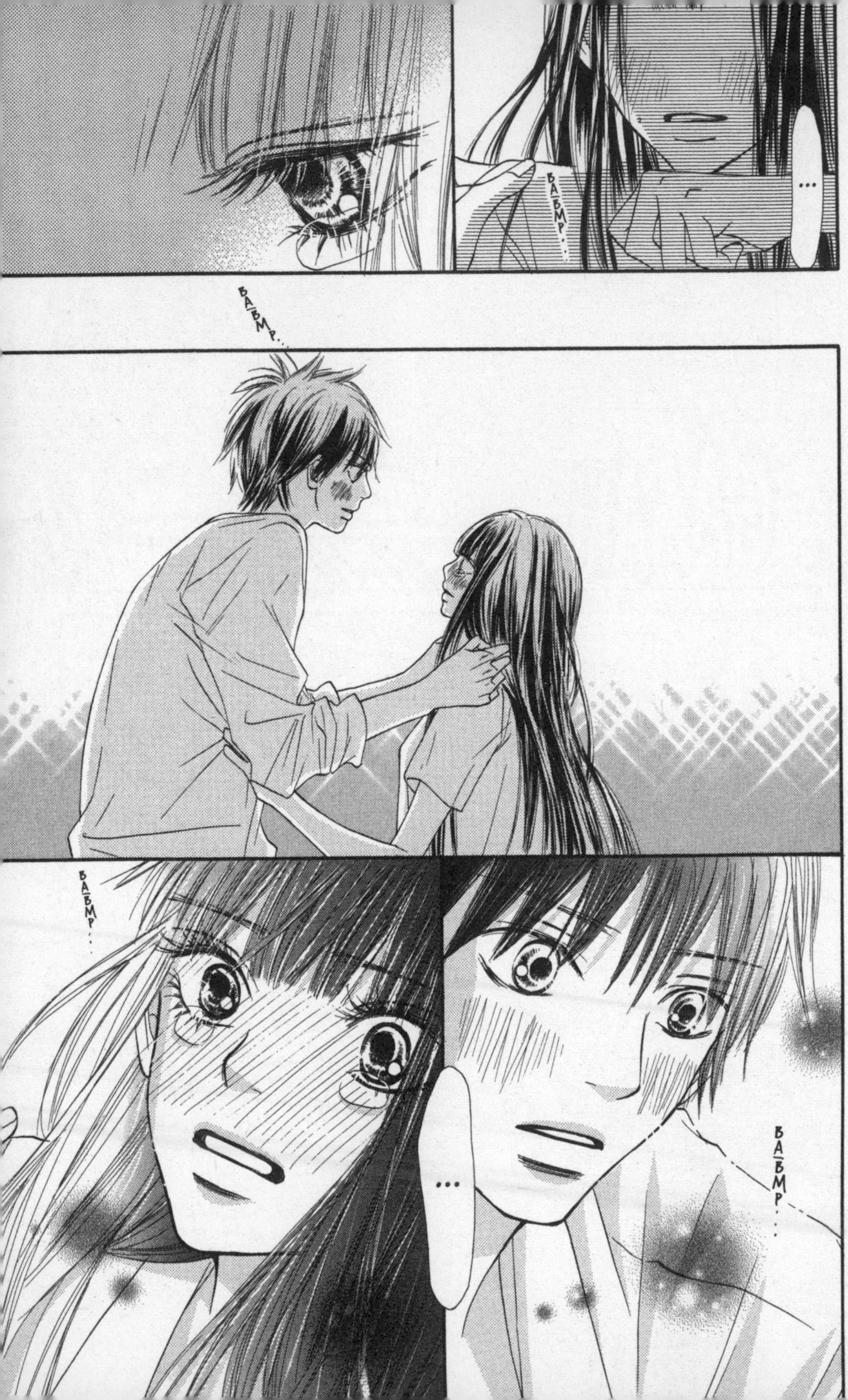

...
BA-BMP...
BA-BMP...
BA-BMP...
...
BA-BMP...

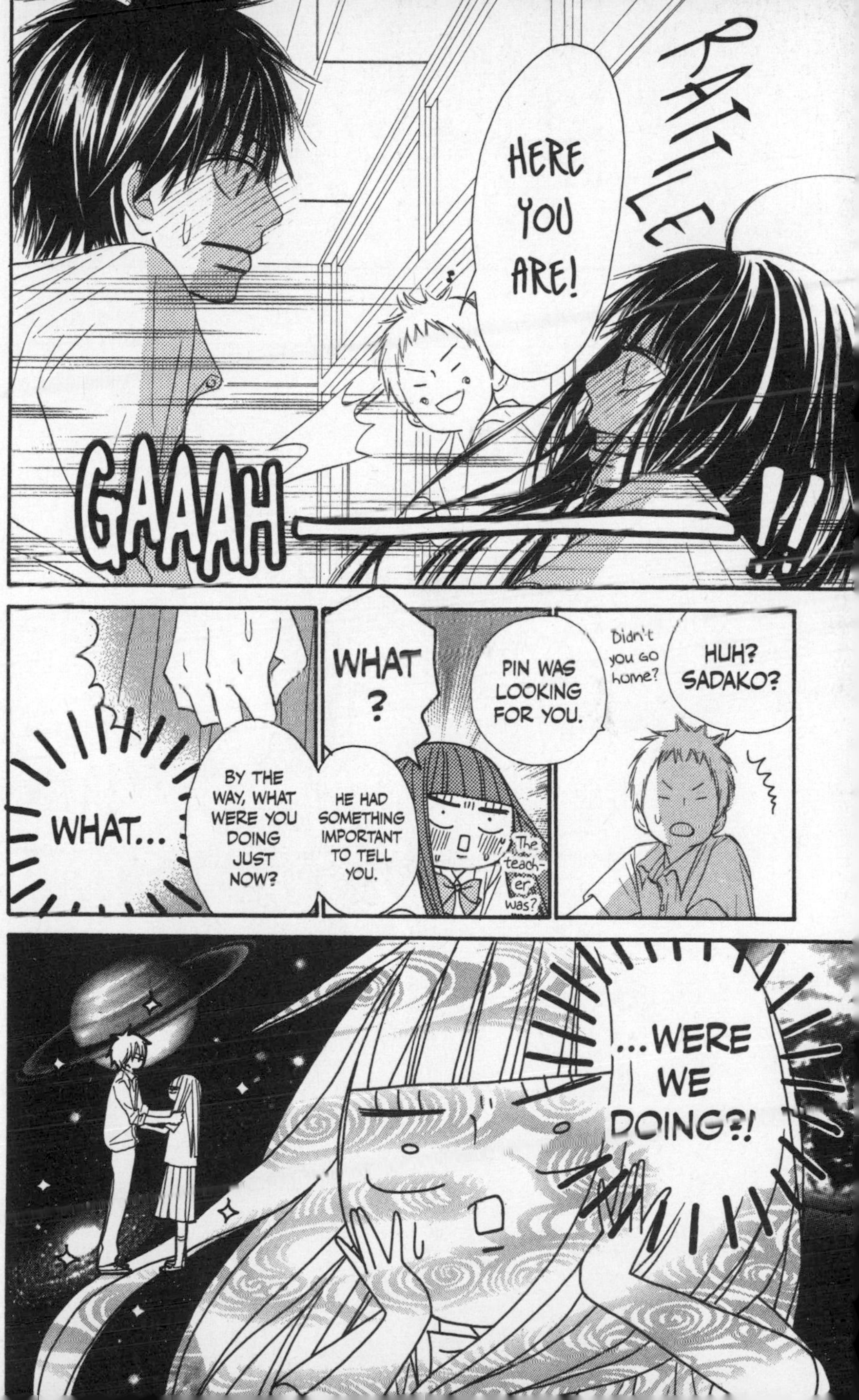
RATTLE
HERE YOU ARE!
GAAAH!!
HUH? SADAKO?
Didn't you go home?
PIN WAS LOOKING FOR YOU.
The teacher was?
WHAT?
HE HAD SOMETHING IMPORTANT TO TELL YOU.
BY THE WAY, WHAT WERE YOU DOING JUST NOW?
WHAT...
...WERE WE DOING?!

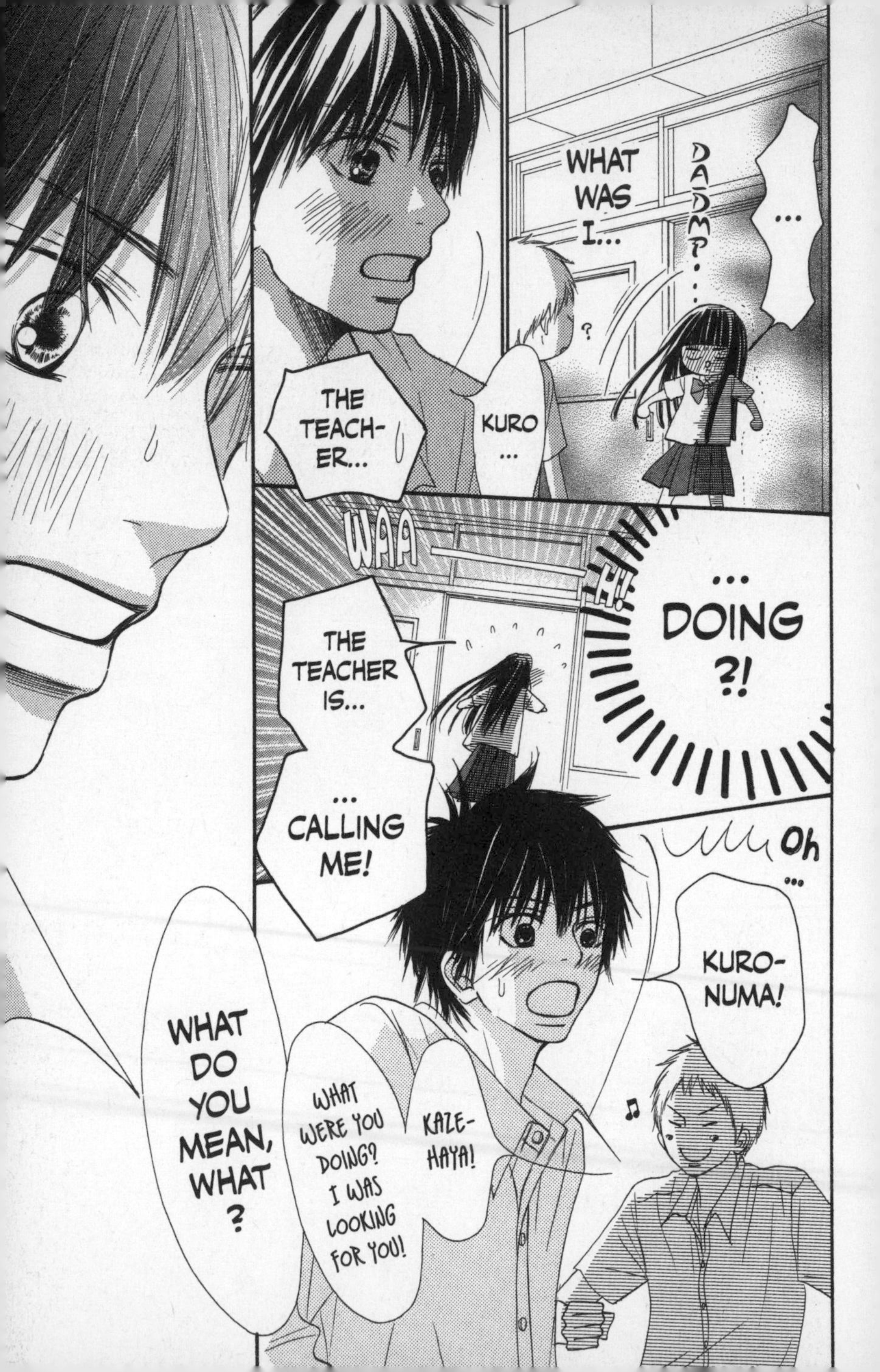
...
DADMP...
WHAT WAS I...
?
KURO...
THE TEACHER...
...DOING?!
WAAH!
THE TEACHER IS...
...CALLING ME!
Oh...
KURO-NUMA!
KAZE-HAYA!
WHAT WERE YOU DOING? I WAS LOOKING FOR YOU!
WHAT DO YOU MEAN, WHAT?

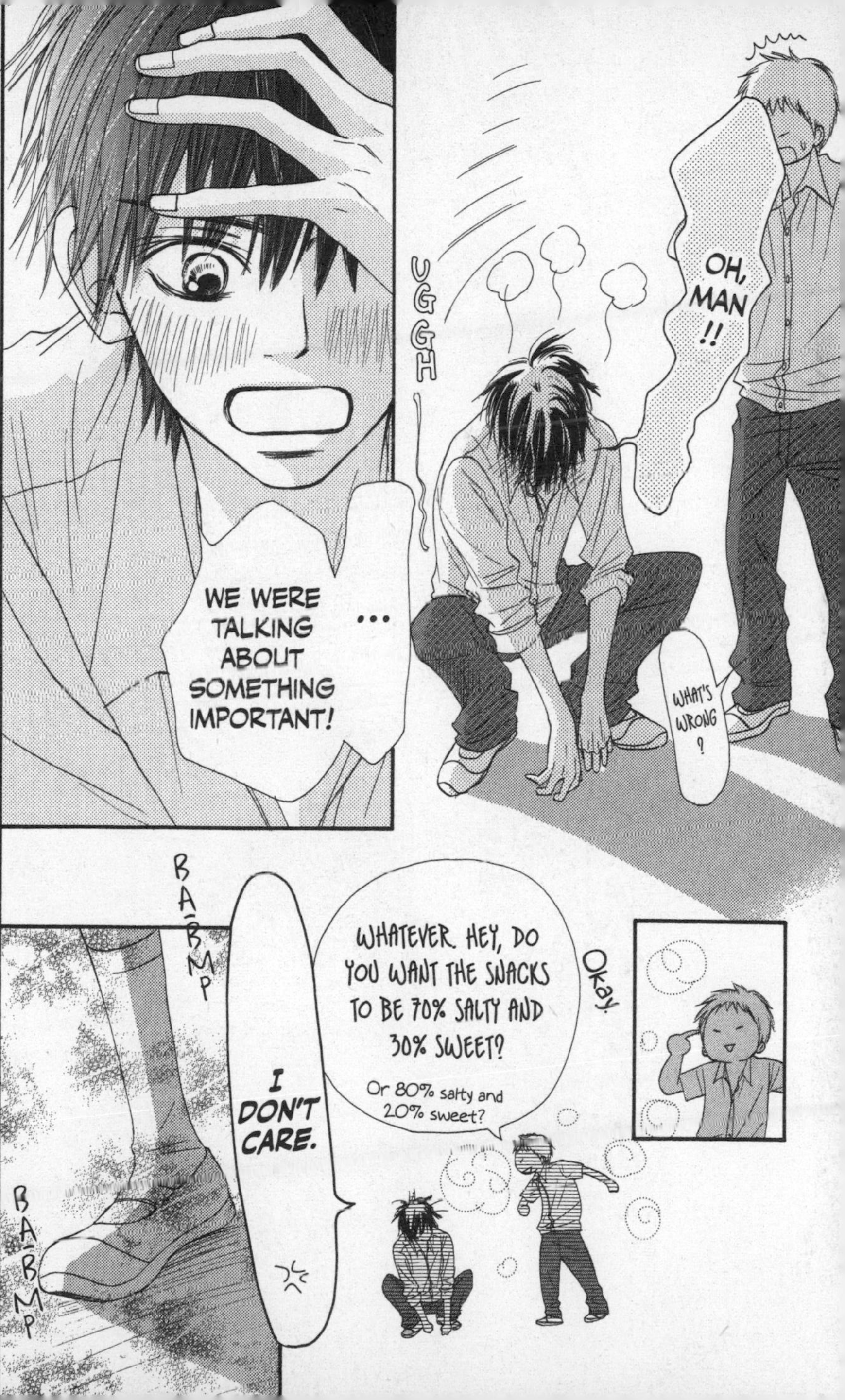
OH, MAN!!
UGGH—
WHAT'S WRONG?
WE WERE TALKING ABOUT SOMETHING IMPORTANT! ...
WHATEVER. HEY, DO YOU WANT THE SNACKS TO BE 70% SALTY AND 30% SWEET?
Or 80% salty and 20% sweet?
Okay.
I DON'T CARE.
BA-BMP
BA-BMP

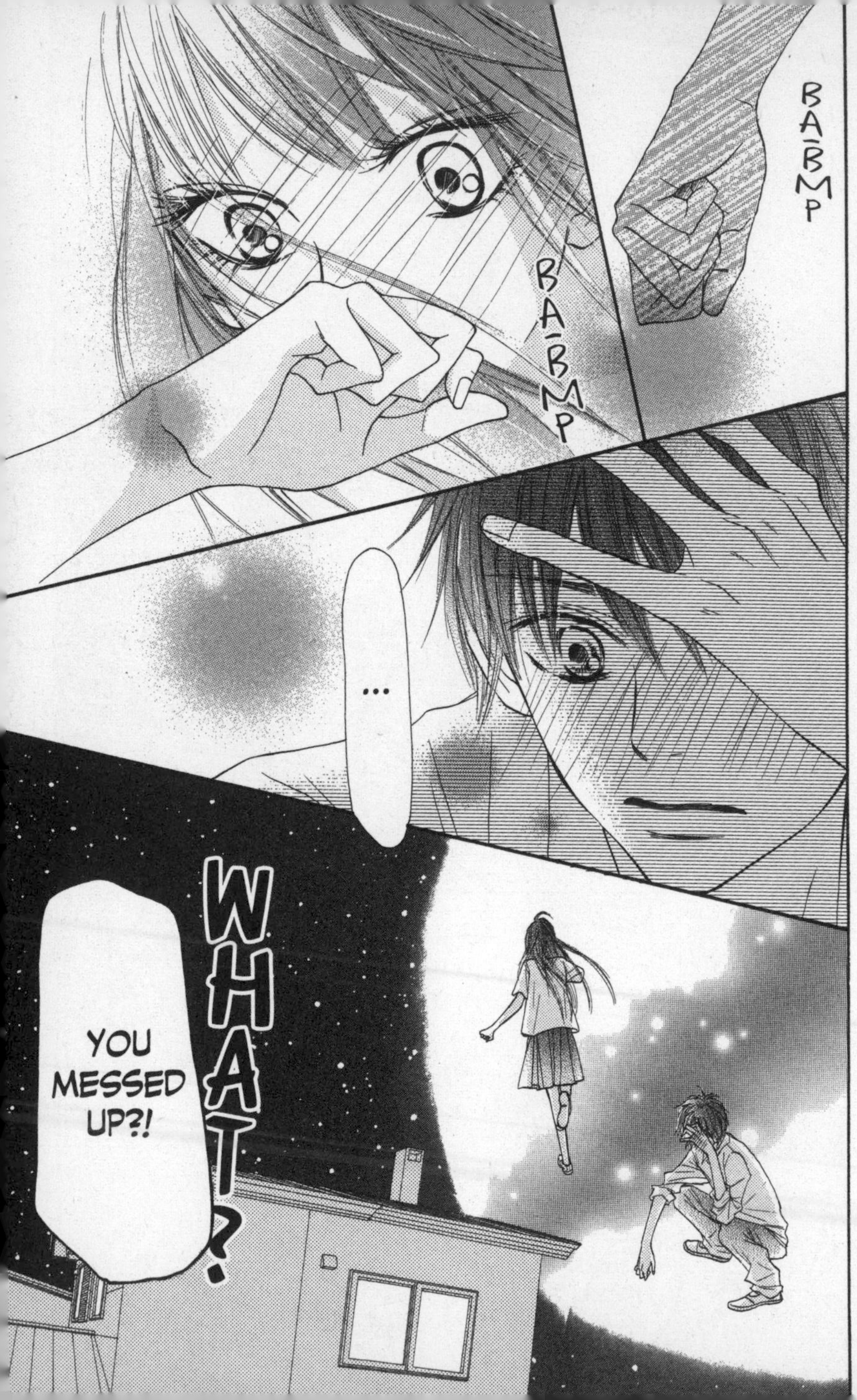
BA-BMP
BA-BMP
...
WHAT?
YOU MESSED UP?!

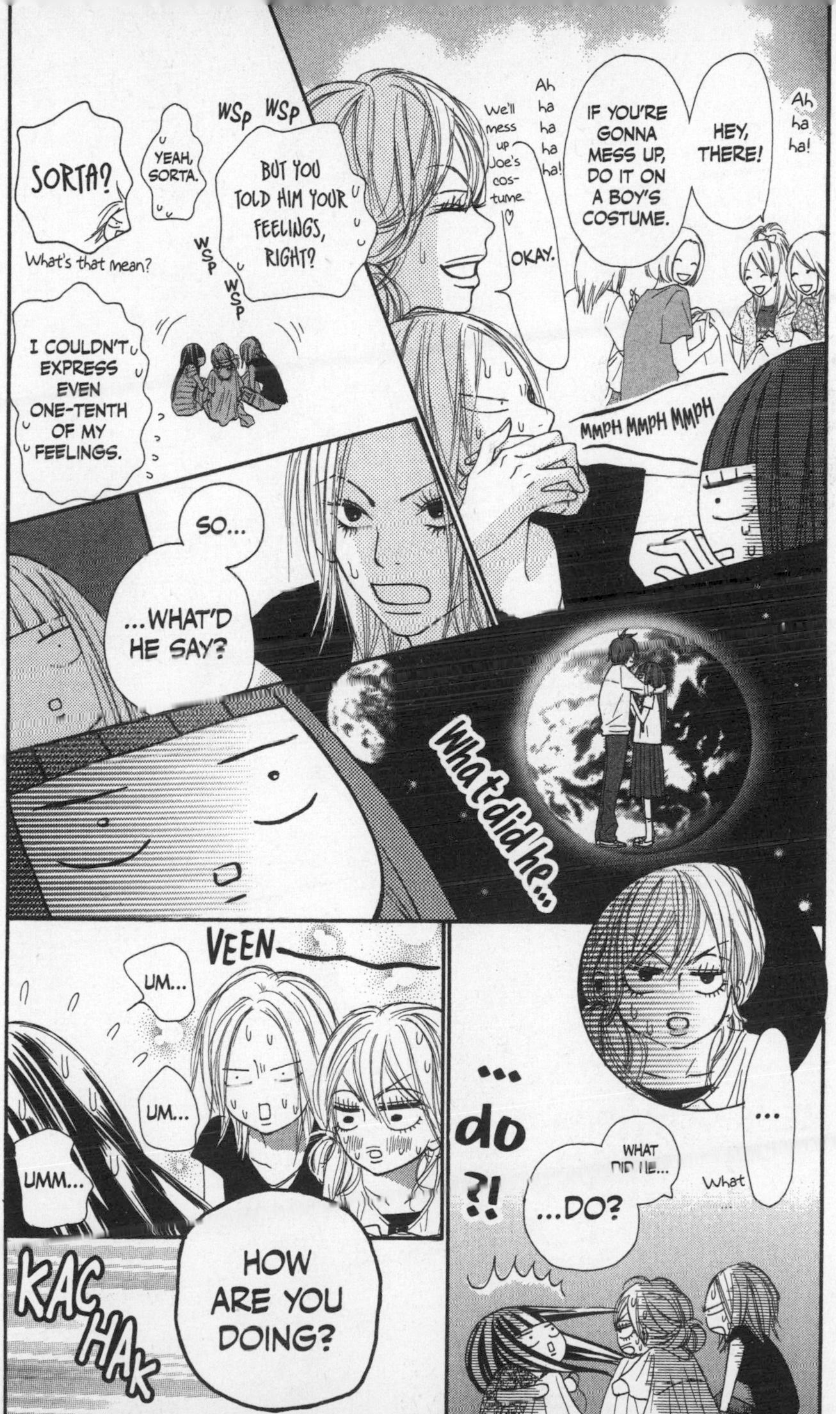
HEY, THERE!
Ah ha ha!
IF YOU'RE GONNA MESS UP, DO IT ON A BOY'S COSTUME.
Ah ha ha ha ha!
We'll mess up Joe's cos-tume ♡
OKAY.
MMPH MMPH MMPH
WSp WSp
BUT YOU TOLD HIM YOUR FEELINGS, RIGHT?
YEAH, SORTA.
SORTA?
What's that mean?
WSP WSP
I COULDN'T EXPRESS EVEN ONE-TENTH OF MY FEELINGS.
SO...
...WHAT'D HE SAY?
What did he...
...
What...
WHAT DID HE...
...DO?
...do?!
VEEN
UM...
UM...
UMM...
HOW ARE YOU DOING?
KACHAK

KARUPIN on JAPAN 1

Hello! How are you? This is Shiina.

Igoyoshinani...
(Persona)
From the Velvet Room

Volume 9 came out in September, but I finished the sidebars in April.

I took care of small things that I could do during maternity leave.

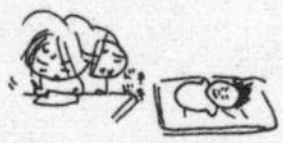

In April, my daughter looked like the Tokuho logo, but in September, when the graphic novel came out...

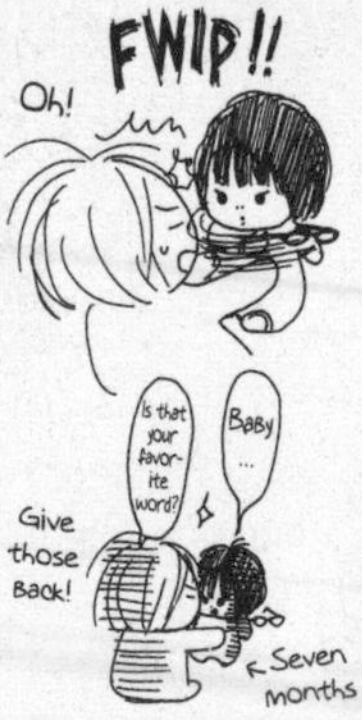
FWIP!!
Oh!
Is that your favorite word?
Baby...
Give those back!
Seven months

She was this big, so I decided never to write the sidebars early again. Her hair that was standing up is lying down now! I wonder what she will be like when this volume comes out.

She'll be one year old. My, how time flies!

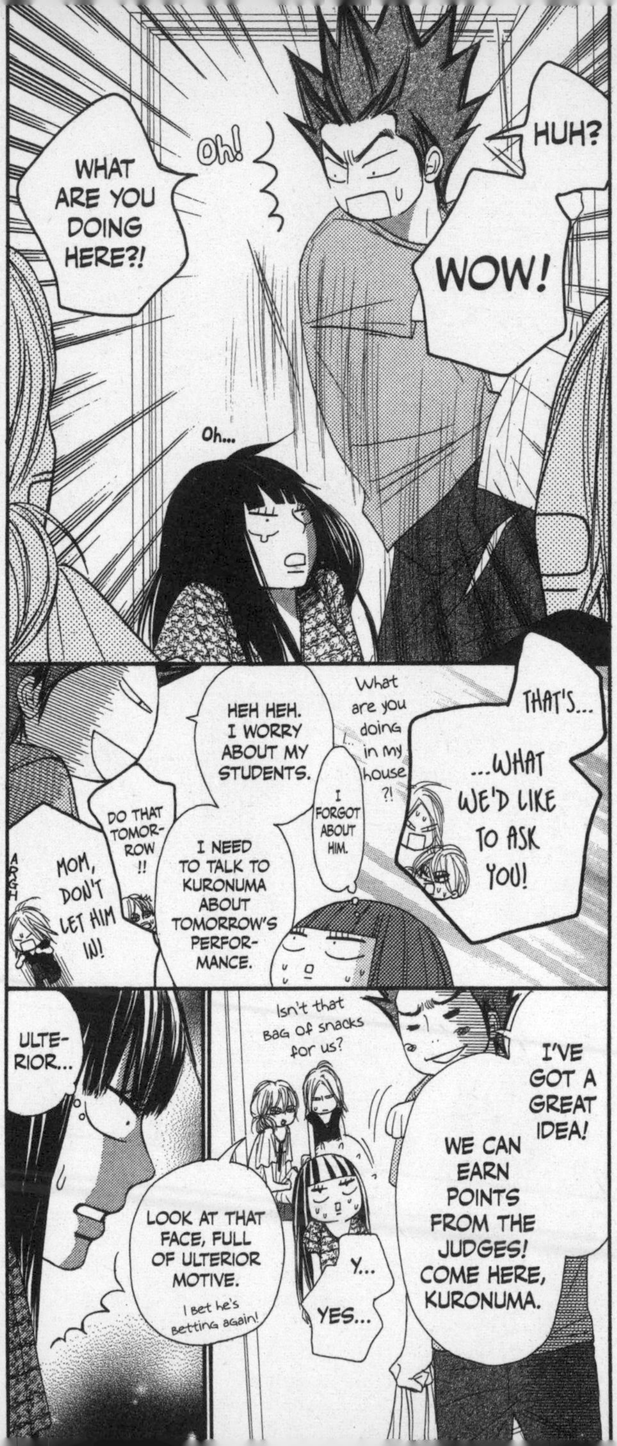
HUH?
WOW!
Oh!
WHAT ARE YOU DOING HERE?!
Oh...
THAT'S...
...WHAT WE'D LIKE TO ASK YOU!
What are you doing in my house?!
I FORGOT ABOUT HIM.
HEH HEH. I WORRY ABOUT MY STUDENTS.
I NEED TO TALK TO KURONUMA ABOUT TOMORROW'S PERFORMANCE.
DO THAT TOMORROW!!
MOM, DON'T LET HIM IN!
ARGH
I'VE GOT A GREAT IDEA!
WE CAN EARN POINTS FROM THE JUDGES! COME HERE, KURONUMA.
Isn't that bag of snacks for us?
Y...
YES...
LOOK AT THAT FACE, FULL OF ULTERIOR MOTIVE.
I bet he's betting again!
ULTERIOR...

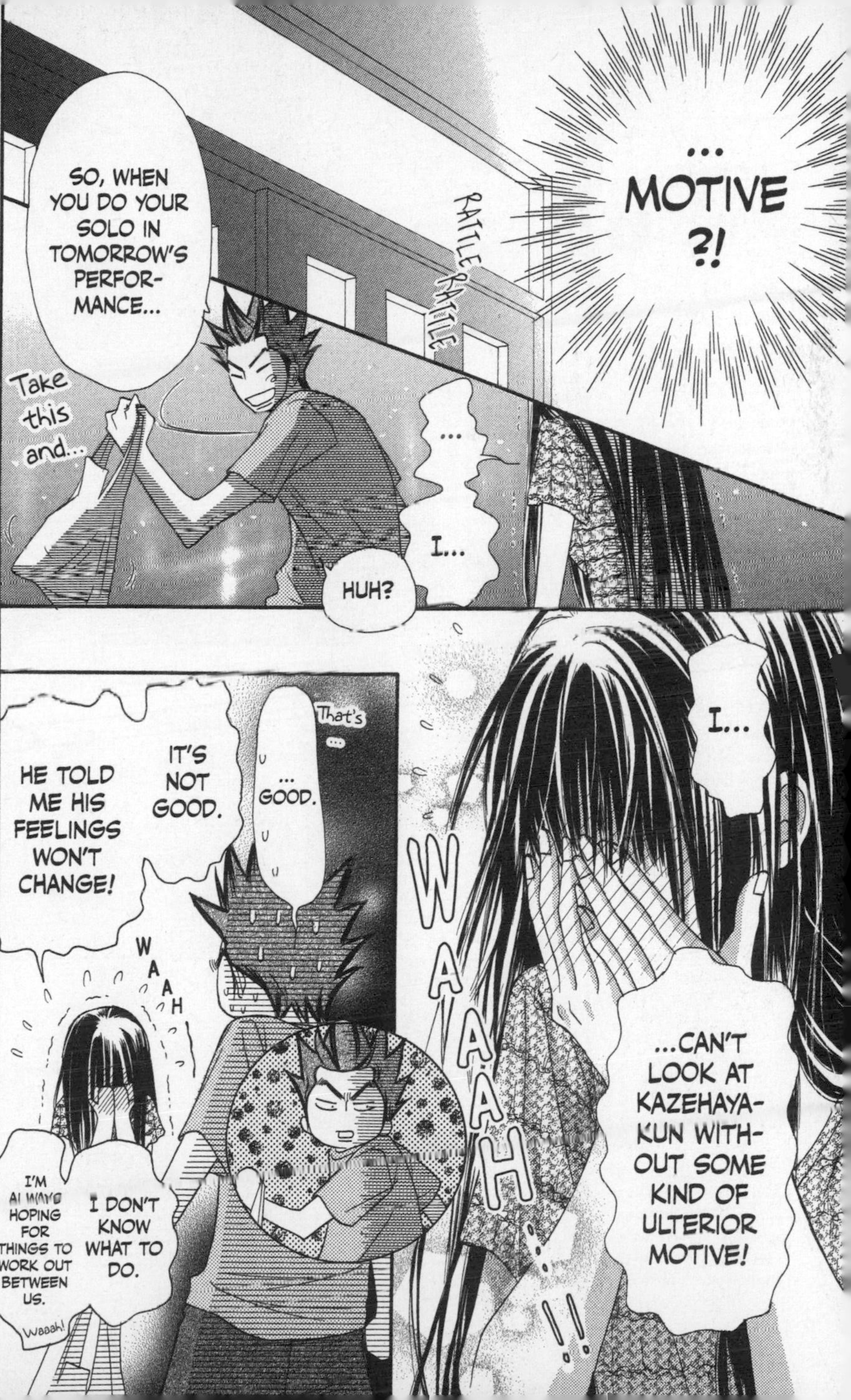
...MOTIVE?!
SO, WHEN YOU DO YOUR SOLO IN TOMORROW'S PERFORMANCE...
Take this and...
RATTLE RATTLE
...
I...
HUH?
I...
...CAN'T LOOK AT KAZEHAYA-KUN WITHOUT SOME KIND OF ULTERIOR MOTIVE!
WAAAAH...!!
That's ...
... GOOD.
IT'S NOT GOOD.
HE TOLD ME HIS FEELINGS WON'T CHANGE!
WAAH
I'M ALWAYS HOPING FOR THINGS TO WORK OUT BETWEEN US.
I DON'T KNOW WHAT TO DO.
Waaah!

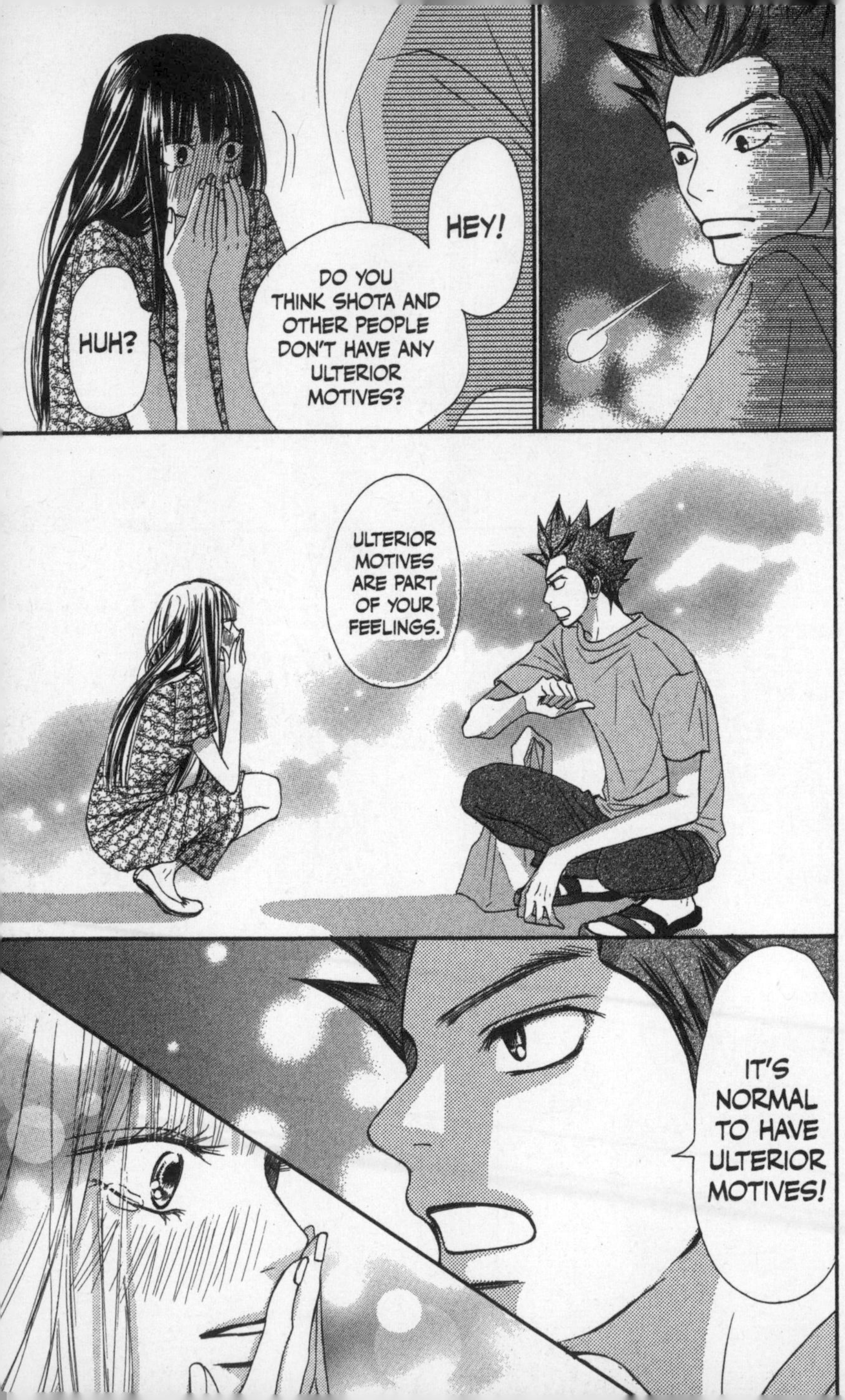
HEY!
DO YOU THINK SHOTA AND OTHER PEOPLE DON'T HAVE ANY ULTERIOR MOTIVES?
HUH?
ULTERIOR MOTIVES ARE PART OF YOUR FEELINGS.
IT'S NORMAL TO HAVE ULTERIOR MOTIVES!

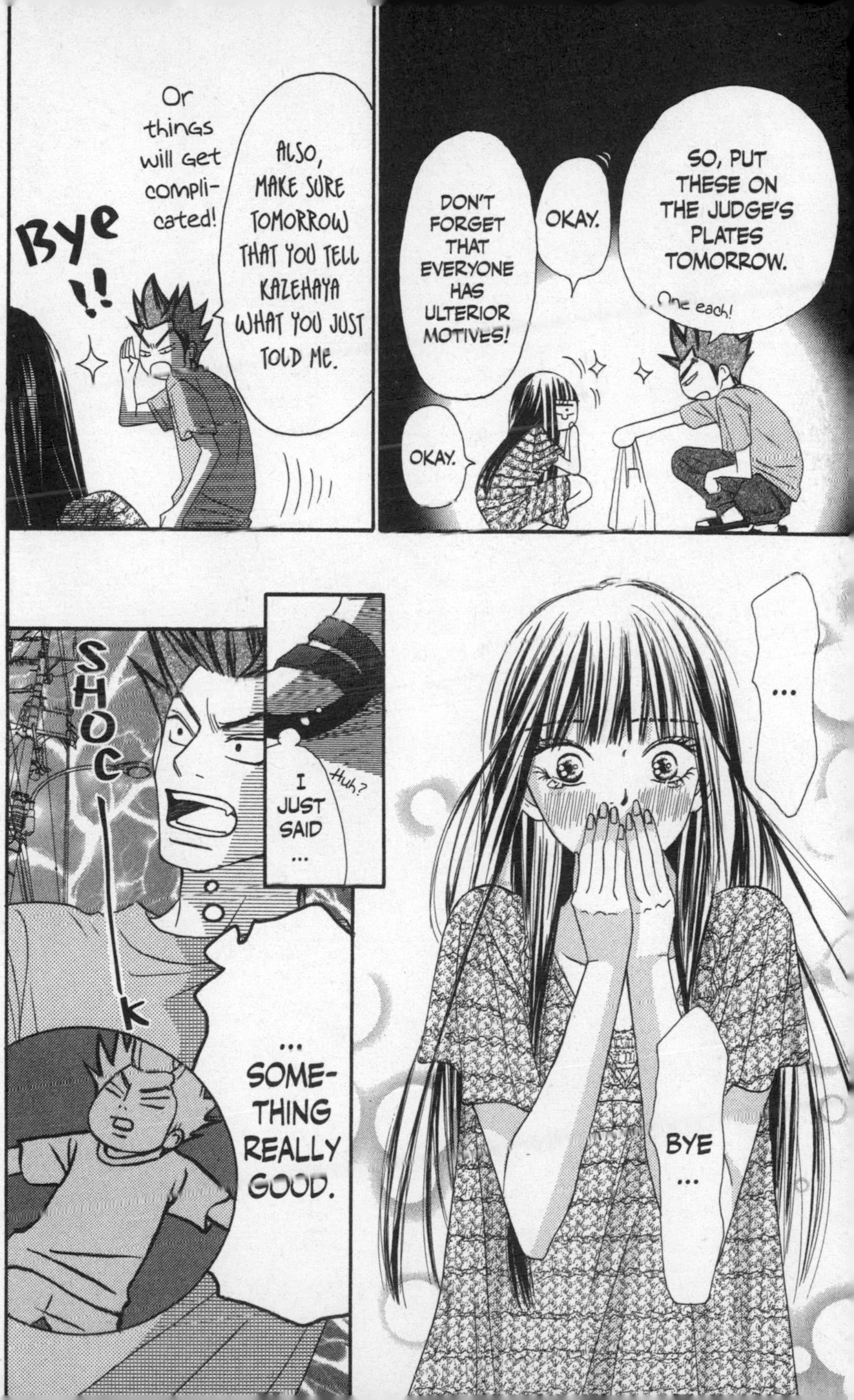
SO, PUT THESE ON THE JUDGE'S PLATES TOMORROW.
One each!
OKAY.
DON'T FORGET THAT EVERYONE HAS ULTERIOR MOTIVES!
OKAY.
ALSO, MAKE SURE TOMORROW THAT YOU TELL KAZEHAYA WHAT YOU JUST TOLD ME.
Or things will get compli-cated!
Bye!!
...
BYE ...
Huh?
I JUST SAID ...
... SOME-THING REALLY GOOD.
SHOCK

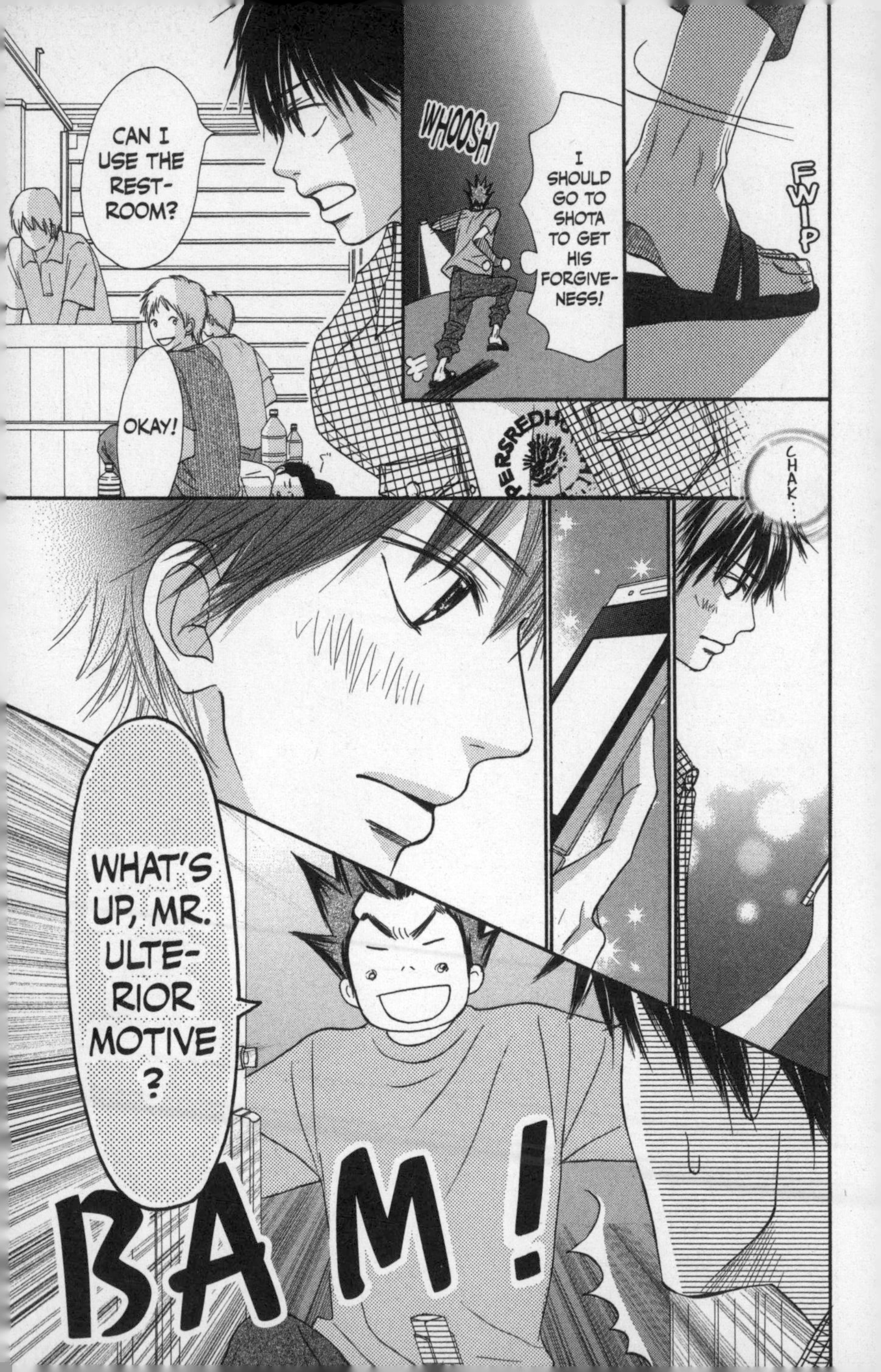
FWIP
WHOOSH
I SHOULD GO TO SHOTA TO GET HIS FORGIVE-NESS!
CAN I USE THE REST-ROOM?
OKAY!
CHAK...
WHAT'S UP, MR. ULTE-RIOR MOTIVE?
BAM!

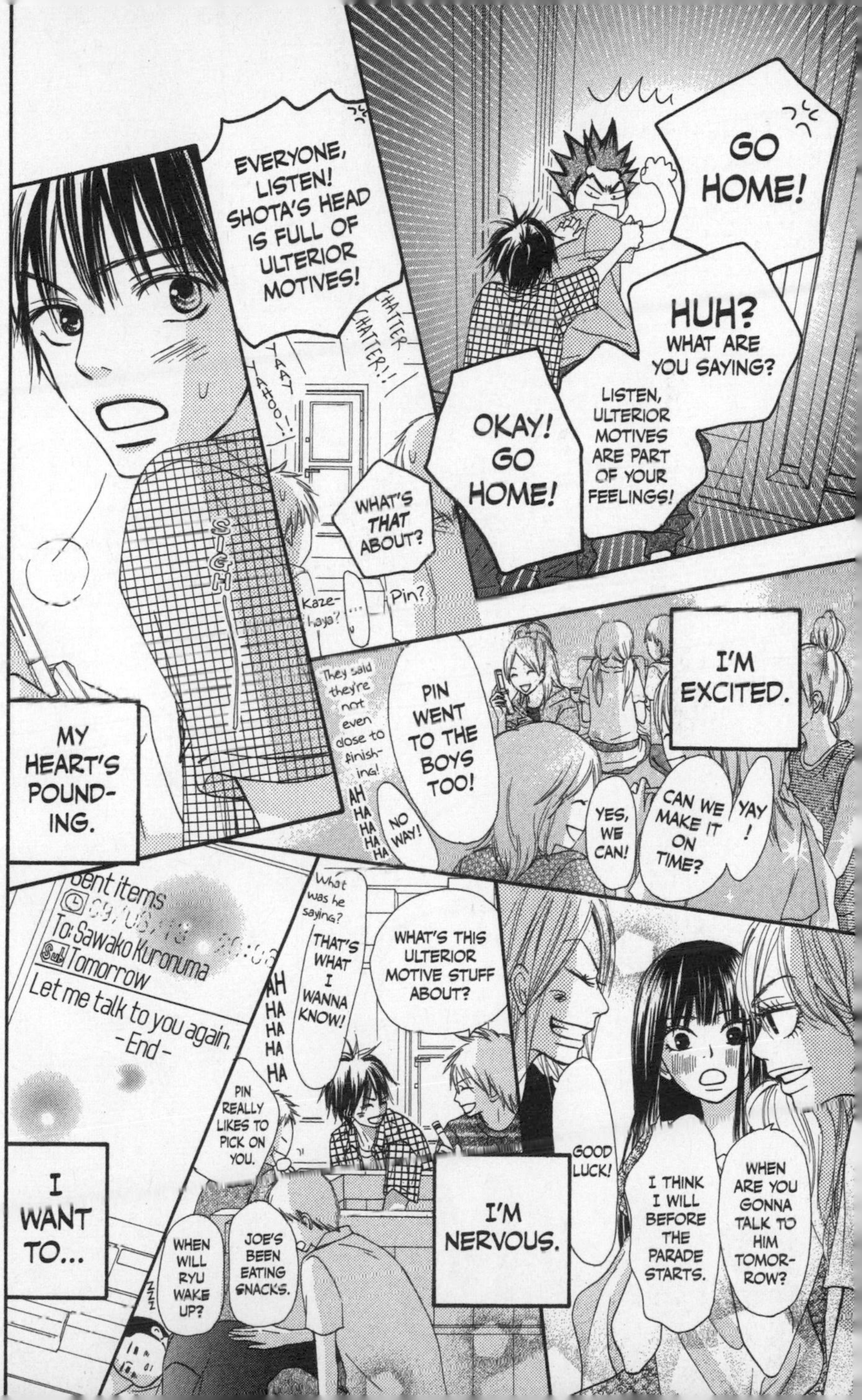

EVERYONE, LISTEN! SHOTA'S HEAD IS FULL OF ULTERIOR MOTIVES!
GO HOME!
HUH? WHAT ARE YOU SAYING?
LISTEN, ULTERIOR MOTIVES ARE PART OF YOUR FEELINGS!
OKAY! GO HOME!
WHAT'S THAT ABOUT?
Pin?
...
Kaze-haya?
CHATTER CHATTER!!
YAAY YAHOO!!
SIGH
MY HEART'S POUND-ING.
I'M EXCITED.
YAY!
CAN WE MAKE IT ON TIME?
YES, WE CAN!
PIN WENT TO THE BOYS TOO!
They said they're not even close to finishing!
NO WAY!
AH HA HA HA HA
WHEN ARE YOU GONNA TALK TO HIM TOMOR-ROW?
I THINK I WILL BEFORE THE PARADE STARTS.
GOOD LUCK!
I'M NERVOUS.
WHAT'S THIS ULTERIOR MOTIVE STUFF ABOUT?
What was he saying?
THAT'S WHAT I WANNA KNOW!
AH HA HA HA HA HA
PIN REALLY LIKES TO PICK ON YOU.
JOE'S BEEN EATING SNACKS.
WHEN WILL RYU WAKE UP?
ZZZ
Sent items
To: Sawako Kuronuma
Sub Tomorrow
Let me talk to you again.
-End-
I WANT TO...

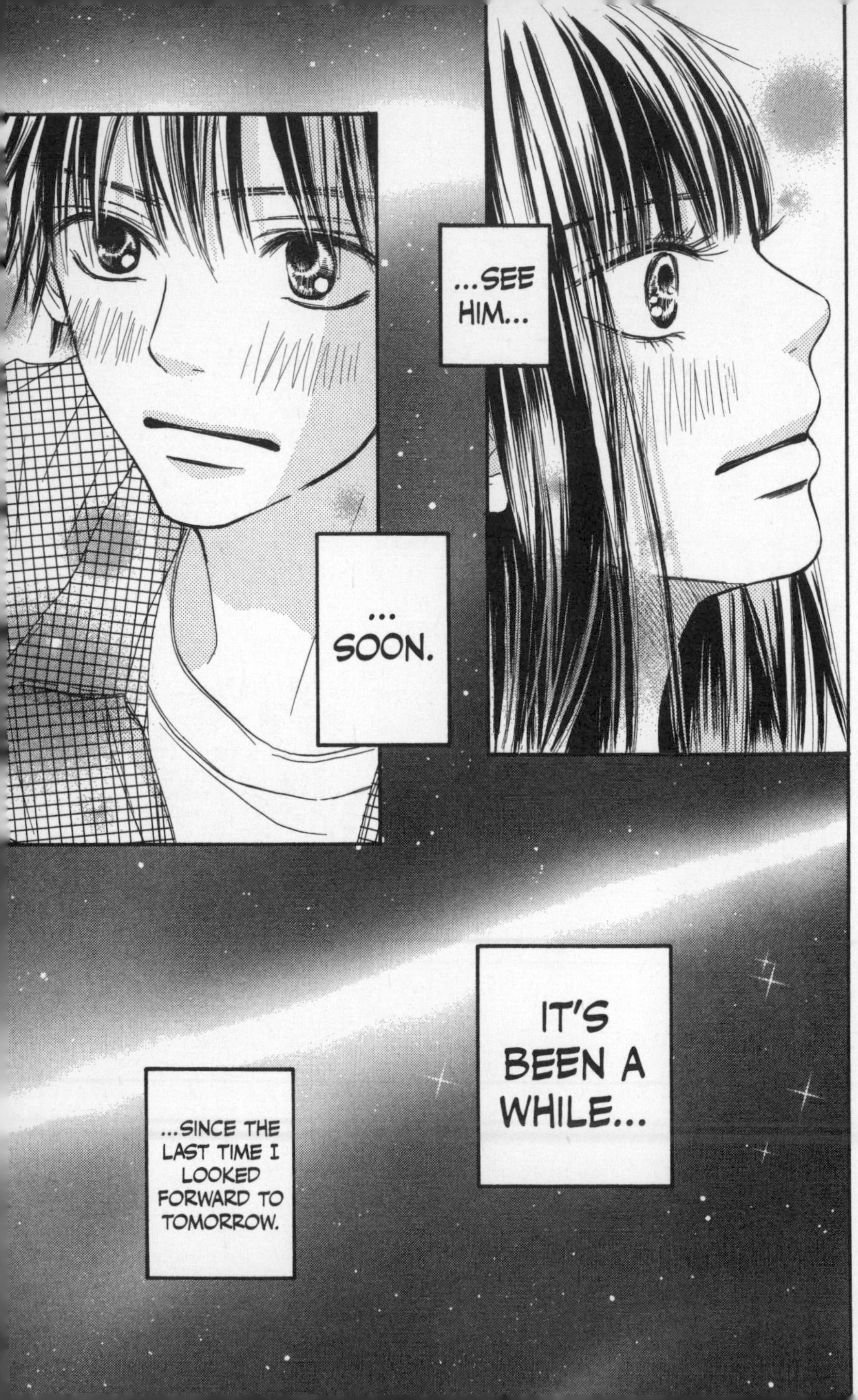
...SEE HIM...
... SOON.
IT'S BEEN A WHILE...
...SINCE THE LAST TIME I LOOKED FORWARD TO TOMORROW.

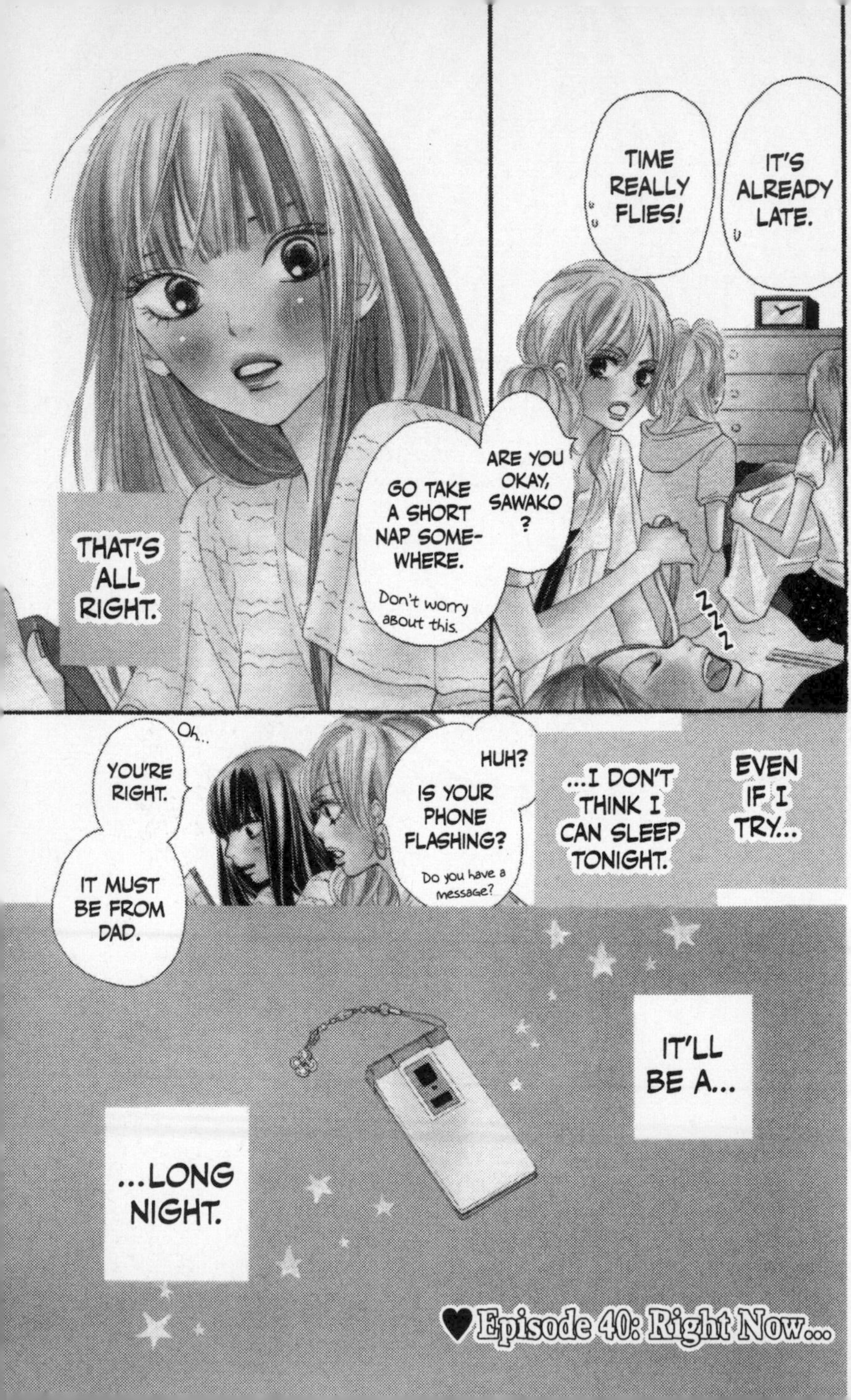
IT'S ALREADY LATE.
TIME REALLY FLIES!
ARE YOU OKAY, SAWAKO?
GO TAKE A SHORT NAP SOME-WHERE.
Don't worry about this.
ZZZ
THAT'S ALL RIGHT.
EVEN IF I TRY...
...I DON'T THINK I CAN SLEEP TONIGHT.
HUH?
IS YOUR PHONE FLASHING?
Do you have a message?
Oh...
YOU'RE RIGHT.
IT MUST BE FROM DAD.
IT'LL BE A...
...LONG NIGHT.
Episode 40: Right Now...

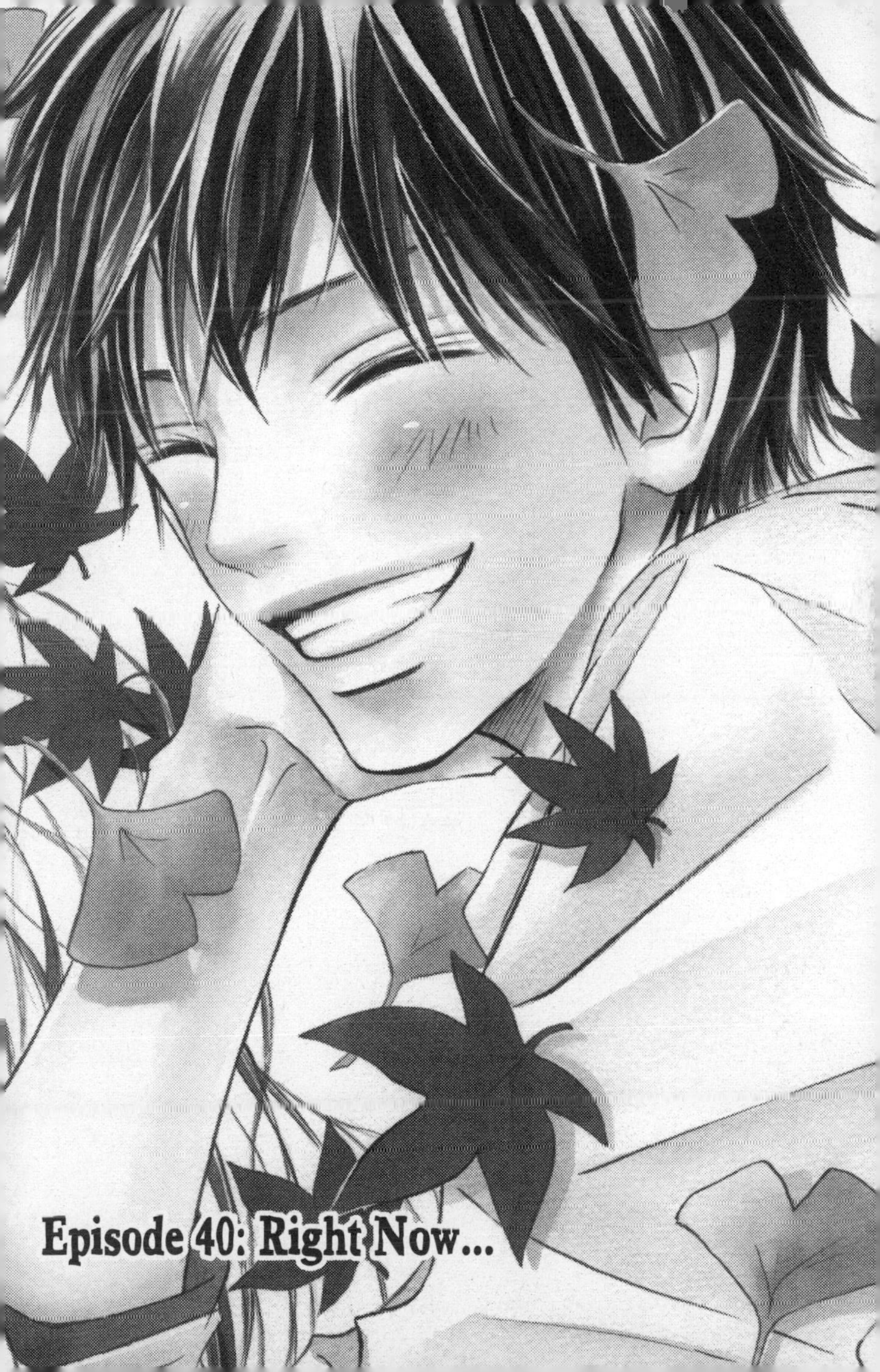
Episode 40: Right Now...

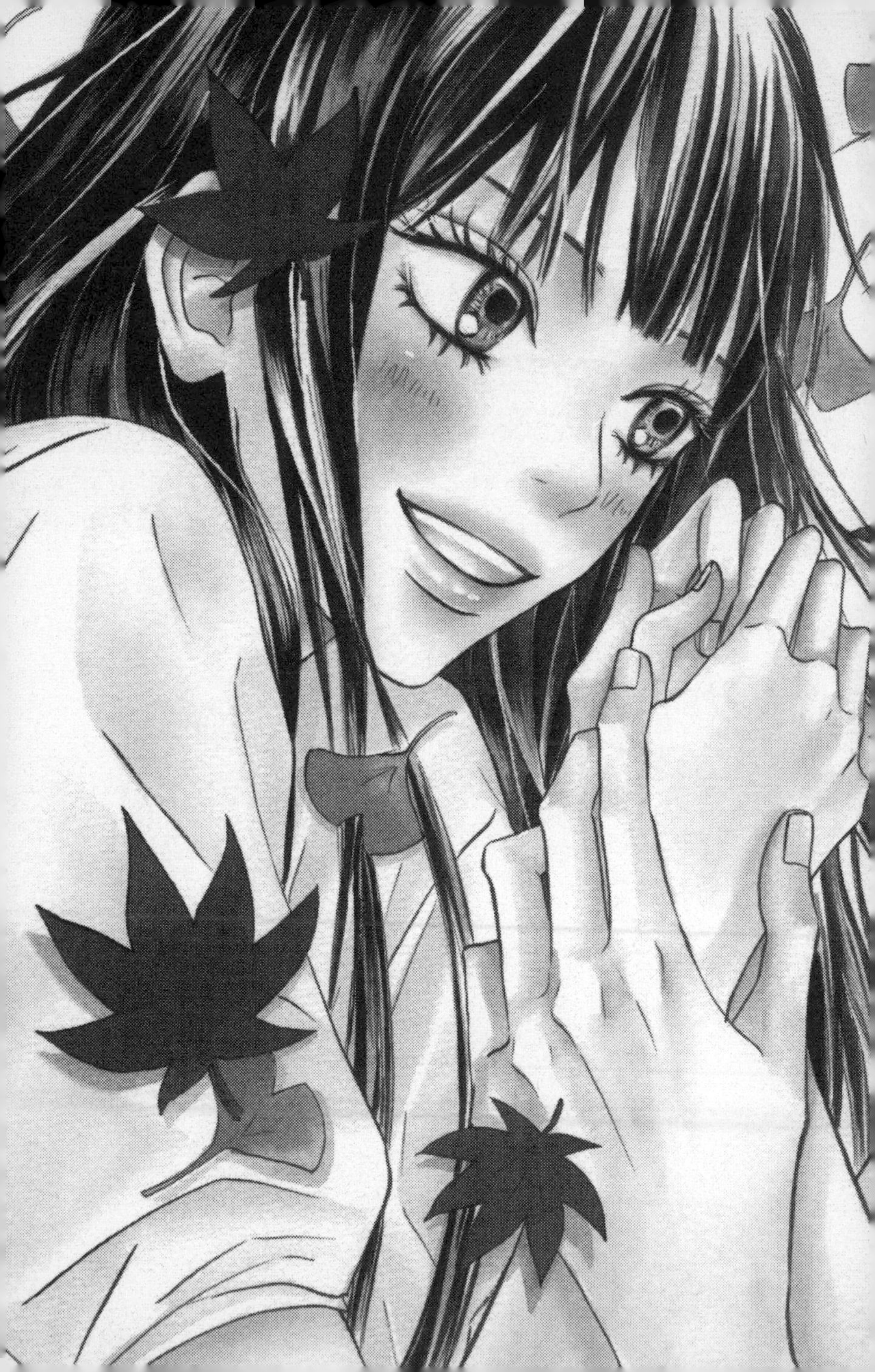

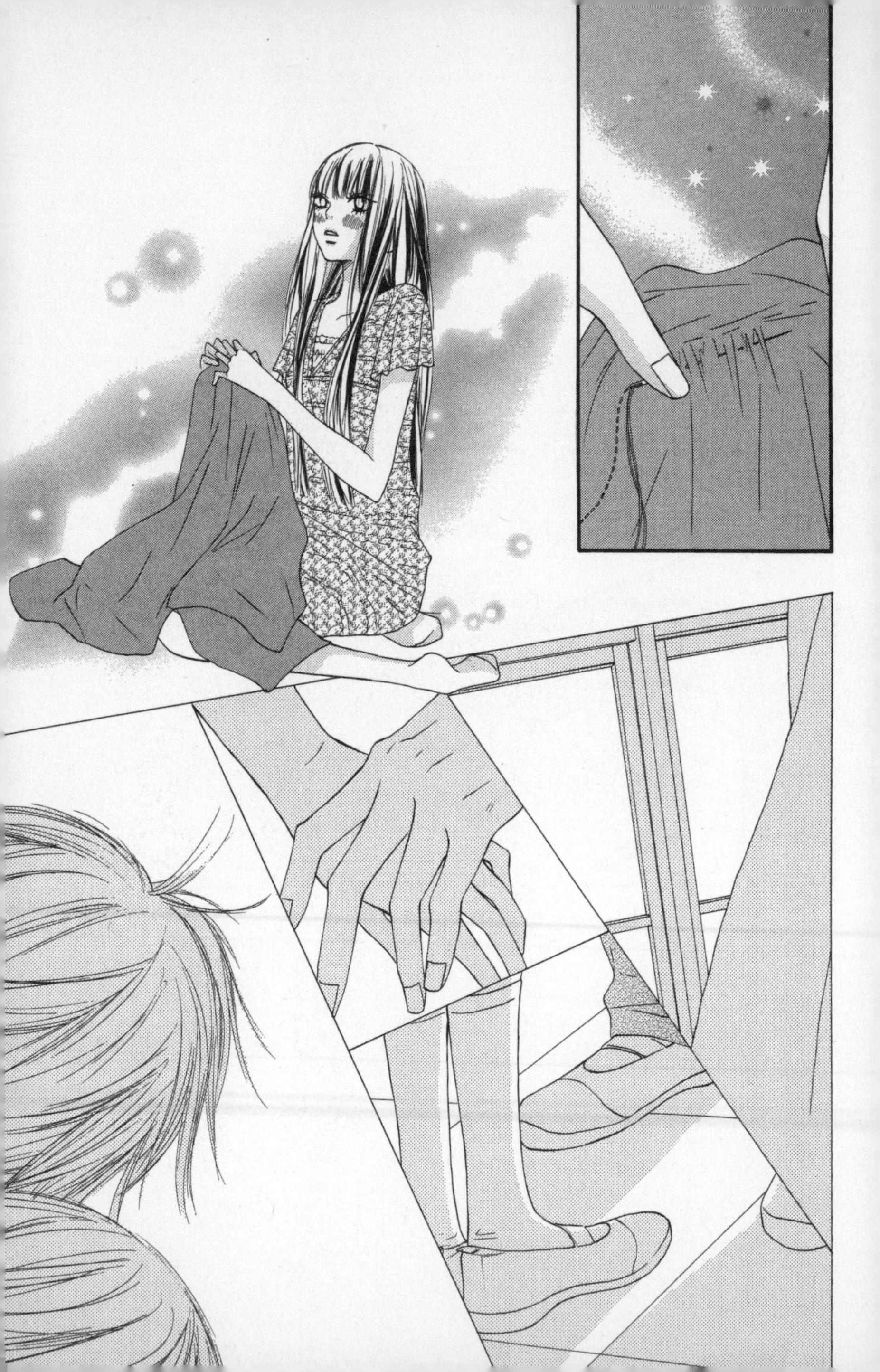

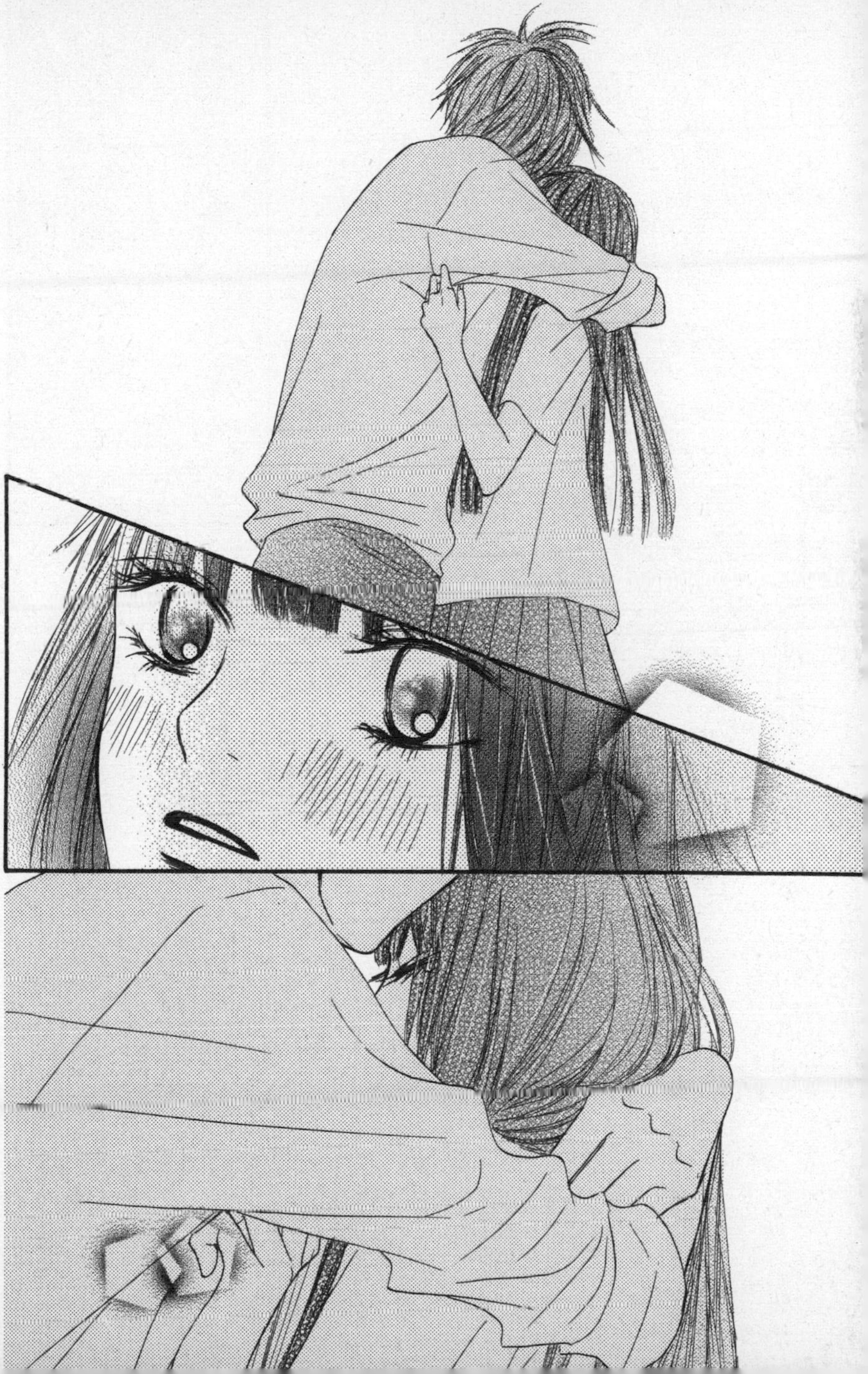

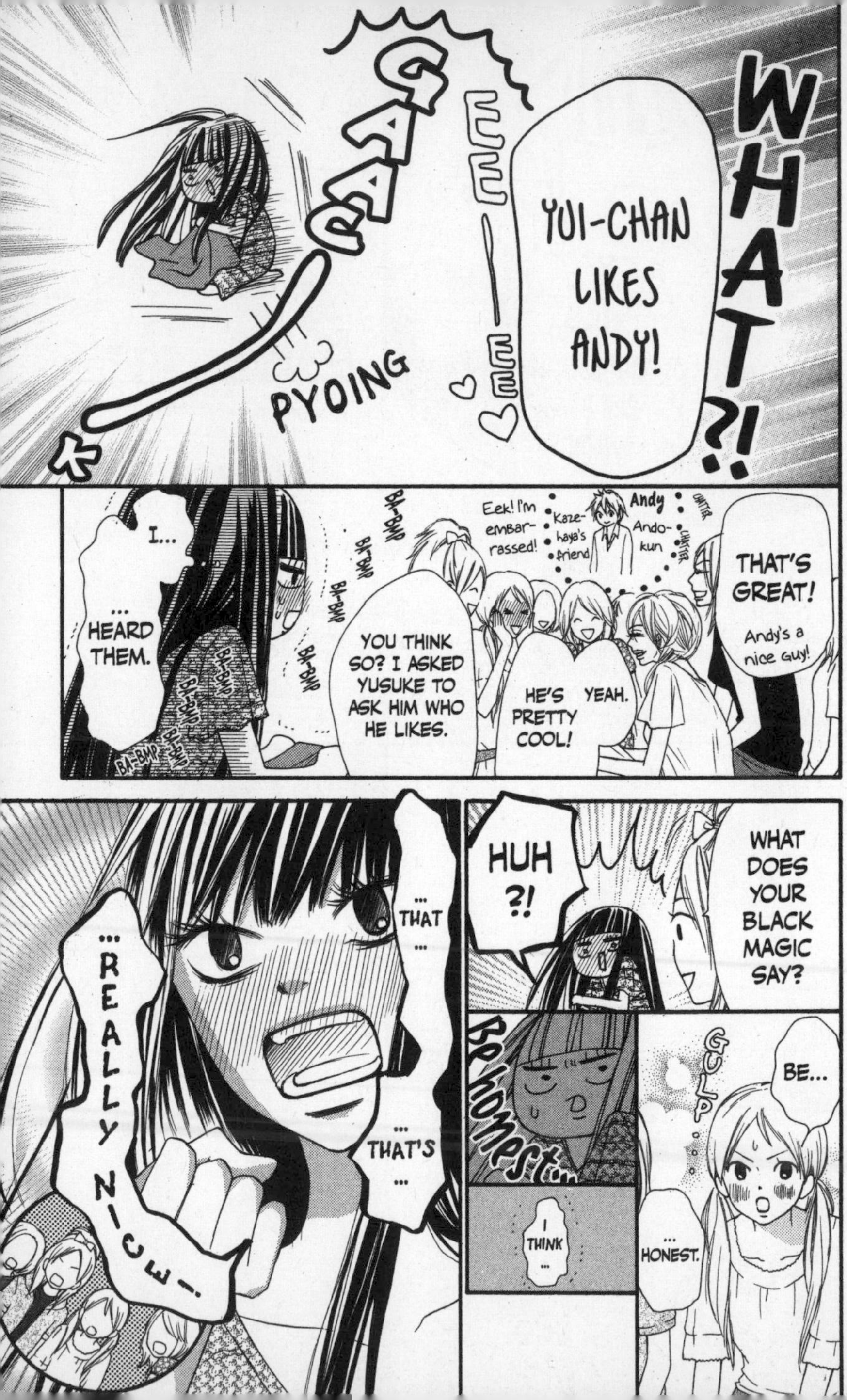
WHAT?!
YUI-CHAN LIKES ANDY!
EEE—EEE
GAAACK
PYOING
THAT'S GREAT!
Andy's a nice Guy!
CHATTER CHATTER
Andy
Ando-kun
Kaze-haya's friend
Eek! I'm embar-rassed!
YEAH.
HE'S PRETTY COOL!
YOU THINK SO? I ASKED YUSUKE TO ASK HIM WHO HE LIKES.
BA-BMP BA-BMP BA-BMP BA-BMP BA-BMP BA-BMP
I...
...HEARD THEM.
WHAT DOES YOUR BLACK MAGIC SAY?
HUH?!
BE...
GULP...
...HONEST.
I THINK...
Be honest...
...THAT...
...THAT'S...
...REALLY NICE—.

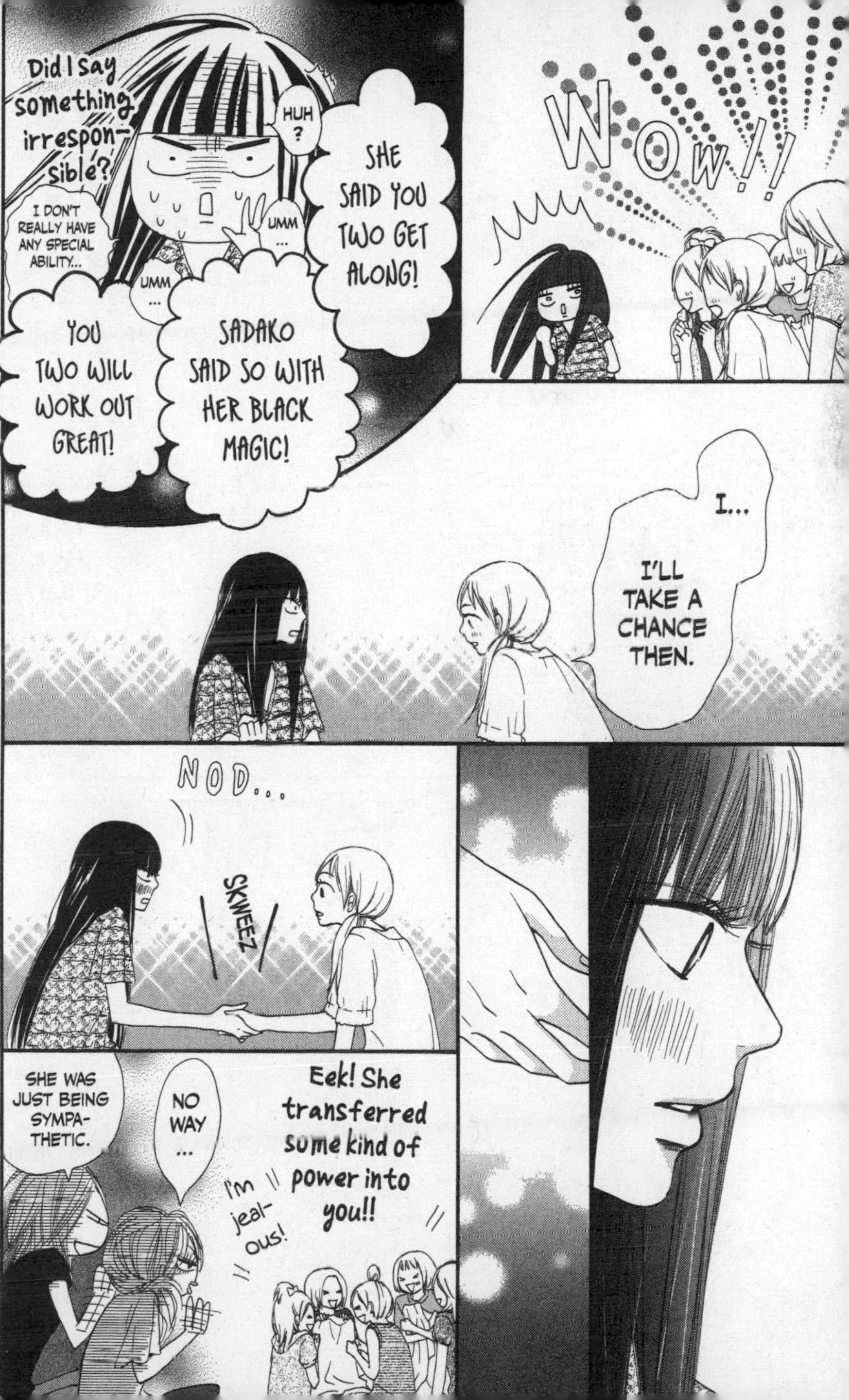
WOW!!
SHE SAID YOU TWO GET ALONG!
HUH?
UMM...
Did I say something irrespon-sible?
I DON'T REALLY HAVE ANY SPECIAL ABILITY...
UMM...
SADAKO SAID SO WITH HER BLACK MAGIC!
YOU TWO WILL WORK OUT GREAT!
I...
I'LL TAKE A CHANCE THEN.
NOD...
SKWEEZ
Eek! She transferred some kind of power into you!!
I'm jeal-ous!
NO WAY...
SHE WAS JUST BEING SYMPA-THETIC.

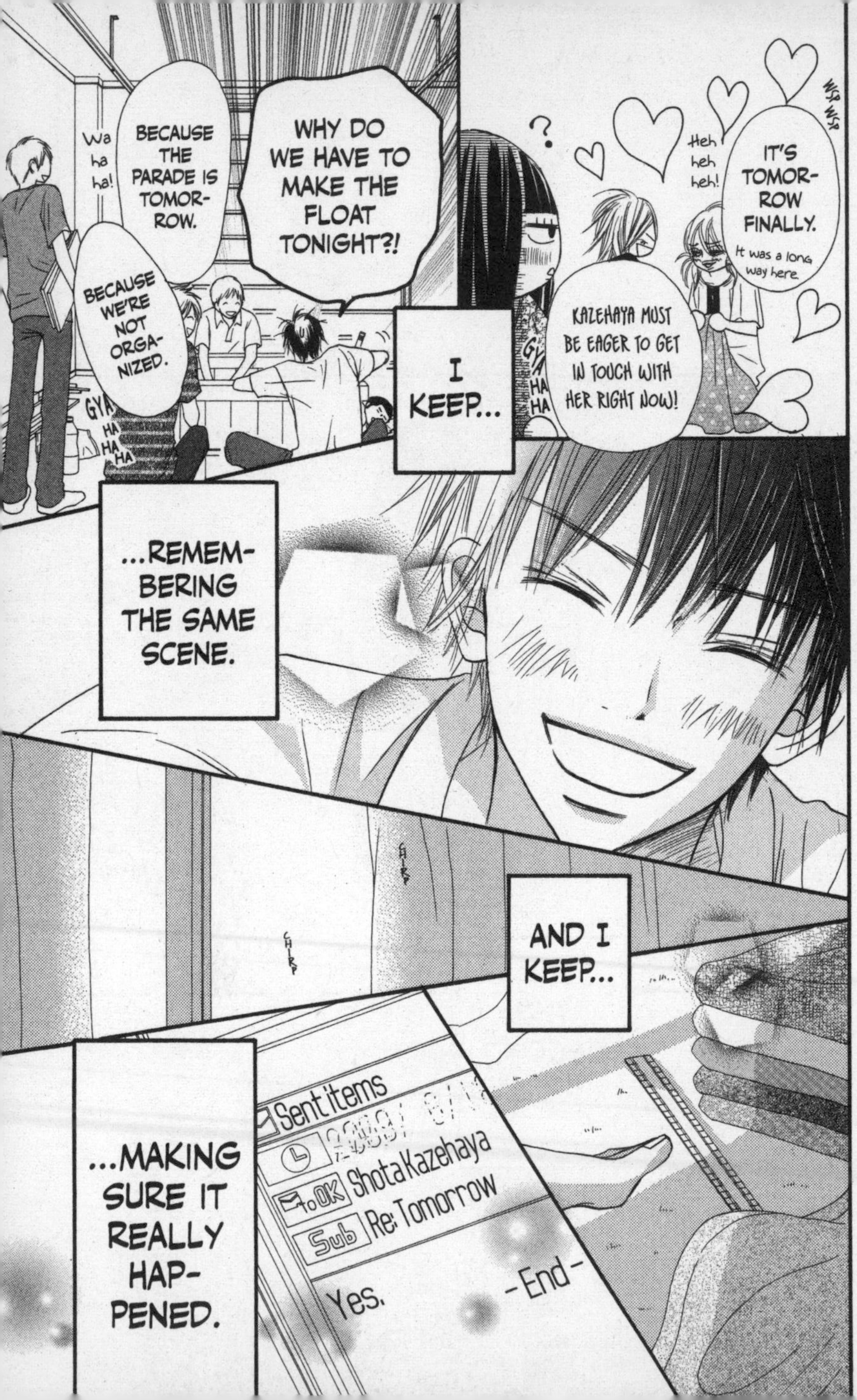
WSP WSP
IT'S TOMORROW FINALLY.
It was a long way here.
Heh heh heh!
KAZEHAYA MUST BE EAGER TO GET IN TOUCH WITH HER RIGHT NOW!
GYA HA HA
WHY DO WE HAVE TO MAKE THE FLOAT TONIGHT?!
BECAUSE THE PARADE IS TOMORROW.
Wa ha ha!
BECAUSE WE'RE NOT ORGANIZED.
GYA HA HA HA
I KEEP...
...REMEMBERING THE SAME SCENE.
CHIRP
CHIRP
AND I KEEP...
...MAKING SURE IT REALLY HAPPENED.
Sent items
Shota Kazehaya
To OK
Sub
Re: Tomorrow
Yes.
-End-

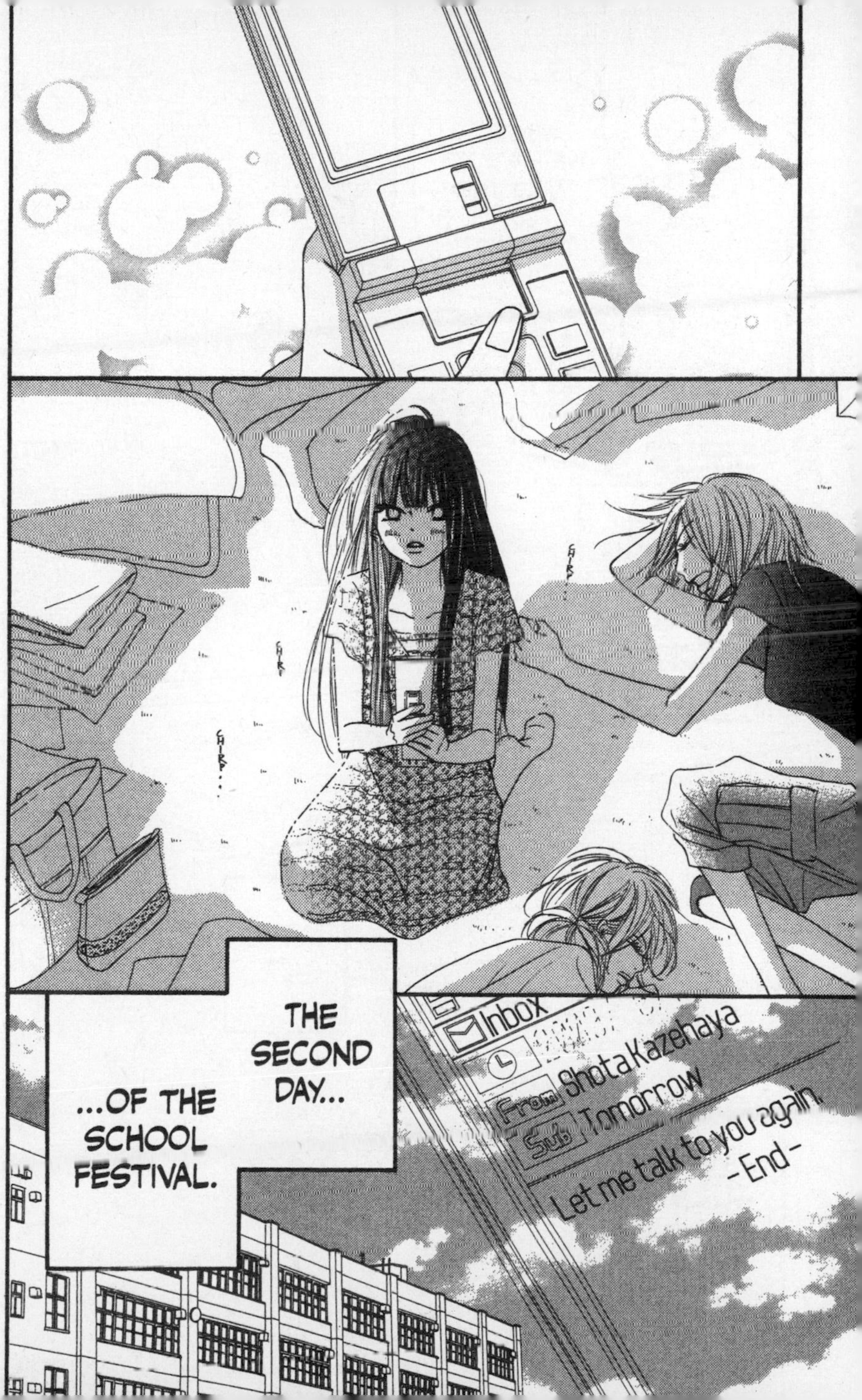
CHIRP...
CHIRP...
CHIRP...
Inbox
From Shota Kazehaya
Sub Tomorrow
Let me talk to you again.
-End-
THE SECOND DAY...
...OF THE SCHOOL FESTIVAL.

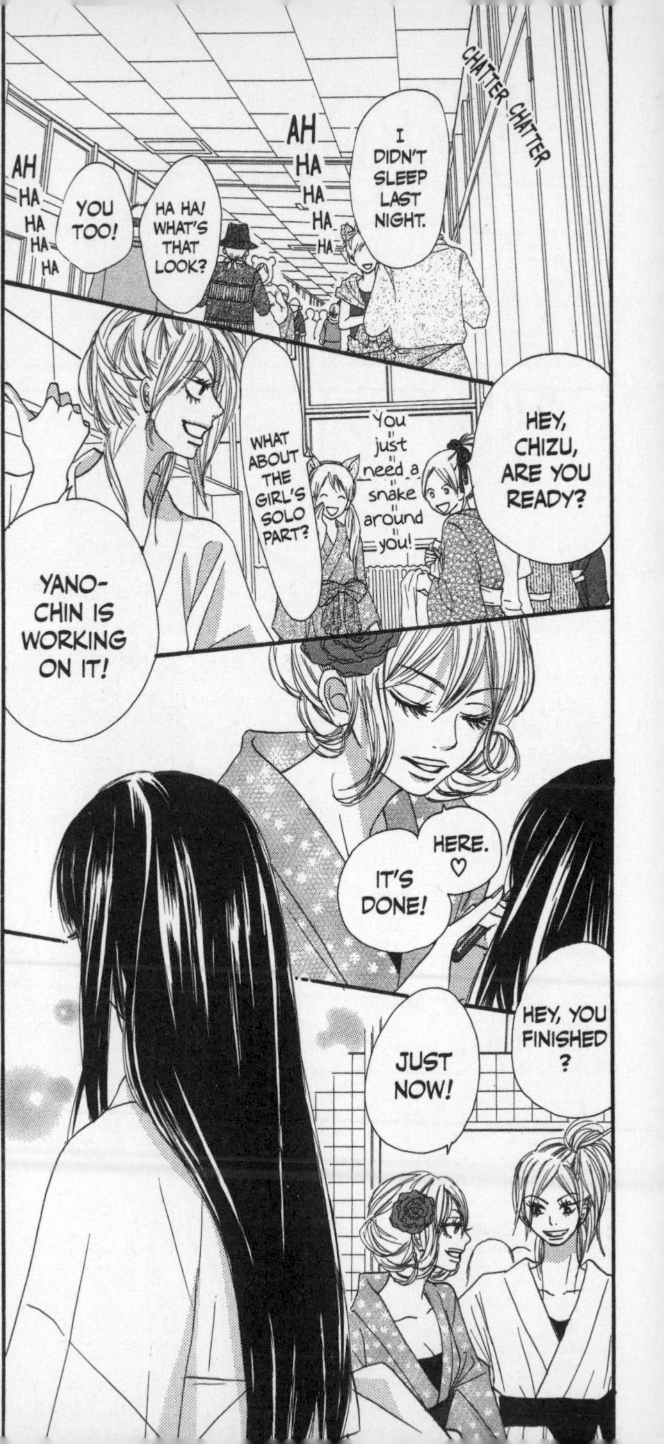
CHATTER CHATTER
I DIDN'T SLEEP LAST NIGHT.
AH HA HA HA HA
HA HA! WHAT'S THAT LOOK?
YOU TOO!
AH HA HA HA HA
HEY, CHIZU, ARE YOU READY?
You just need a snake around you!
WHAT ABOUT THE GIRL'S SOLO PART?
YANO-CHIN IS WORKING ON IT!
HERE. ♡
IT'S DONE!
HEY, YOU FINISHED?
JUST NOW!

KARUPIN on JAPAN 2

That's right! I also worked on the front pages for Episode 40 around April and May. But at the same time, I was drawing a cover design for the DS game too. One of the ideas was Kazehaya and Sawako lying on fallen leaves. Huh? Maybe it was just leaves? Anyway, although that picture didn't become the cover, it was really cute, so I used it for the graphic novel. Thank you to the staff who let me use it.

All of the pictures were nice!

In the picture for the cover of the DS game, Kazehaya is putting his arm around Sawako's shoulders. I think. I was going to copy it, but it didn't work. (laugh) I just wrote "(laugh)." Recently, I like to do this when I write emails. It's useful! By the way, my handwriting looks like a worm crawling along the ground. I jumped from one topic to the next again!

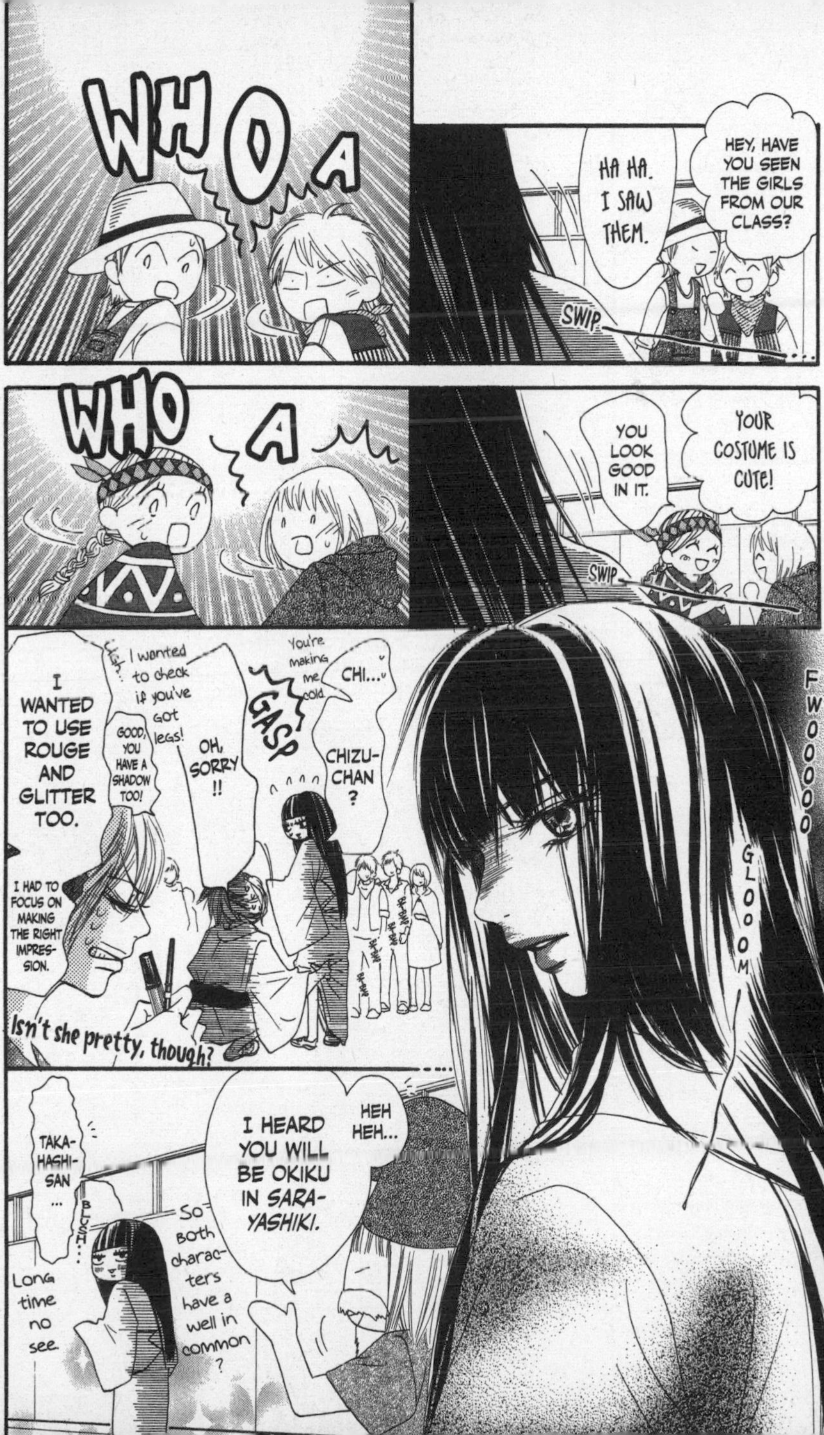
HEY, HAVE YOU SEEN THE GIRLS FROM OUR CLASS?
HA HA. I SAW THEM.
SWIP...
WHOA
YOUR COSTUME IS CUTE!
YOU LOOK GOOD IN IT.
SWIP
WHOA
FWOOOOOO
GLOOOM
CHIZU-CHAN?
CHI...
You're making me cold.
GASP
OH, SORRY!!
I wanted to check if you've got legs!
GOOD, YOU HAVE A SHADOW TOO!
I WANTED TO USE ROUGE AND GLITTER TOO.
I HAD TO FOCUS ON MAKING THE RIGHT IMPRESSION.
Isn't she pretty, though?
HEH HEH...
I HEARD YOU WILL BE OKIKU IN SARA-YASHIKI.
So both characters have a well in common?
TAKAHASHI-SAN...
BLUSH...
Long time no see.

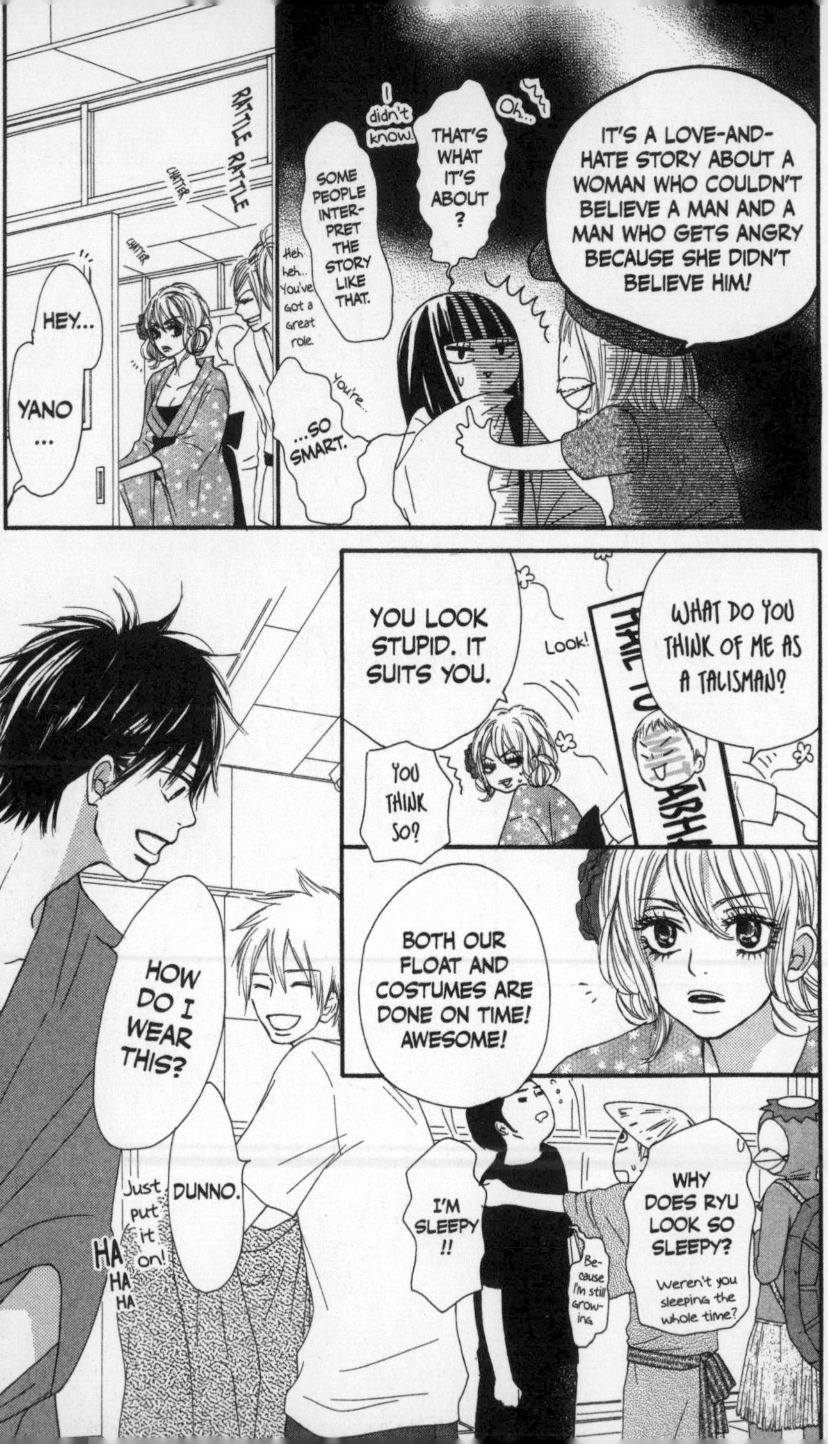
IT'S A LOVE-AND-HATE STORY ABOUT A WOMAN WHO COULDN'T BELIEVE A MAN AND A MAN WHO GETS ANGRY BECAUSE SHE DIDN'T BELIEVE HIM!
Oh...
THAT'S WHAT IT'S ABOUT?
I didn't know.
SOME PEOPLE INTERPRET THE STORY LIKE THAT.
Heh heh... You've got a great role.
You're...
...SO SMART.
RATTLE RATTLE
CHATTER
CHATTER
HEY...
YANO...
WHAT DO YOU THINK OF ME AS A TALISMAN?
Look!
YOU LOOK STUPID. IT SUITS YOU.
YOU THINK SO?
BOTH OUR FLOAT AND COSTUMES ARE DONE ON TIME! AWESOME!
WHY DOES RYU LOOK SO SLEEPY?
Weren't you sleeping the whole time?
Because I'm still growing.
I'M SLEEPY!!
HOW DO I WEAR THIS?
DUNNO.
Just put it on!
HA HA HA

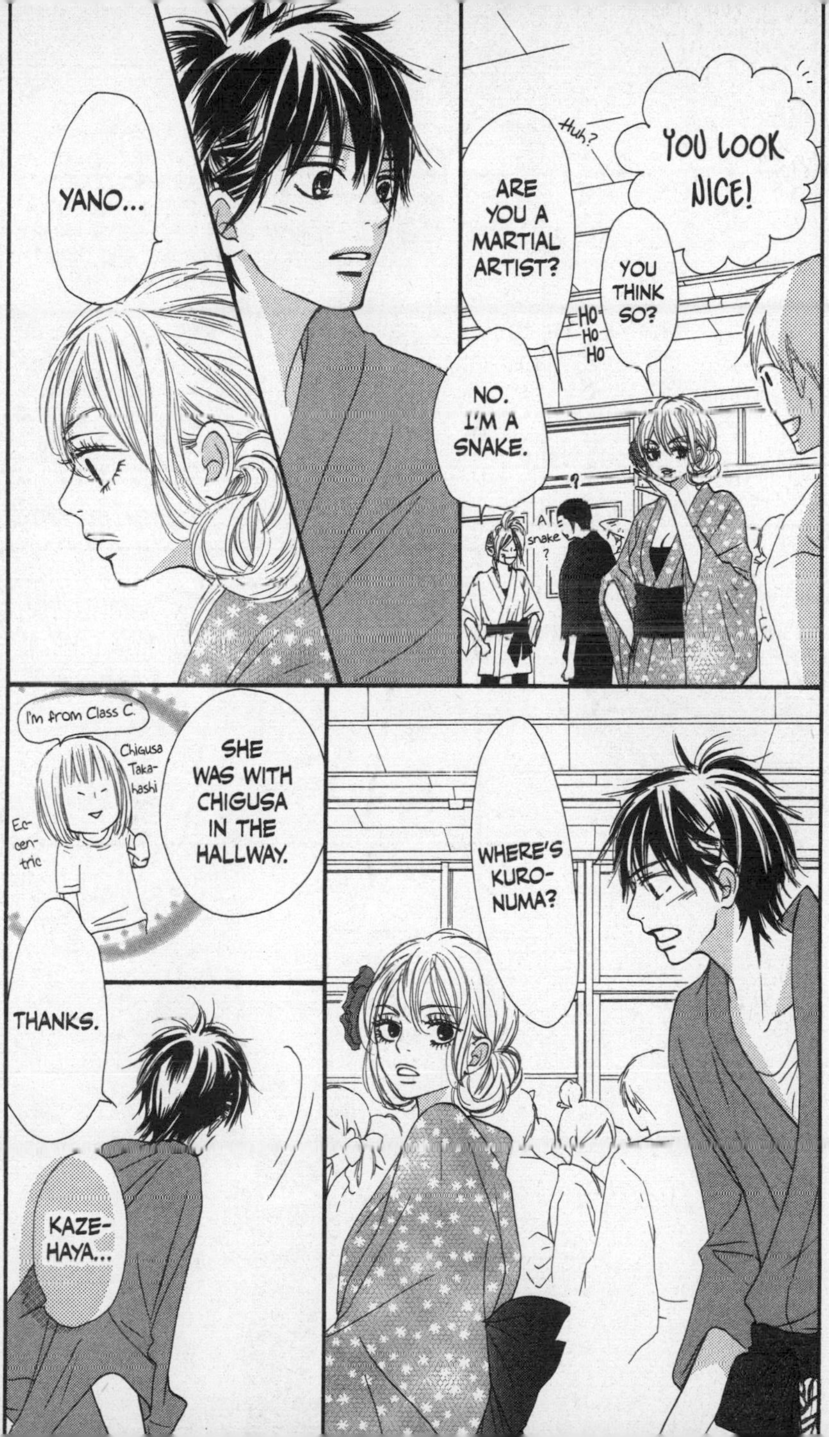
YOU LOOK NICE!
YOU THINK SO?
HO HO HO
Huh?
ARE YOU A MARTIAL ARTIST?
NO. I'M A SNAKE.
?
A snake?
YANO...
WHERE'S KURO-NUMA?
SHE WAS WITH CHIGUSA IN THE HALLWAY.
I'm from Class C.
Chigusa Takahashi
Ec-cen-tric
THANKS.
KAZE-HAYA...

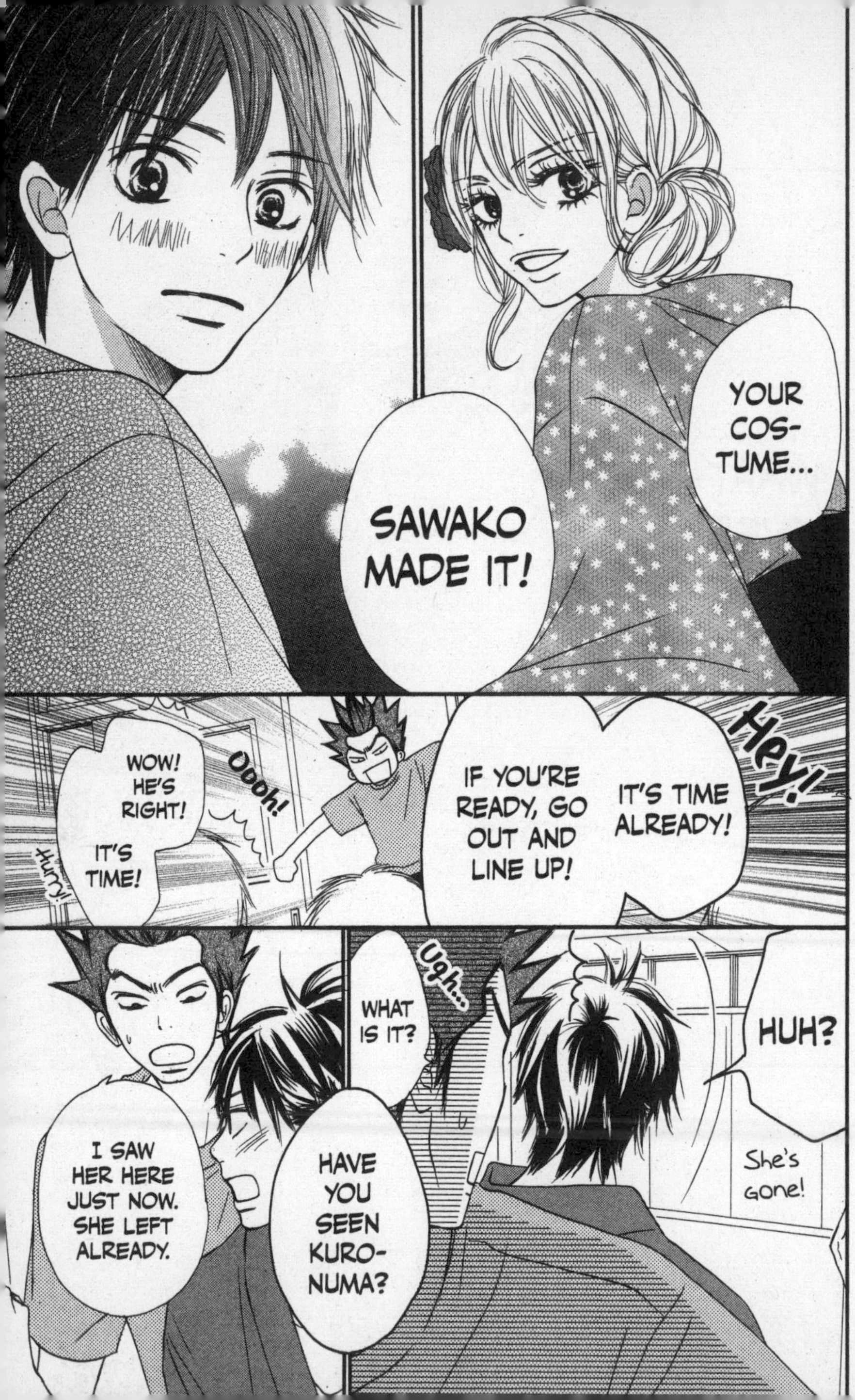
YOUR COS-TUME...
SAWAKO MADE IT!
Hey!
IT'S TIME ALREADY!
IF YOU'RE READY, GO OUT AND LINE UP!
Oooh!
WOW! HE'S RIGHT!
IT'S TIME!
Hurry!
HUH?
She's gone!
Ugh...
WHAT IS IT?
HAVE YOU SEEN KURO-NUMA?
I SAW HER HERE JUST NOW. SHE LEFT ALREADY.

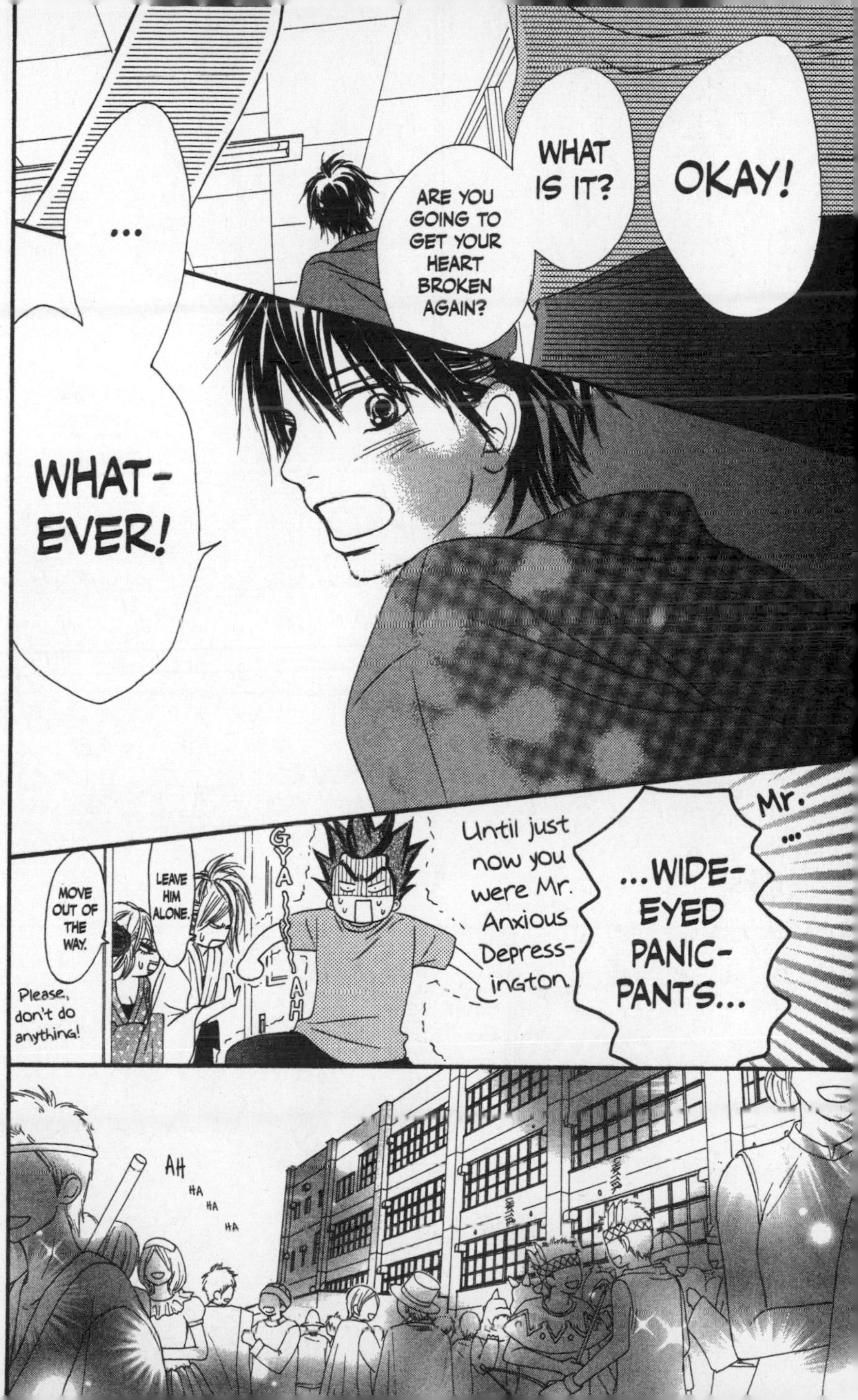
OKAY!
WHAT IS IT?
ARE YOU GOING TO GET YOUR HEART BROKEN AGAIN?
...
WHAT-EVER!
Mr. ...
...WIDE-EYED PANIC-PANTS...
Until just now you were Mr. Anxious Depress-ington.
GYA-AH
LEAVE HIM ALONE.
MOVE OUT OF THE WAY.
Please, don't do anything!
AH HA HA HA

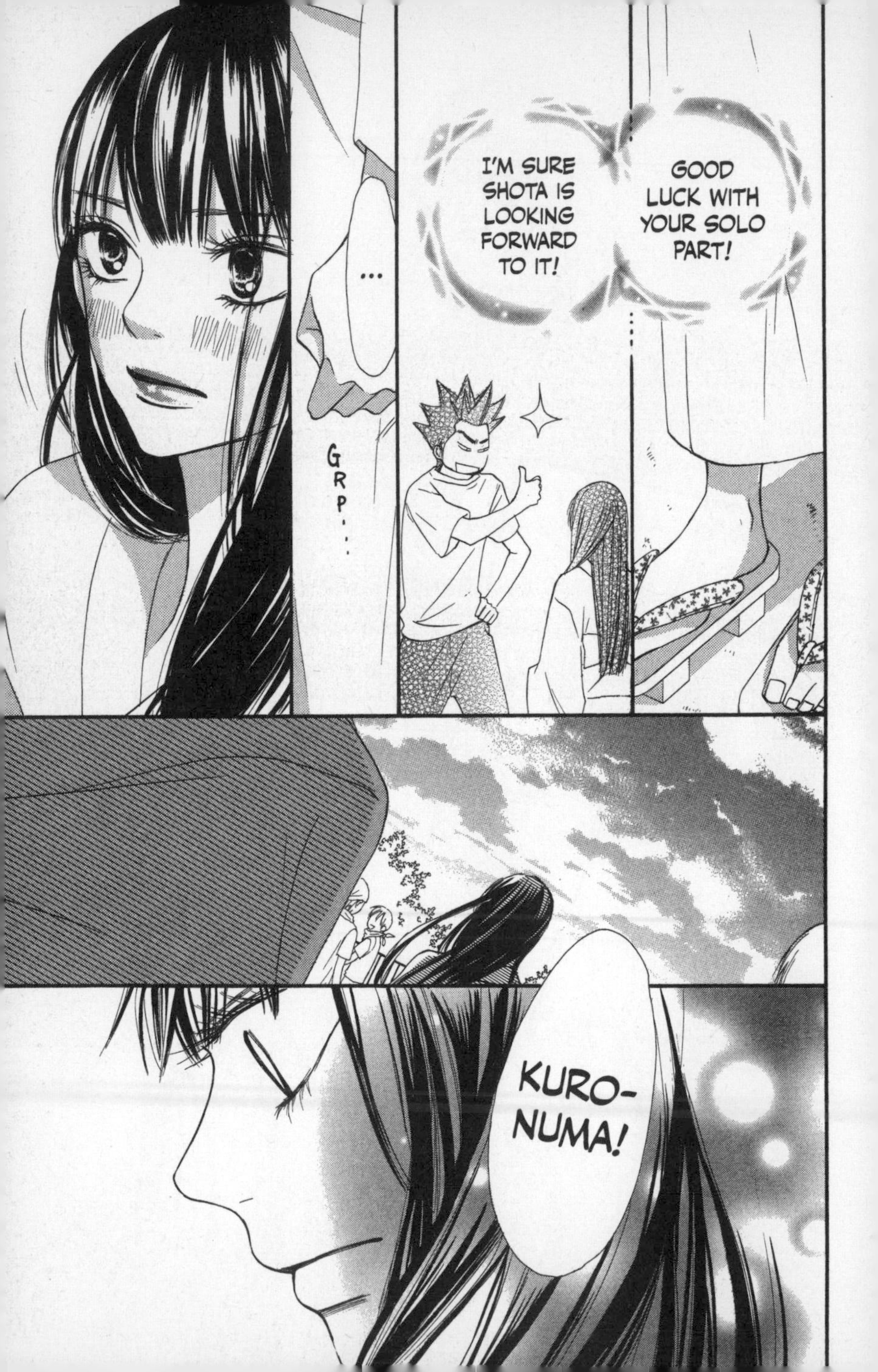
GOOD LUCK WITH YOUR SOLO PART!
I'M SURE SHOTA IS LOOKING FORWARD TO IT!
...
GRP...
KURO-NUMA!

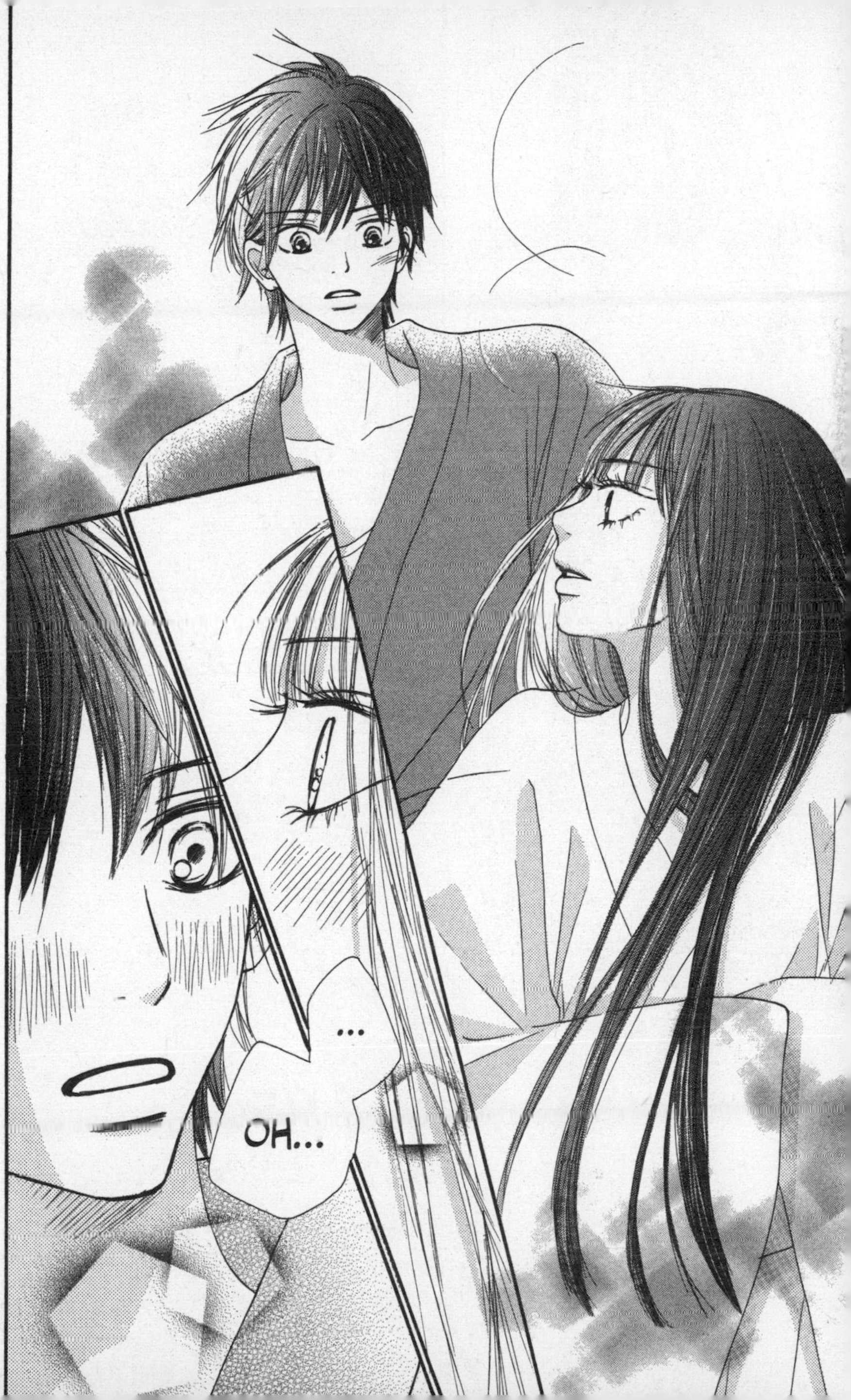
...
OH...

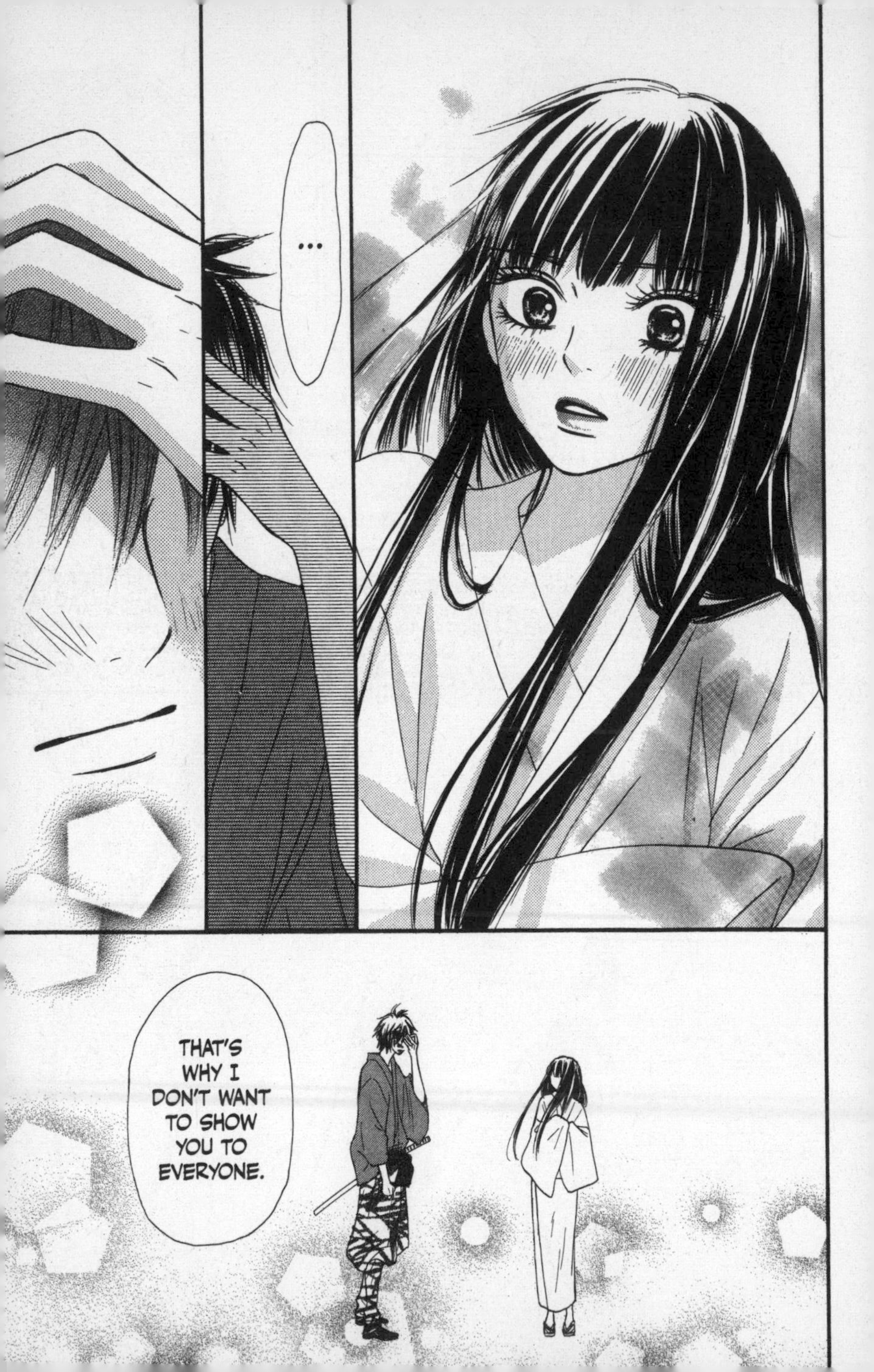
...
THAT'S WHY I DON'T WANT TO SHOW YOU TO EVERYONE.

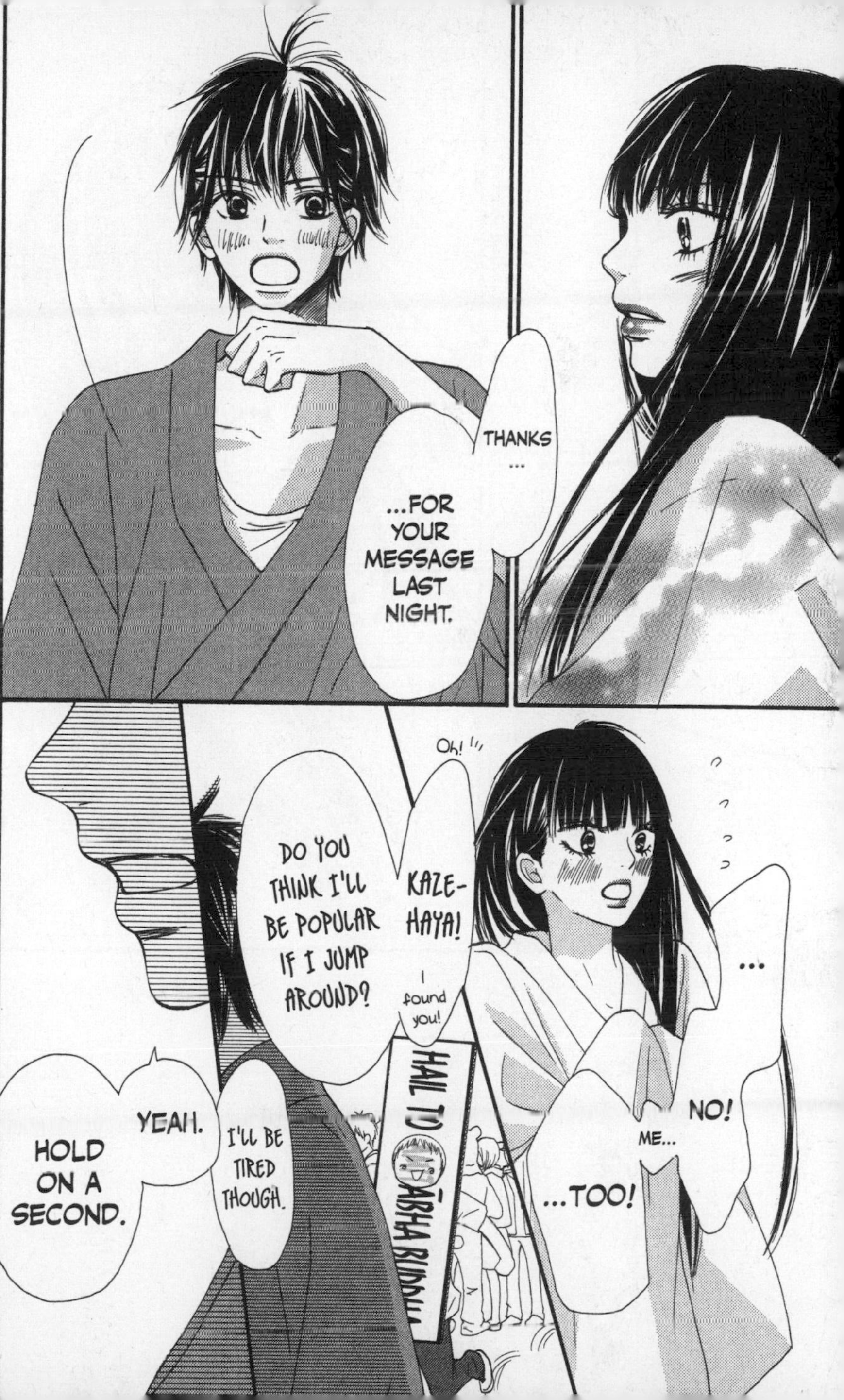

THANKS...
...FOR YOUR MESSAGE LAST NIGHT.
Oh!
KAZE-HAYA!
I found you!
DO YOU THINK I'LL BE POPULAR IF I JUMP AROUND?
...
NO!
ME...
...TOO!
HAIL TO
I'LL BE TIRED THOUGH.
YEAH.
HOLD ON A SECOND.

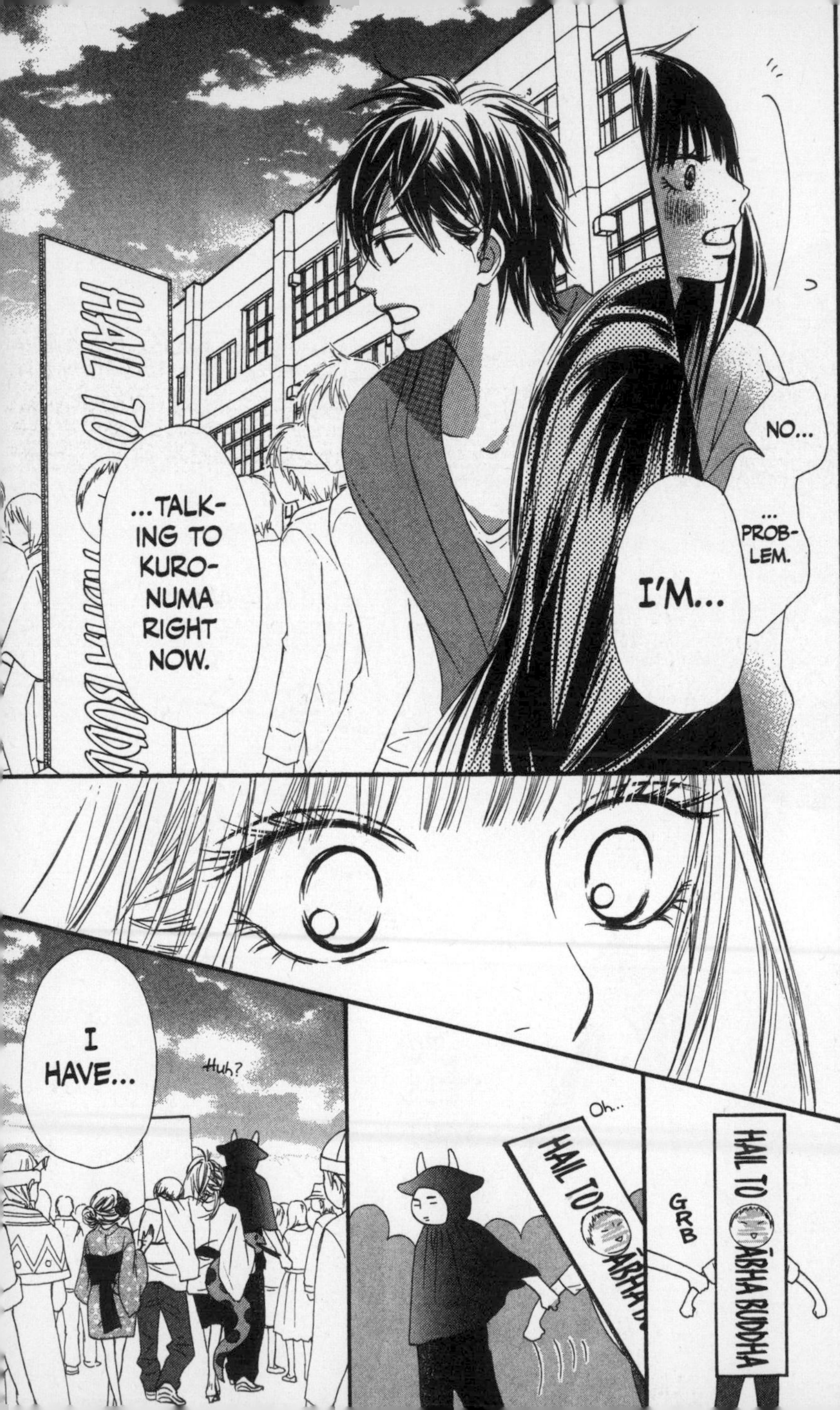
NO... ...PROB-LEM.
I'M...
...TALK-ING TO KURO-NUMA RIGHT NOW.
HAIL TO
HAIL TO ĀBHA BUDDHA
GRB
Oh...
HAIL TO
I HAVE...
Huh?

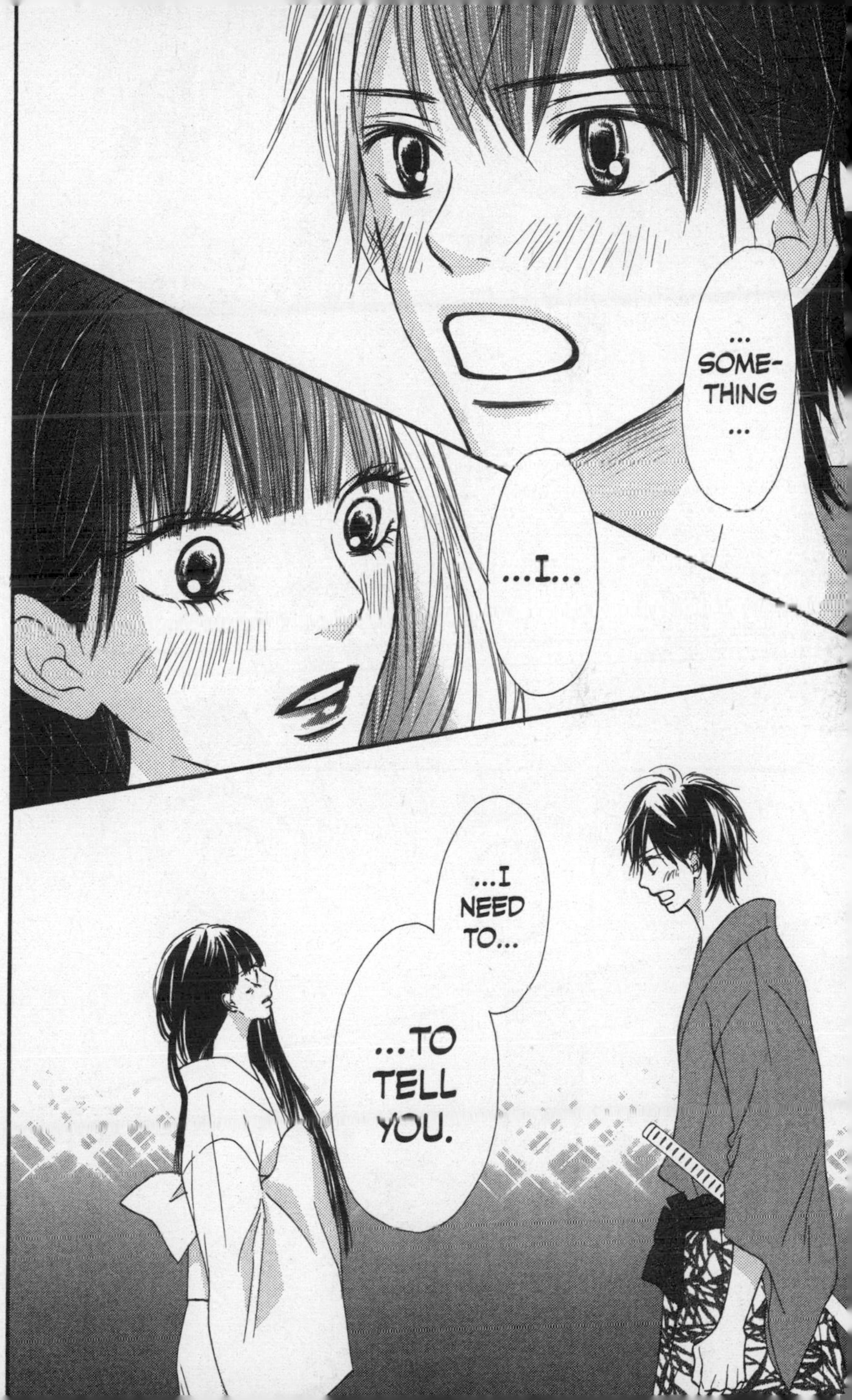
...SOME-THING...
...I...
...I NEED TO...
...TO TELL YOU.

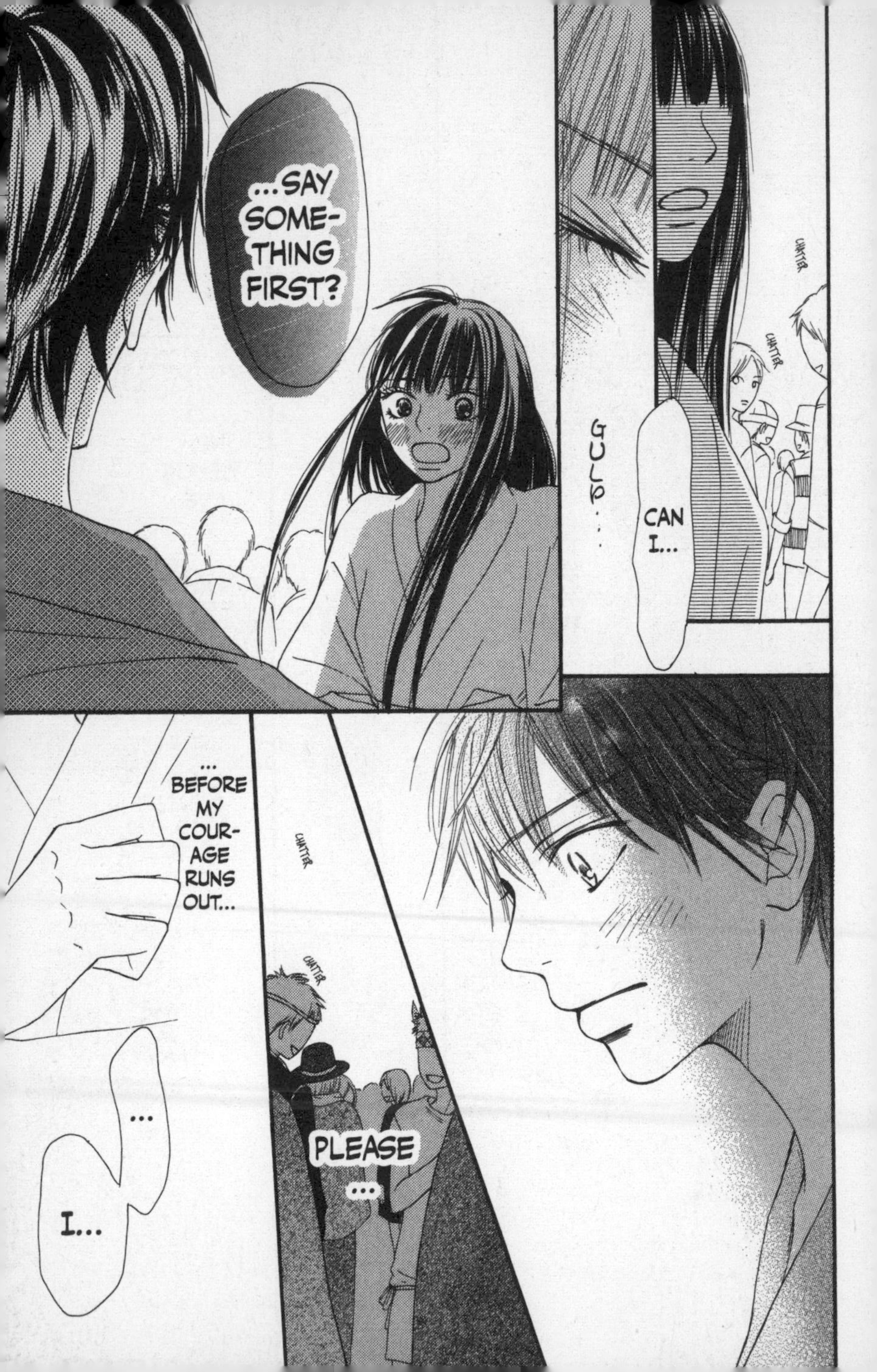
CHATTER
CHATTER
GULP...
CAN I...
...SAY SOMETHING FIRST?
CHATTER
CHATTER
PLEASE...
...BEFORE MY COURAGE RUNS OUT...
...
I...

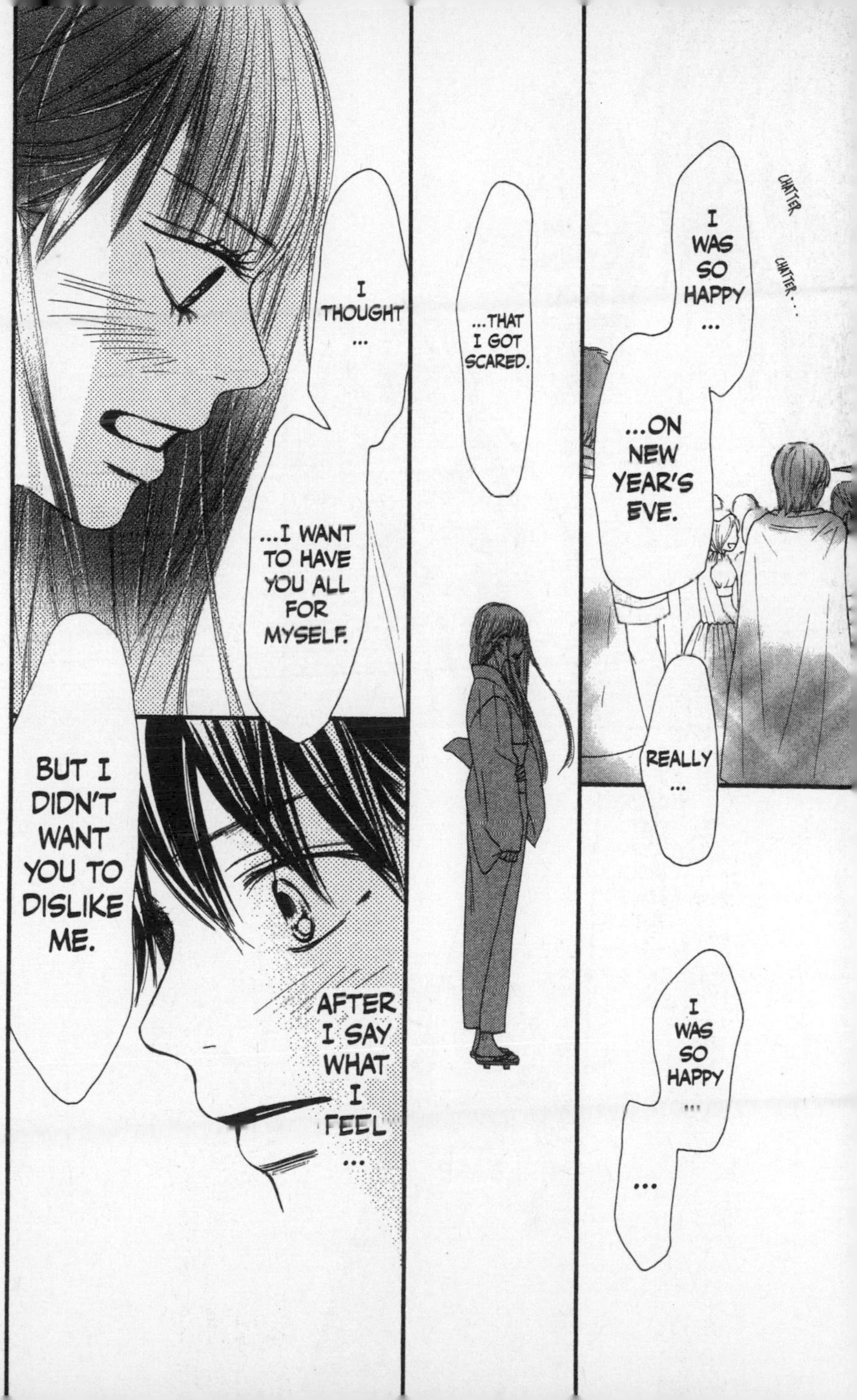
CHATTER
CHATTER...
I WAS SO HAPPY ...
...ON NEW YEAR'S EVE.
REALLY ...
I WAS SO HAPPY ...
...
...THAT I GOT SCARED.
I THOUGHT ...
...I WANT TO HAVE YOU ALL FOR MYSELF.
AFTER I SAY WHAT I FEEL ...
BUT I DIDN'T WANT YOU TO DISLIKE ME.

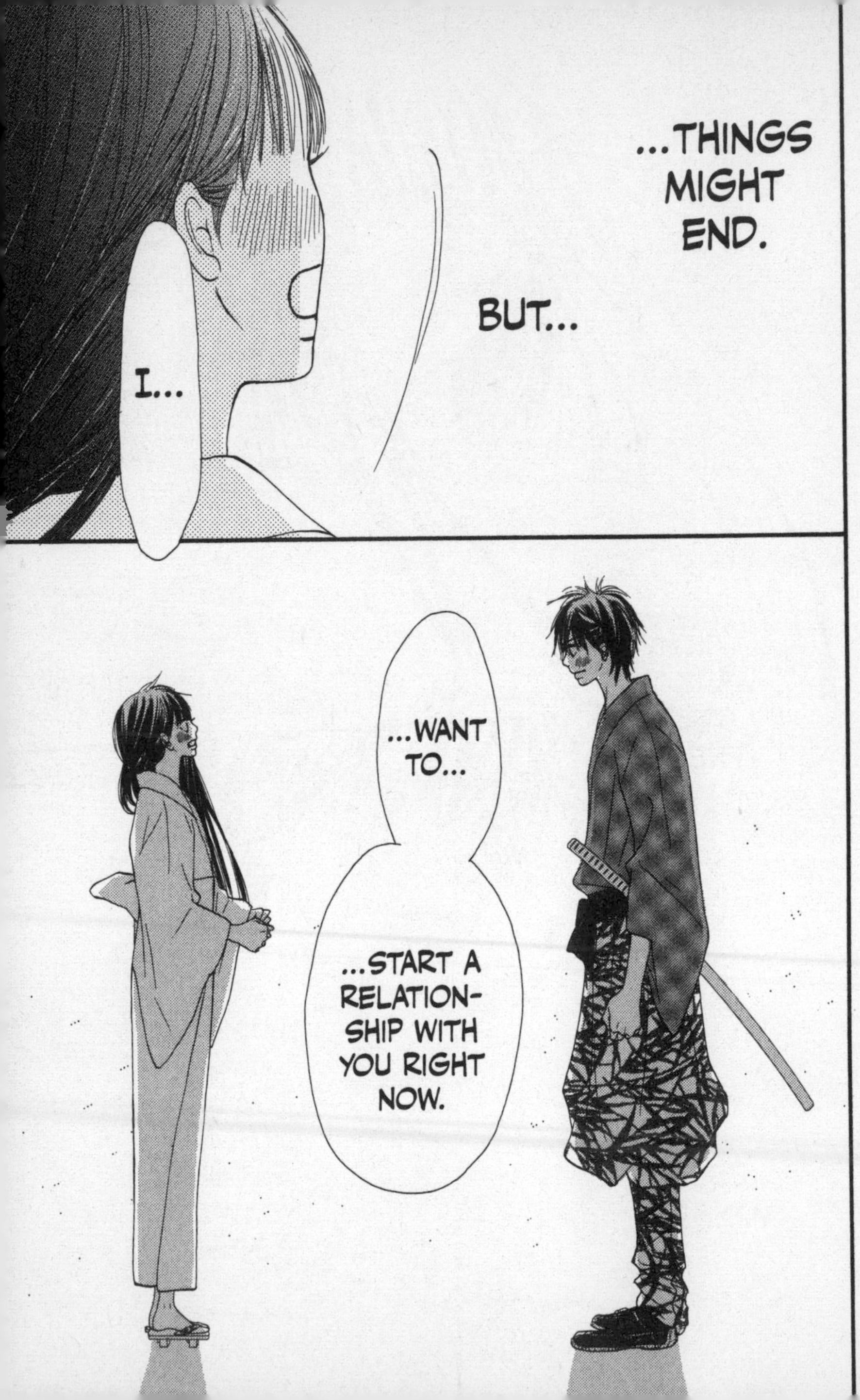
...THINGS MIGHT END.
BUT...
I...
...WANT TO...
...START A RELATIONSHIP WITH YOU RIGHT NOW.

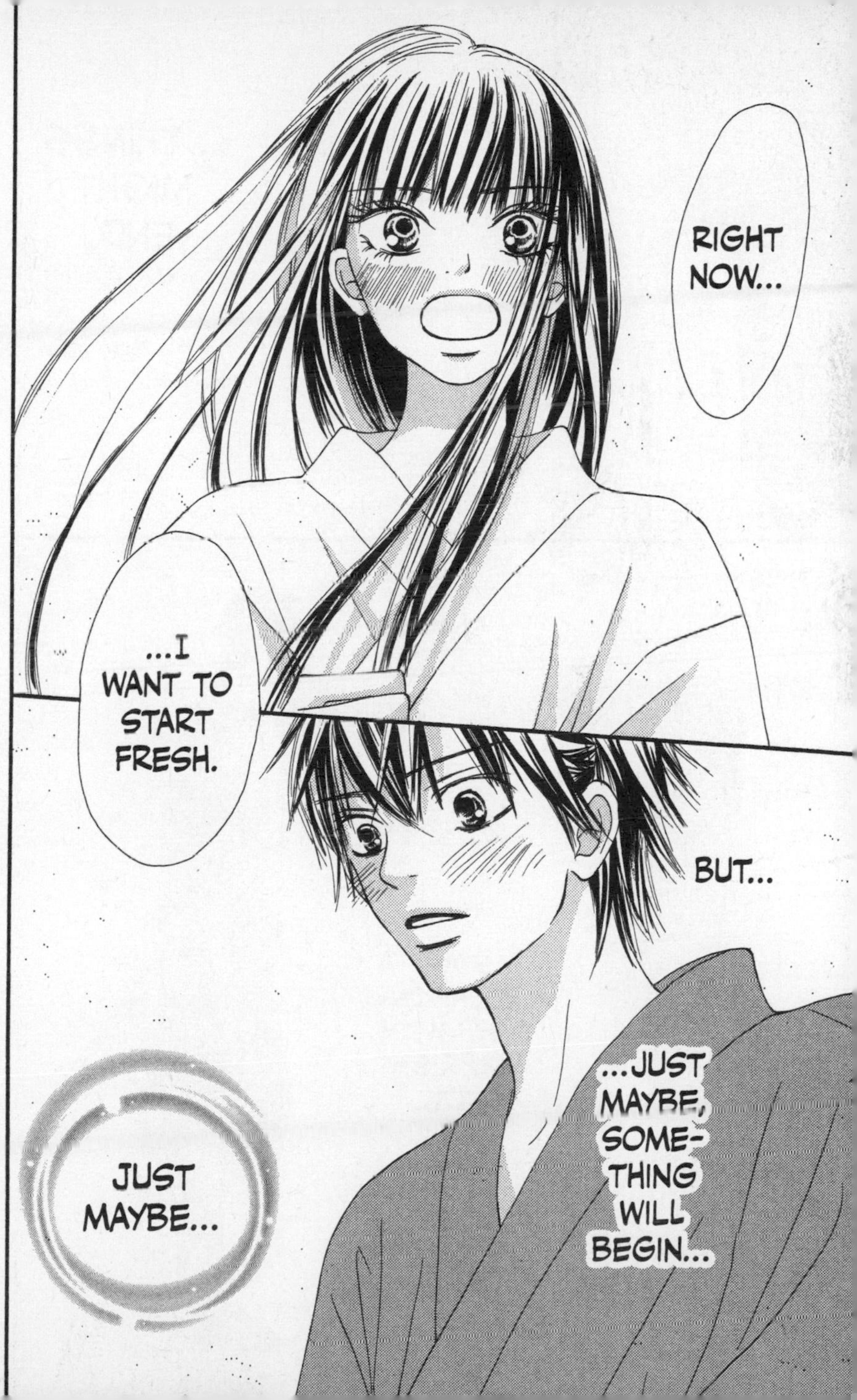
RIGHT NOW...
...I WANT TO START FRESH.
BUT...
...JUST MAYBE, SOME-THING WILL BEGIN...
JUST MAYBE...

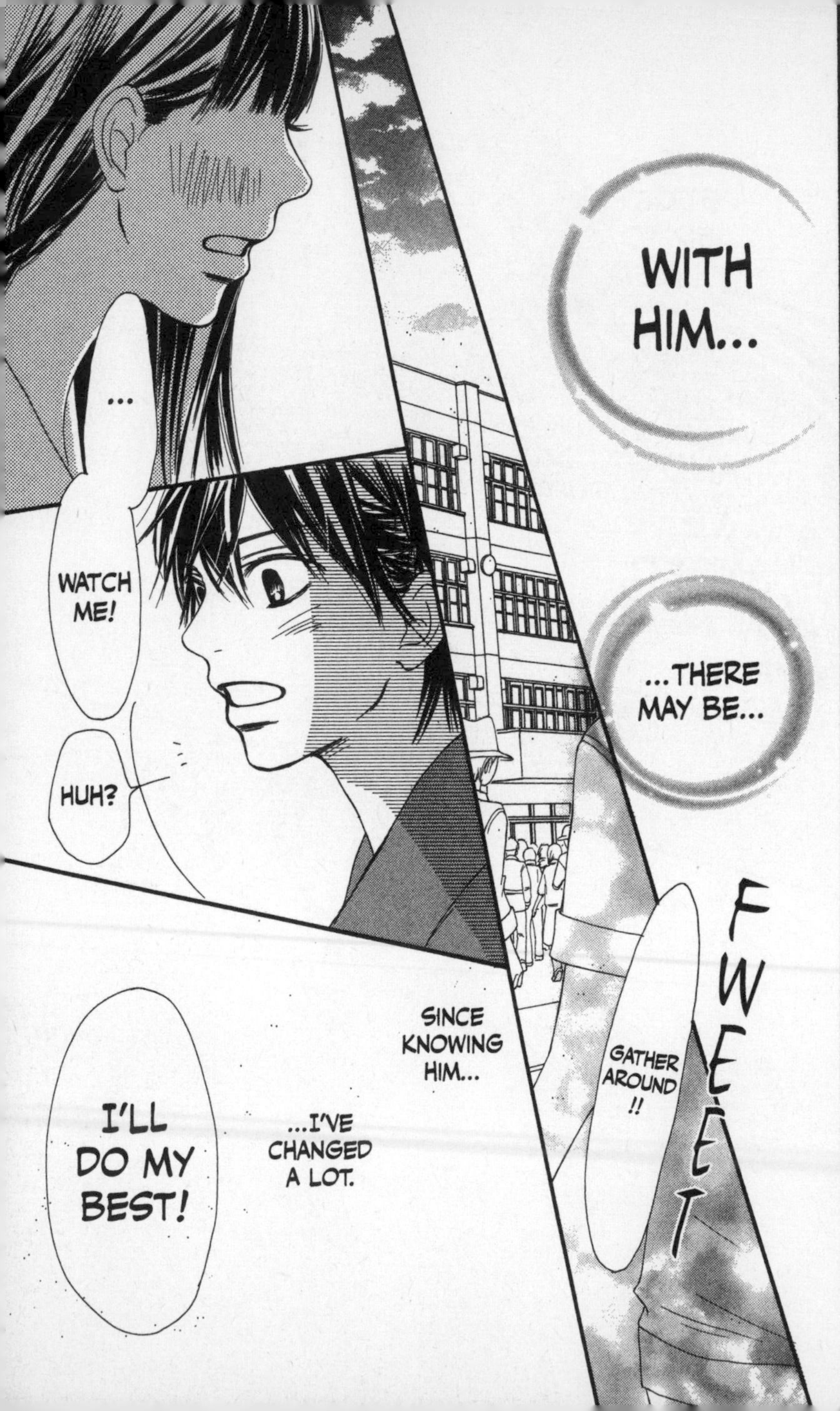
WITH HIM...
...THERE MAY BE...
...
WATCH ME!
HUH?
FWEET
GATHER AROUND !!
SINCE KNOWING HIM...
...I'VE CHANGED A LOT.
I'LL DO MY BEST!

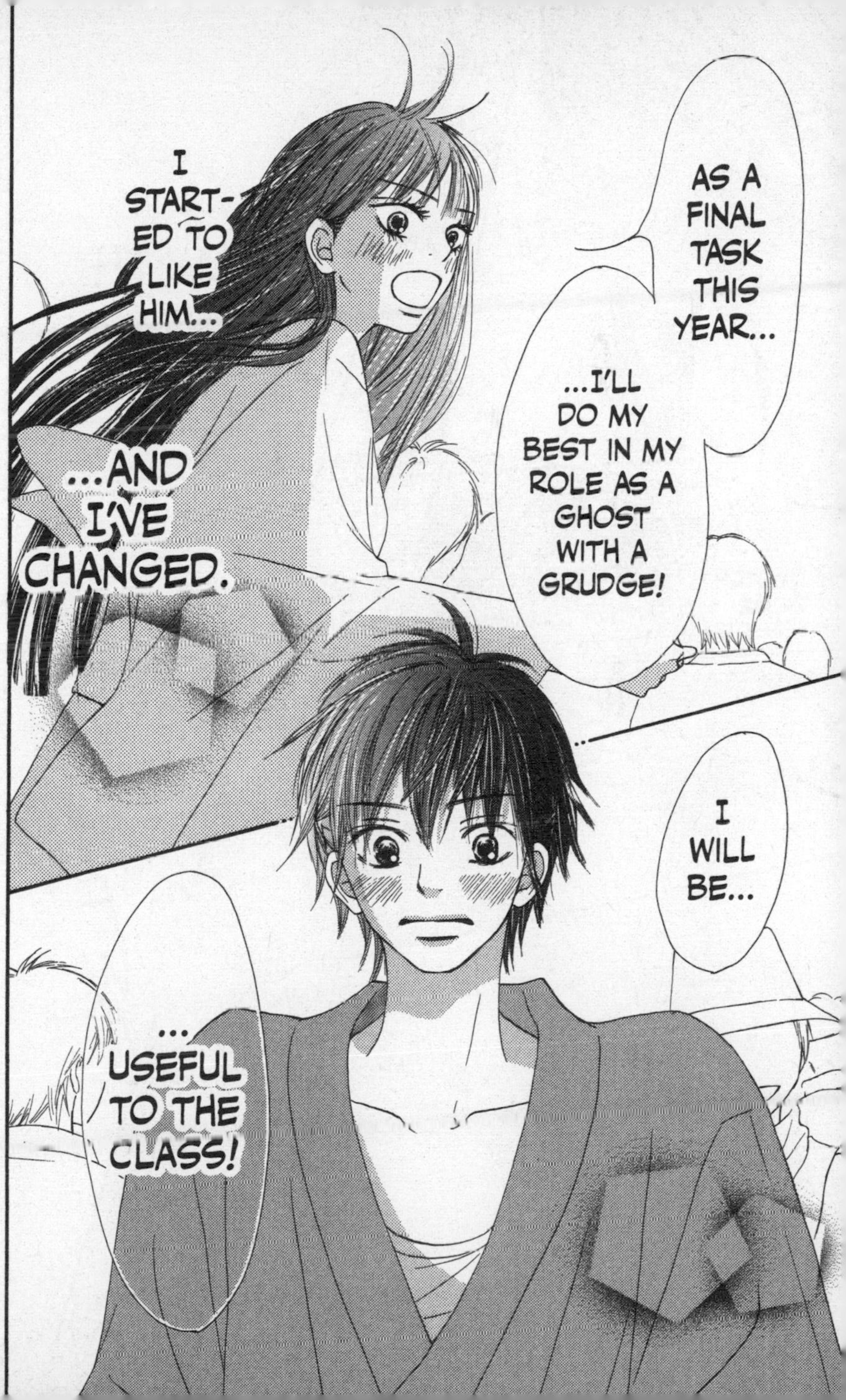
AS A FINAL TASK THIS YEAR...
...I'LL DO MY BEST IN MY ROLE AS A GHOST WITH A GRUDGE!
I START-ED TO LIKE HIM...
...AND I'VE CHANGED.
I WILL BE...
...USEFUL TO THE CLASS!

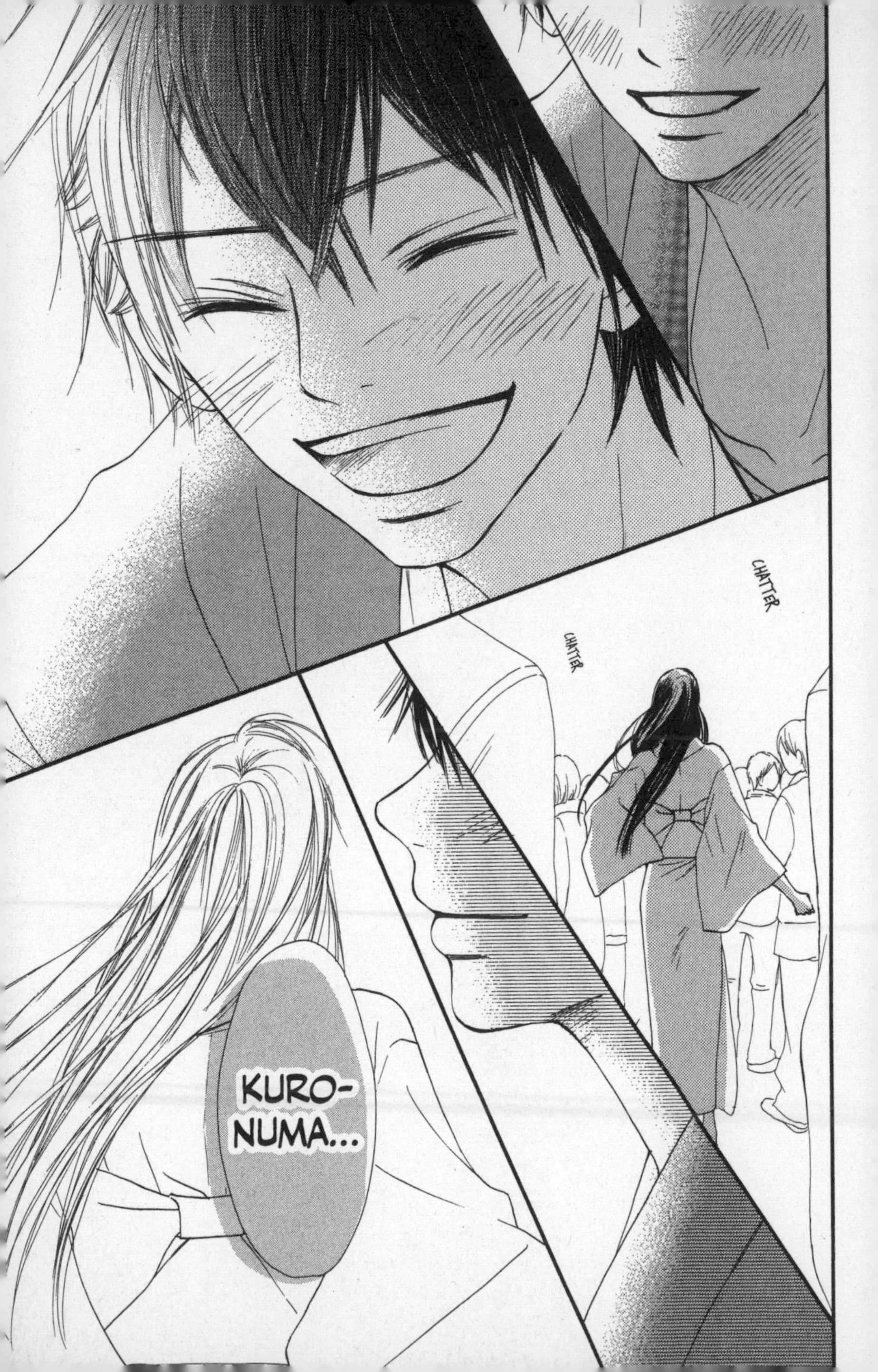
CHATTER
CHATTER
KURO-
NUMA...

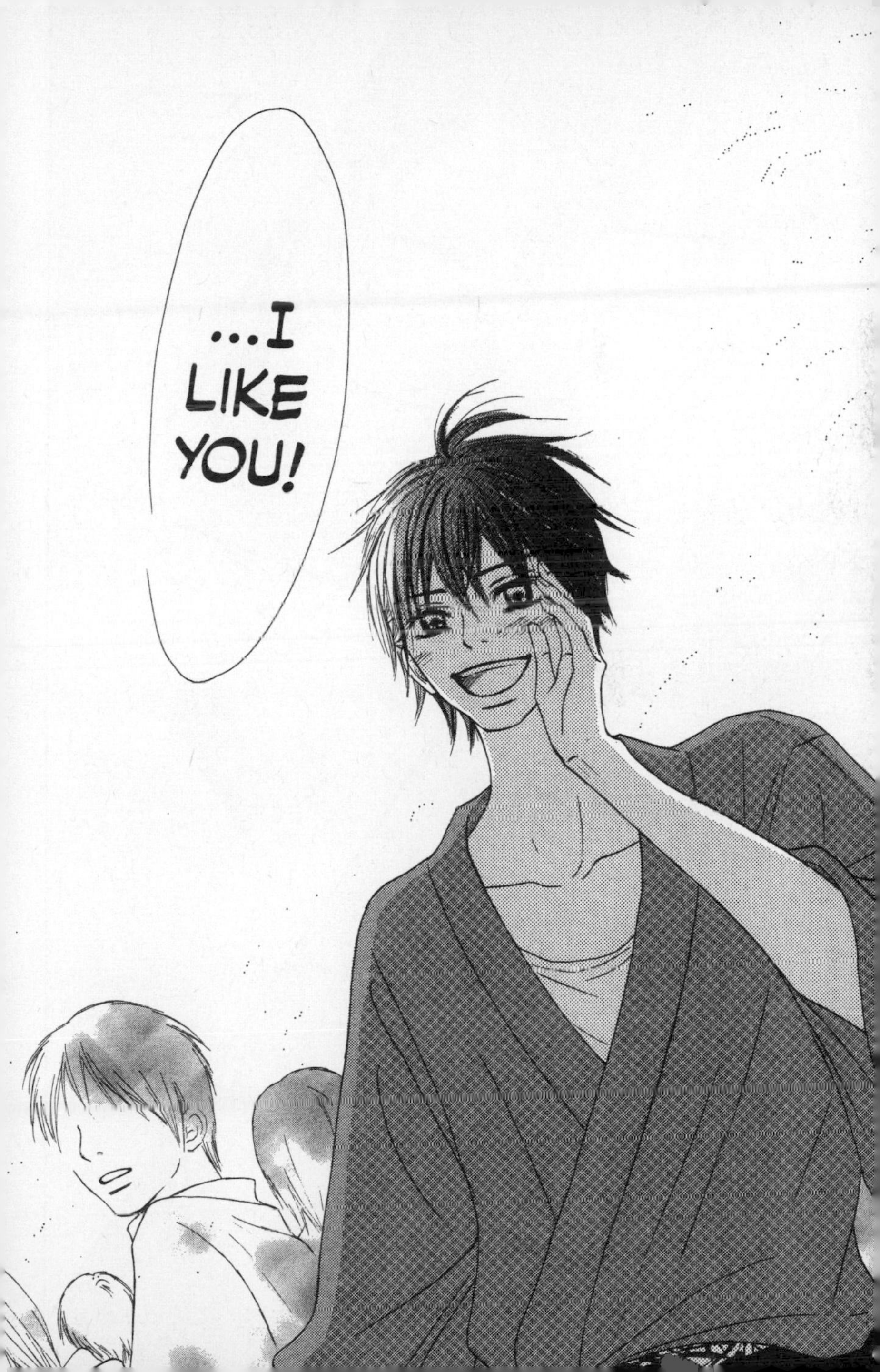
...I LIKE YOU!

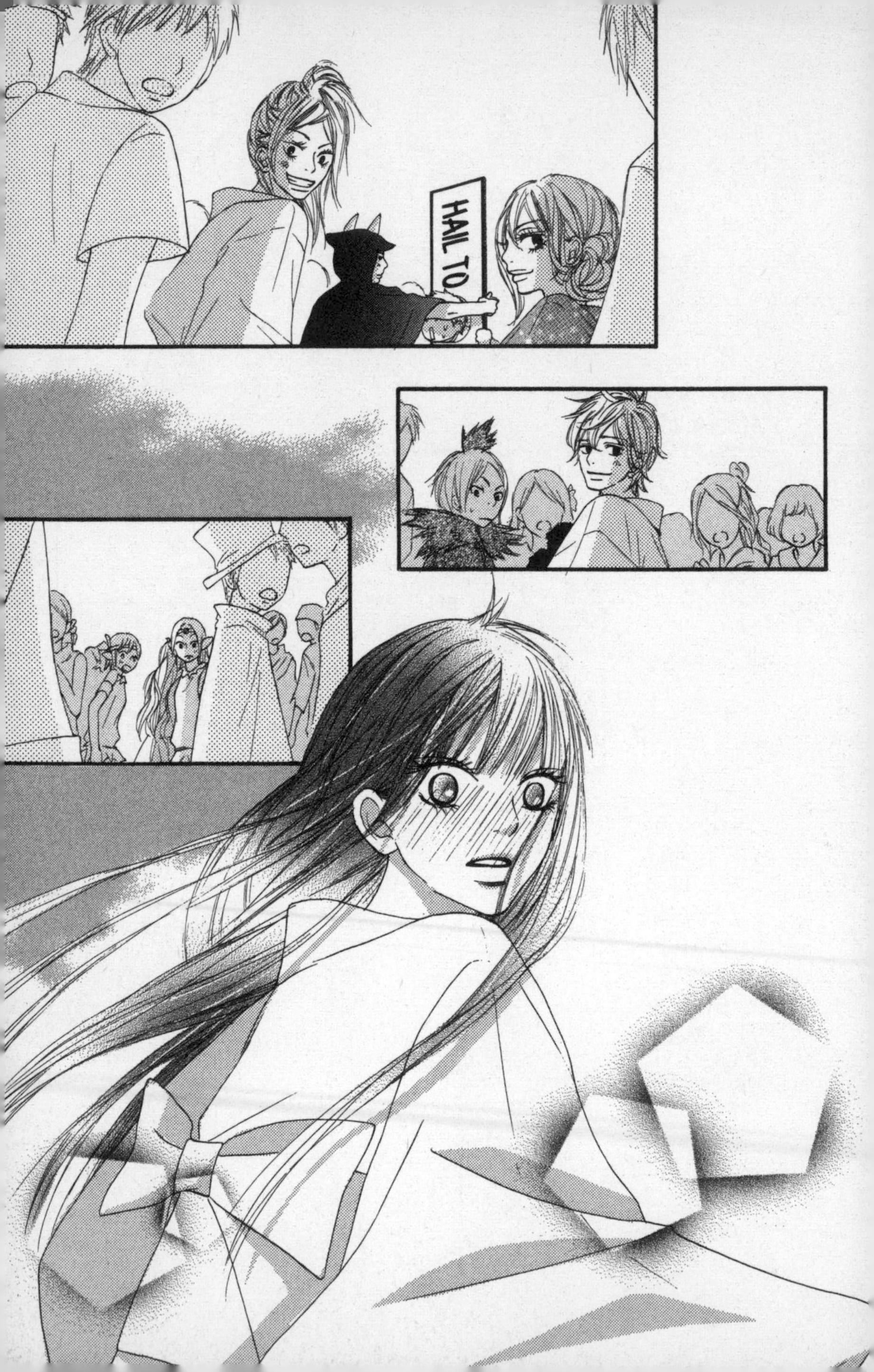
HAIL TO

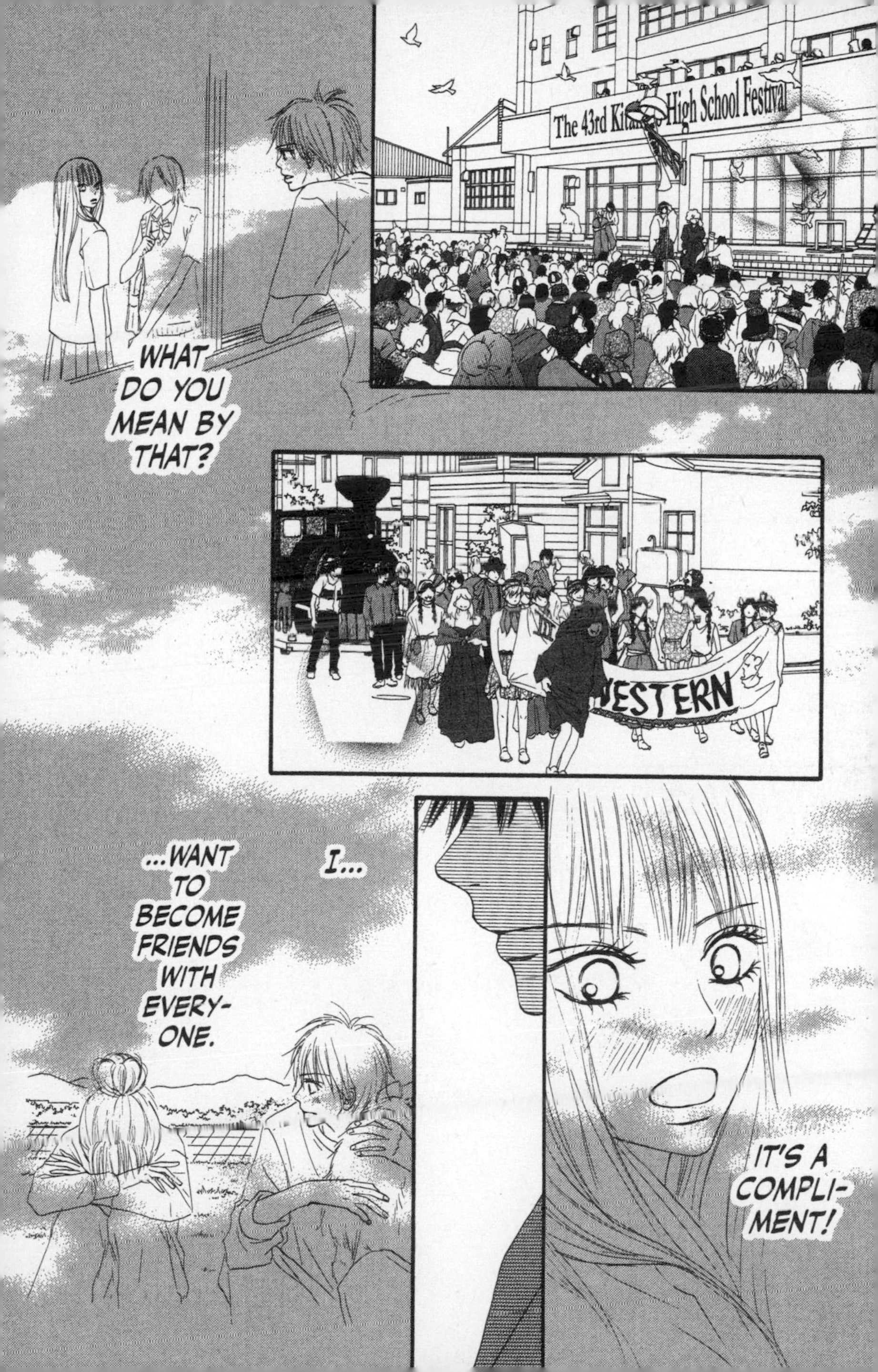
The 43rd Kita High School Festival
WHAT DO YOU MEAN BY THAT?
WESTERN
IT'S A COMPLI-MENT!
I...
...WANT TO BECOME FRIENDS WITH EVERY-ONE.

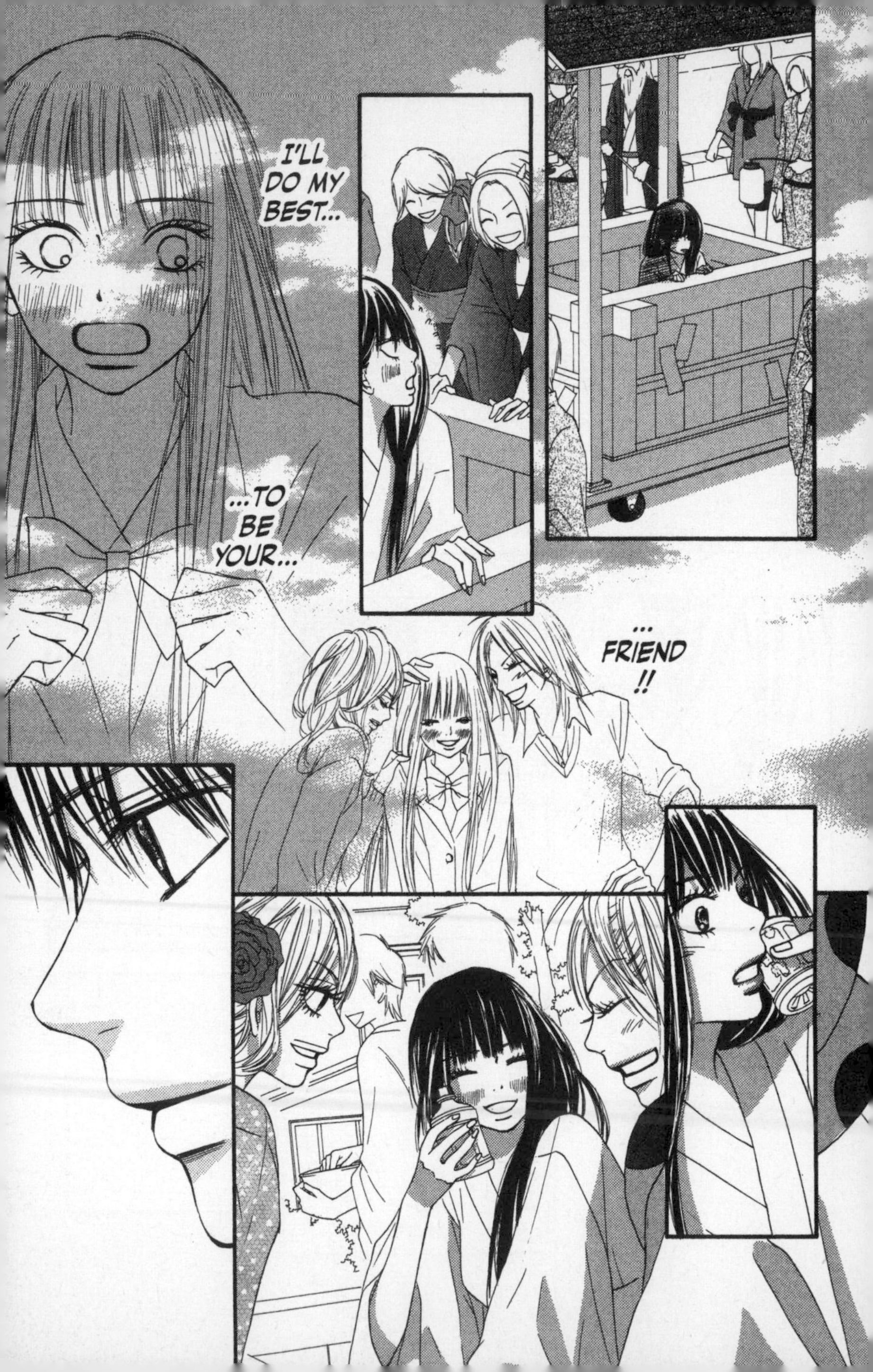
I'LL DO MY BEST...
...TO BE YOUR...
... FRIEND !!

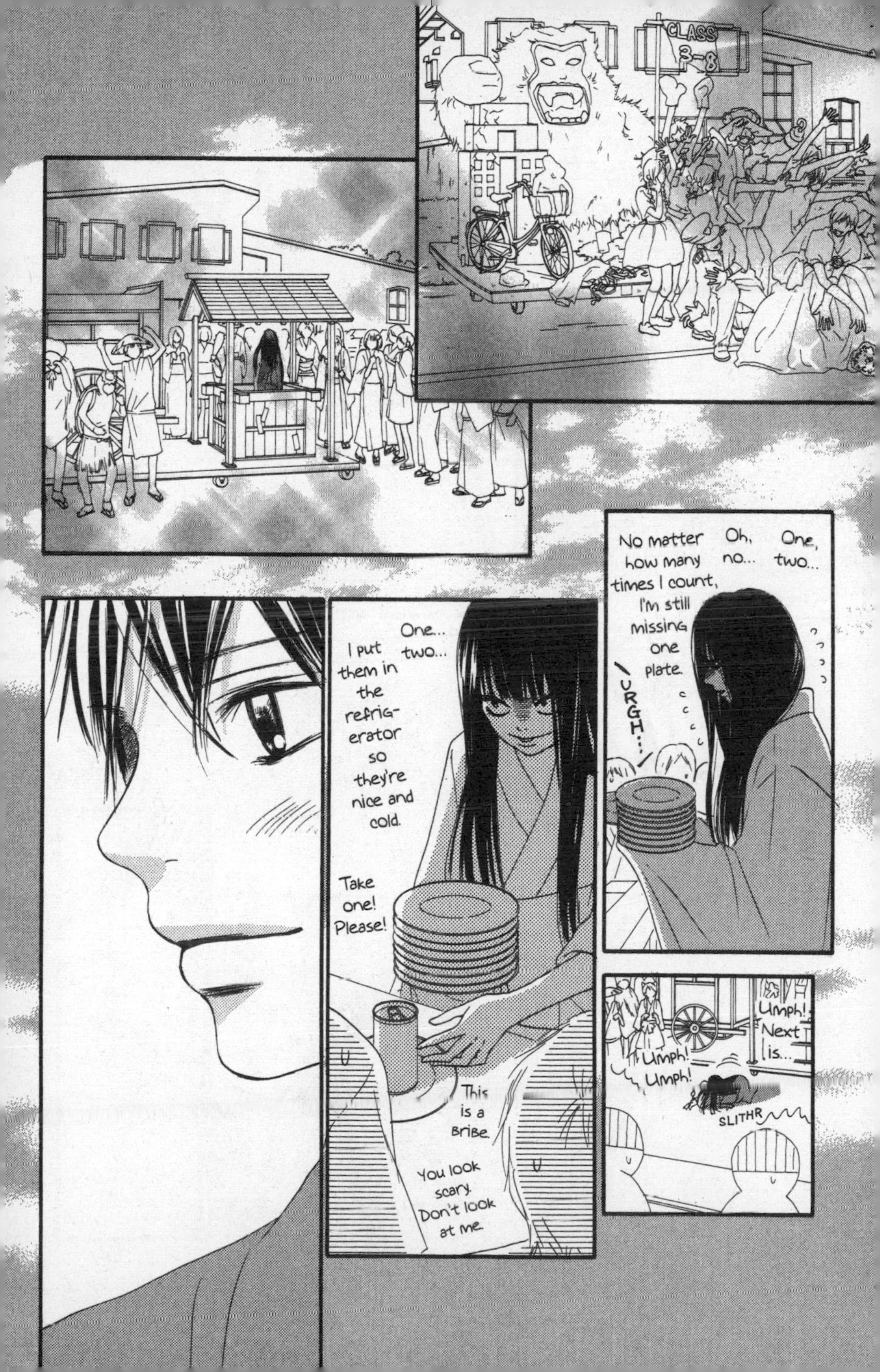
CLASS 3-8
One, two...
Oh, no...
No matter how many times I count, I'm still missing one plate.
URGH...
Umph! Next is...
Umph! Umph!
SLITHR
One... two...
I put them in the refrigerator so they're nice and cold.
Take one! Please!
This is a bribe.
You look scary. Don't look at me.

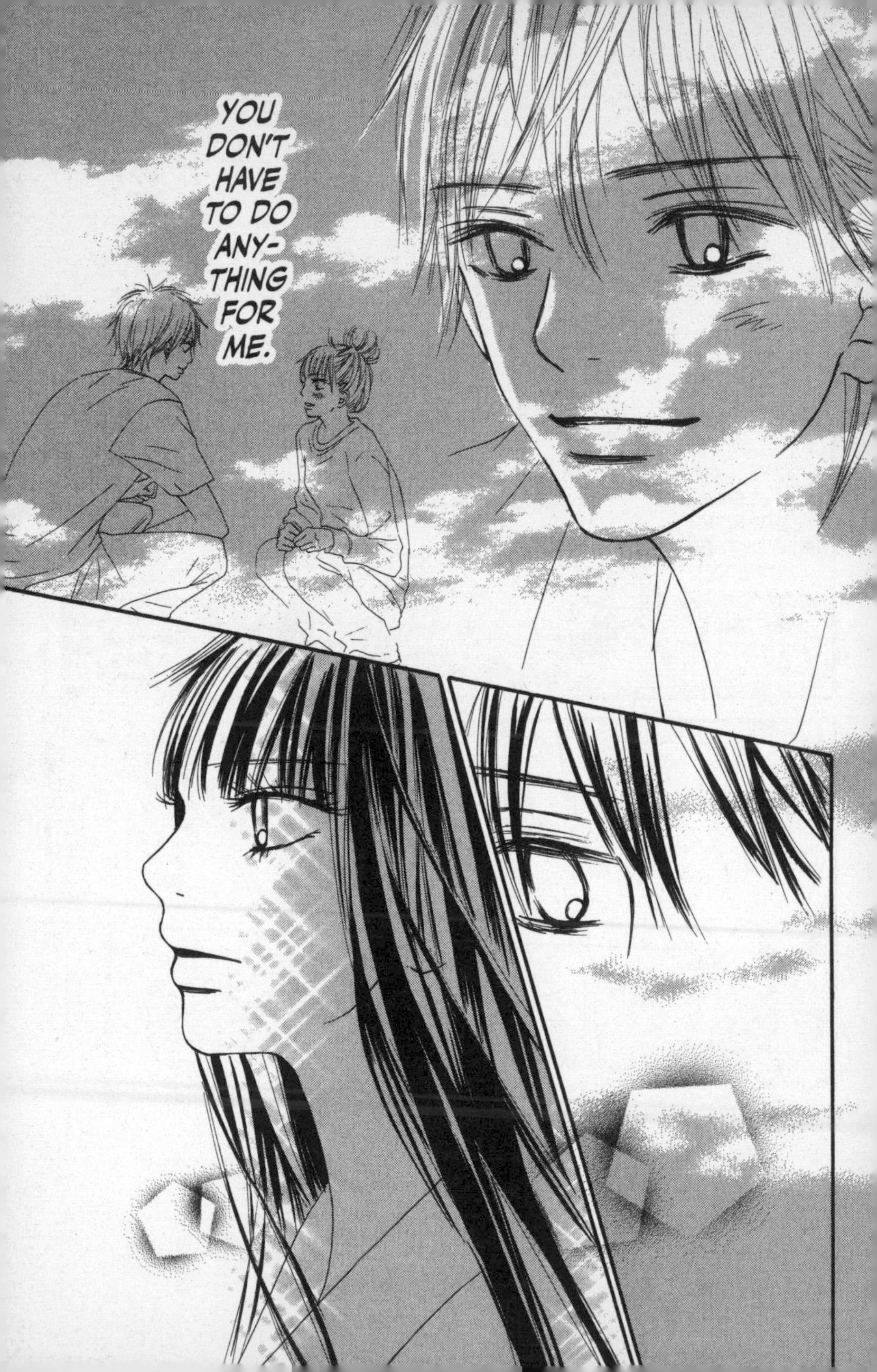
YOU DON'T HAVE TO DO ANY-THING FOR ME.

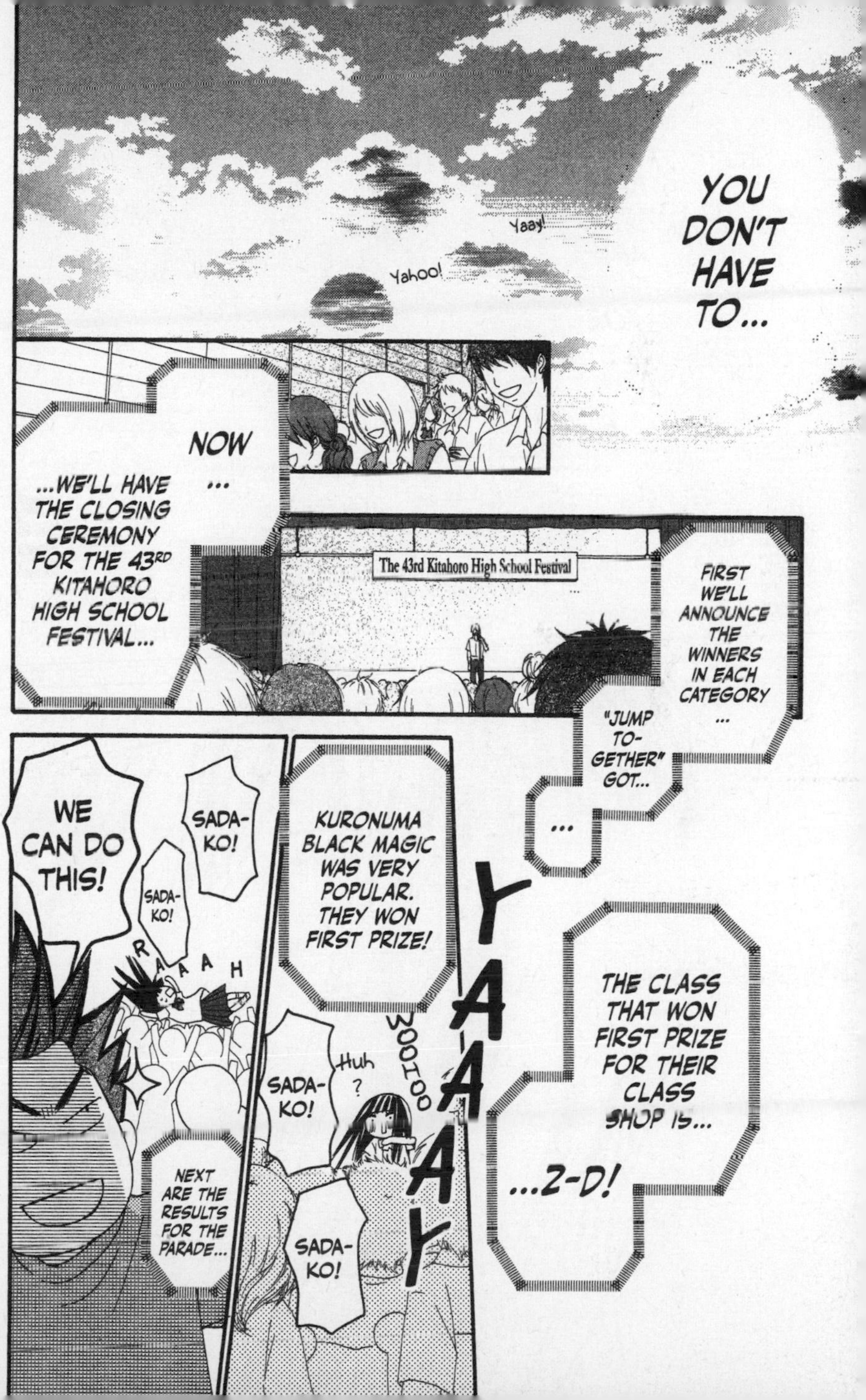
YOU DON'T HAVE TO...
Yaay!
Yahoo!
NOW ...
...WE'LL HAVE THE CLOSING CEREMONY FOR THE 43RD KITAHORO HIGH SCHOOL FESTIVAL...
The 43rd Kitahoro High School Festival
FIRST WE'LL ANNOUNCE THE WINNERS IN EACH CATEGORY ...
"JUMP TO-GETHER" GOT...
...
THE CLASS THAT WON FIRST PRIZE FOR THEIR CLASS SHOP IS...
...2-D!
YAAAAY
KURONUMA BLACK MAGIC WAS VERY POPULAR. THEY WON FIRST PRIZE!
WOOHOO
Huh ?
SADA-KO!
SADA-KO!
WE CAN DO THIS!
SADA-KO!
SADA-KO!
RAAAH
NEXT ARE THE RESULTS FOR THE PARADE...

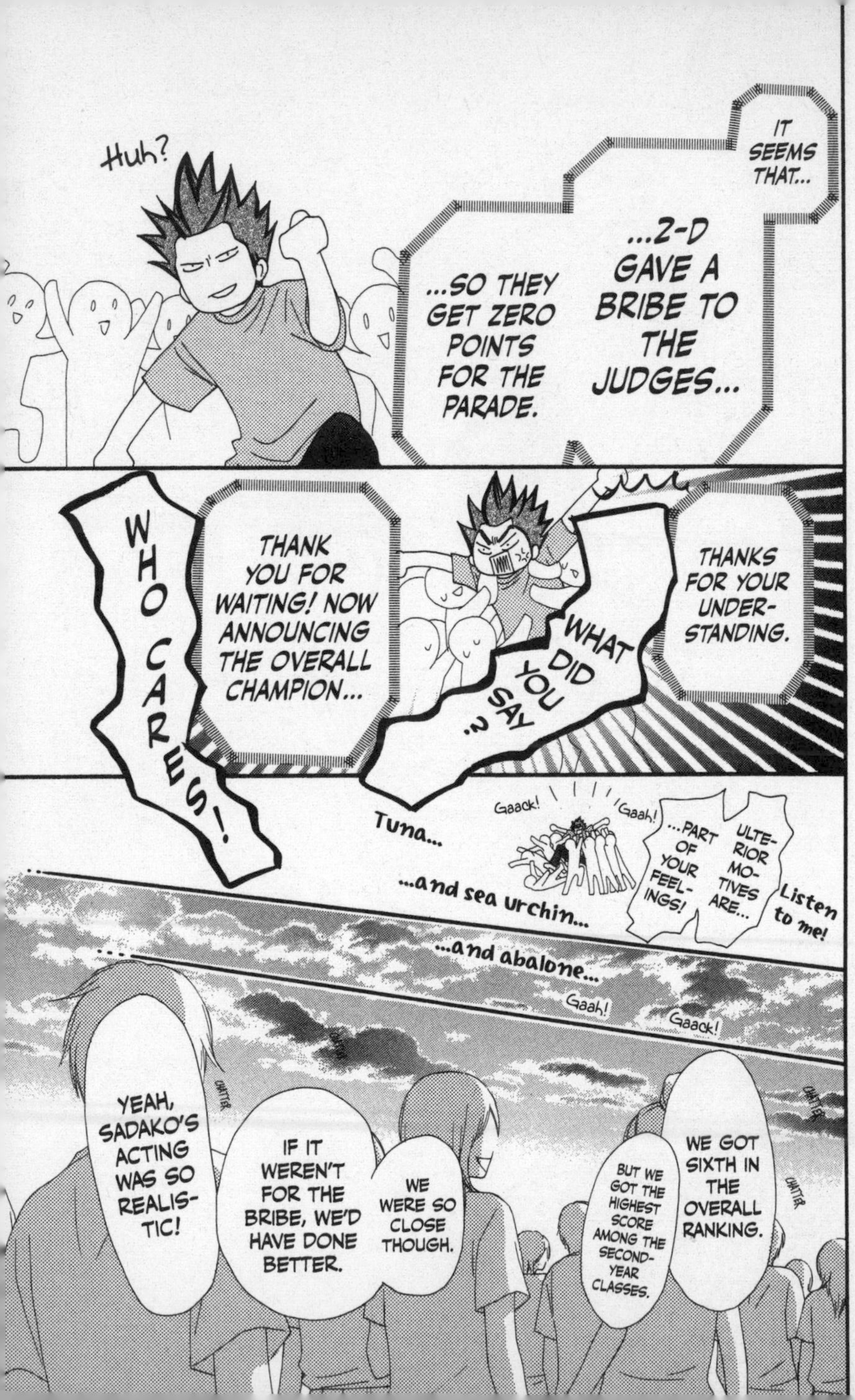
IT SEEMS THAT...
...2-D GAVE A BRIBE TO THE JUDGES...
...SO THEY GET ZERO POINTS FOR THE PARADE.
Huh?
THANKS FOR YOUR UNDER-STANDING.
WHAT DID YOU SAY?
THANK YOU FOR WAITING! NOW ANNOUNCING THE OVERALL CHAMPION...
WHO CARES!
Listen to me!
ULTE-RIOR MO-TIVES ARE...
...PART OF YOUR FEEL-INGS!
Gaah!
Gaack!
Tuna...
...and sea urchin...
...and abalone...
Gaah!
Gaack!
WE GOT SIXTH IN THE OVERALL RANKING.
BUT WE GOT THE HIGHEST SCORE AMONG THE SECOND-YEAR CLASSES.
WE WERE SO CLOSE THOUGH.
IF IT WEREN'T FOR THE BRIBE, WE'D HAVE DONE BETTER.
YEAH, SADAKO'S ACTING WAS SO REALIS-TIC!

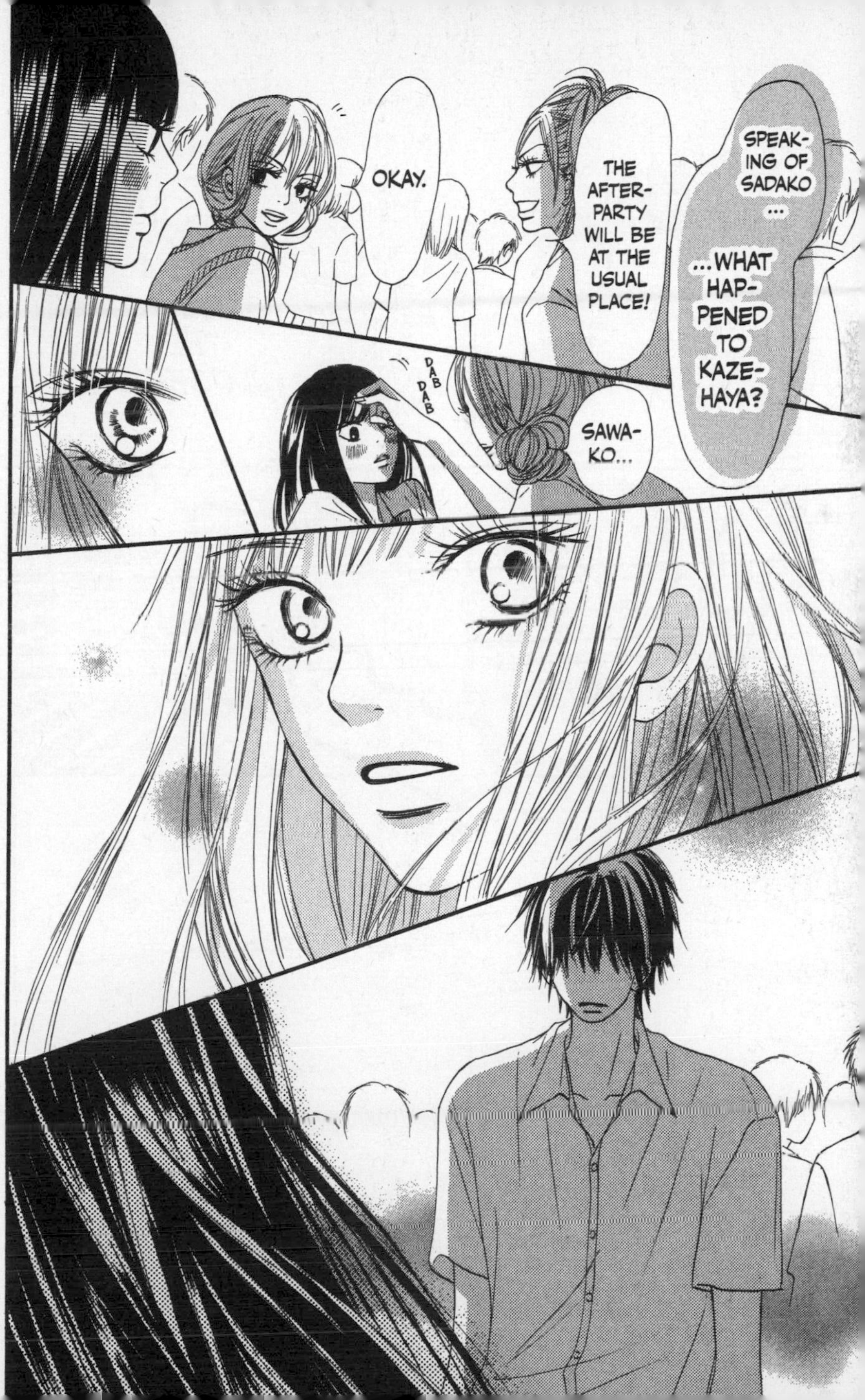
SPEAK-ING OF SADAKO ... ...WHAT HAP-PENED TO KAZE-HAYA?
THE AFTER-PARTY WILL BE AT THE USUAL PLACE!
OKAY.
SAWA-KO...
DAB DAB

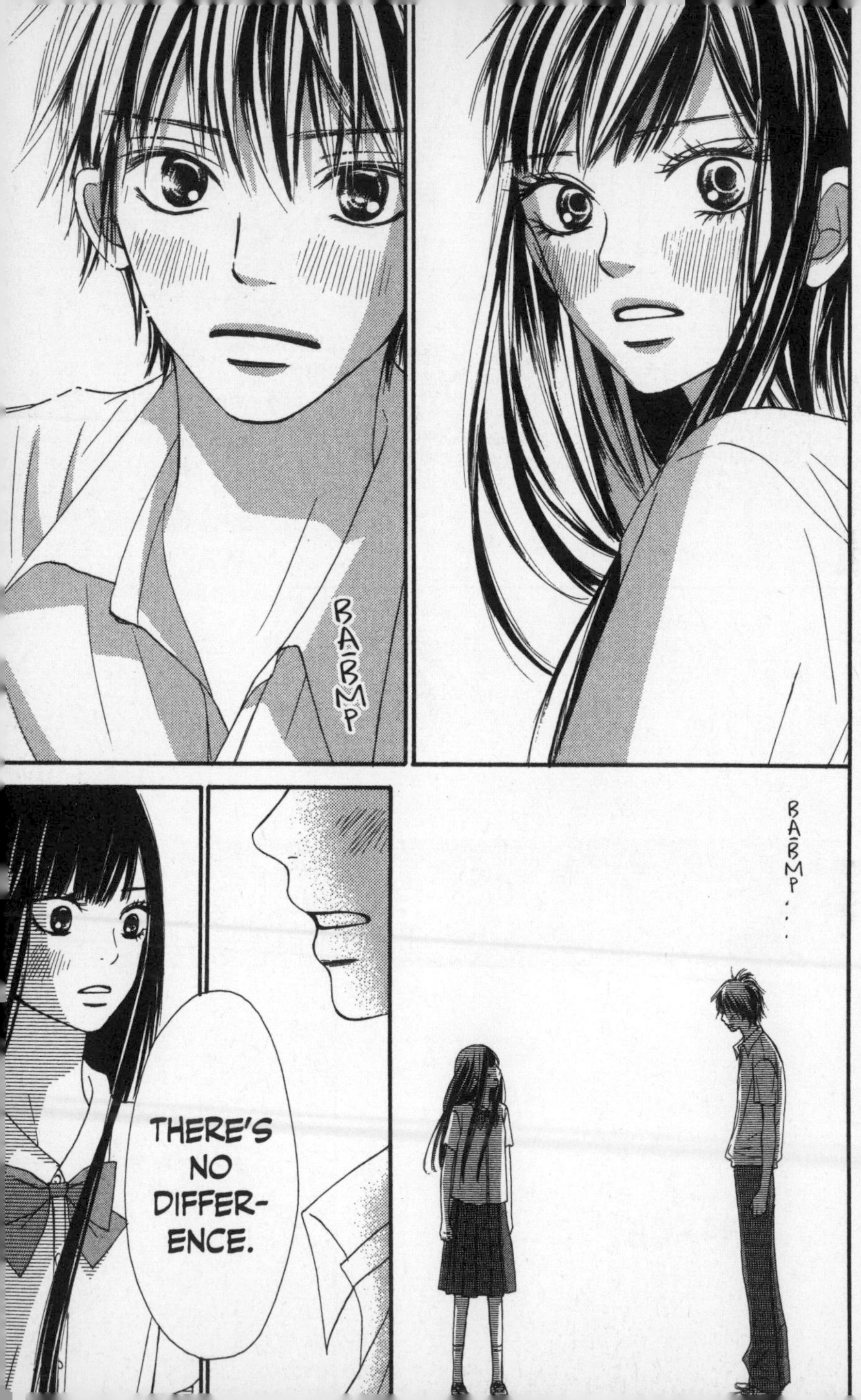
BA-BUMP
BA-BUMP...
THERE'S NO DIFFER-ENCE.

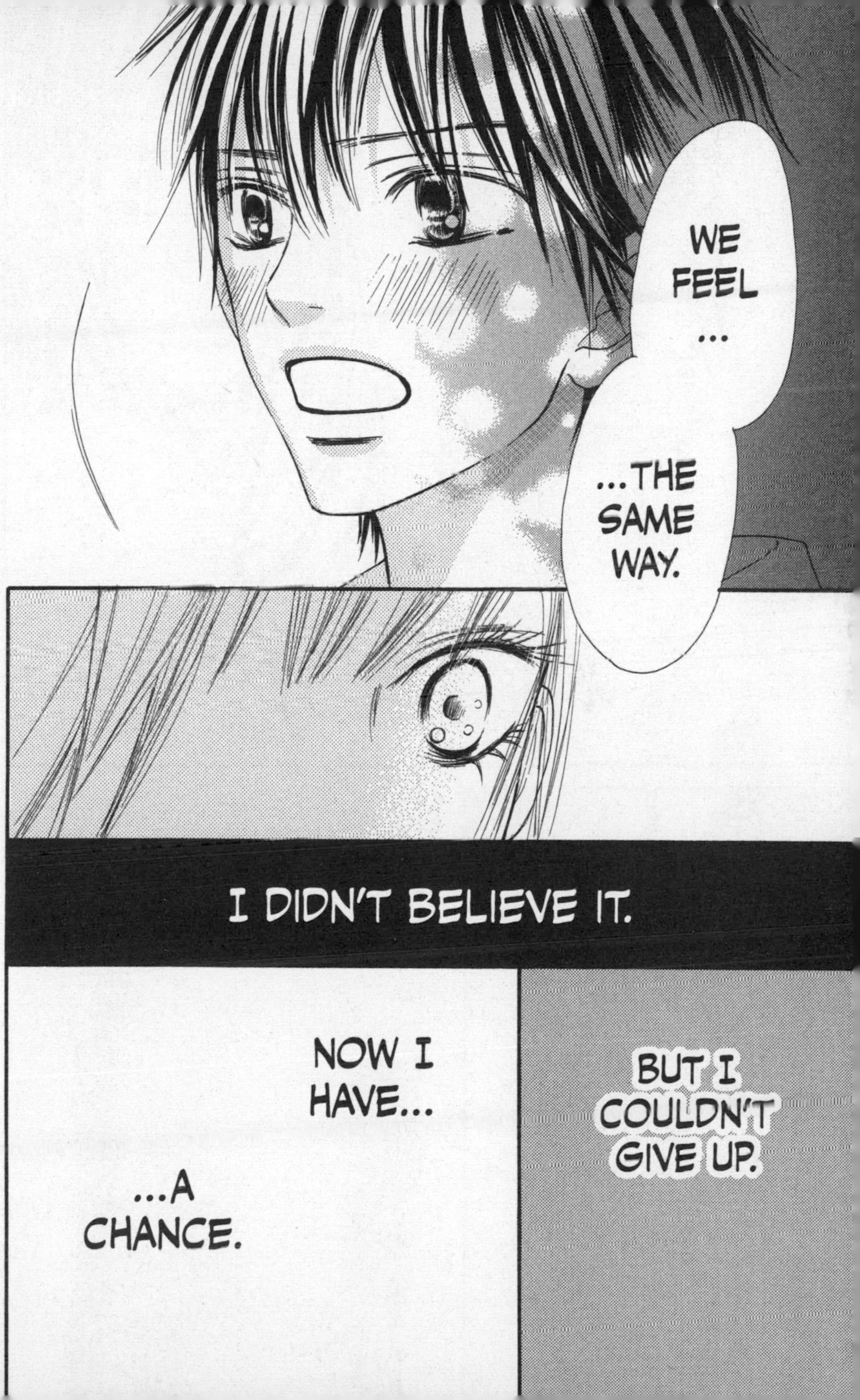
WE FEEL ...
...THE SAME WAY.
I DIDN'T BELIEVE IT.
BUT I COULDN'T GIVE UP.
NOW I HAVE...
...A CHANCE.

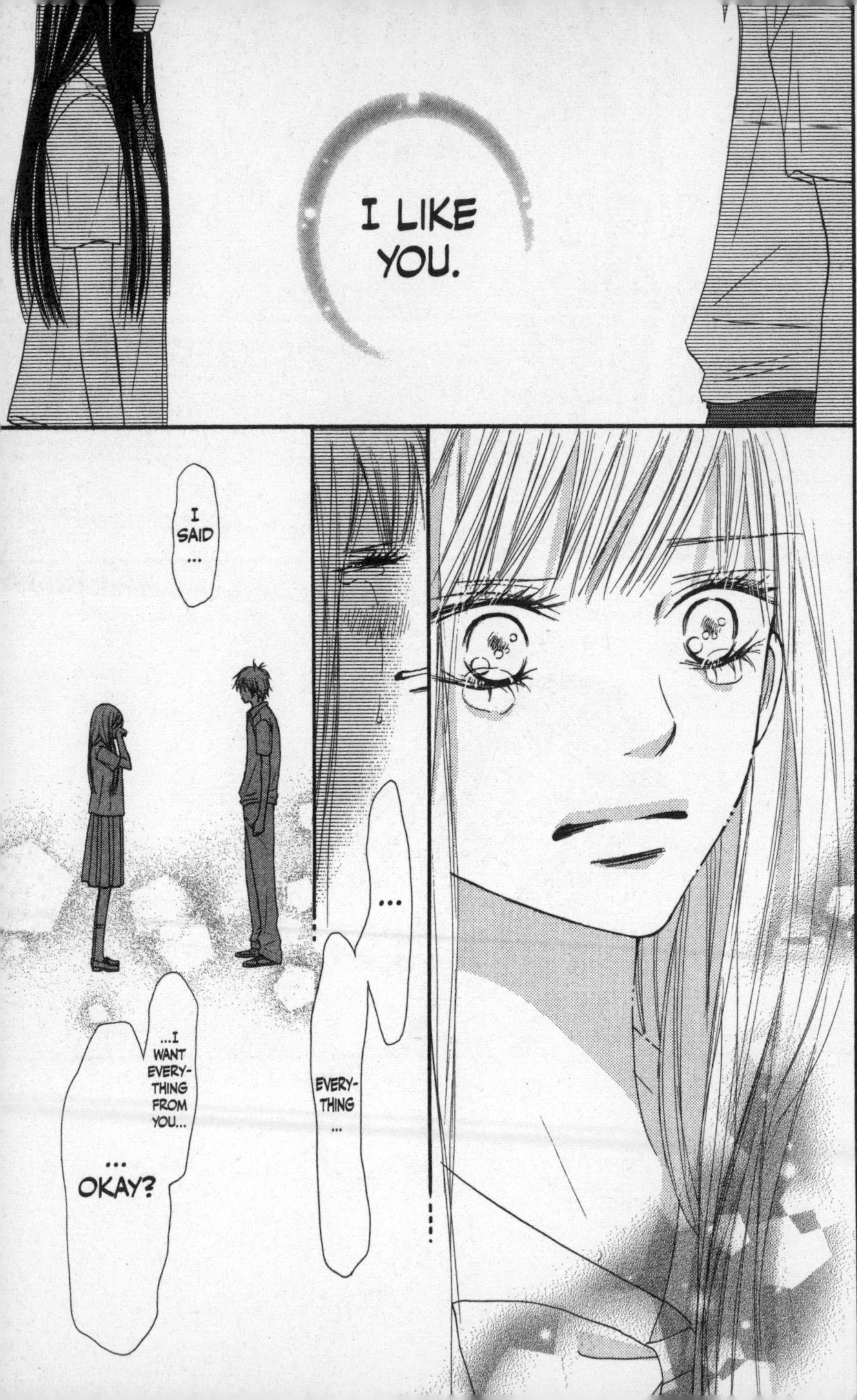
I LIKE YOU.
...
EVERY-THING ...
I SAID ...
...I WANT EVERY-THING FROM YOU...
... OKAY?

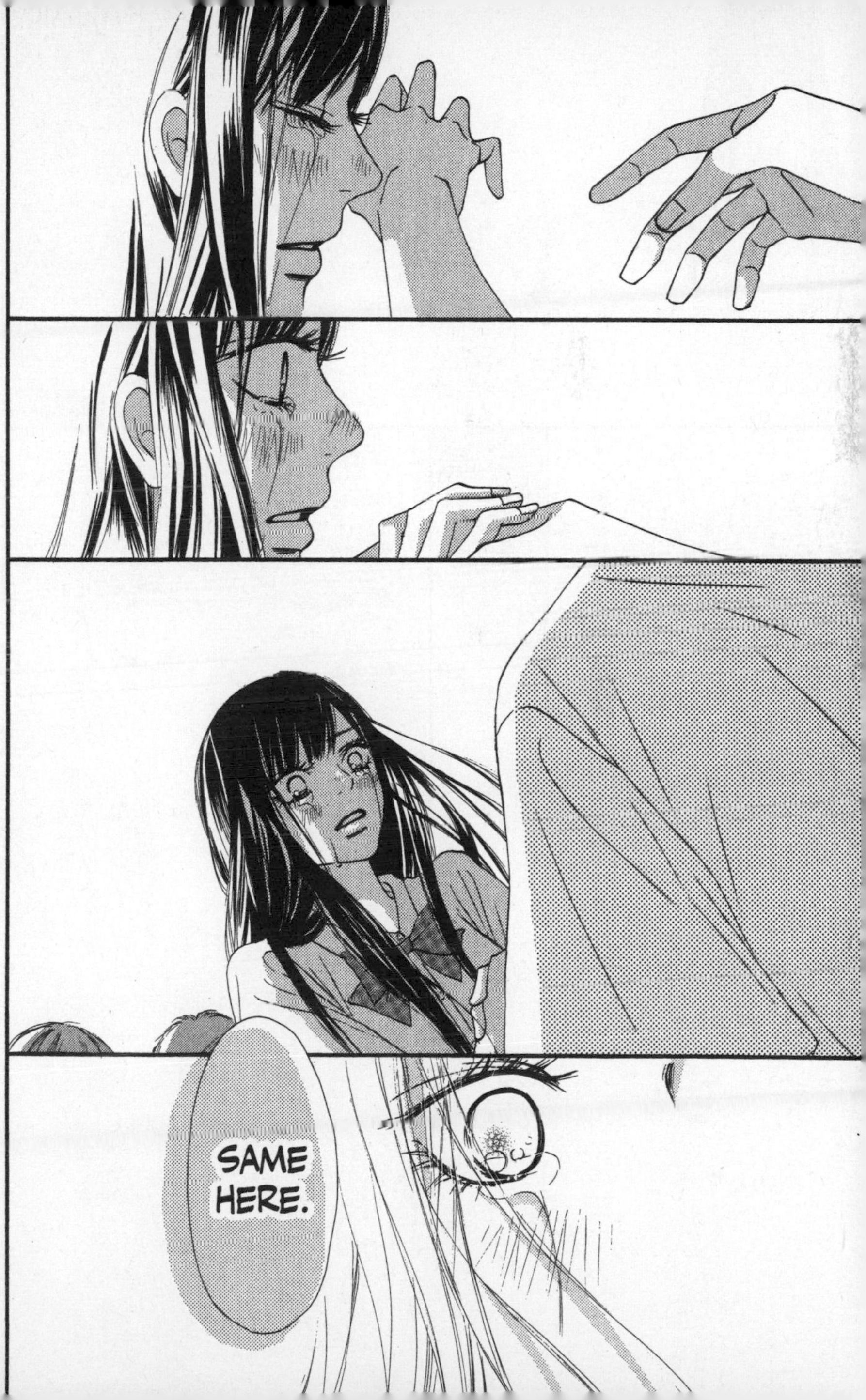
SAME HERE.

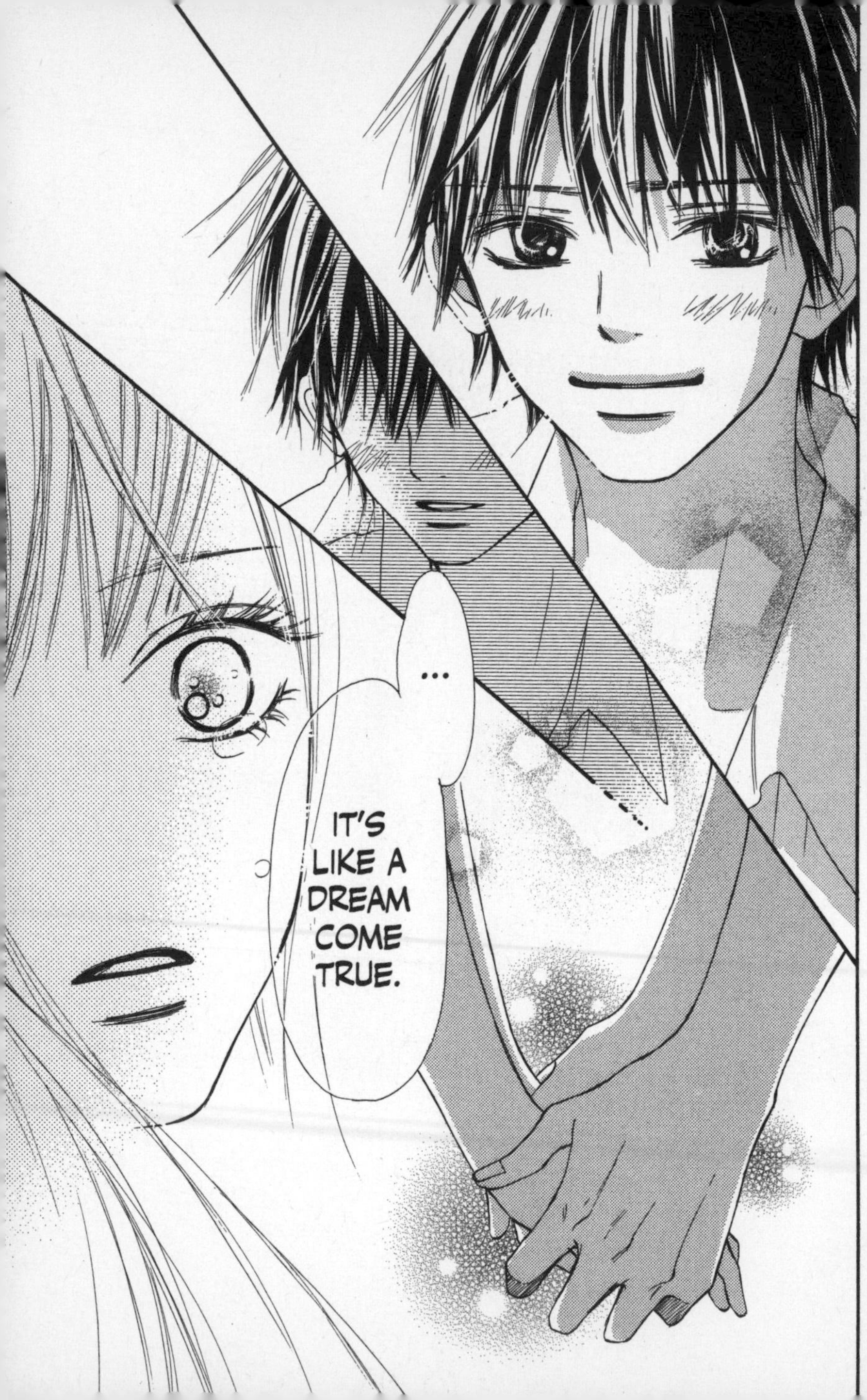
...
IT'S LIKE A DREAM COME TRUE.

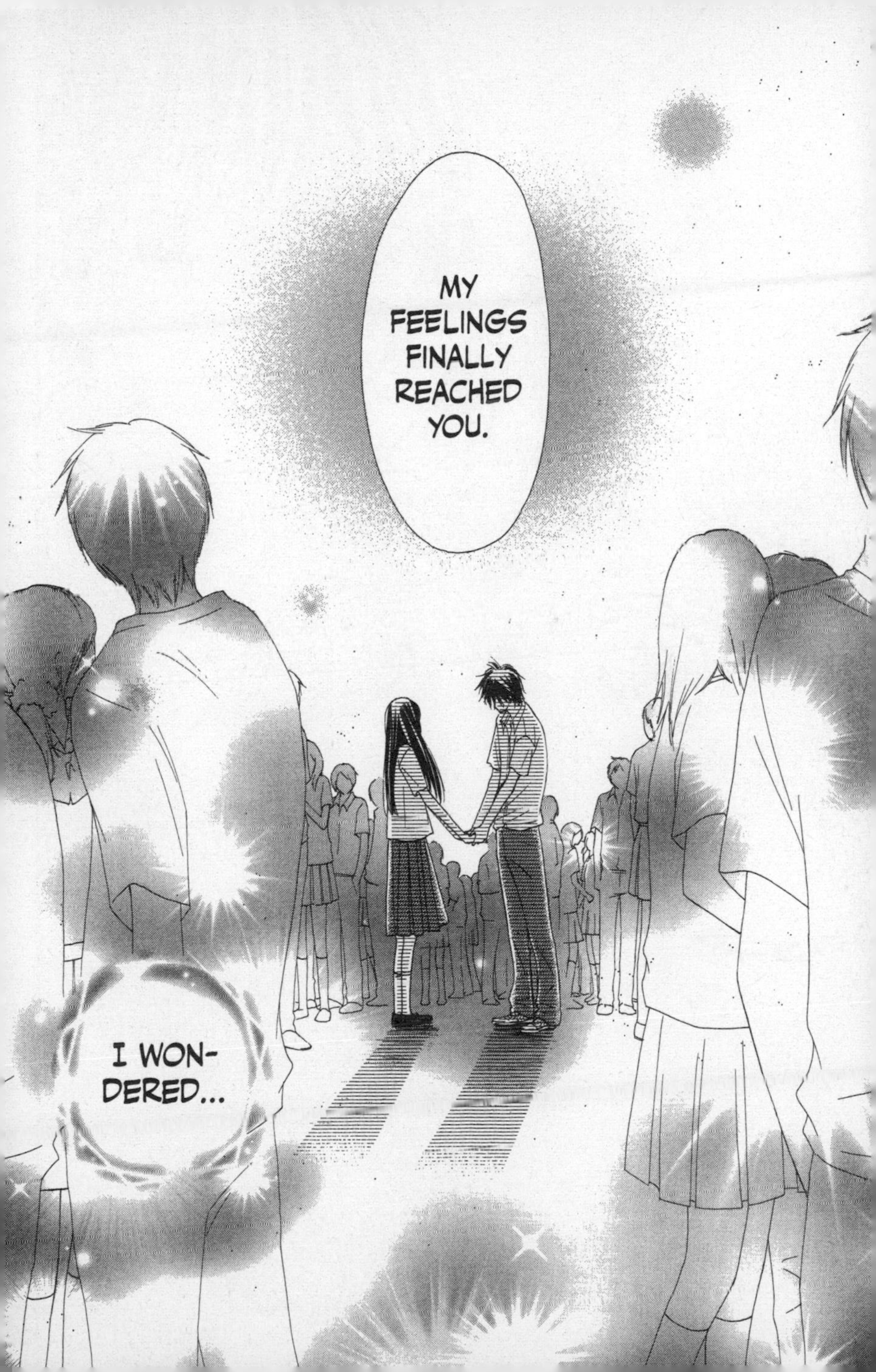
MY FEELINGS FINALLY REACHED YOU.
I WON-DERED...

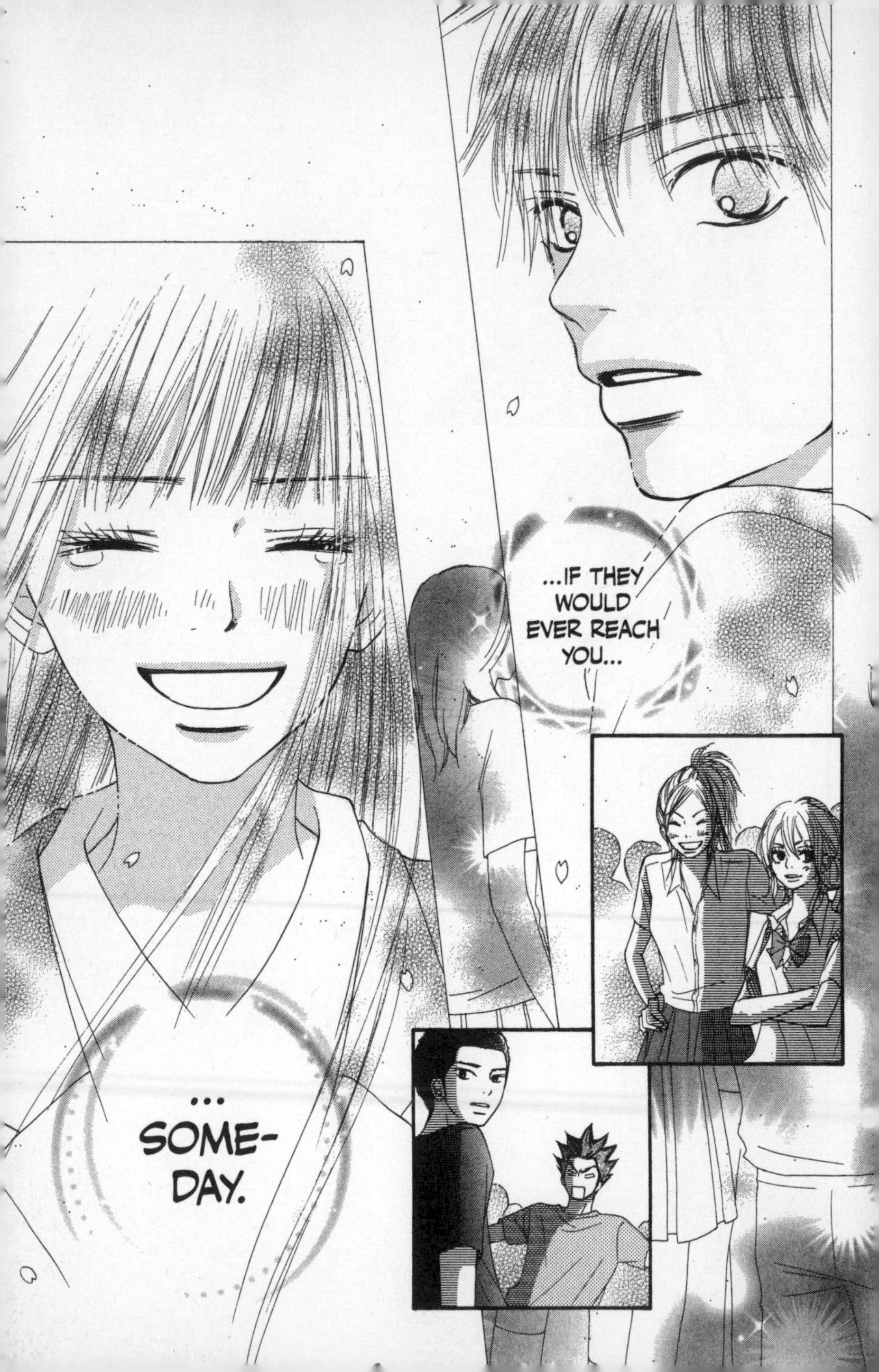
...IF THEY WOULD EVER REACH YOU...
... SOME-DAY.

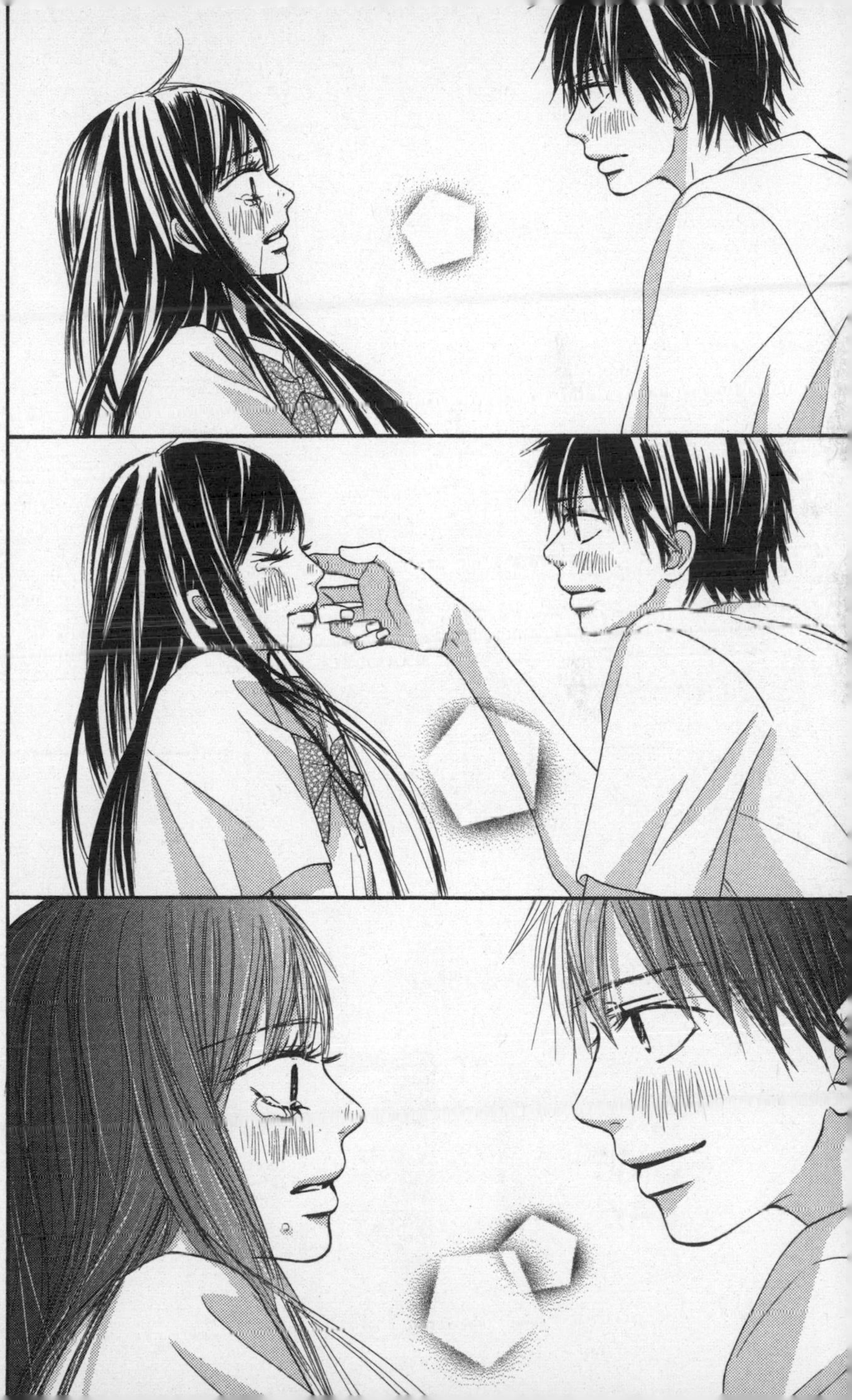

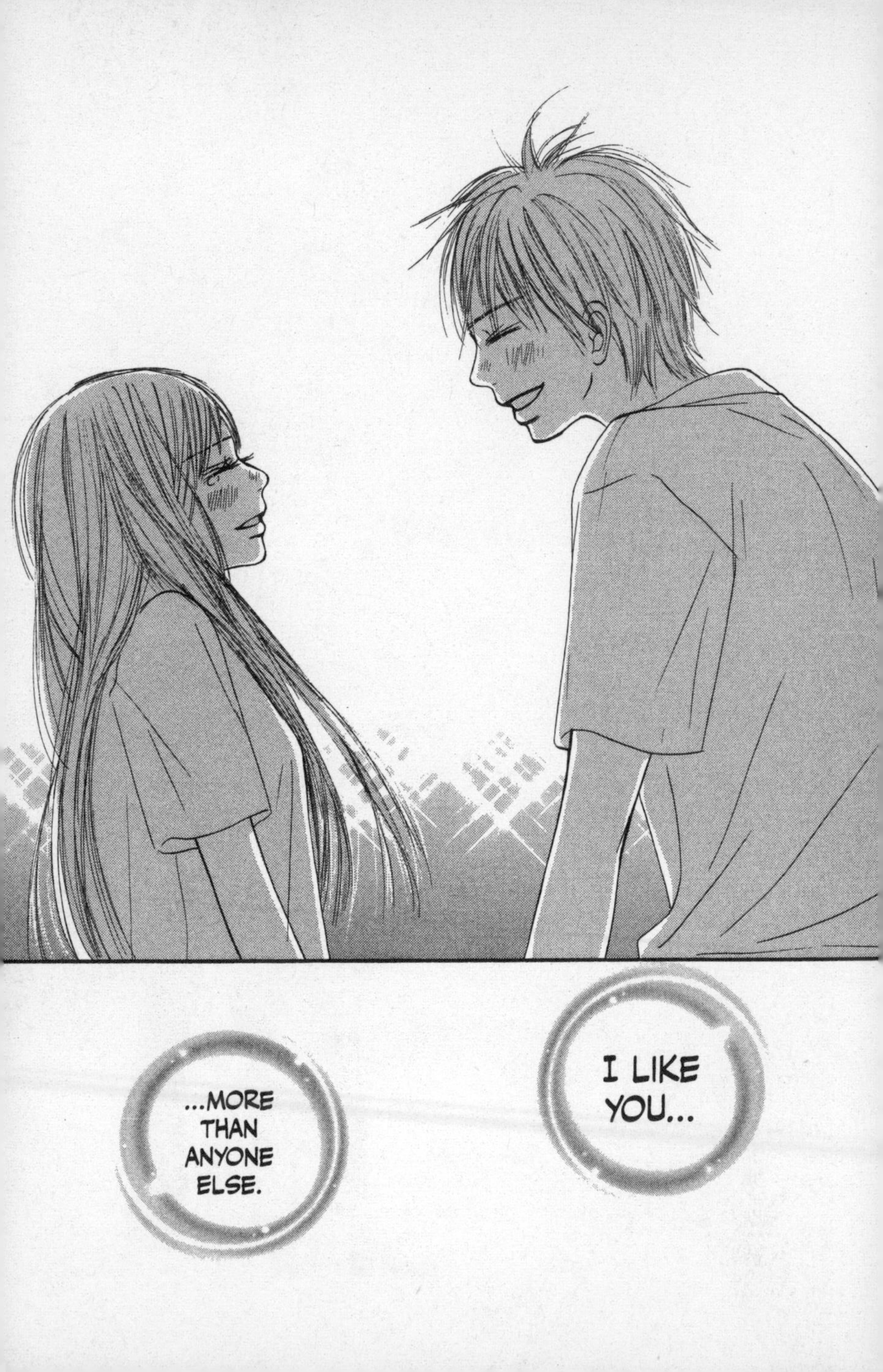
I LIKE YOU...
...MORE THAN ANYONE ELSE.

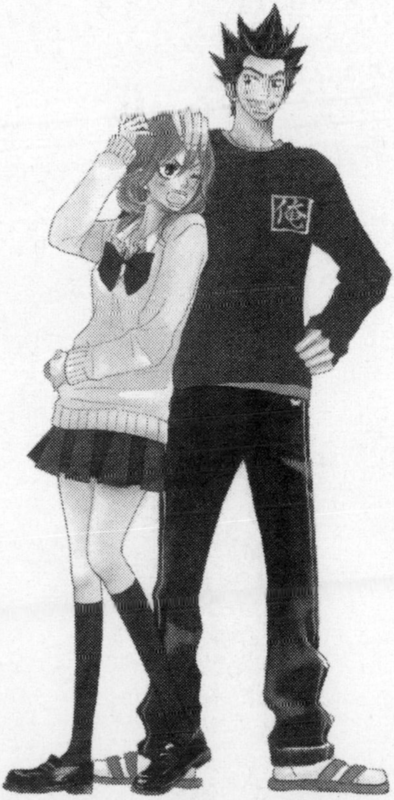
俺

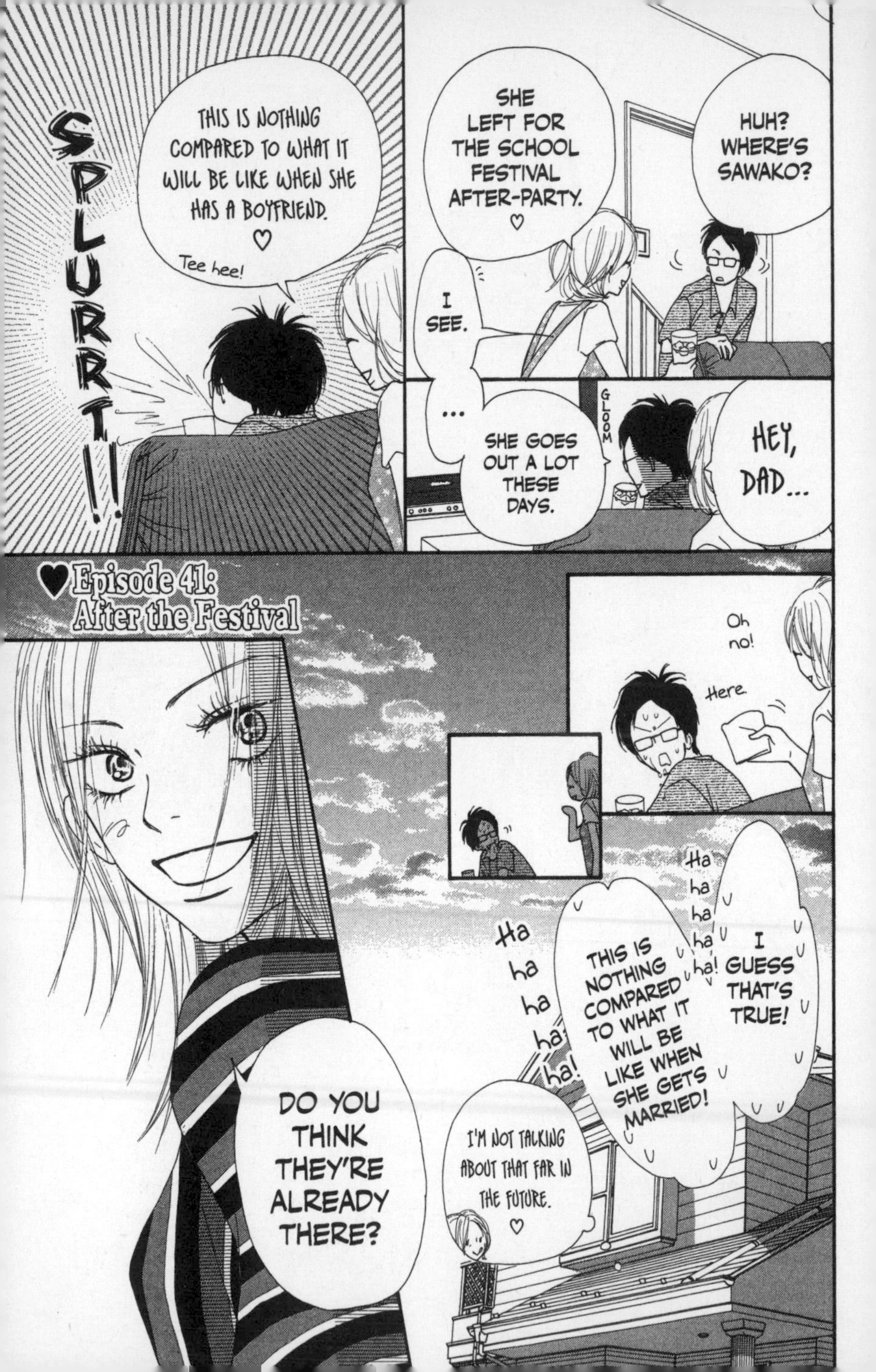
HUH? WHERE'S SAWAKO?
SHE LEFT FOR THE SCHOOL FESTIVAL AFTER-PARTY. ♡
I SEE.
HEY, DAD...
SHE GOES OUT A LOT THESE DAYS.
GLOOM
...
THIS IS NOTHING COMPARED TO WHAT IT WILL BE LIKE WHEN SHE HAS A BOYFRIEND. ♡
Tee hee!
SPLURRT!!
♥Episode 41: After the Festival
Oh no!
Here.
Ha ha ha ha ha!
I GUESS THAT'S TRUE!
THIS IS NOTHING COMPARED TO WHAT IT WILL BE LIKE WHEN SHE GETS MARRIED!
Ha ha ha ha ha!
I'M NOT TALKING ABOUT THAT FAR IN THE FUTURE. ♡
DO YOU THINK THEY'RE ALREADY THERE?

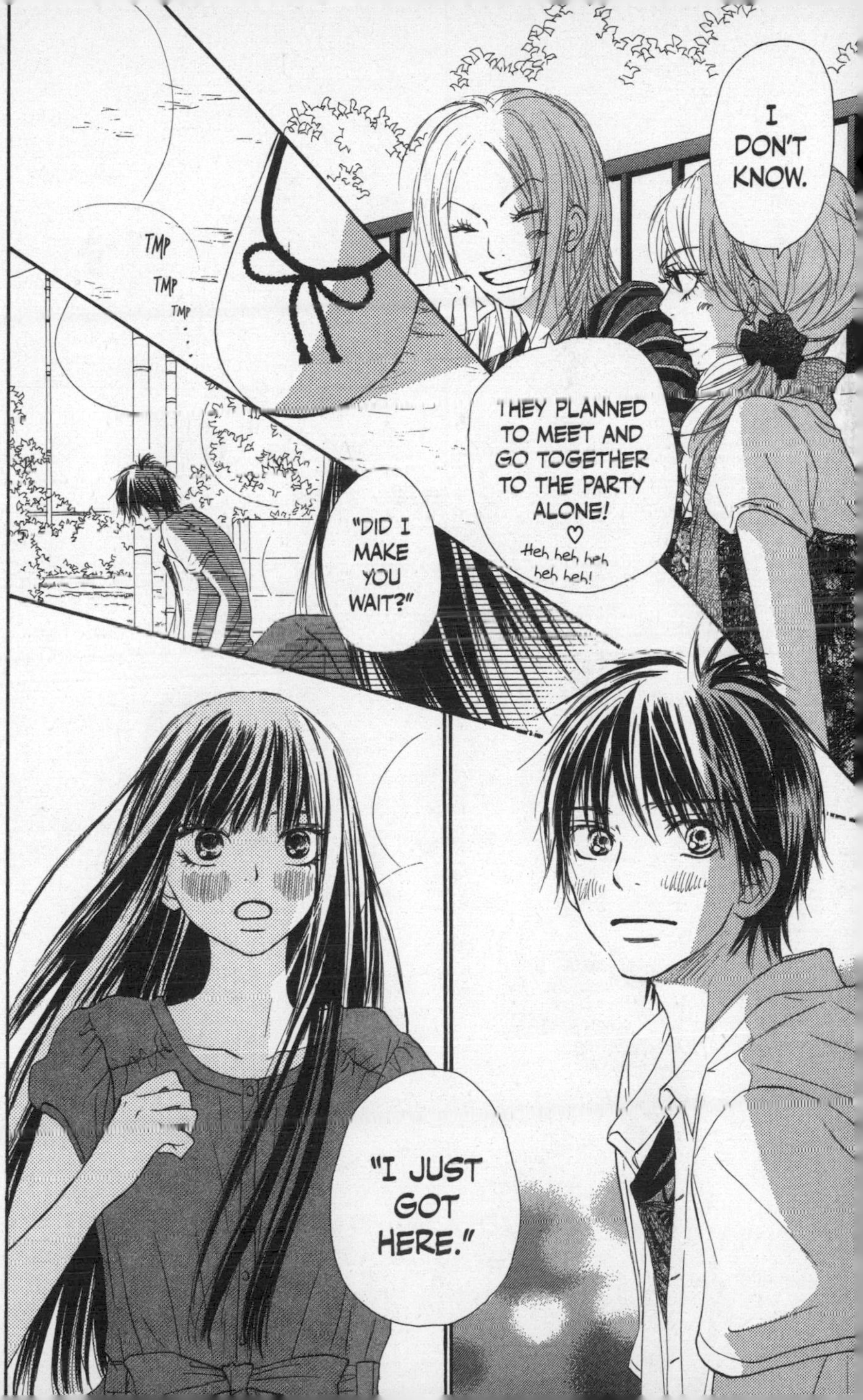
I DON'T KNOW.
THEY PLANNED TO MEET AND GO TOGETHER TO THE PARTY ALONE! ♡
Heh heh heh heh heh!
TMP
TMP
TMP
"DID I MAKE YOU WAIT?"
"I JUST GOT HERE."

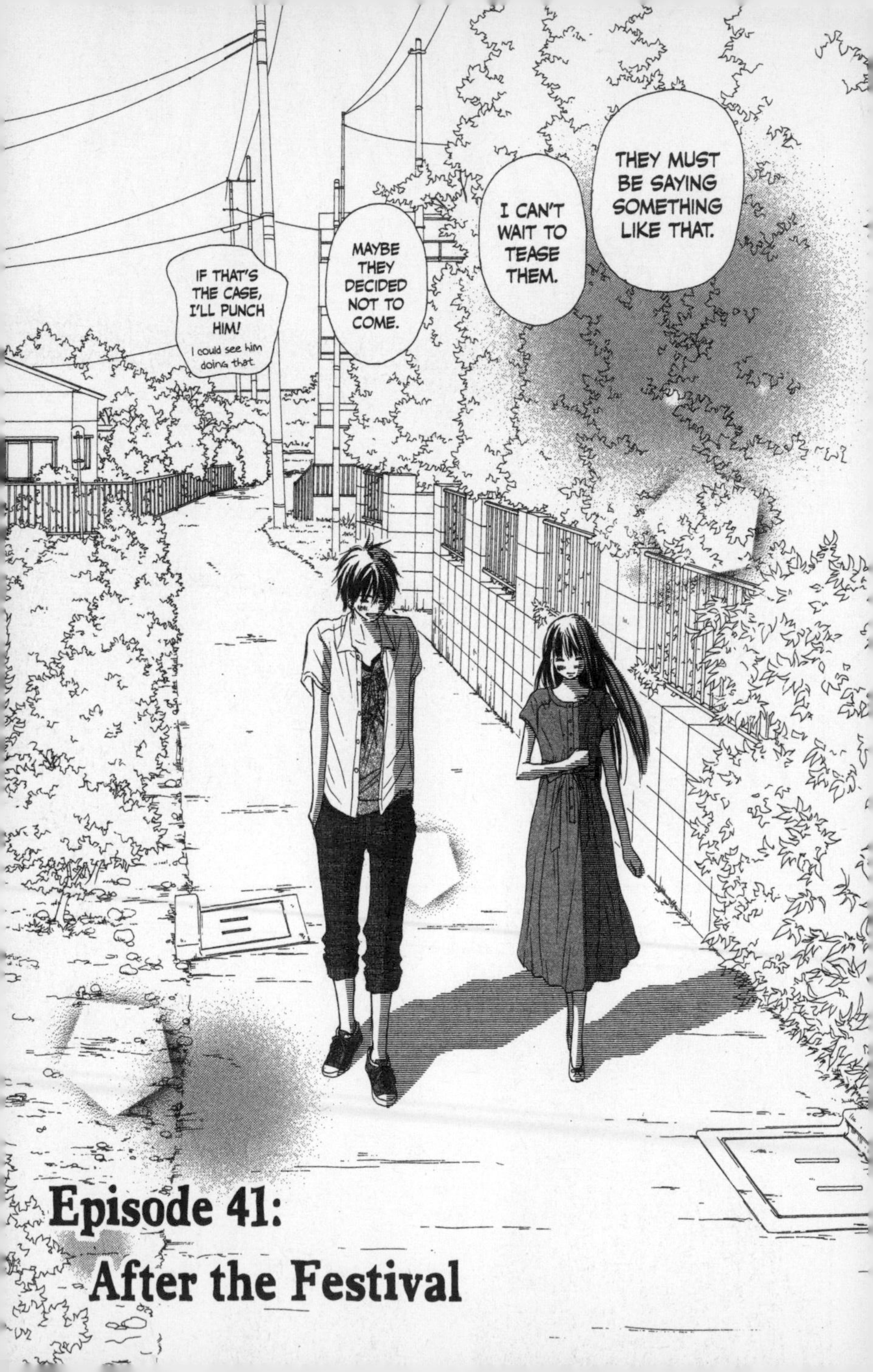
THEY MUST BE SAYING SOMETHING LIKE THAT.
I CAN'T WAIT TO TEASE THEM.
MAYBE THEY DECIDED NOT TO COME.
IF THAT'S THE CASE, I'LL PUNCH HIM!
I could see him doing that.

Episode 41: After the Festival

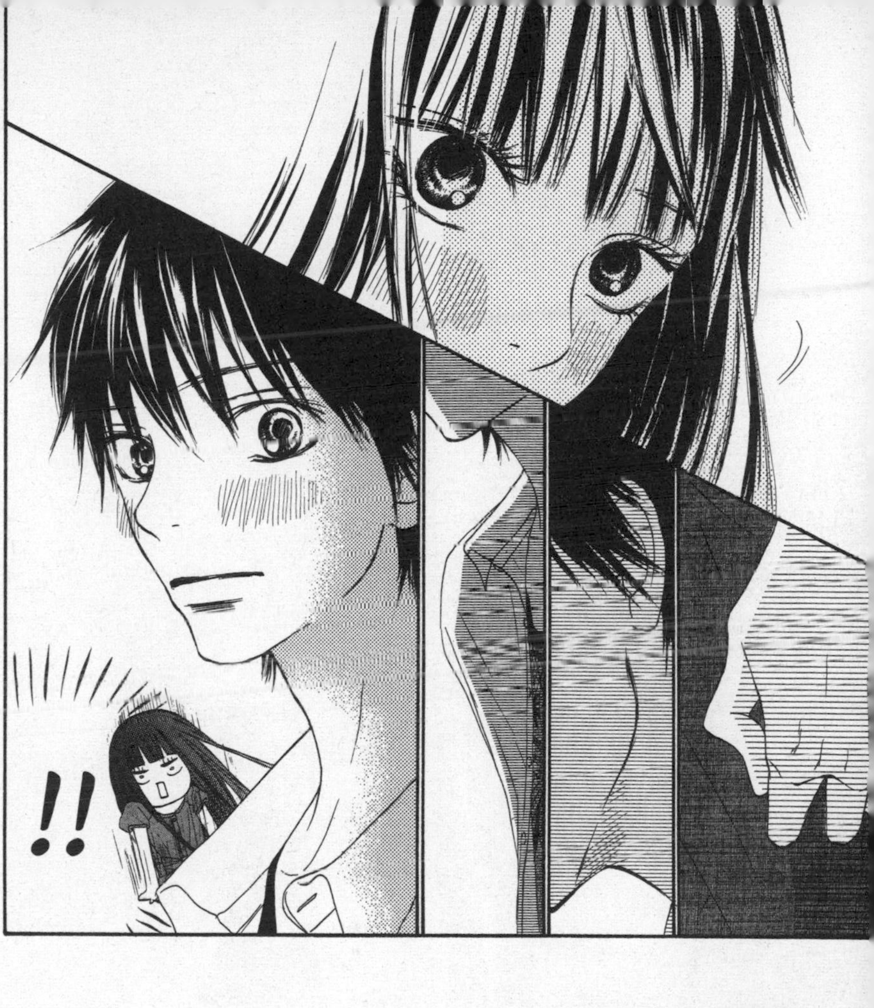
!!

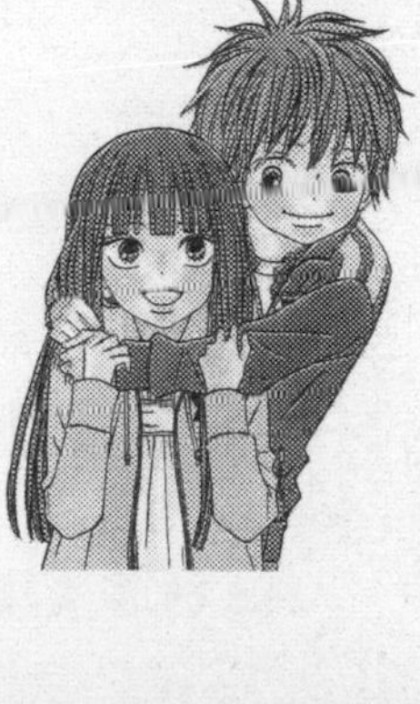

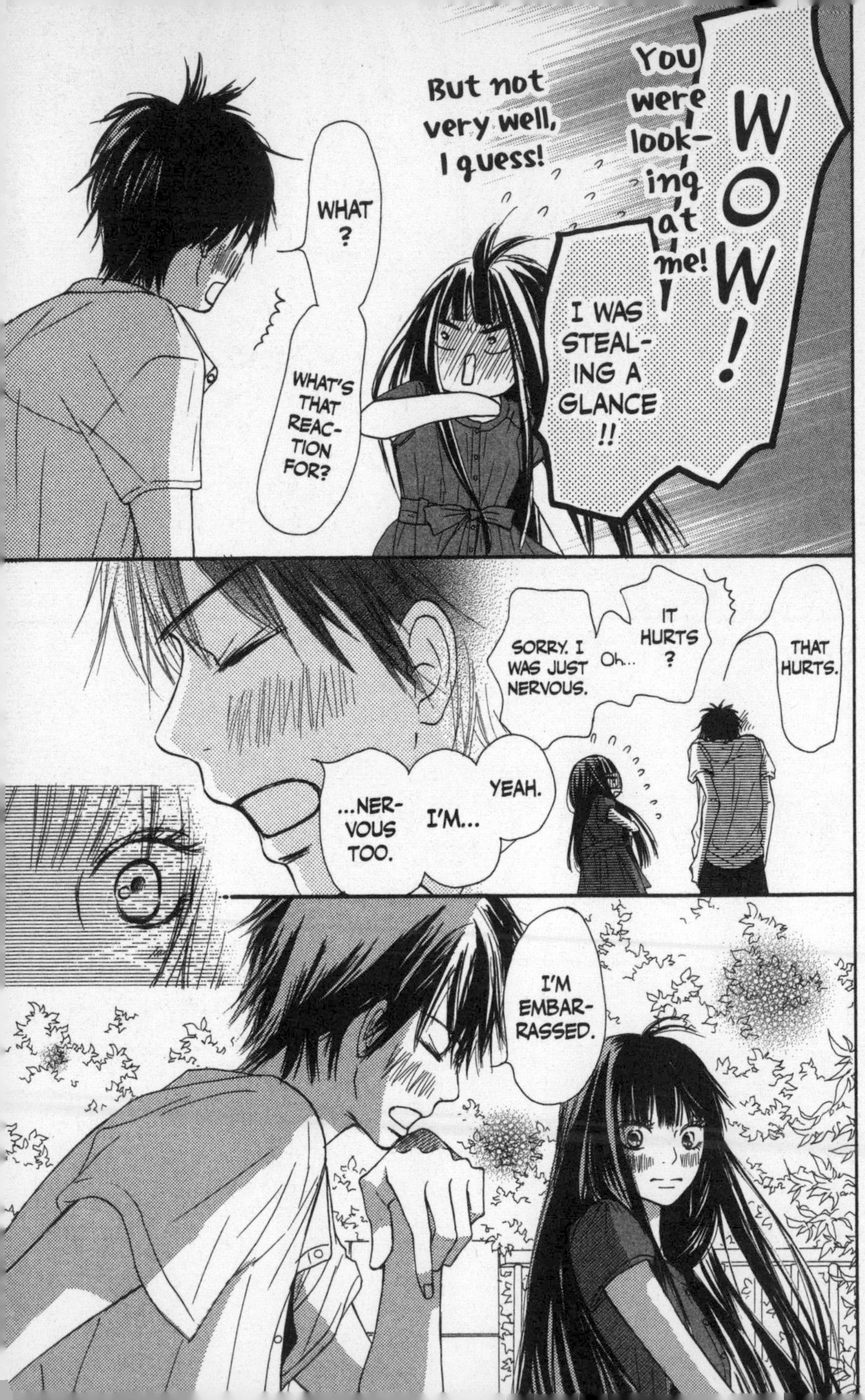
WOW!
You were looking at me!
I WAS STEALING A GLANCE!!
But not very well, I guess!
WHAT?
WHAT'S THAT REACTION FOR?
THAT HURTS.
IT HURTS?
Oh...
SORRY. I WAS JUST NERVOUS.
YEAH.
I'M...
...NERVOUS TOO.
I'M EMBARRASSED.

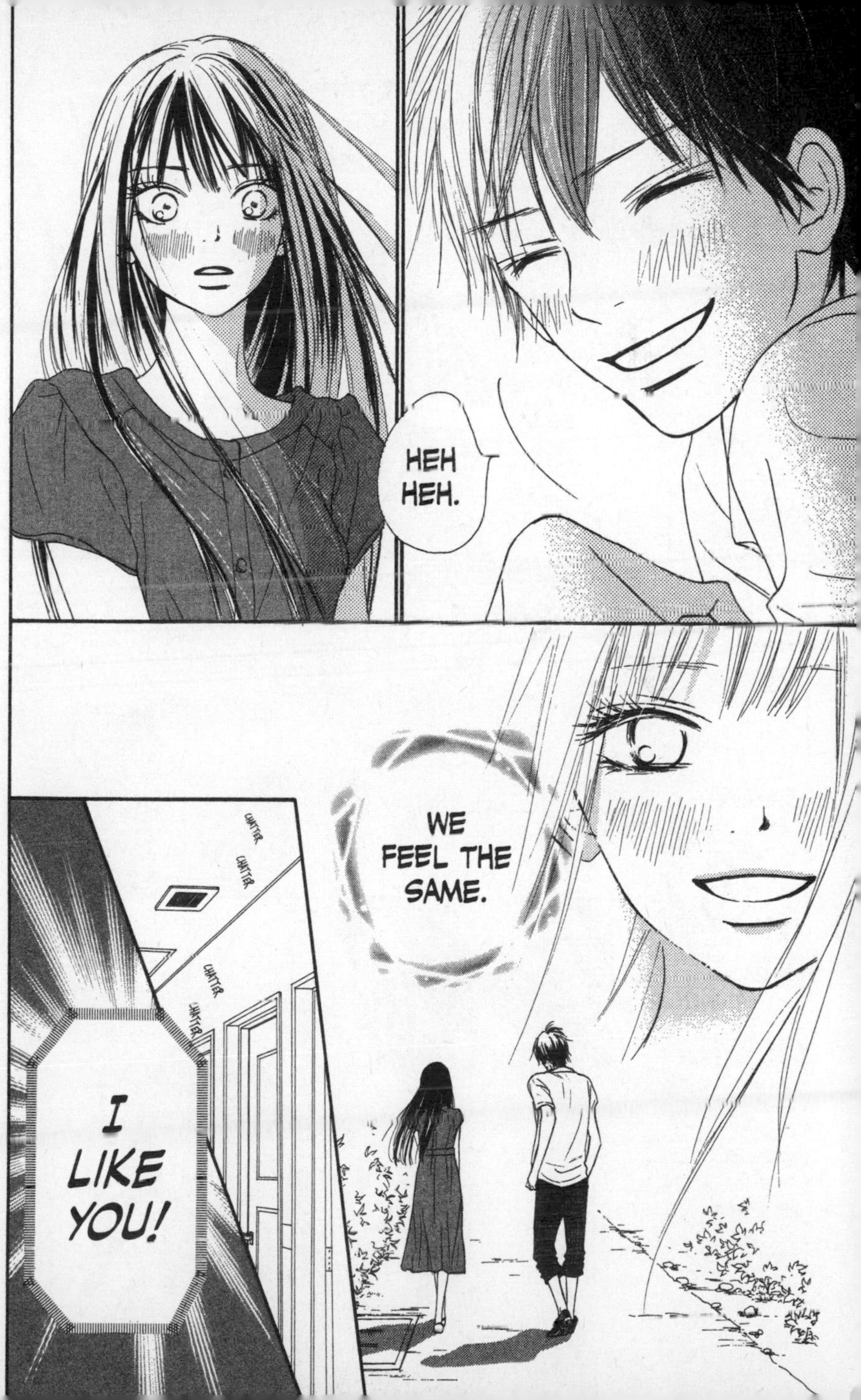
HEH HEH.
WE FEEL THE SAME.
CHATTER CHATTER
CHATTER CHATTER
I LIKE YOU!

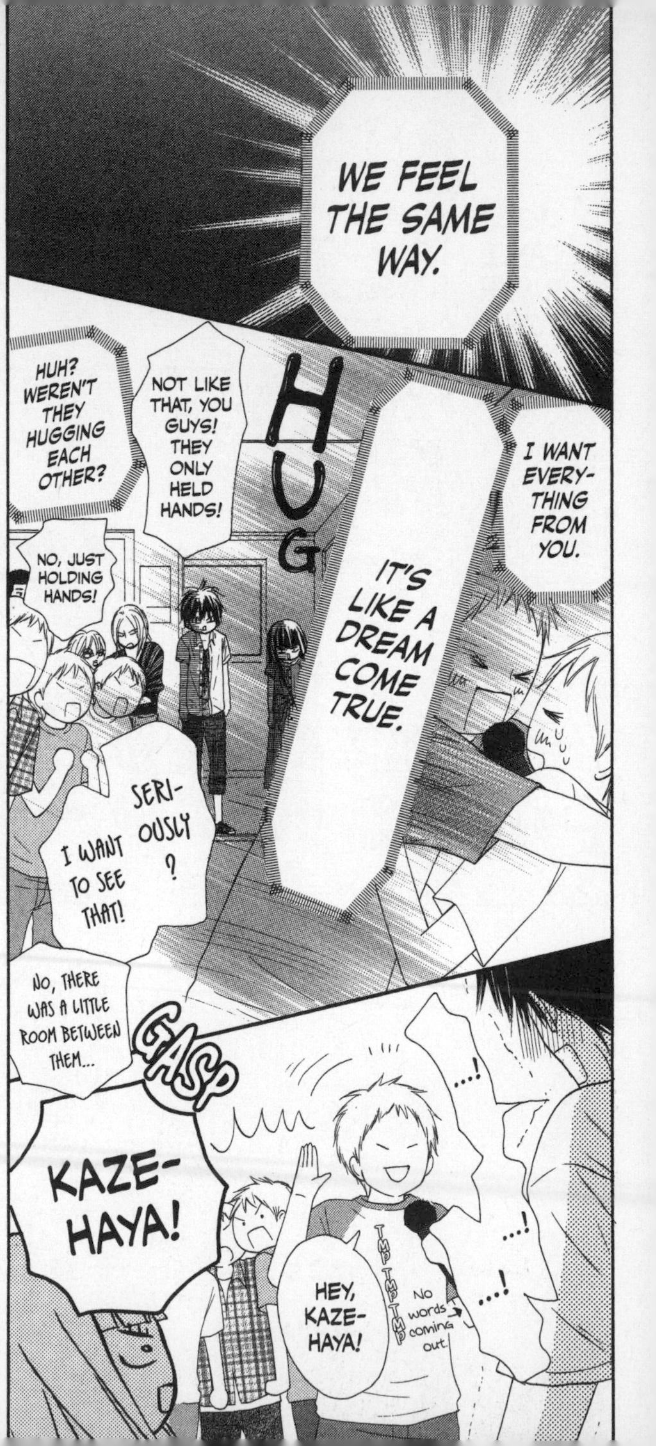
WE FEEL THE SAME WAY.
I WANT EVERY-THING FROM YOU.
IT'S LIKE A DREAM COME TRUE.
HUG
NOT LIKE THAT, YOU GUYS! THEY ONLY HELD HANDS!
HUH? WEREN'T THEY HUGGING EACH OTHER?
NO, JUST HOLDING HANDS!
SERI-OUSLY ?
I WANT TO SEE THAT!
NO, THERE WAS A LITTLE ROOM BETWEEN THEM...
...!
...!
...!
No words coming out.
TMP TMP TMP TMP
HEY, KAZE-HAYA!
GASP
KAZE-HAYA!

KARUPIN on JAPAN 3

Anyway, there were lots of fun events to celebrate the anime version of *Kimi ni Todoke*, such as Harajuku Jack and a preview screening of the first episode! Great!

I wanted to go...

I had a chance to meet Chara-san.

What do you think? Should I wear this?

Eek!♡

?

But I started having a fever two days before the event. (Why me?) It was about 104° F...

What is this?

I didn't have enough blankets to keep me warm even though it was summer.
When I went to see the doctor, I had tonsillitis. The last time I had that was when I was in kindergarten.

Why...now...?

I rarely catch cold since I work at home. But why such awful timing? Why tonsillitis?

Conclusion Bad luck

But it's just like me.

Sorry, Chara-san, that I couldn't go.

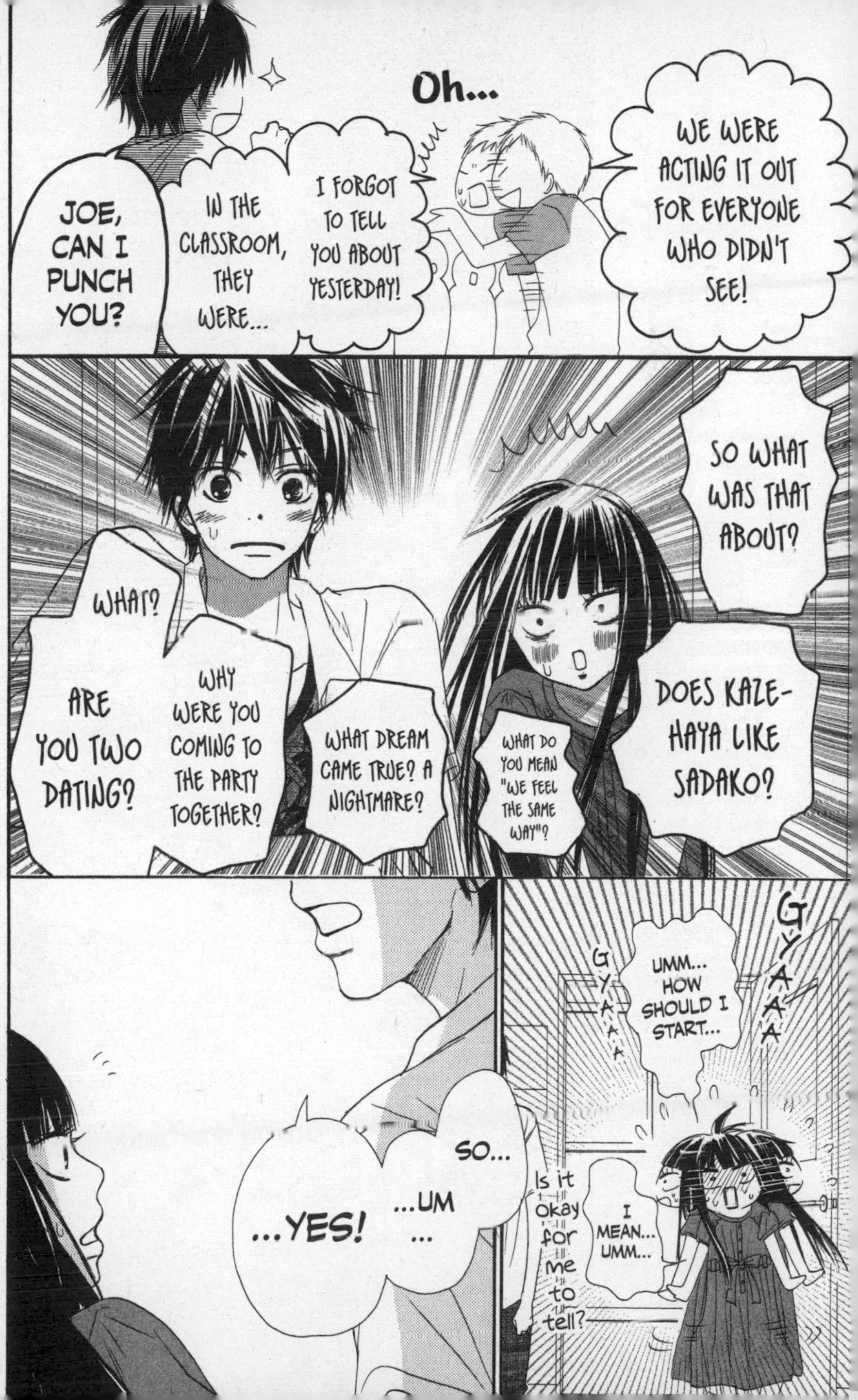

WE WERE ACTING IT OUT FOR EVERYONE WHO DIDN'T SEE!
Oh...
I FORGOT TO TELL YOU ABOUT YESTERDAY!
IN THE CLASSROOM, THEY WERE...
JOE, CAN I PUNCH YOU?
SO WHAT WAS THAT ABOUT?
DOES KAZE-HAYA LIKE SADAKO?
WHAT DO YOU MEAN "WE FEEL THE SAME WAY"?
WHAT DREAM CAME TRUE? A NIGHTMARE?
WHY WERE YOU COMING TO THE PARTY TOGETHER?
WHAT?
ARE YOU TWO DATING?
GYAAAA
UMM... HOW SHOULD I START...
GYAAAA
I MEAN... UMM...
Is it okay for me to tell?
SO...
...UM ...
...YES!

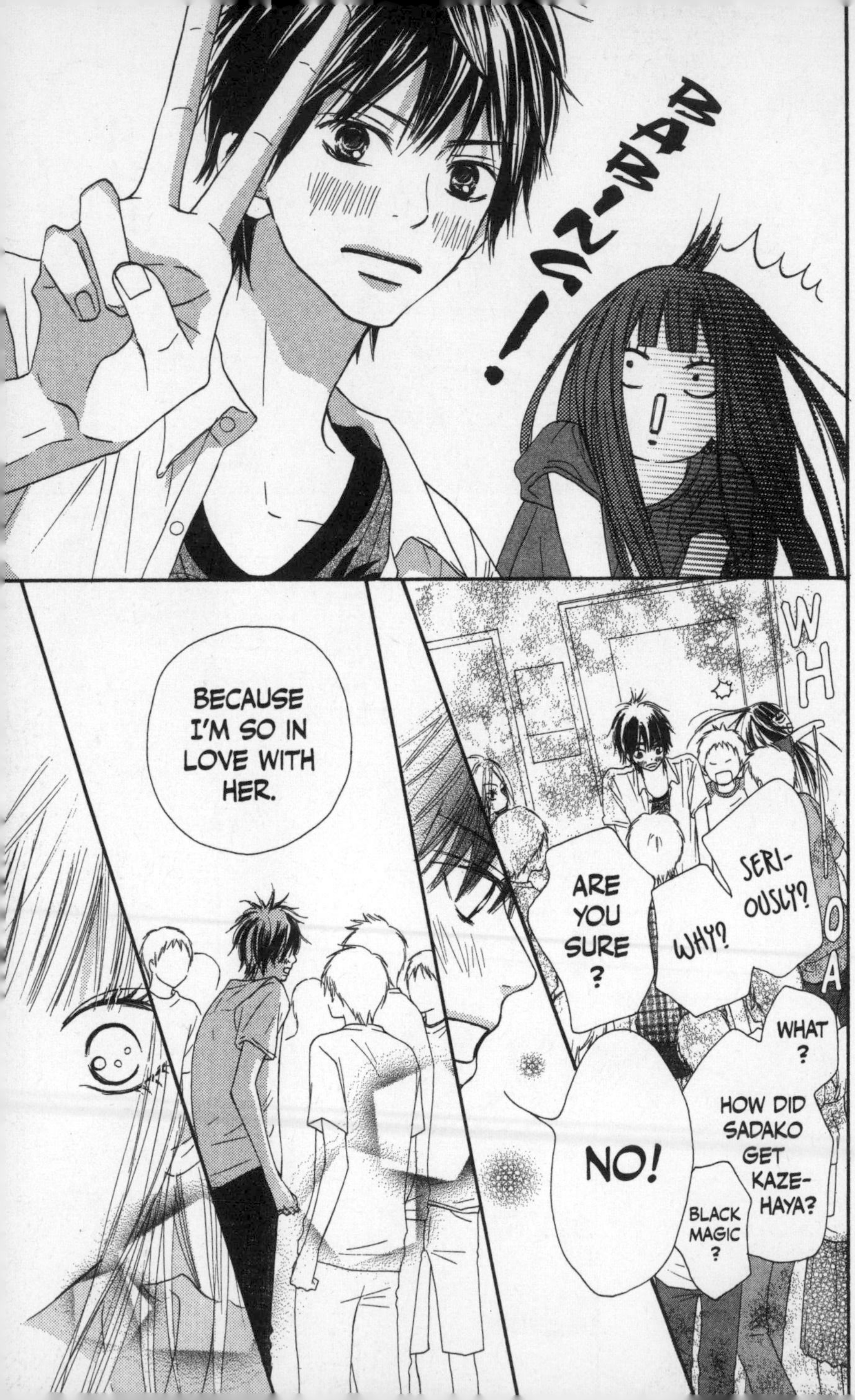
BABING!
WHOA
SERI-OUSLY?
ARE YOU SURE?
WHY?
WHAT?
HOW DID SADAKO GET KAZE-HAYA?
NO!
BLACK MAGIC?
BECAUSE I'M SO IN LOVE WITH HER.

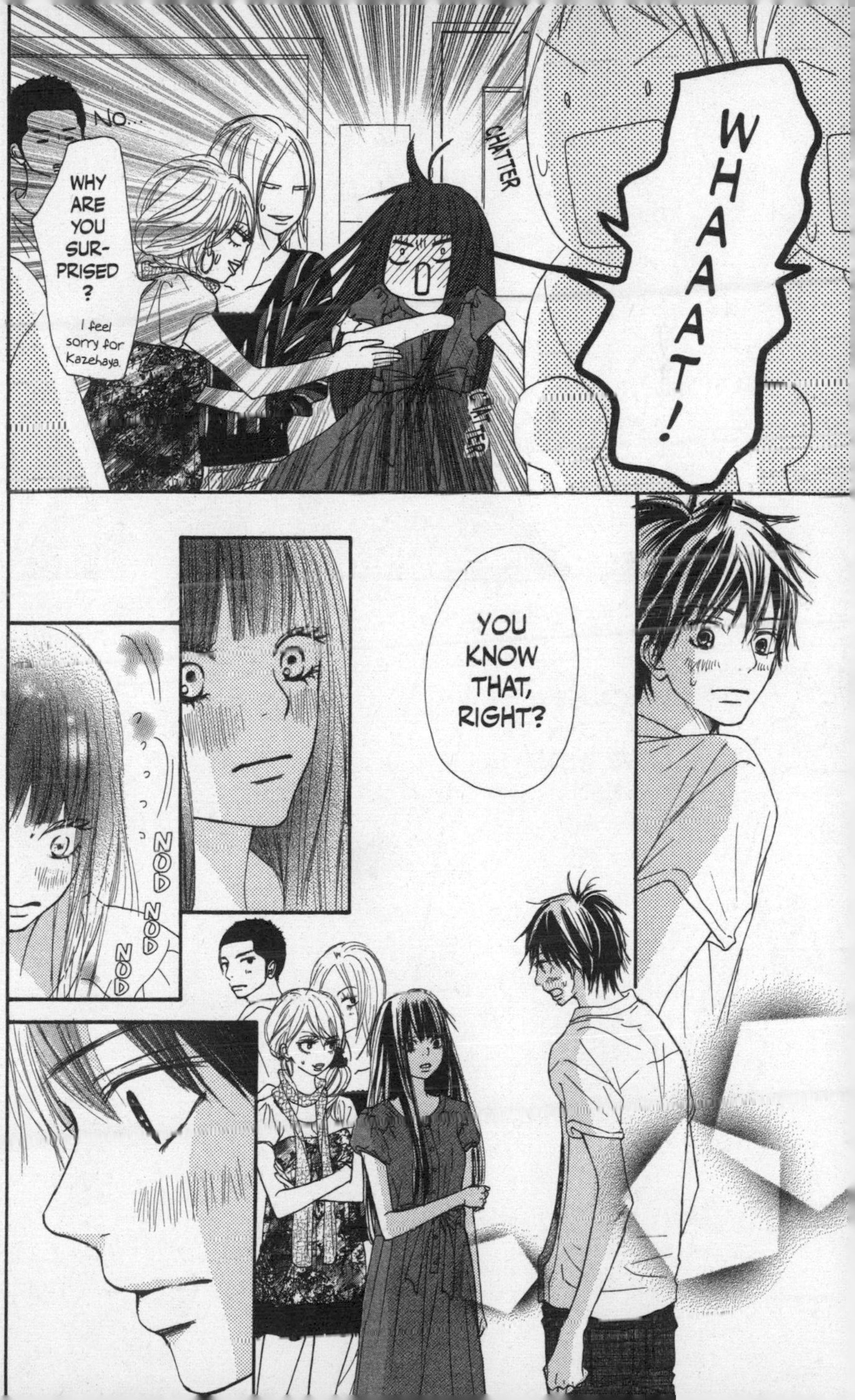
WHAAAT!
CHATTER
NO...
WHY ARE YOU SUR-PRISED?
I feel sorry for Kazehaya.
CHATTER
YOU KNOW THAT, RIGHT?
NOD NOD NOD

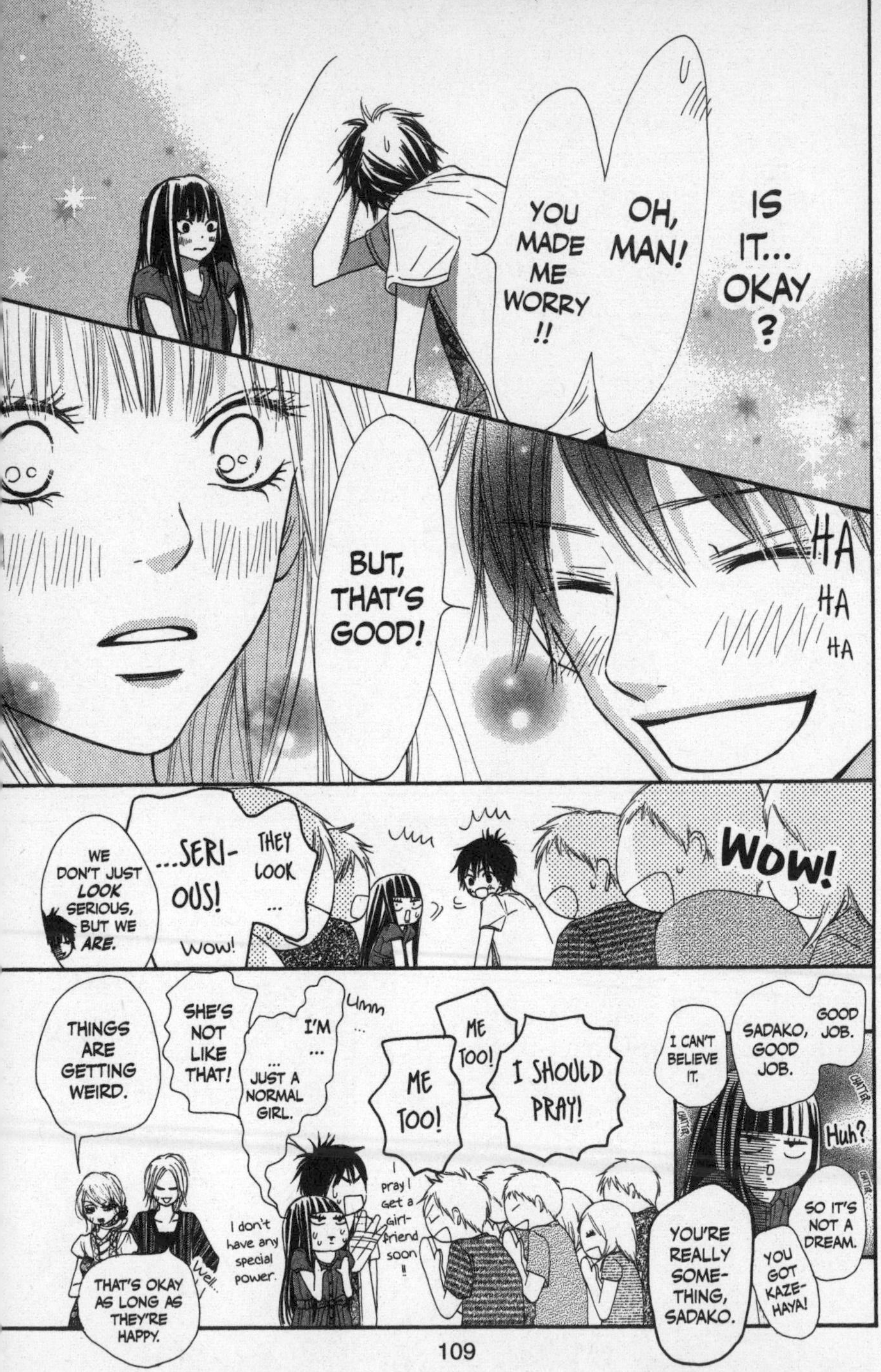
IS IT... OKAY?
OH, MAN!
YOU MADE ME WORRY !!
HA HA HA
BUT, THAT'S GOOD!
WOW!
THEY LOOK ...
...SERI-OUS!
WOW!
WE DON'T JUST *LOOK* SERIOUS, BUT WE *ARE*.
GOOD JOB.
SADAKO, GOOD JOB.
I CAN'T BELIEVE IT.
Huh?
SO IT'S NOT A DREAM.
YOU GOT KAZE-HAYA!
YOU'RE REALLY SOME-THING, SADAKO.
I SHOULD PRAY!
ME TOO!
ME TOO!
I pray I get a Girl-friend soon !!
Umm ...
I'M ... JUST A NORMAL GIRL.
I don't have any special power.
SHE'S NOT LIKE THAT!
THINGS ARE GETTING WEIRD.
Well...
THAT'S OKAY AS LONG AS THEY'RE HAPPY.

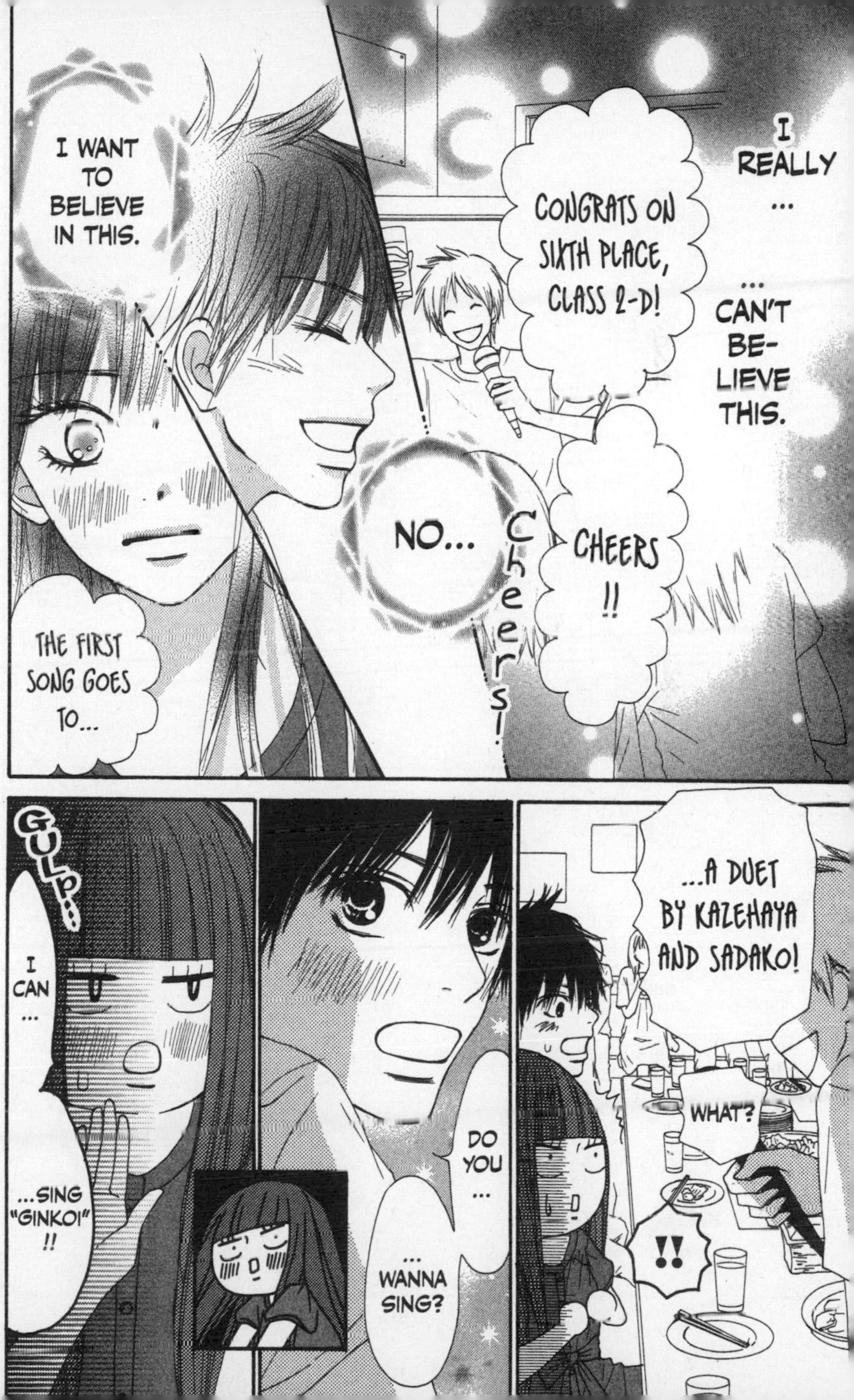
I REALLY ... ... CAN'T BE-LIEVE THIS.
CONGRATS ON SIXTH PLACE, CLASS 2-D!
CHEERS !!
Cheers!
NO...
I WANT TO BELIEVE IN THIS.
THE FIRST SONG GOES TO...
...A DUET BY KAZEHAYA AND SADAKO!
WHAT?
!!
DO YOU ...
... WANNA SING?
GULP...
I CAN ...
...SING "GINKOI" !!

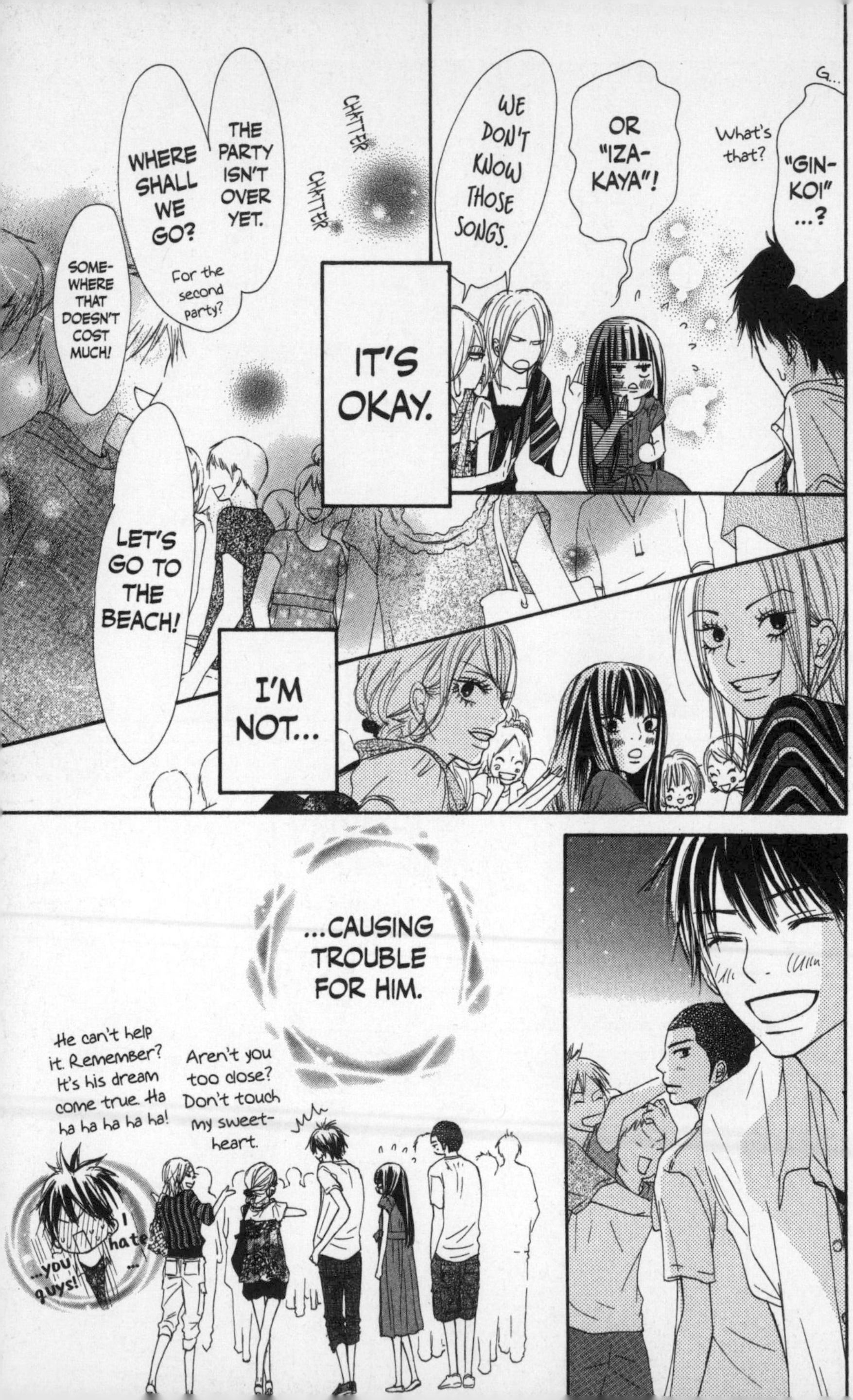
G...
What's that?
"GIN-KOI" ...?
OR "IZA-KAYA"!
WE DON'T KNOW THOSE SONGS.
IT'S OKAY.
CHATTER
CHATTER
THE PARTY ISN'T OVER YET.
WHERE SHALL WE GO?
For the second party?
SOME-WHERE THAT DOESN'T COST MUCH!
LET'S GO TO THE BEACH!
I'M NOT...
...CAUSING TROUBLE FOR HIM.
Aren't you too close? Don't touch my sweet-heart.
He can't help it. Remember? It's his dream come true. Ha ha ha ha ha ha!
I hate...
...you guys!

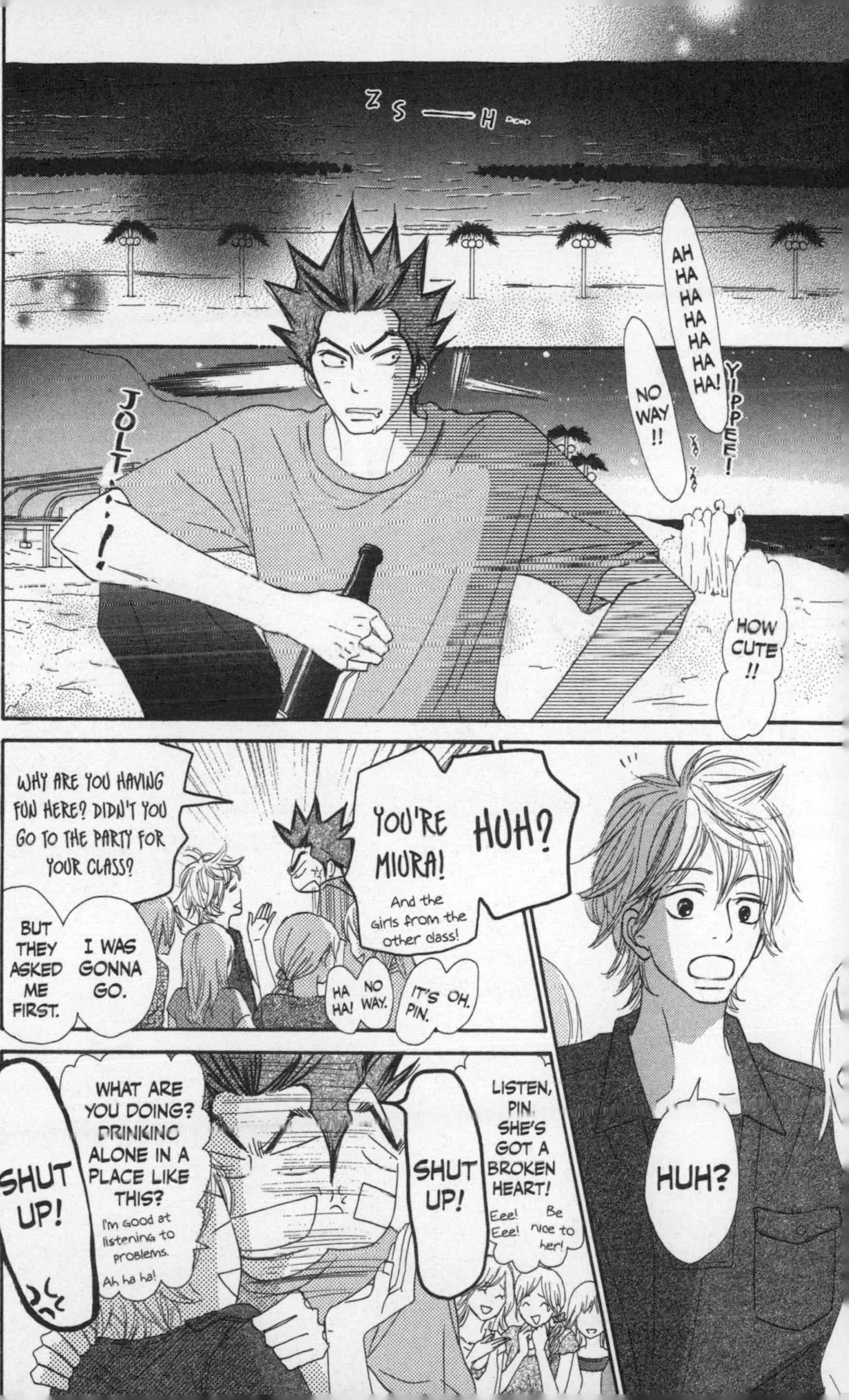
ZS—H
AH HA HA HA HA HA HA!
YIPPEE!
NO WAY!!
HOW CUTE!!
JOLT…!
HUH?
YOU'RE MIURA!
HUH?
And the girls from the other class!
WHY ARE YOU HAVING FUN HERE? DIDN'T YOU GO TO THE PARTY FOR YOUR CLASS?
I WAS GONNA GO.
BUT THEY ASKED ME FIRST.
IT'S OH. PIN.
NO WAY.
HA HA!
LISTEN, PIN, SHE'S GOT A BROKEN HEART!
Be nice to her!
Eee! Eee!
SHUT UP!
WHAT ARE YOU DOING? DRINKING ALONE IN A PLACE LIKE THIS?
I'm good at listening to problems.
Ah ha ha!
SHUT UP!

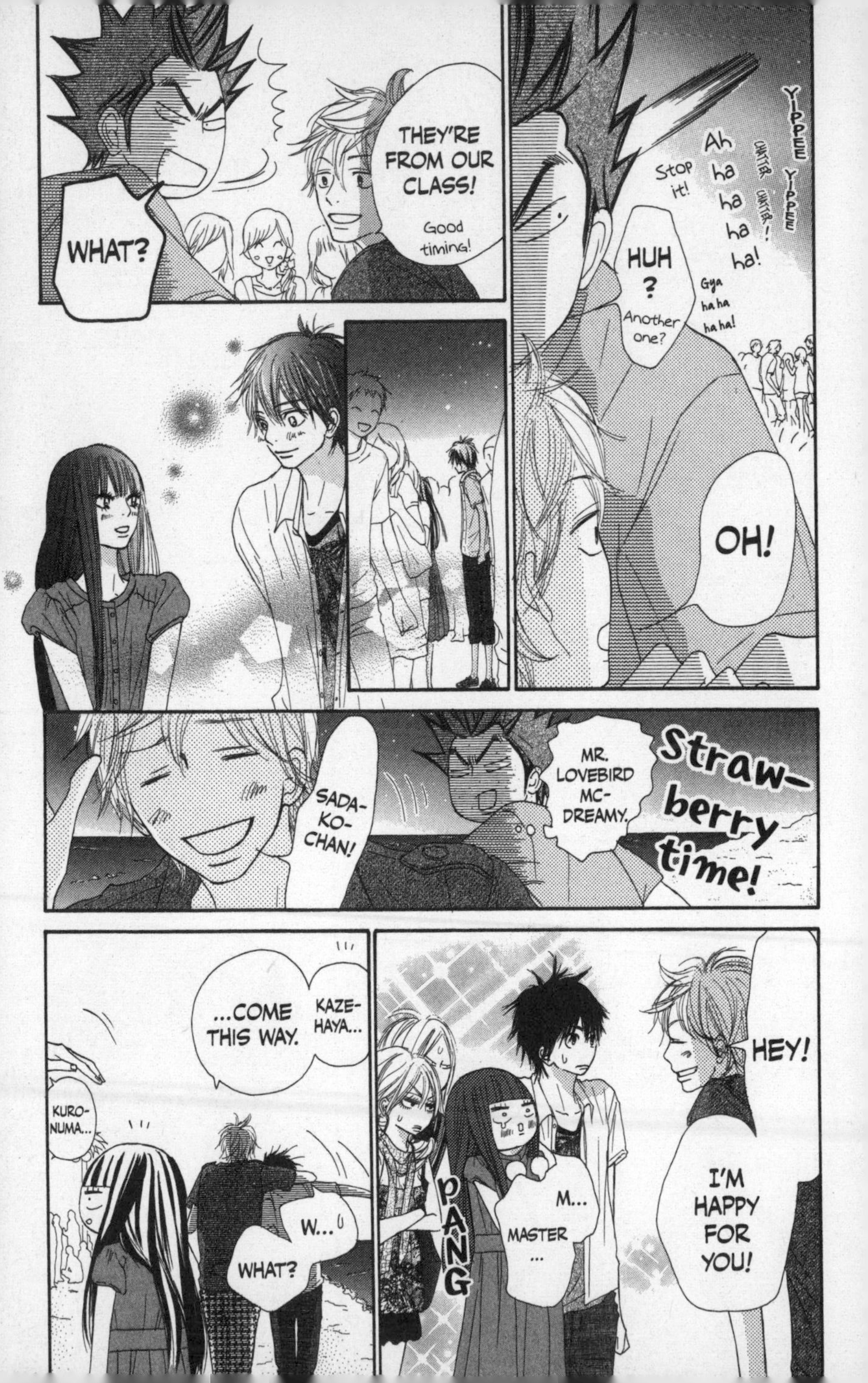
YIPPEE YIPPEE
Ah ha ha ha ha!
CHATTER CHATTER
Stop it!
HUH? Another one?
Gya ha ha ha ha!
OH!
THEY'RE FROM OUR CLASS! Good timing!
WHAT?
Straw-berry time!
MR. LOVEBIRD MC-DREAMY.
SADAKO-CHAN!
HEY!
I'M HAPPY FOR YOU!
M... MASTER ...
PANG
KAZE-HAYA...
...COME THIS WAY.
W... WHAT?
KURO-NUMA...

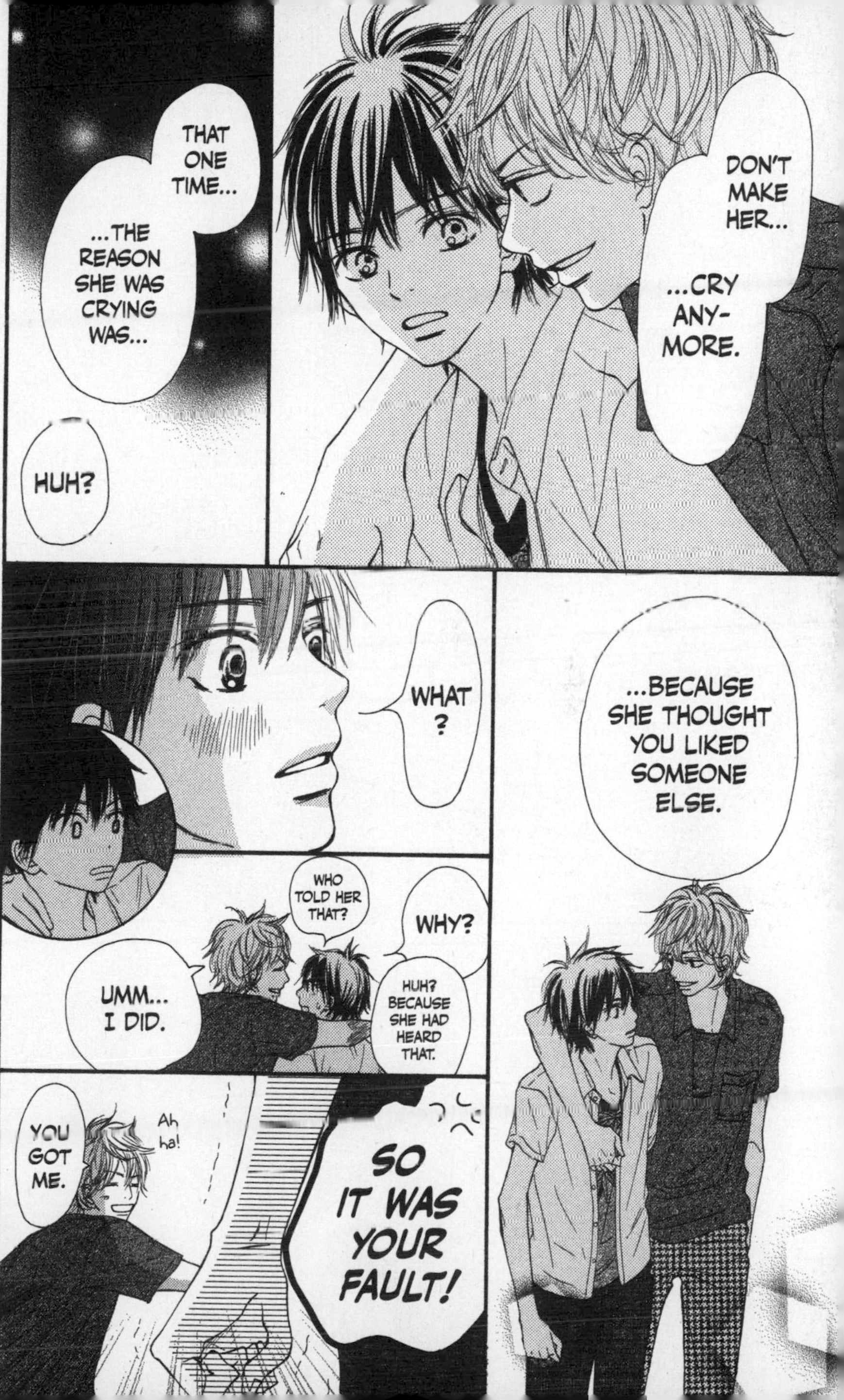
DON'T MAKE HER...
...CRY ANYMORE.
THAT ONE TIME...
...THE REASON SHE WAS CRYING WAS...
HUH?
...BECAUSE SHE THOUGHT YOU LIKED SOMEONE ELSE.
WHAT?
WHY?
HUH? BECAUSE SHE HAD HEARD THAT.
WHO TOLD HER THAT?
UMM... I DID.
SO IT WAS YOUR FAULT!
Ah ha!
YOU GOT ME.

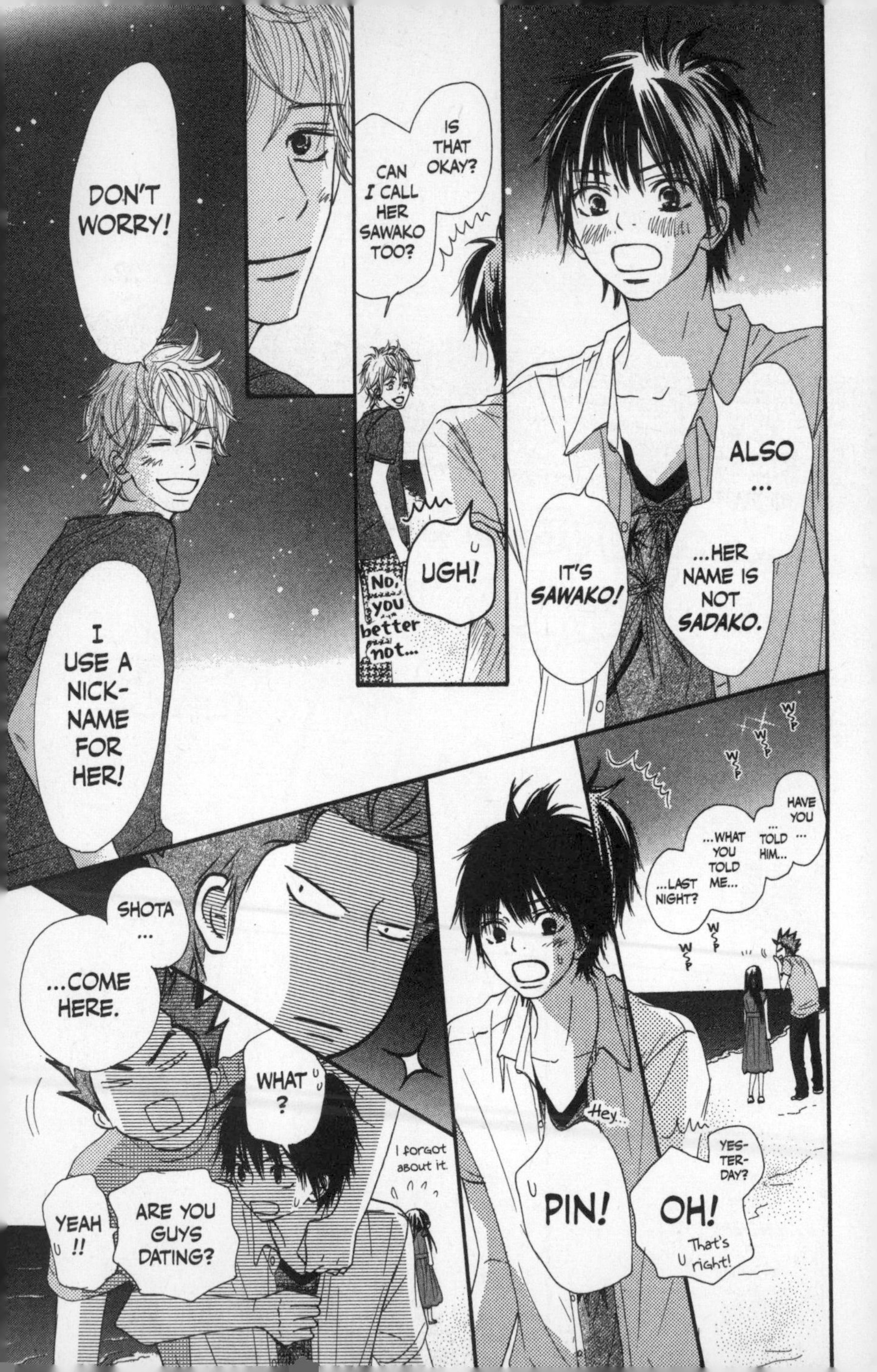
ALSO ...
...HER NAME IS NOT SADAKO.
IT'S SAWAKO!
IS THAT OKAY?
CAN I CALL HER SAWAKO TOO?
UGH!
No, you better not...
DON'T WORRY!
I USE A NICKNAME FOR HER!
WSP WSP WSP
HAVE YOU ... TOLD HIM...
...WHAT YOU TOLD ME...
...LAST NIGHT?
WSP WSP
Hey...
YESTERDAY?
OH!
That's right!
PIN!
SHOTA ...
...COME HERE.
WHAT?
ARE YOU GUYS DATING?
YEAH !!
I forgot about it.

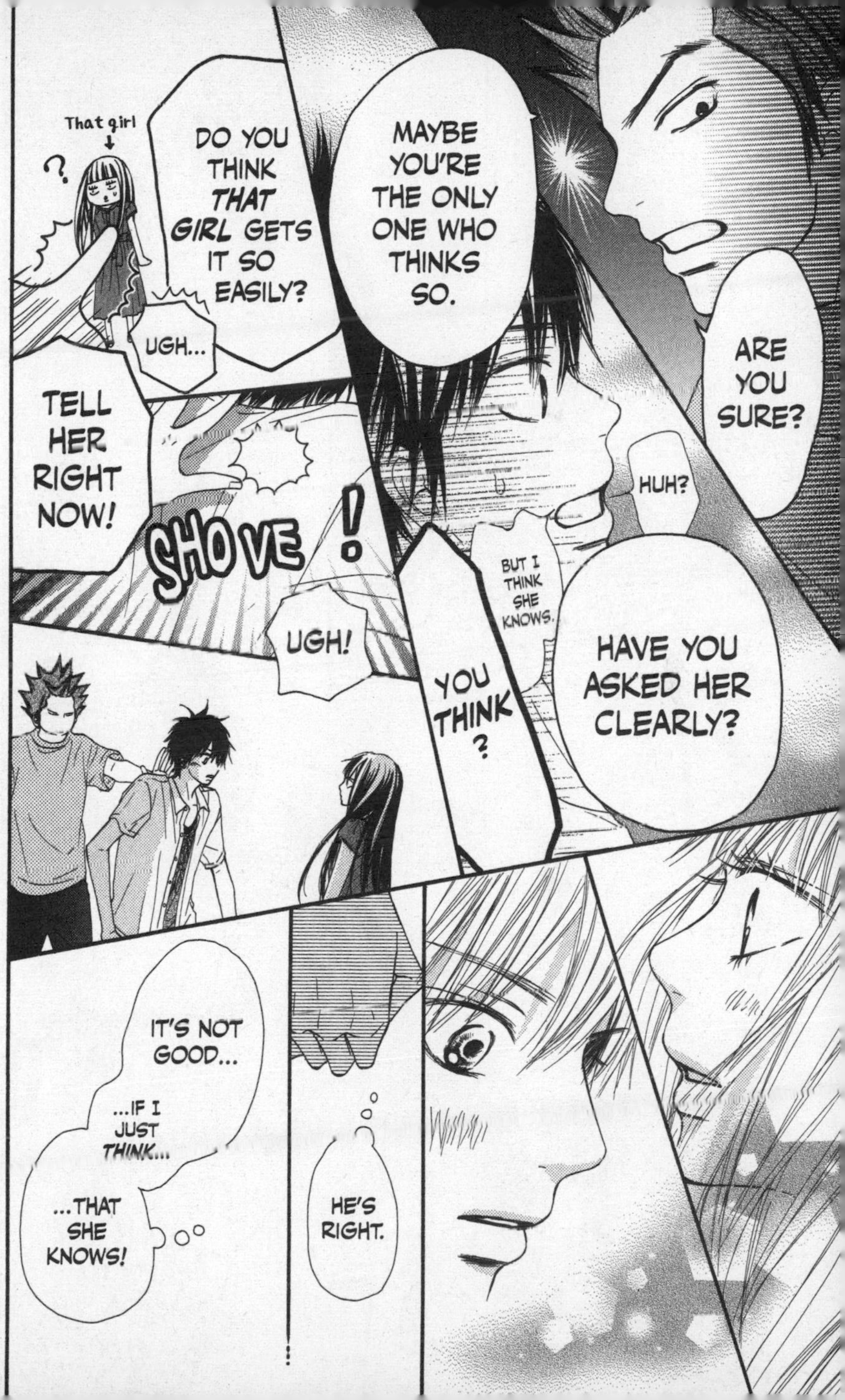
ARE YOU SURE?
HUH?
HAVE YOU ASKED HER CLEARLY?
BUT I THINK SHE KNOWS.
YOU THINK?
MAYBE YOU'RE THE ONLY ONE WHO THINKS SO.
DO YOU THINK *THAT GIRL* GETS IT SO EASILY?
That girl
UGH...
TELL HER RIGHT NOW!
SHOVE
!
UGH!
HE'S RIGHT.
IT'S NOT GOOD...
...IF I JUST *THINK*...
...THAT SHE KNOWS!

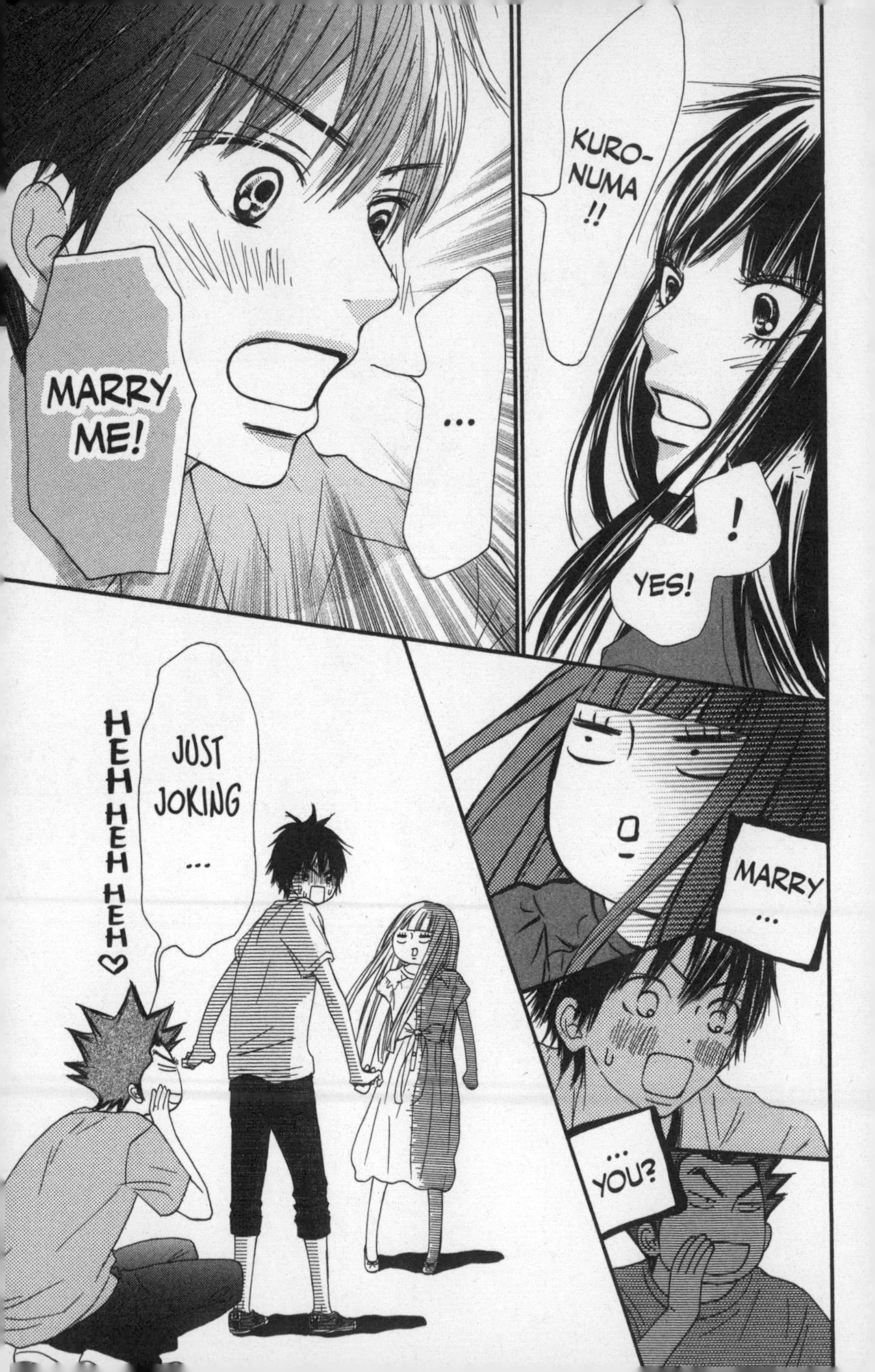
KURO-NUMA !!
!
YES!
...
MARRY ME!
MARRY ...
... YOU?
JUST JOKING ...
HEH HEH HEH HEH ♡

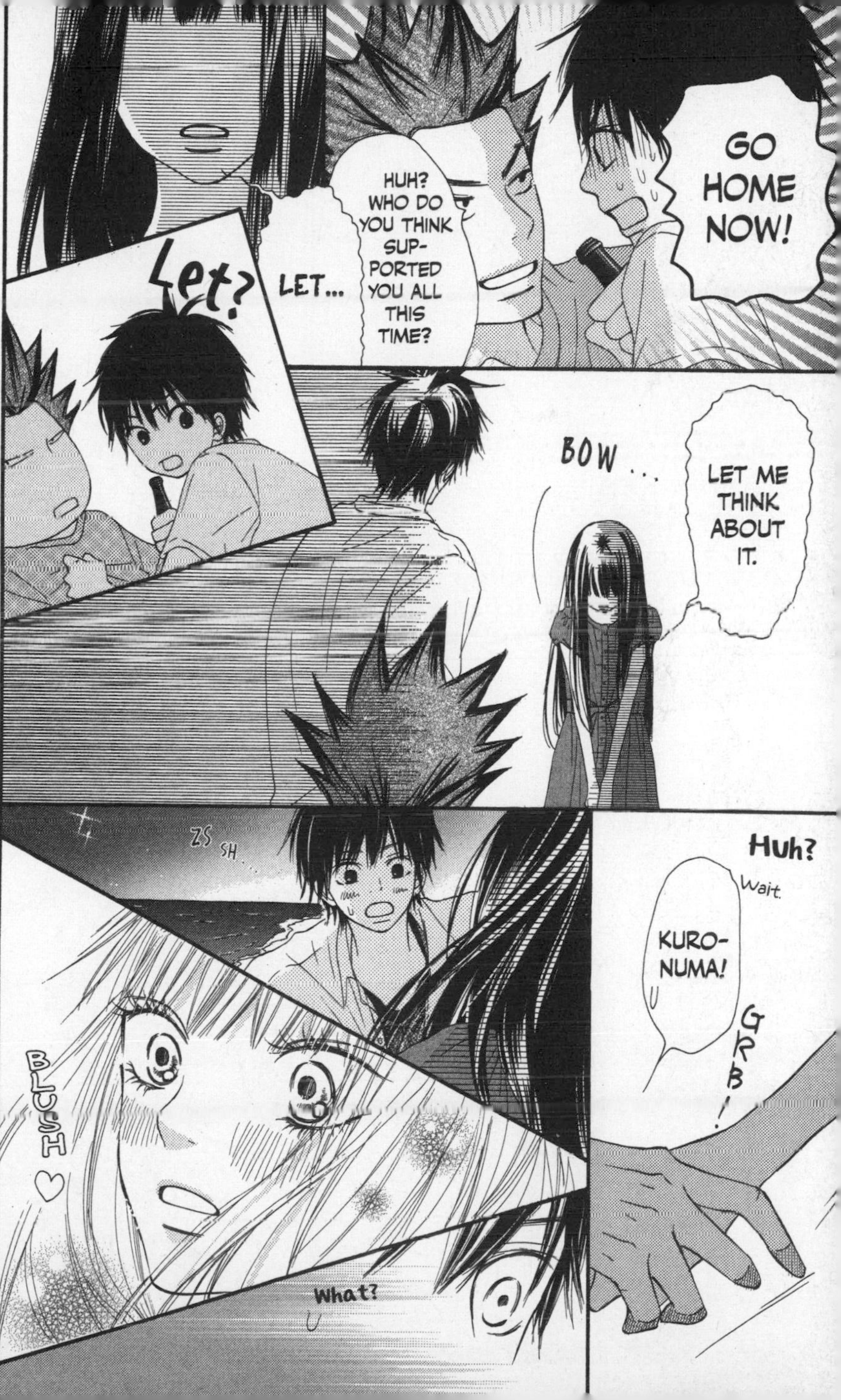
GO HOME NOW!
HUH? WHO DO YOU THINK SUP-PORTED YOU ALL THIS TIME?
LET...
Let?
LET ME THINK ABOUT IT.
BOW...
Huh?
Wait.
KURO-NUMA!
GRB!
ZSSH...
BLUSH ♥
What?

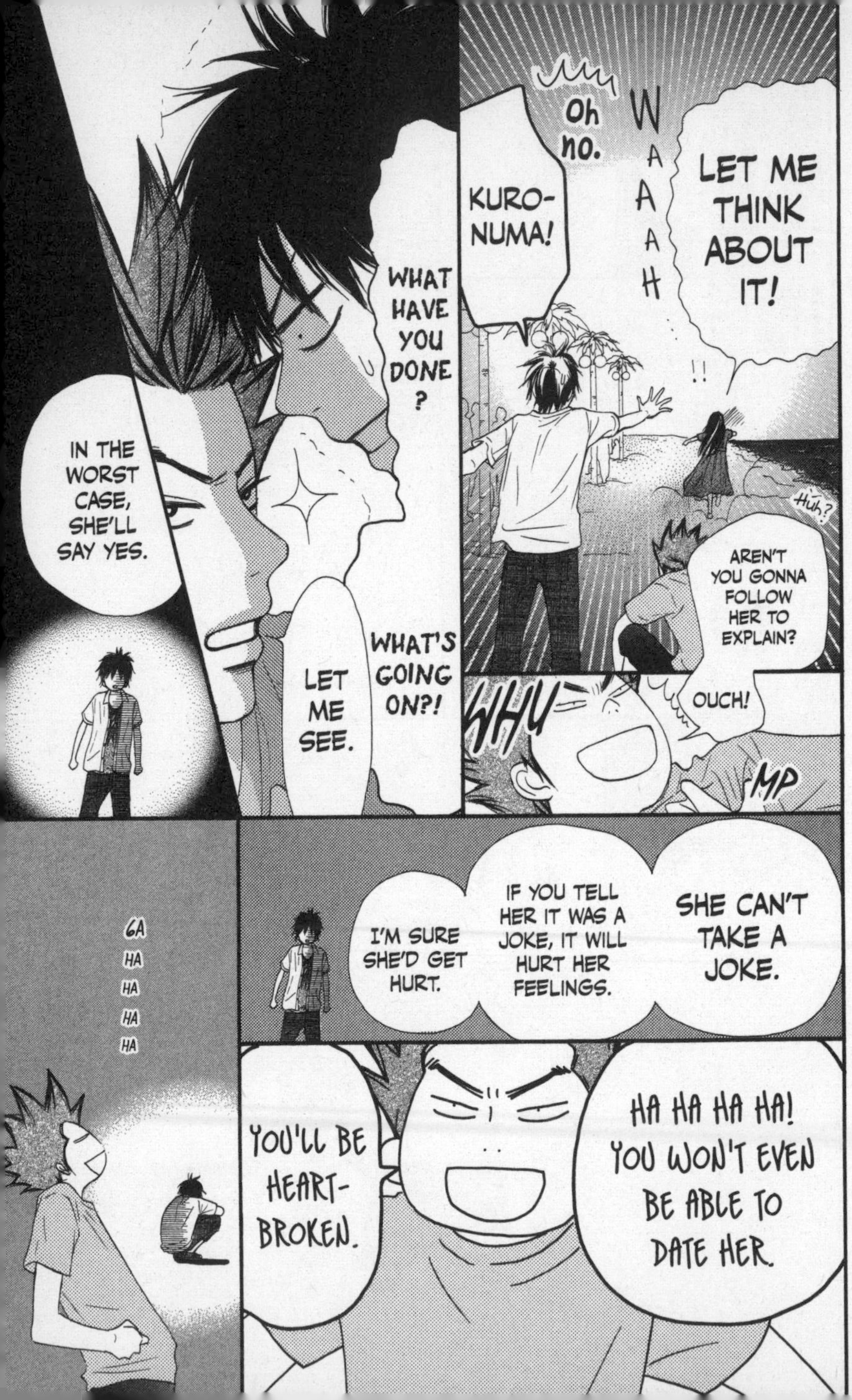
LET ME THINK ABOUT IT!
WAAAH
Oh no.
KURO-NUMA!
!!
Huh?
AREN'T YOU GONNA FOLLOW HER TO EXPLAIN?
OUCH!
WHUMP
WHAT HAVE YOU DONE?
WHAT'S GOING ON?!
LET ME SEE.
IN THE WORST CASE, SHE'LL SAY YES.
SHE CAN'T TAKE A JOKE.
IF YOU TELL HER IT WAS A JOKE, IT WILL HURT HER FEELINGS.
I'M SURE SHE'D GET HURT.
HA HA HA HA! YOU WON'T EVEN BE ABLE TO DATE HER.
YOU'LL BE HEART-BROKEN.
GA HA HA HA HA

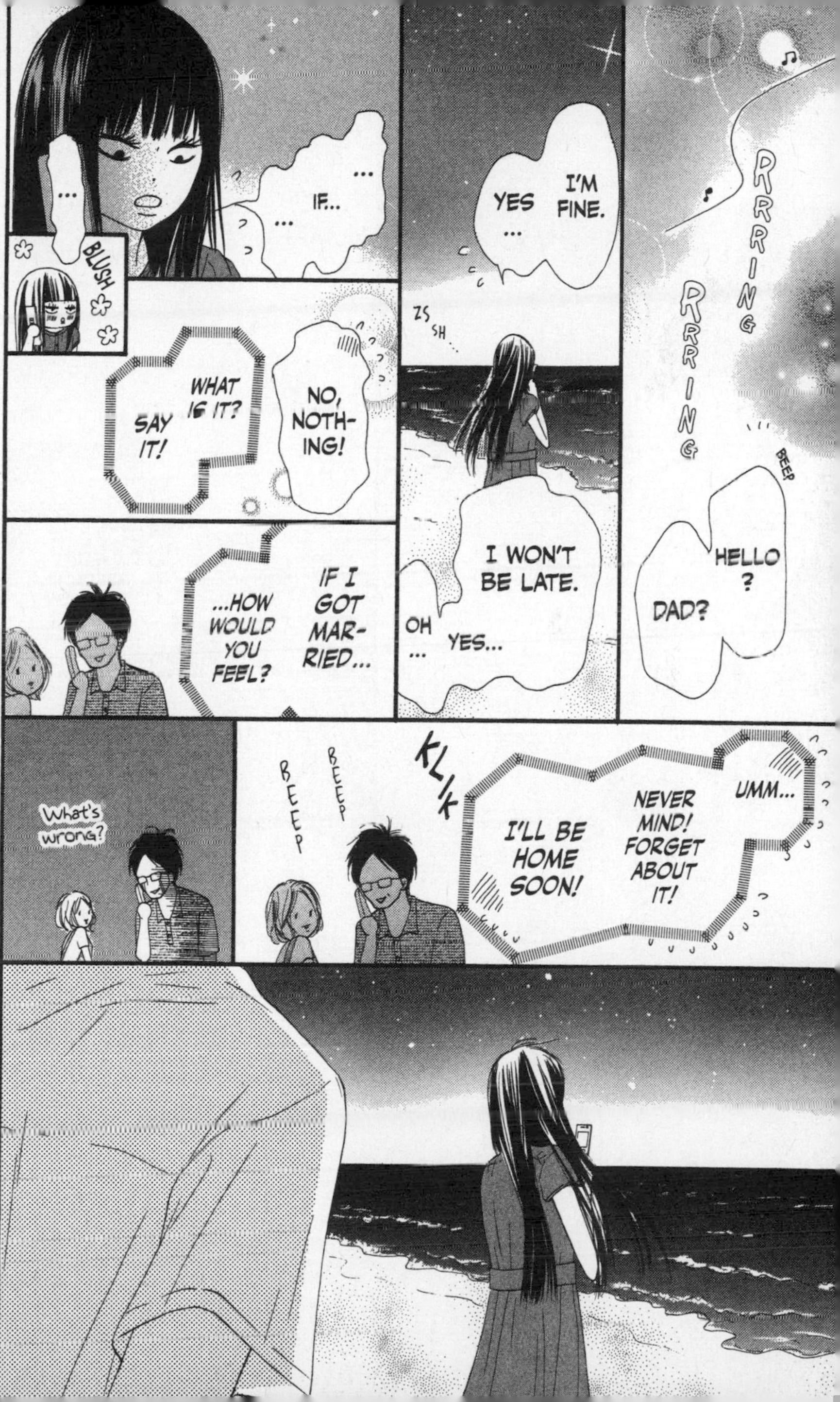
RRRING RRRING
BEEP
HELLO?
DAD?
I'M FINE.
YES...
ZSSH...
I WON'T BE LATE.
YES...
OH...
...
IF...
...
...
BLUSH
NO, NOTHING!
WHAT IS IT?
SAY IT!
IF I GOT MARRIED...
...HOW WOULD YOU FEEL?
KLIK
UMM...
NEVER MIND! FORGET ABOUT IT!
I'LL BE HOME SOON!
BEEP BEEP
What's wrong?

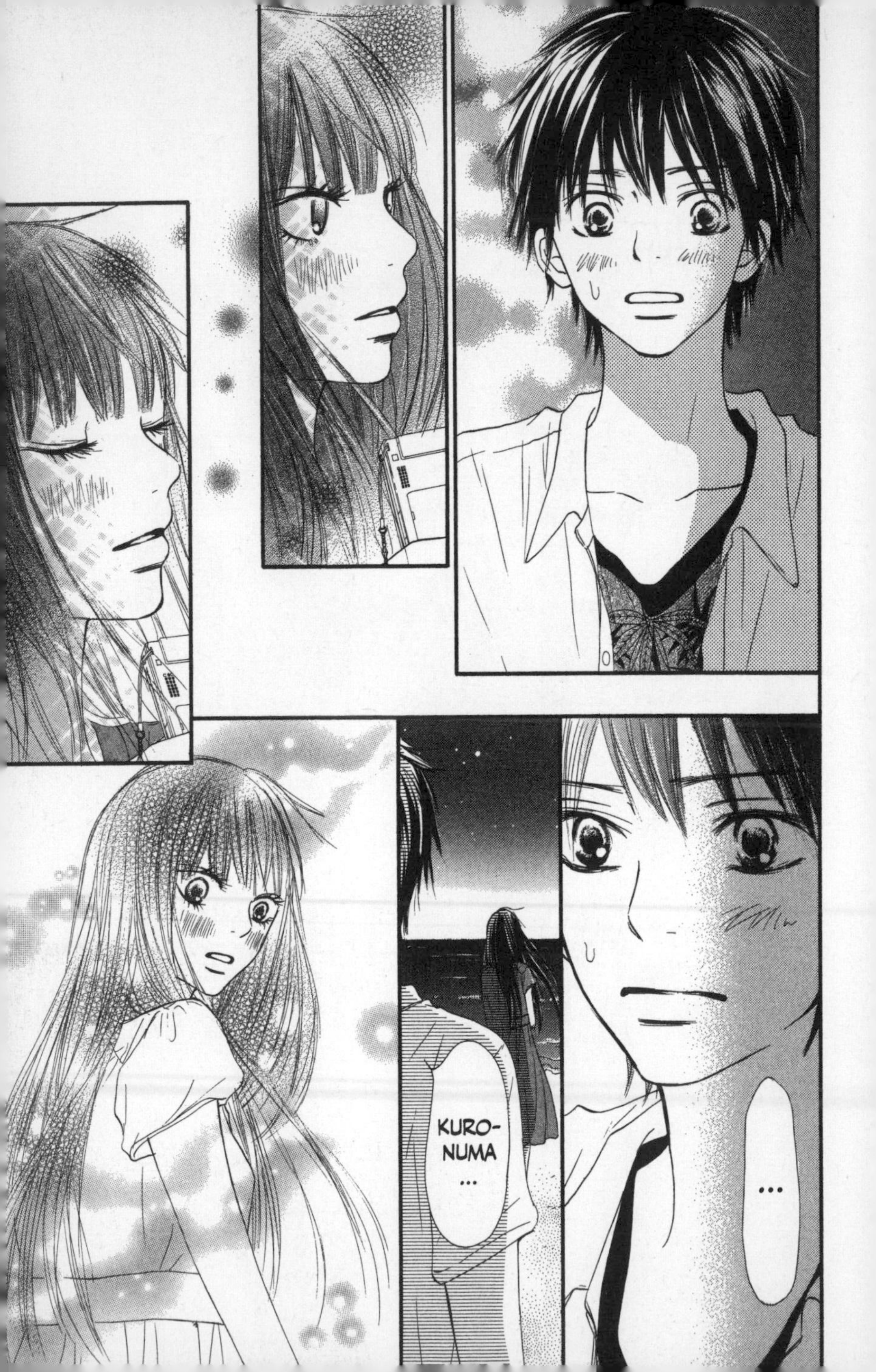
...
KURO-NUMA ...

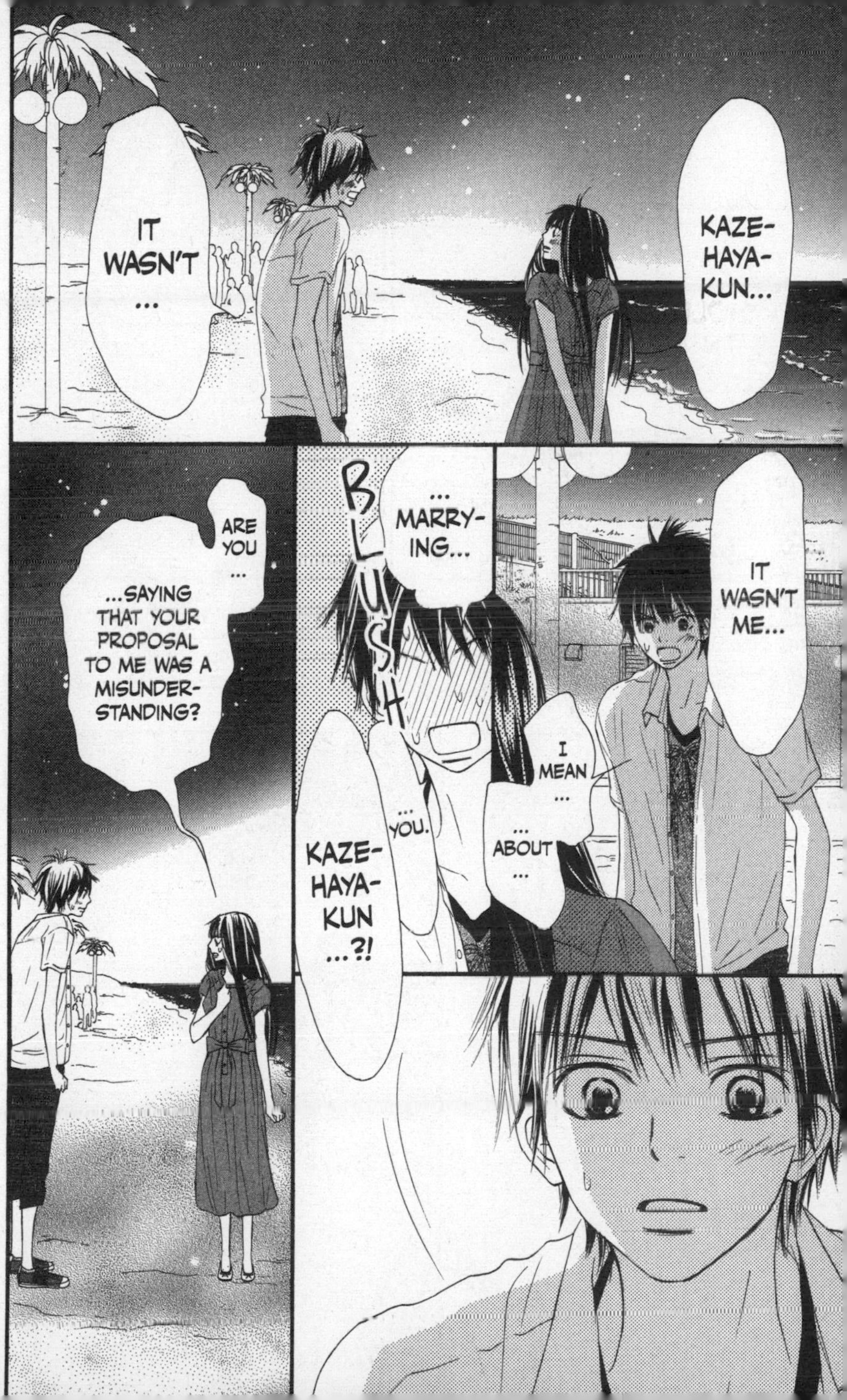
KAZE-HAYA-KUN...
IT WASN'T ...
IT WASN'T ME...
I MEAN ...
... ABOUT ...
... MARRY-ING...
BLUSH
... YOU.
KAZE-HAYA-KUN ...?!
ARE YOU ...
...SAYING THAT YOUR PROPOSAL TO ME WAS A MISUNDER-STANDING?

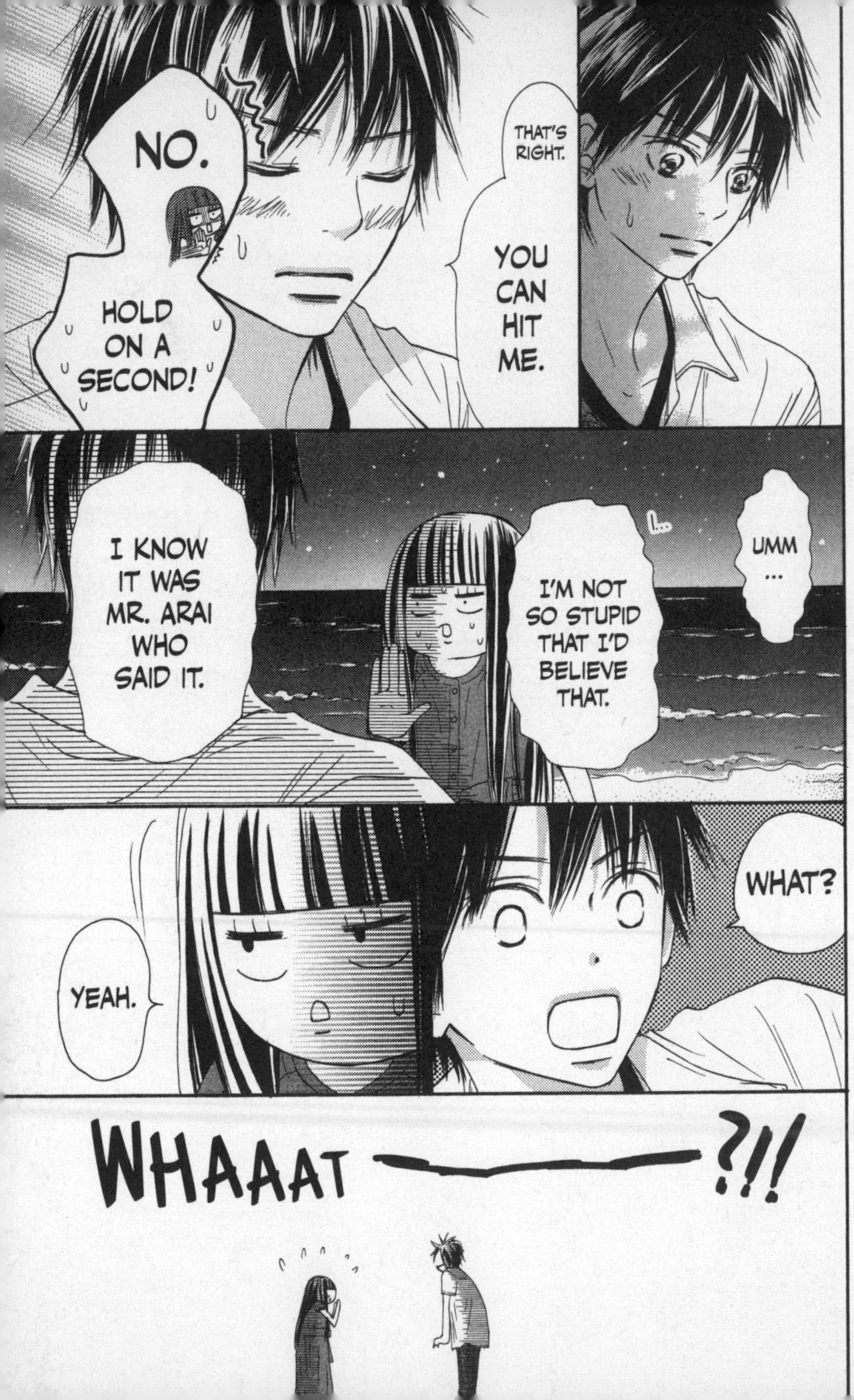
THAT'S RIGHT.
YOU CAN HIT ME.
NO.
HOLD ON A SECOND!
UMM ...
I...
I'M NOT SO STUPID THAT I'D BELIEVE THAT.
I KNOW IT WAS MR. ARAI WHO SAID IT.
WHAT?
YEAH.
WHAAAT——?!!

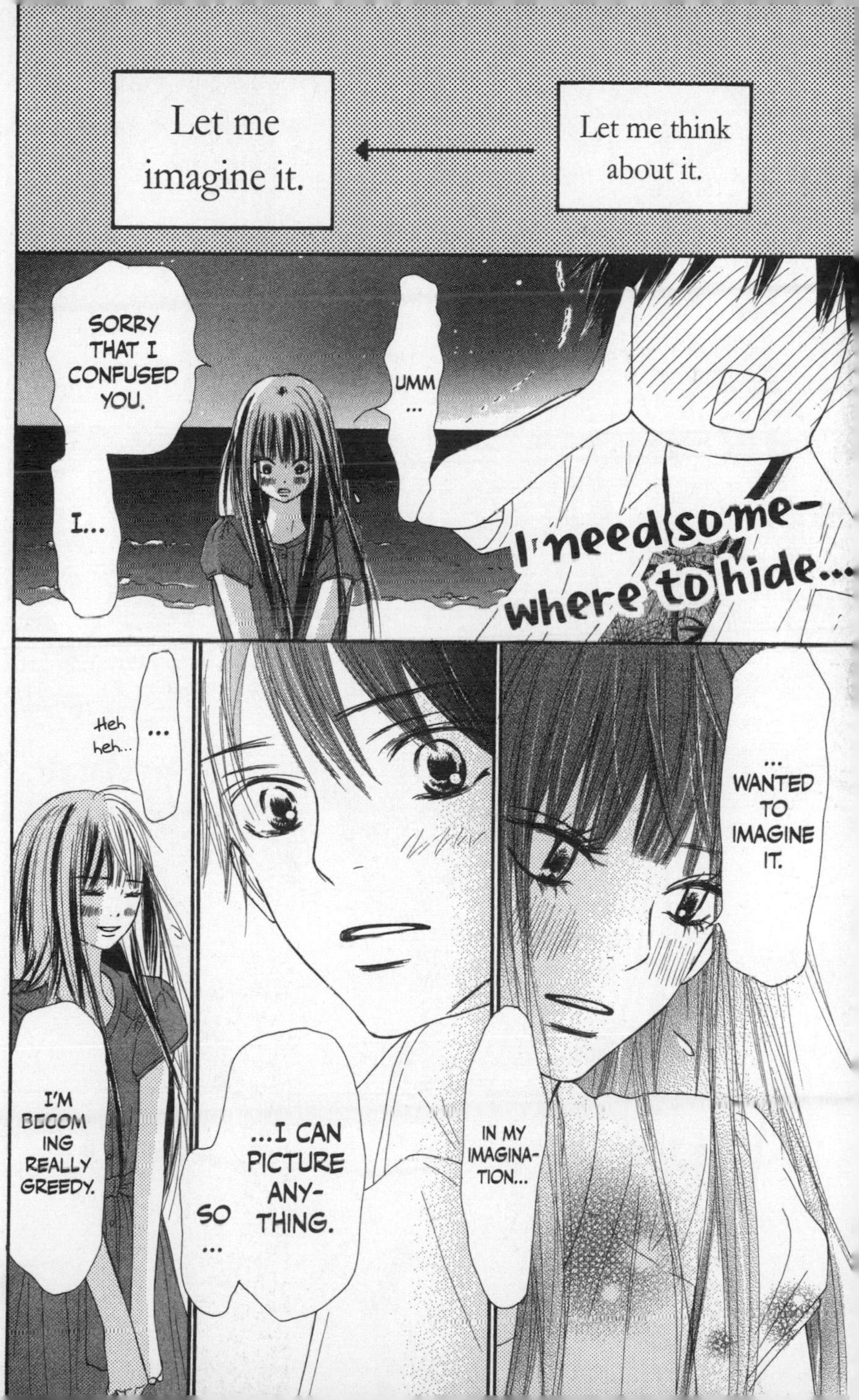

Let me think about it.
Let me imagine it.
I need some-where to hide...
UMM ...
SORRY THAT I CONFUSED YOU.
I...
... WANTED TO IMAGINE IT.
IN MY IMAGINA-TION...
...I CAN PICTURE ANY-THING.
SO ...
heh heh...
...
I'M BECOM ING REALLY GREEDY.

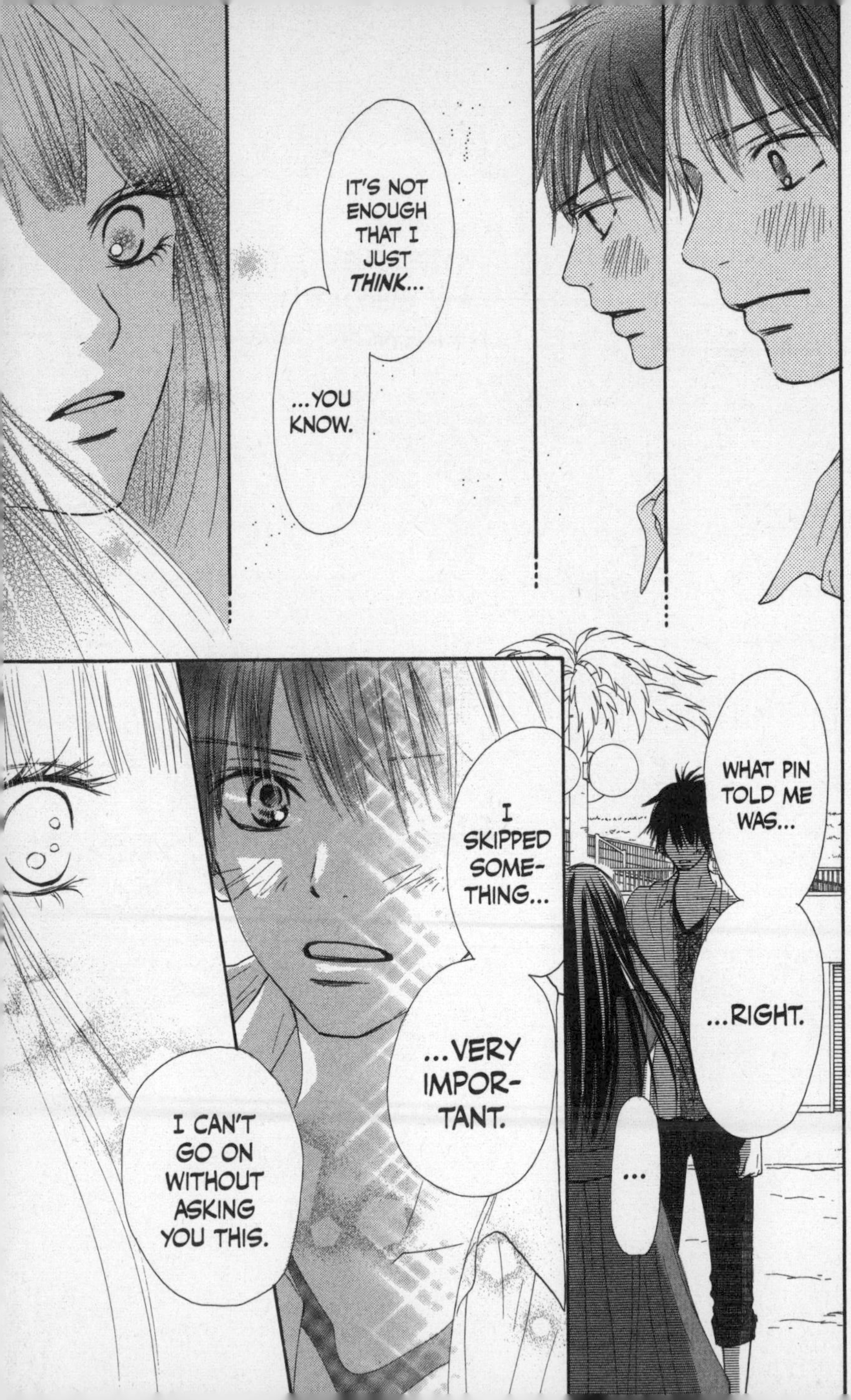
IT'S NOT ENOUGH THAT I JUST *THINK*...
...YOU KNOW.
WHAT PIN TOLD ME WAS...
...RIGHT.
...
I SKIPPED SOME-THING...
...VERY IMPOR-TANT.
I CAN'T GO ON WITHOUT ASKING YOU THIS.

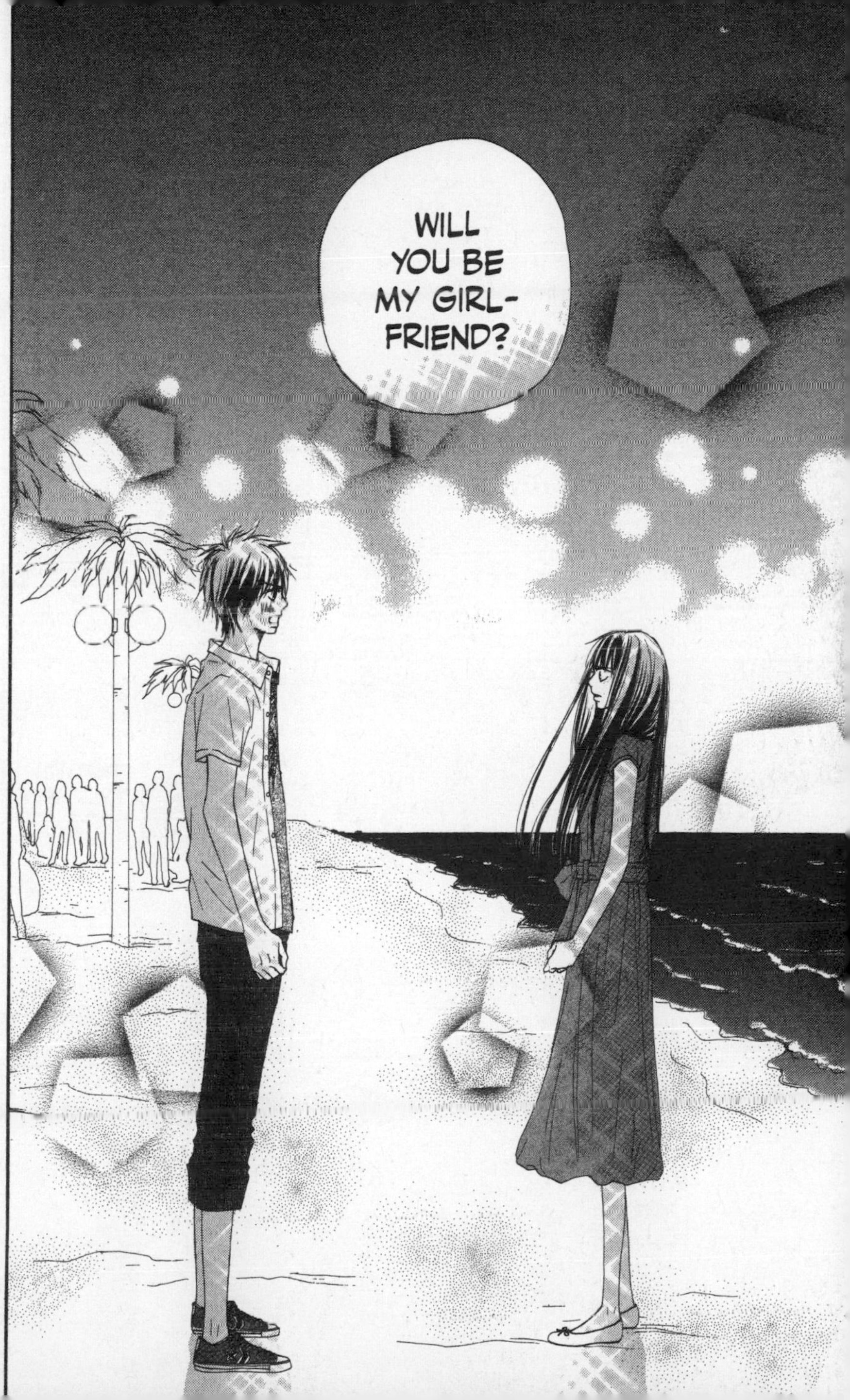
WILL YOU BE MY GIRL-FRIEND?

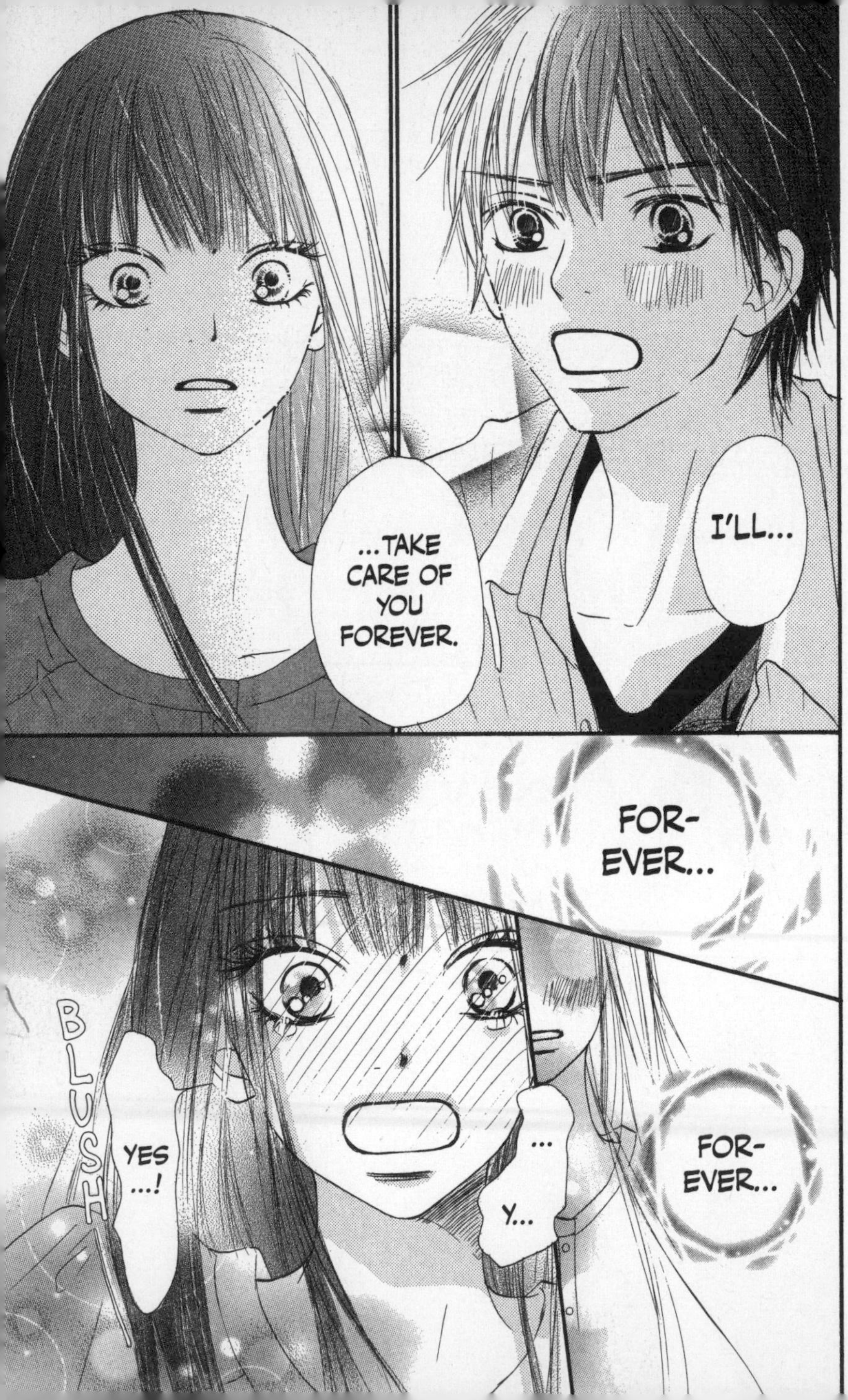
I'LL...
...TAKE CARE OF YOU FOREVER.
FOR-EVER...
FOR-EVER...
...
Y...
BLUSH
YES ...!

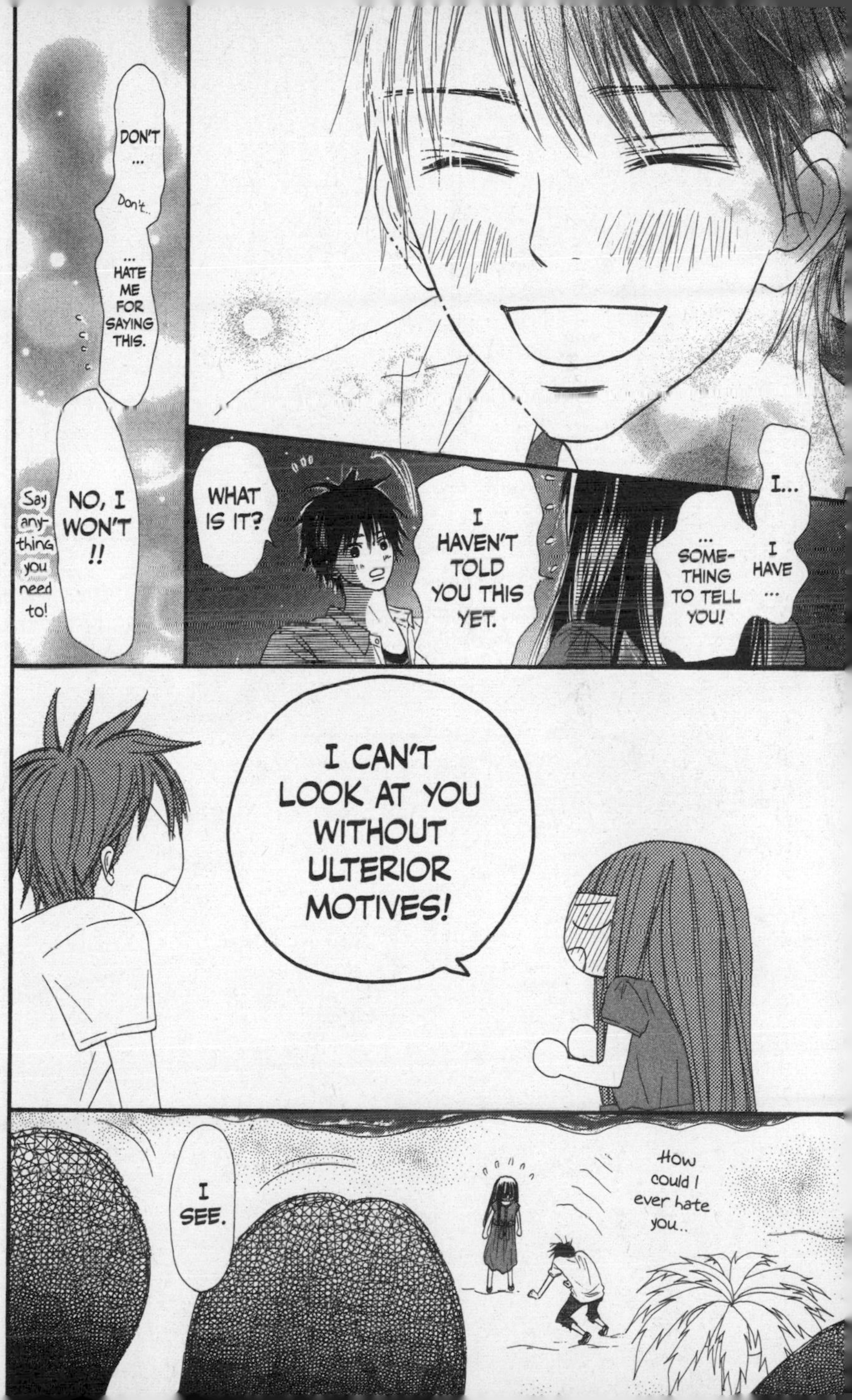
I...
I HAVE ...
... SOMETHING TO TELL YOU!
I HAVEN'T TOLD YOU THIS YET.
WHAT IS IT?
DON'T ...
Don't..
... HATE ME FOR SAYING THIS.
NO, I WON'T !!
Say anything you need to!
I CAN'T LOOK AT YOU WITHOUT ULTERIOR MOTIVES!
How could I ever hate you..
I SEE.

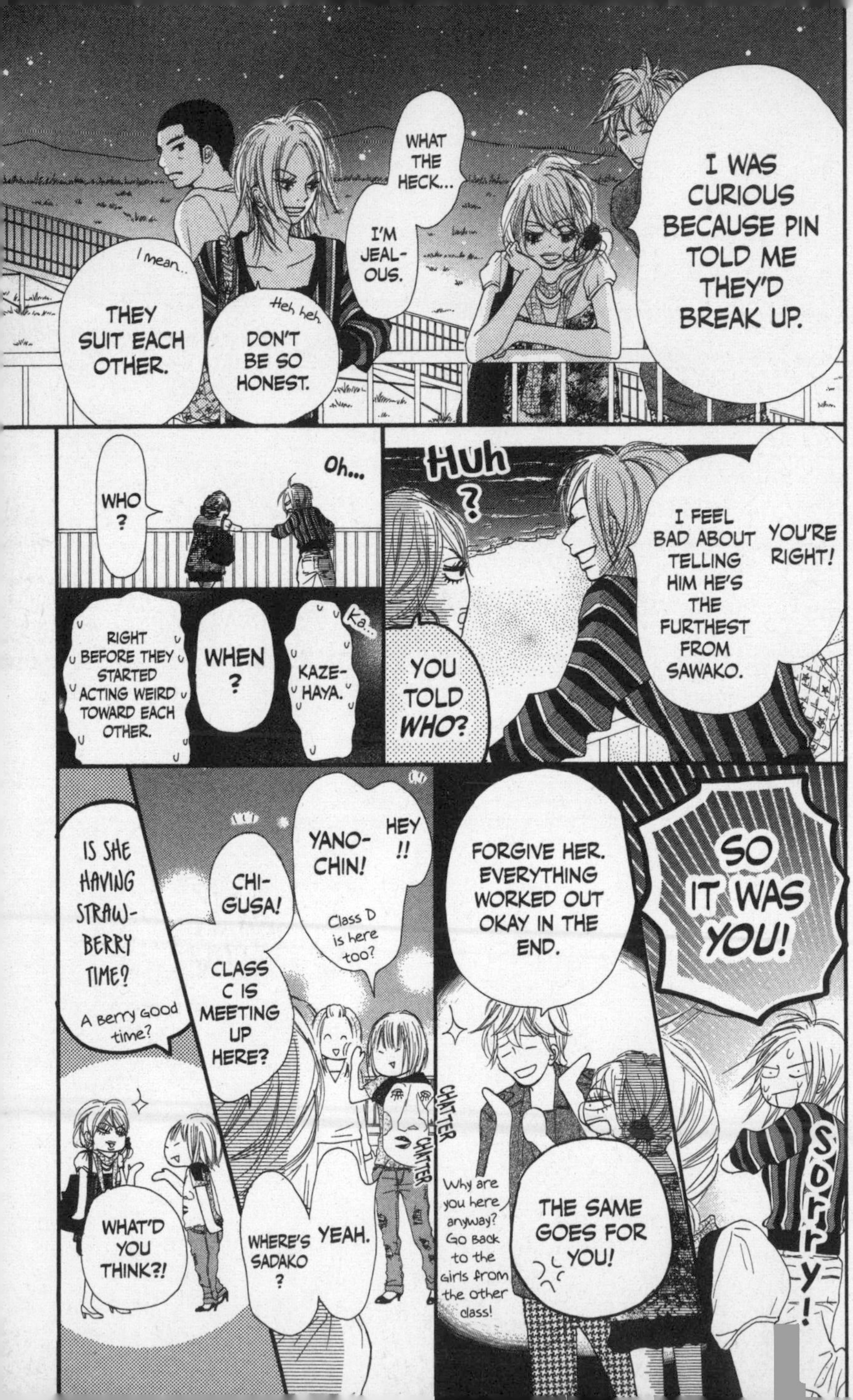

I WAS CURIOUS BECAUSE PIN TOLD ME THEY'D BREAK UP.
WHAT THE HECK...
I'M JEAL-OUS.
I mean...
THEY SUIT EACH OTHER.
Heh heh.
DON'T BE SO HONEST.
YOU'RE RIGHT!
I FEEL BAD ABOUT TELLING HIM HE'S THE FURTHEST FROM SAWAKO.
Huh ?
YOU TOLD WHO?
Oh...
WHO ?
Ka...
KAZE-HAYA.
WHEN ?
RIGHT BEFORE THEY STARTED ACTING WEIRD TOWARD EACH OTHER.
SO IT WAS YOU!
Sorry!
FORGIVE HER. EVERYTHING WORKED OUT OKAY IN THE END.
THE SAME GOES FOR YOU!
Why are you here anyway? Go back to the girls from the other class!
HEY!!
YANO-CHIN!
Class D is here too?
CHI-GUSA!
CLASS C IS MEETING UP HERE?
IS SHE HAVING STRAW-BERRY TIME?
A berry good time?
CHATTER
CHATTER
YEAH.
WHERE'S SADAKO ?
WHAT'D YOU THINK?!

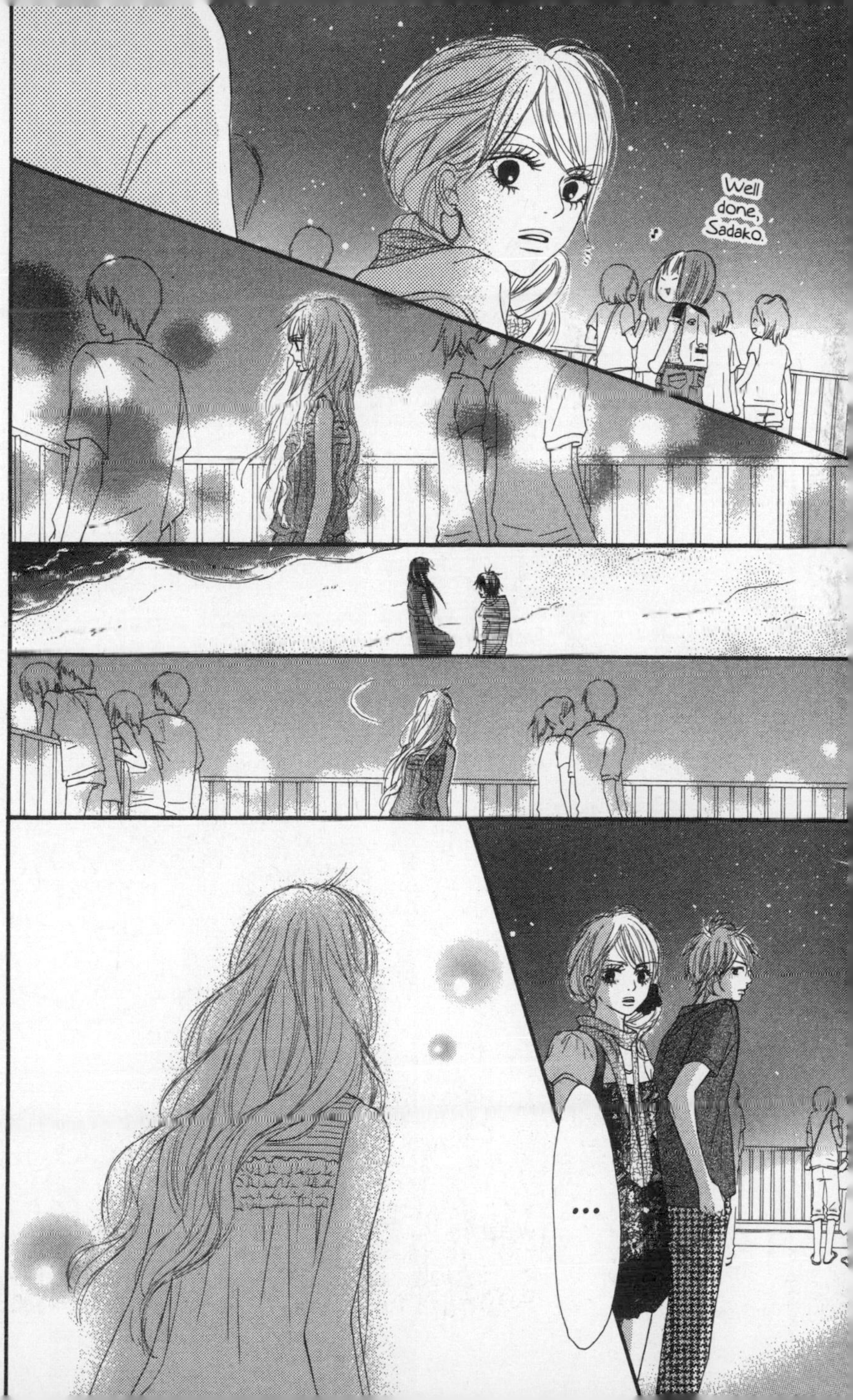
Well done, Sadako.
...

Episode 42: Sawako and Kurumi

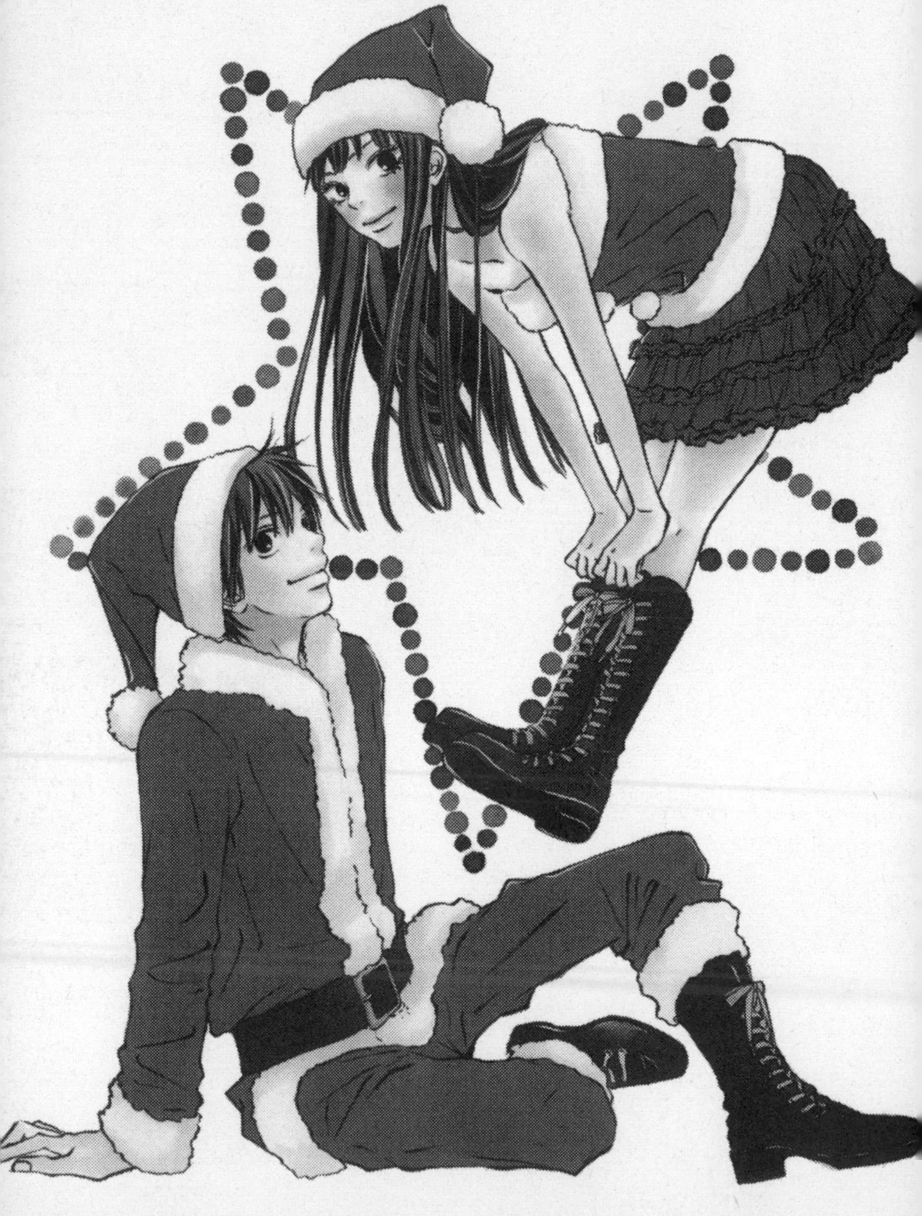

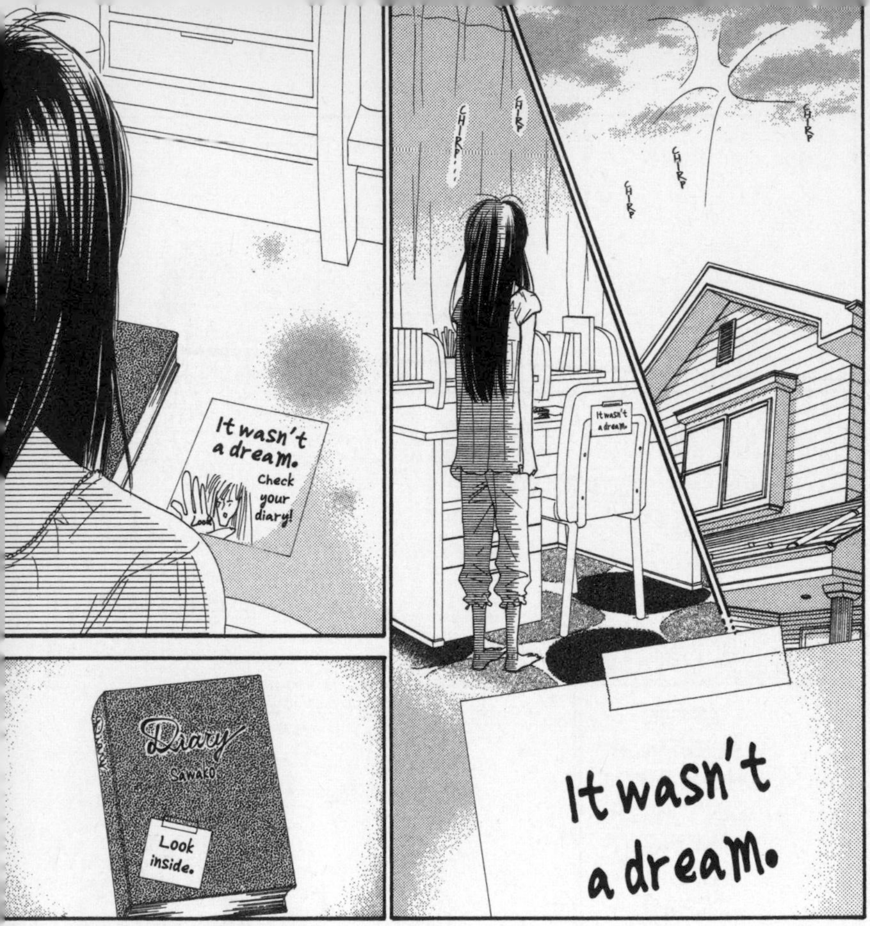
CHIRP...
CHIRP
CHIRP
CHIRP
CHIRP
It wasn't a dream.
It wasn't a dream.
It wasn't a dream.
Check your diary!
Diary
SAWAKO
Look inside.

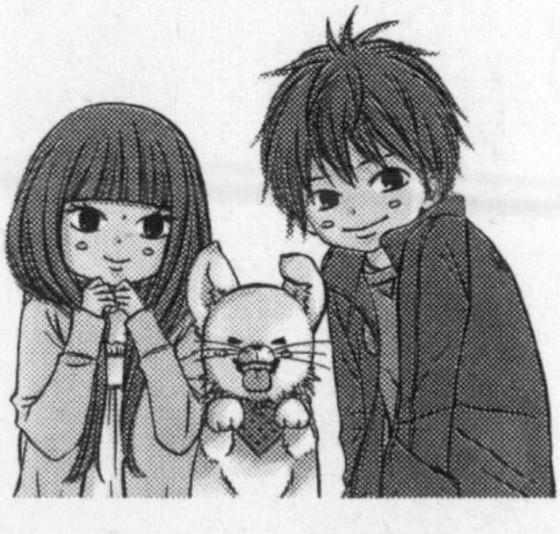

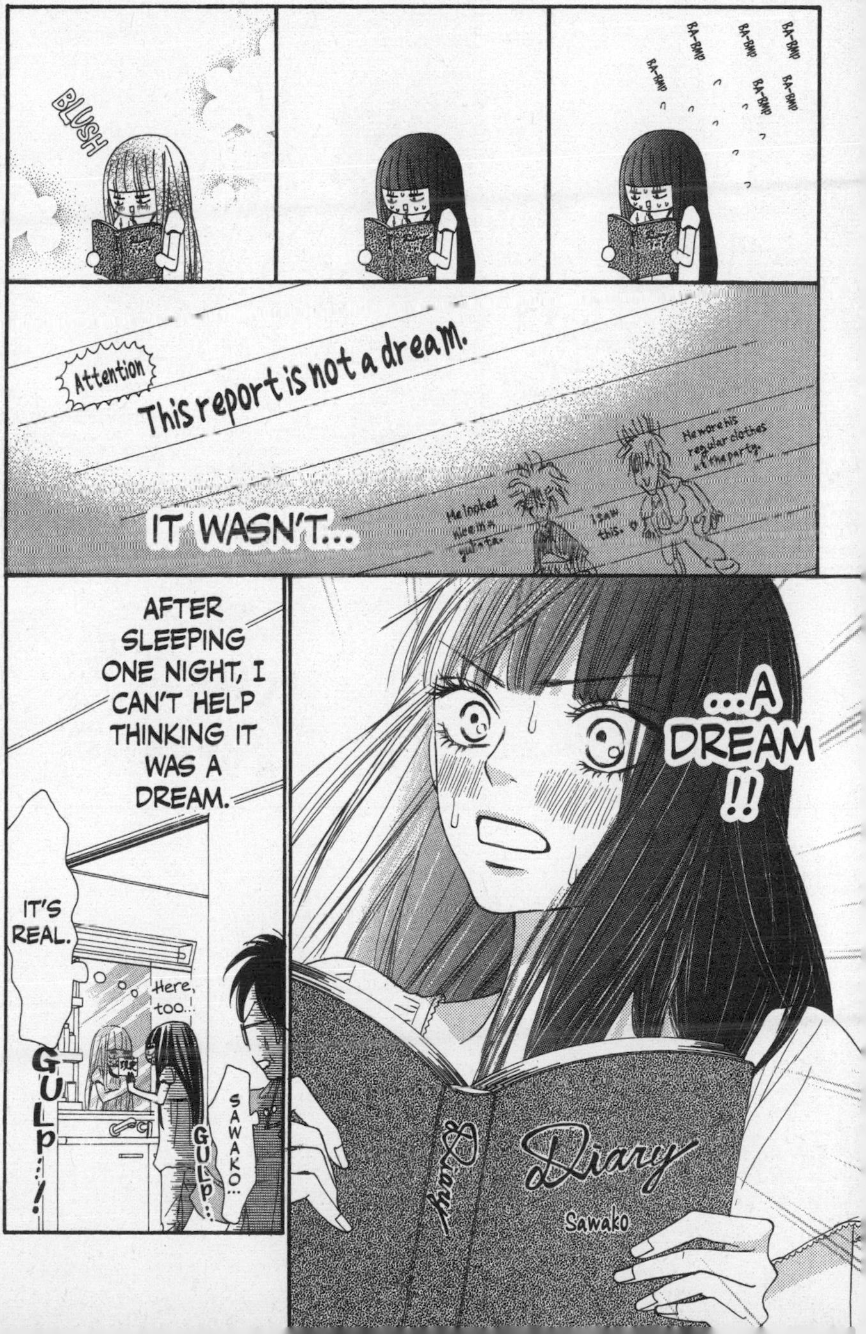
BA-BUMP
BA-BUMP
BA-BUMP
BA-BUMP
BA-BUMP
BLUSH
Attention
This report is not a dream.
He wore his regular clothes at the party.
I saw this.
IT WASN'T...
...A DREAM!!
Diary
Diary
Sawako
AFTER SLEEPING ONE NIGHT, I CAN'T HELP THINKING IT WAS A DREAM.
IT'S REAL.
Here, too...
GULP...!
SAWAKO...
GULP...

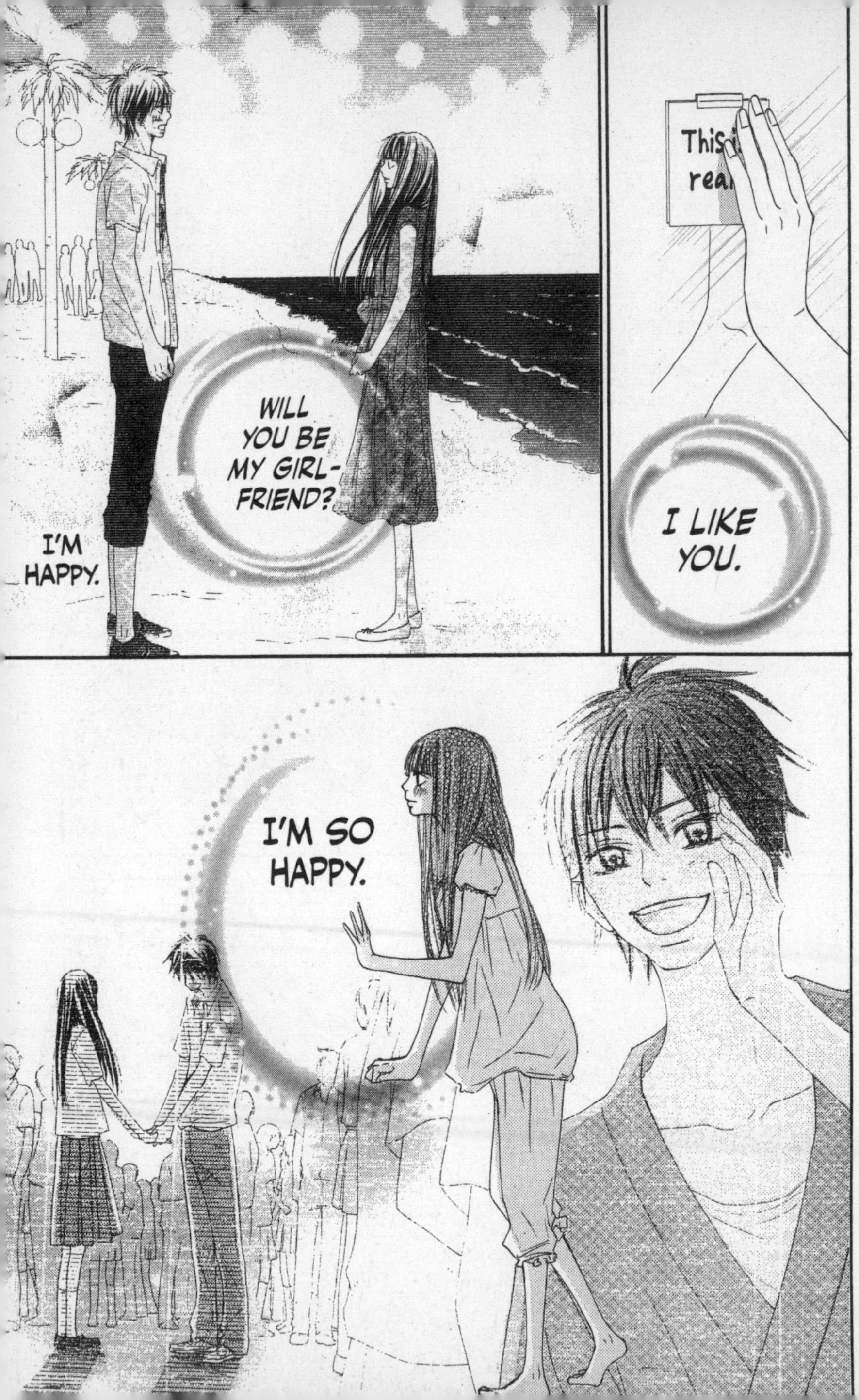
I LIKE YOU.
WILL YOU BE MY GIRL-FRIEND?
I'M HAPPY.
I'M SO HAPPY.

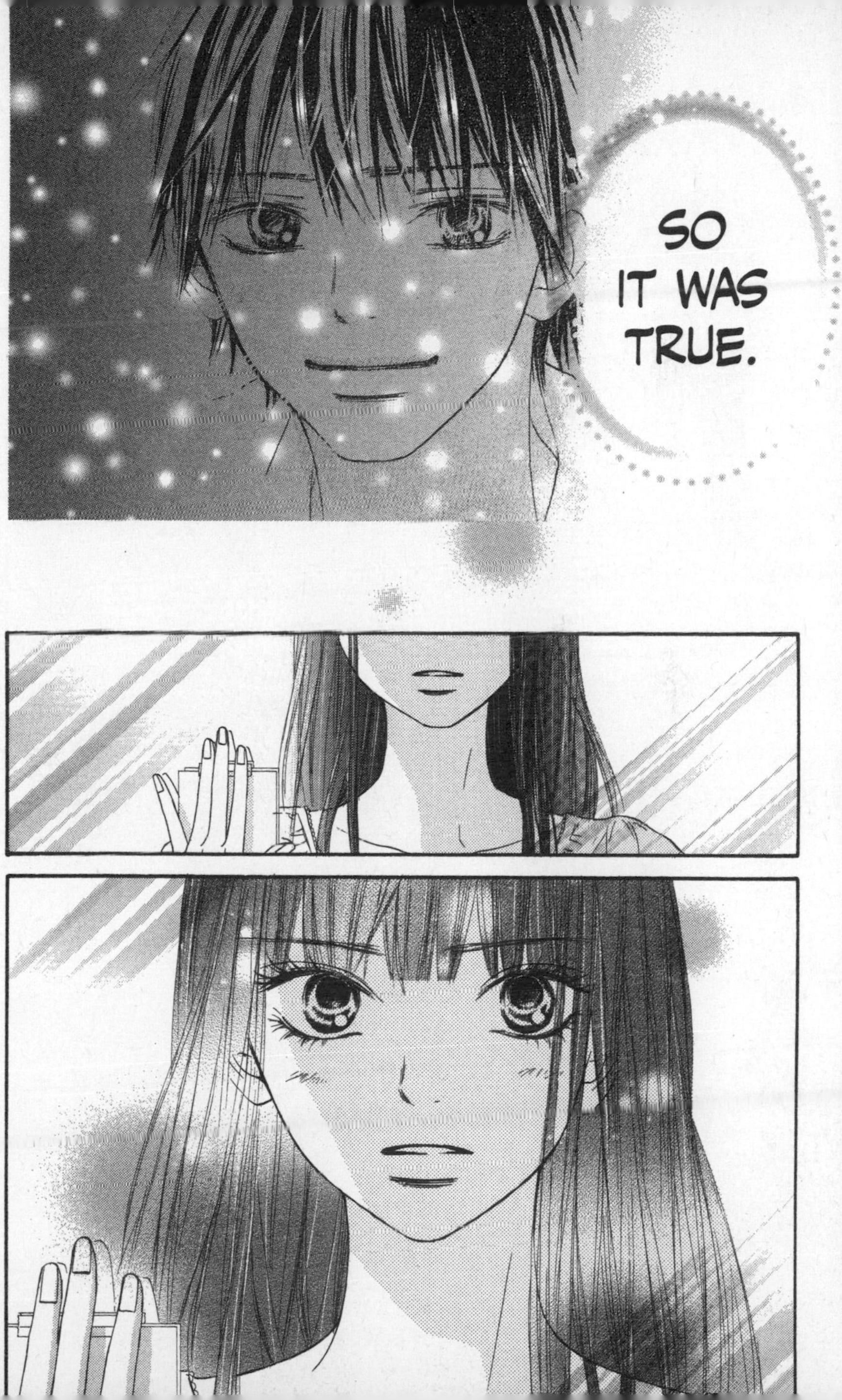
SO IT WAS TRUE.

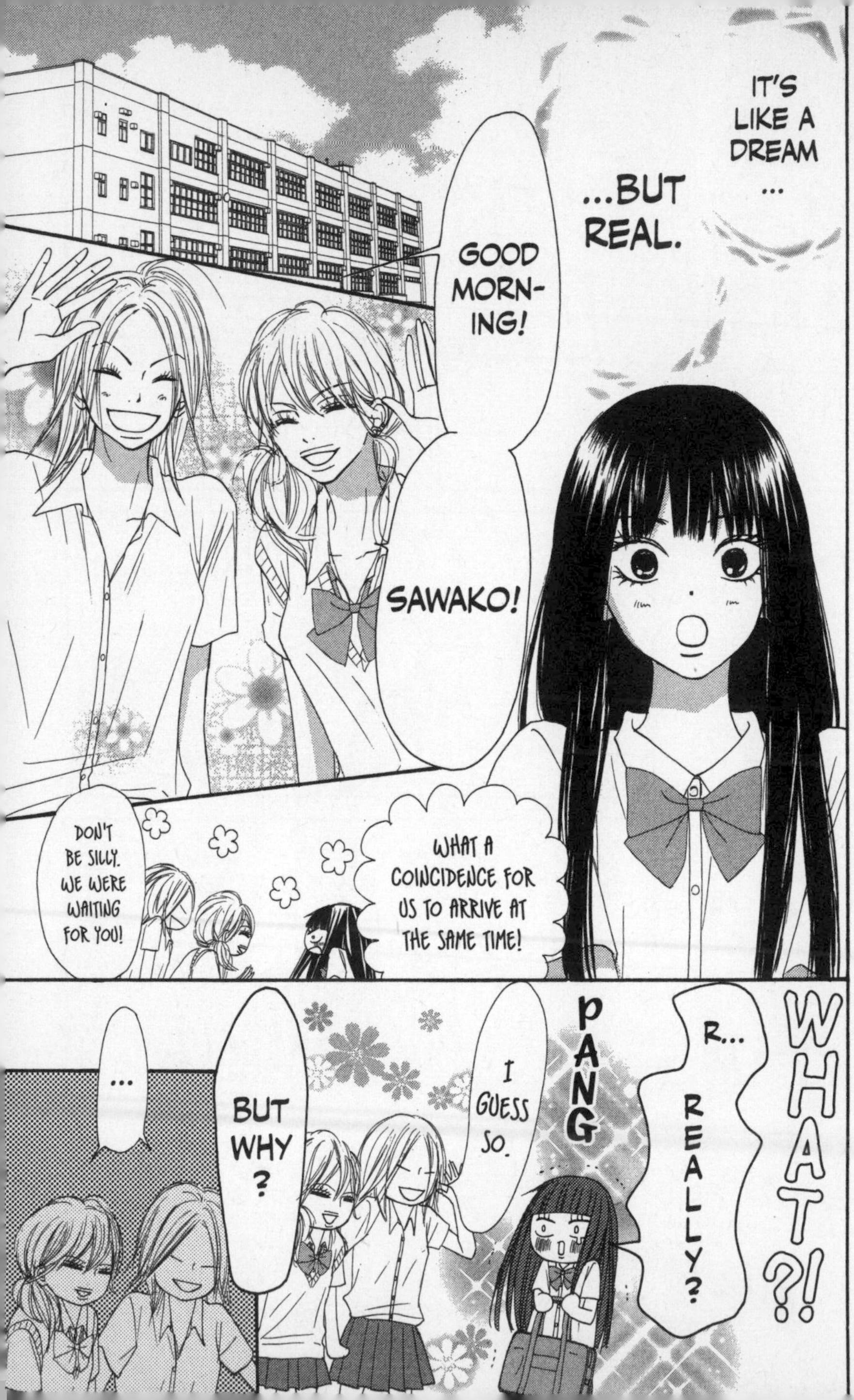
IT'S LIKE A DREAM ...
...BUT REAL.
GOOD MORNING!
SAWAKO!
WHAT A COINCIDENCE FOR US TO ARRIVE AT THE SAME TIME!
DON'T BE SILLY. WE WERE WAITING FOR YOU!
WHAT?!
R... REALLY?
PANG
I GUESS SO.
BUT WHY?
...

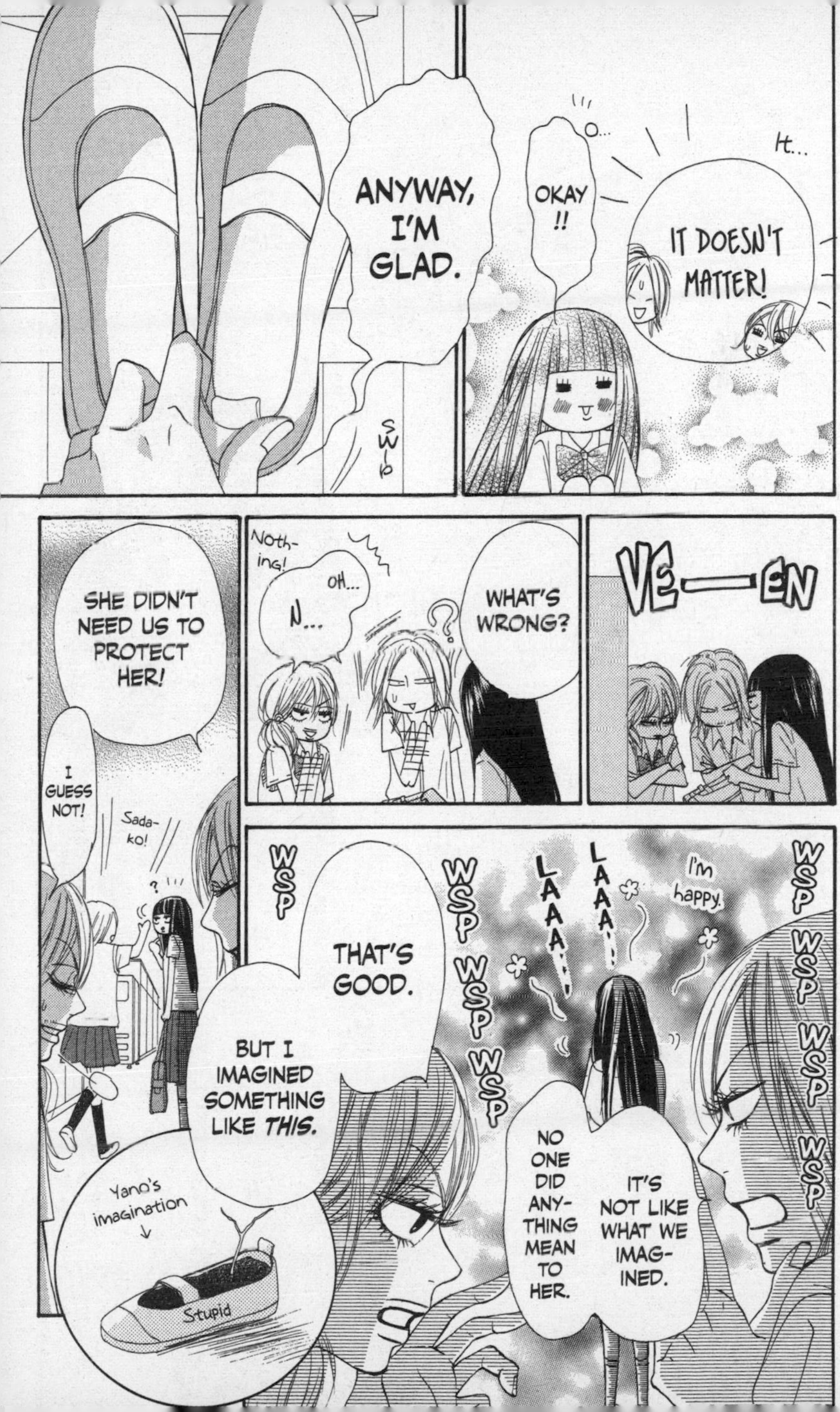
It...
IT DOESN'T MATTER!
O...
OKAY!!
ANYWAY, I'M GLAD.
SWIP
VE—EN
WHAT'S WRONG?
OH...
N...
Noth-ing!
WSP WSP WSP WSP WSP
I'm happy.
LAAAA...
LAAAA...
WSP WSP WSP
WSP
THAT'S GOOD.
IT'S NOT LIKE WHAT WE IMAG-INED.
NO ONE DID ANY-THING MEAN TO HER.
BUT I IMAGINED SOMETHING LIKE *THIS.*
Yano's imagination
Stupid
SHE DIDN'T NEED US TO PROTECT HER!
I GUESS NOT!
Sada-ko!

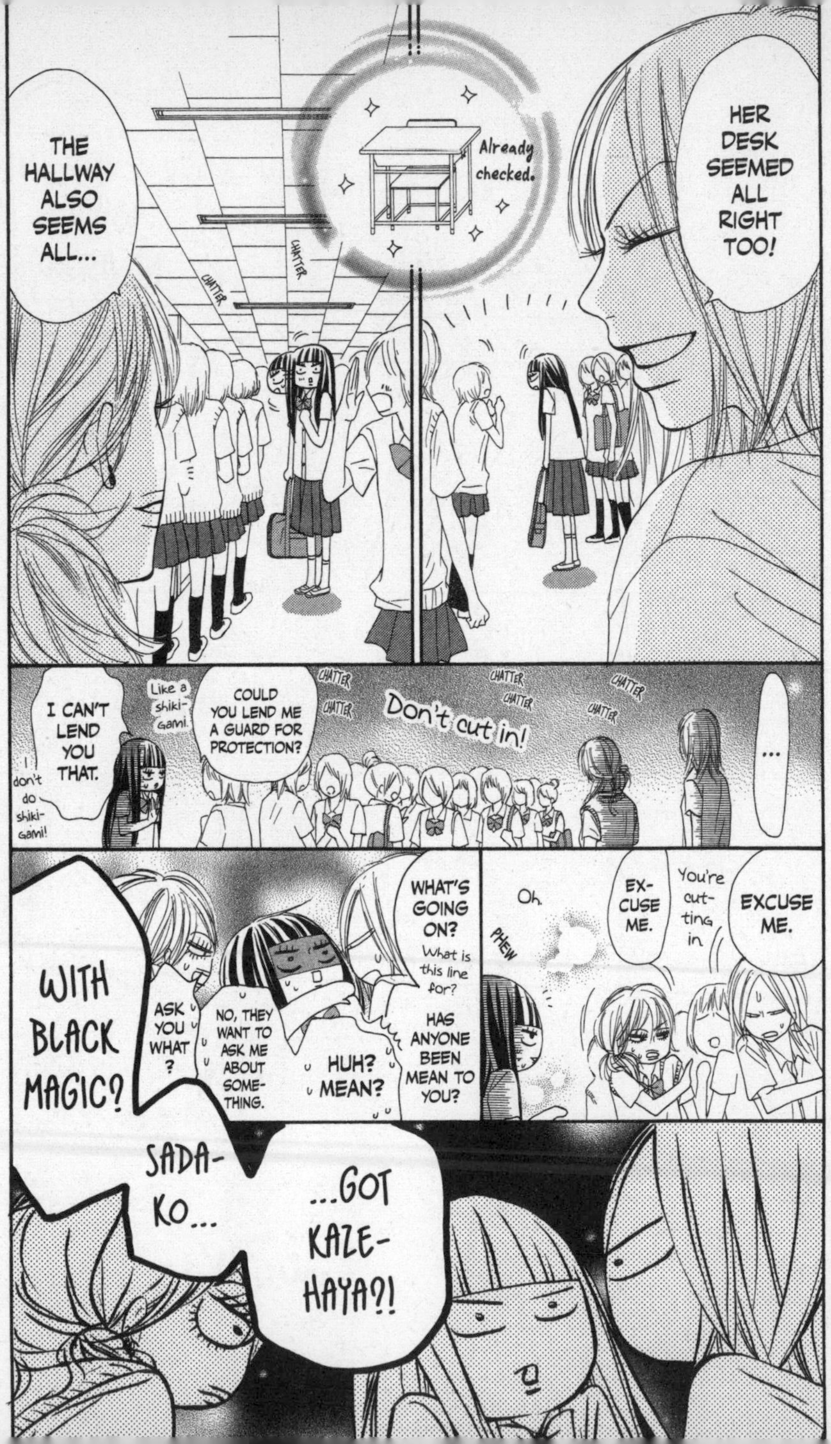

HER DESK SEEMED ALL RIGHT TOO!
Already checked.
THE HALLWAY ALSO SEEMS ALL...
CHATTER
CHATTER
...
CHATTER
CHATTER
CHATTER
CHATTER
CHATTER
CHATTER
Don't cut in!
COULD YOU LEND ME A GUARD FOR PROTECTION?
Like a shiki-Gami.
I CAN'T LEND YOU THAT.
I don't do shiki-Gami!
EXCUSE ME.
You're cut-ting in
EX-CUSE ME.
Oh.
PHEW
WHAT'S GOING ON?
What is this line for?
HAS ANYONE BEEN MEAN TO YOU?
HUH? MEAN?
NO, THEY WANT TO ASK ME ABOUT SOME-THING.
ASK YOU WHAT?
WITH BLACK MAGIC?
SADA-KO...
...GOT KAZE-HAYA?!

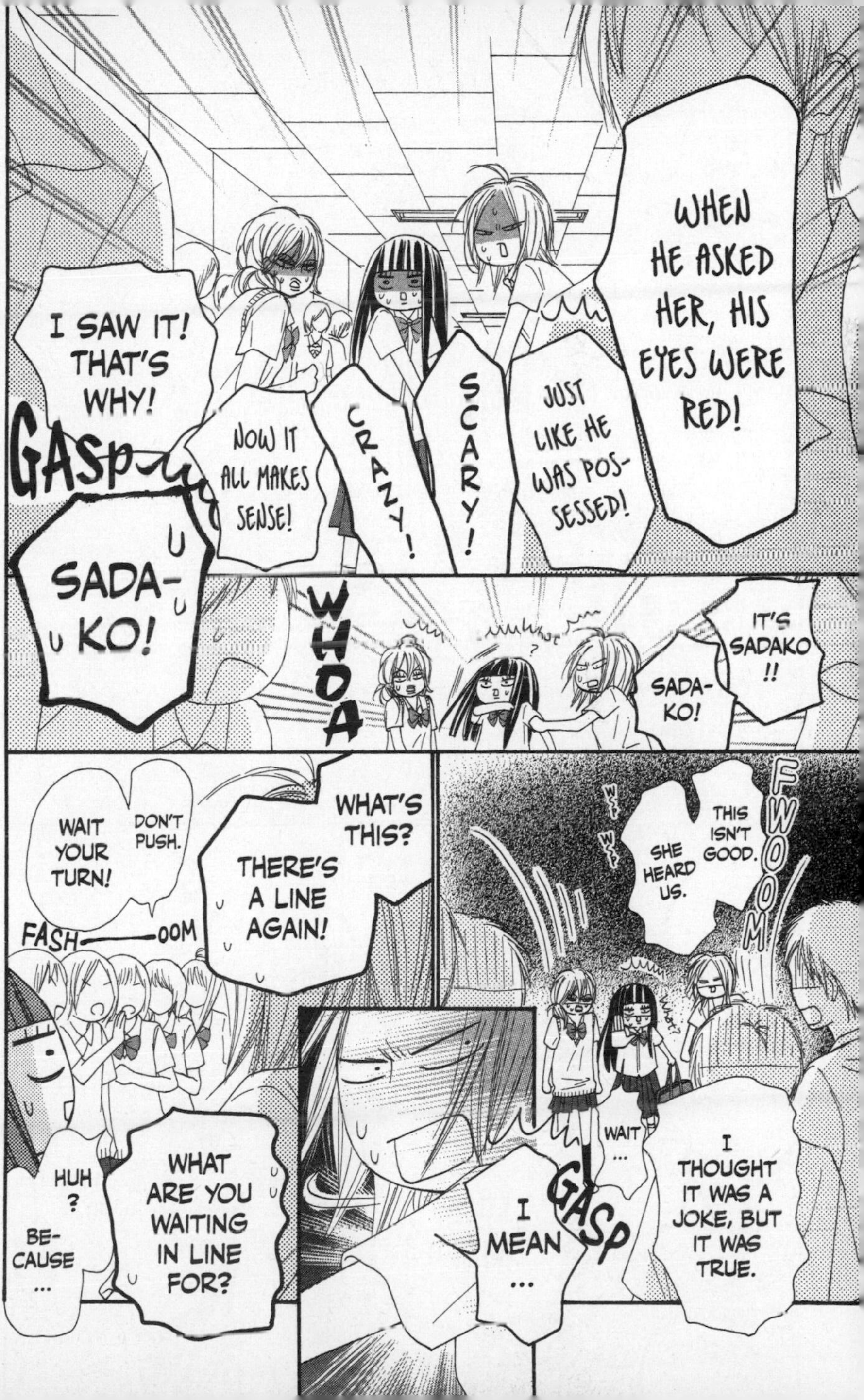
WHEN HE ASKED HER, HIS EYES WERE RED!
JUST LIKE HE WAS POS-SESSED!
SCARY!
CRAZY!
NOW IT ALL MAKES SENSE!
I SAW IT! THAT'S WHY!
GASP
SADA-KO!
IT'S SADAKO!!
SADA-KO!
WHOA
FWOOOM
THIS ISN'T GOOD.
SHE HEARD US.
WSP WSP
WHAT'S THIS?
THERE'S A LINE AGAIN!
DON'T PUSH.
WAIT YOUR TURN!
FASH——OOM
I THOUGHT IT WAS A JOKE, BUT IT WAS TRUE.
WAIT ...
GASP
I MEAN ...
WHAT ARE YOU WAITING IN LINE FOR?
HUH?
BE-CAUSE ...

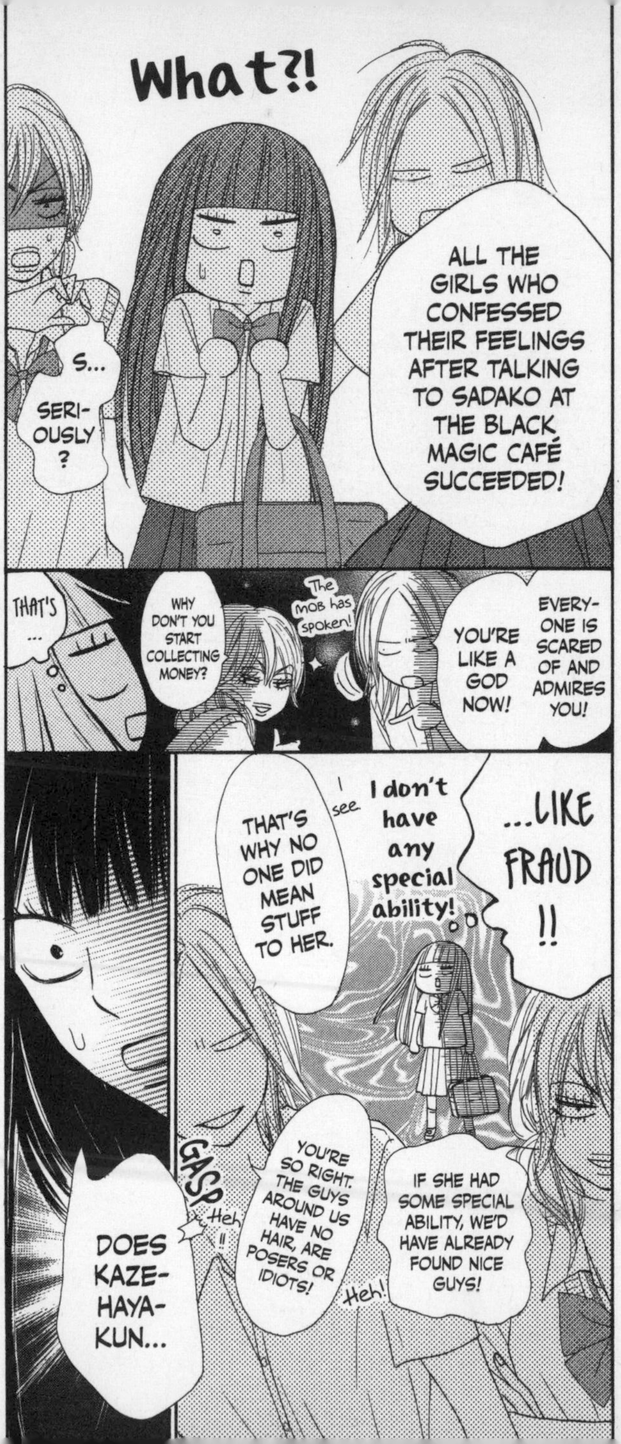
What?!
ALL THE GIRLS WHO CONFESSED THEIR FEELINGS AFTER TALKING TO SADAKO AT THE BLACK MAGIC CAFÉ SUCCEEDED!
S... SERI-OUSLY ?
EVERY-ONE IS SCARED OF AND ADMIRES YOU!
YOU'RE LIKE A GOD NOW!
The mob has spoken!
WHY DON'T YOU START COLLECTING MONEY?
THAT'S ...
...LIKE FRAUD !!
I don't have any special ability!
I see.
THAT'S WHY NO ONE DID MEAN STUFF TO HER.
IF SHE HAD SOME SPECIAL ABILITY, WE'D HAVE ALREADY FOUND NICE GUYS!
Heh!
YOU'RE SO RIGHT. THE GUYS AROUND US HAVE NO HAIR, ARE POSERS OR IDIOTS!
Heh !!
GASP
DOES KAZE-HAYA-KUN...

KARUPIN on JAPAN 4

Anyway, the animation is great in every way. If you have the chance, please watch it! It's better than the manga! ♡

Some characters got names when the anime was created.

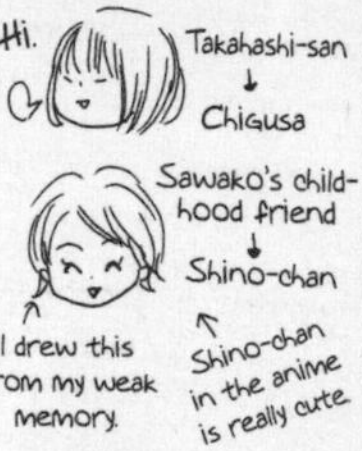
Hi.
Takahashi-san
↓
Chigusa
Sawako's child-hood friend
↓
Shino-chan
I drew this from my weak memory.
Shino-chan in the anime is really cute

The staff named those two and the girls from class A. I use Takahashi-san's name in the manga, as well! Thanks!

By the way, as soon as I started writing again, my daughter was hospitalized. (She's okay now.) I stayed at the hospital almost two weeks with her. While I was with her, the DVD of the anime arrived at home. I really wanted to watch it.

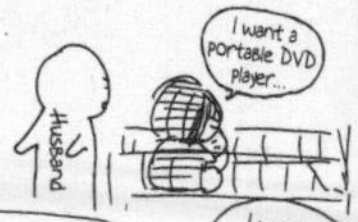
I want a portable DVD player...
Husband

So he bought one using points at the electronics shop. But the next day, my daughter was allowed to go home temporarily and then completely. In the end, I got a portable DVD player for no reason! Ha ha! That was nice. See ya!

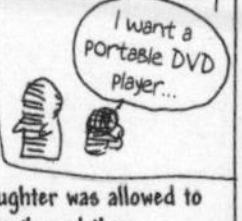
I want a portable DVD player...

What an unbelievable way to end my comments...

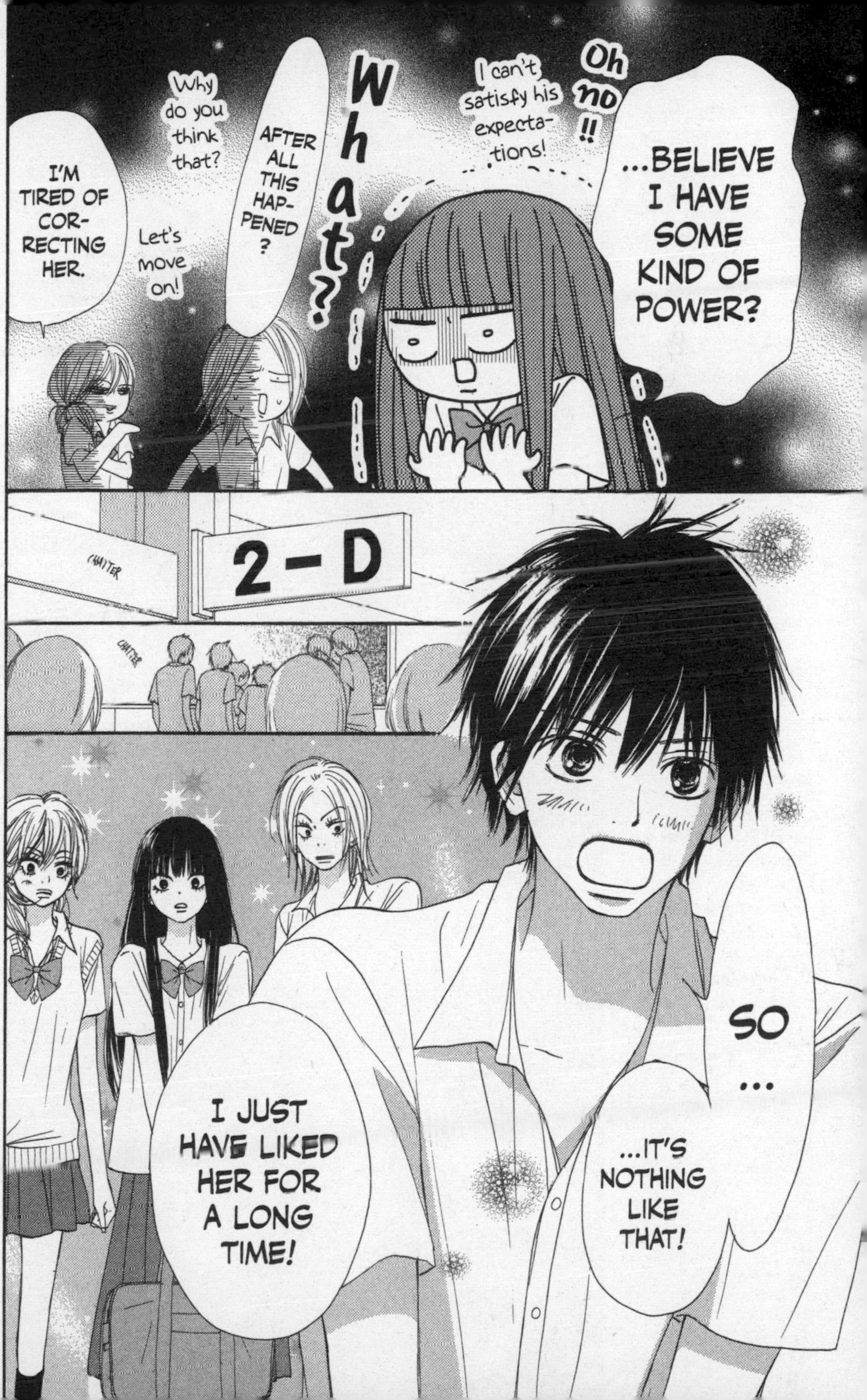
...BELIEVE I HAVE SOME KIND OF POWER?
Oh no!!
I can't satisfy his expectations!
What?
AFTER ALL THIS HAPPENED?
Why do you think that?
Let's move on!
I'M TIRED OF CORRECTING HER.
2-D
CHATTER
CHATTER
SO ...
...IT'S NOTHING LIKE THAT!
I JUST HAVE LIKED HER FOR A LONG TIME!

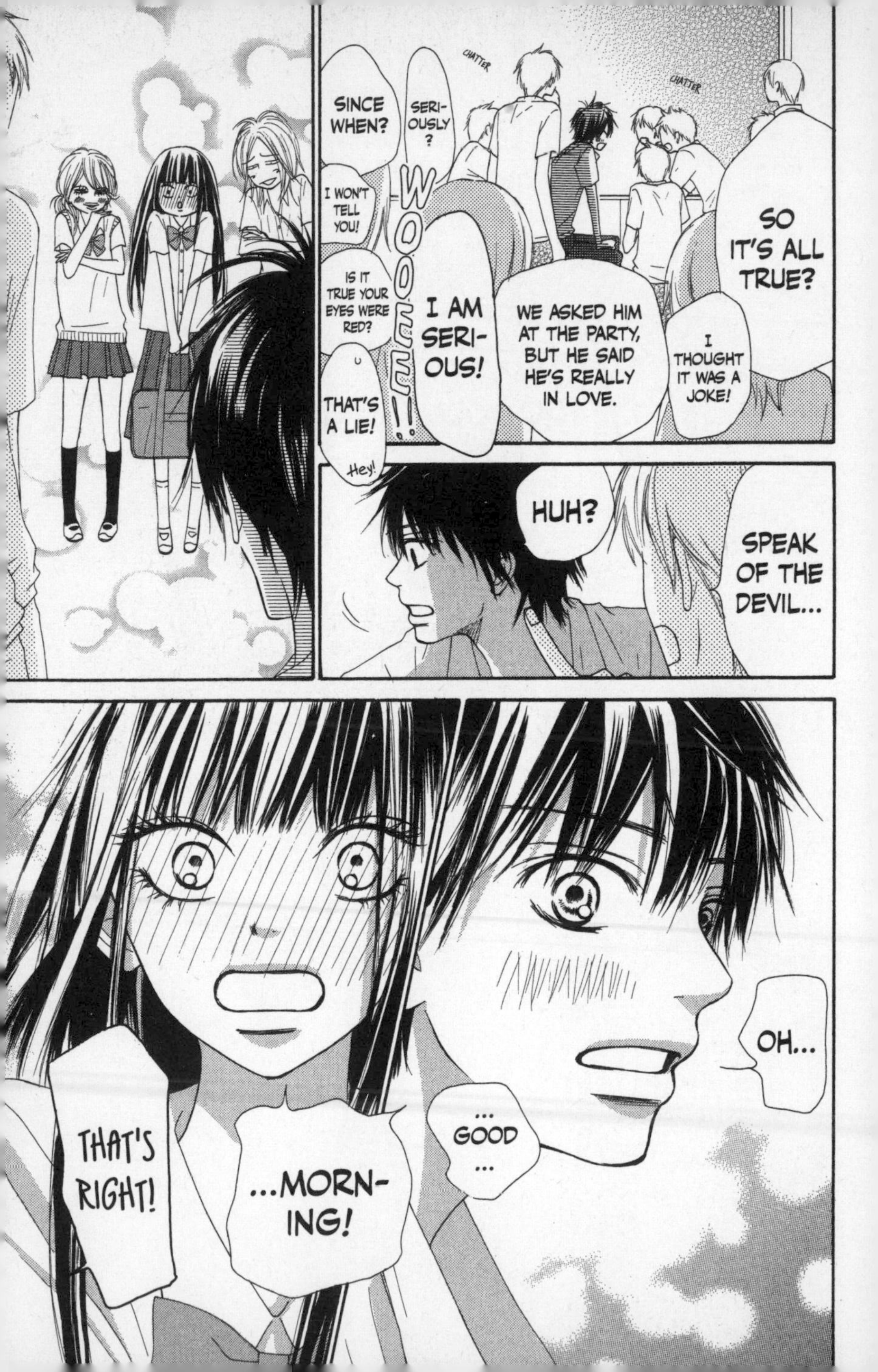
CHATTER
CHATTER
SO IT'S ALL TRUE?
I THOUGHT IT WAS A JOKE!
WE ASKED HIM AT THE PARTY, BUT HE SAID HE'S REALLY IN LOVE.
I AM SERI-OUS!
SERI-OUSLY?
SINCE WHEN?
I WON'T TELL YOU!
WOOEE!!
IS IT TRUE YOUR EYES WERE RED?
THAT'S A LIE!
Hey!
SPEAK OF THE DEVIL...
HUH?
OH...
...GOOD...
...MORN-ING!
THAT'S RIGHT!

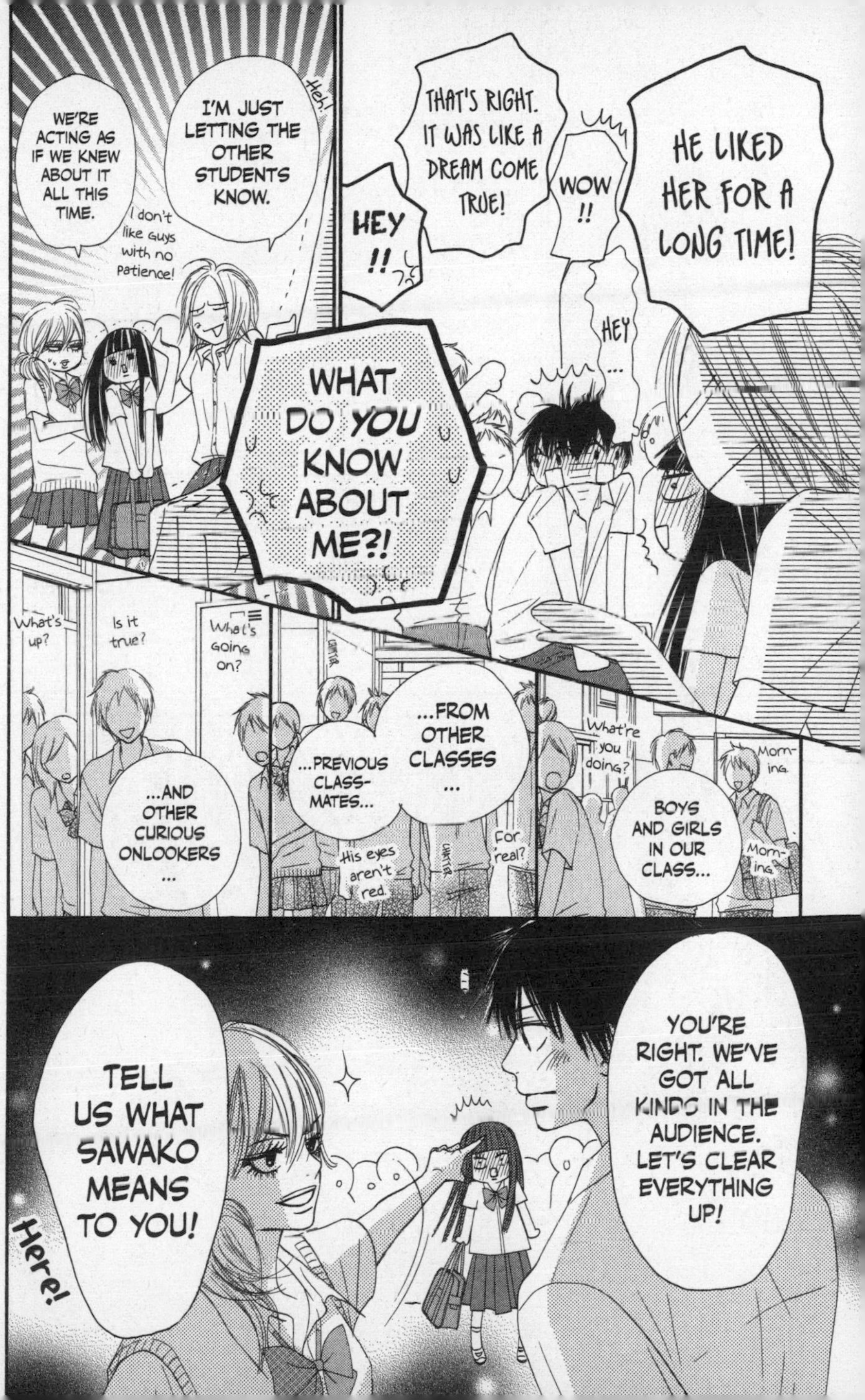
HE LIKED HER FOR A LONG TIME!
WOW!!
THAT'S RIGHT. IT WAS LIKE A DREAM COME TRUE!
HEY!!
HEY...
WHAT DO YOU KNOW ABOUT ME?!
Heh!
I'M JUST LETTING THE OTHER STUDENTS KNOW.
WE'RE ACTING AS IF WE KNEW ABOUT IT ALL THIS TIME.
I don't like guys with no patience!
Morn-ing.
What're you doing?
BOYS AND GIRLS IN OUR CLASS...
Morn-ing.
...FROM OTHER CLASSES...
...PREVIOUS CLASS-MATES...
For real?
His eyes aren't red.
What's going on?
Is it true?
What's up?
...AND OTHER CURIOUS ONLOOKERS...
YOU'RE RIGHT. WE'VE GOT ALL KINDS IN THE AUDIENCE. LET'S CLEAR EVERYTHING UP!
TELL US WHAT SAWAKO MEANS TO YOU!
Here!

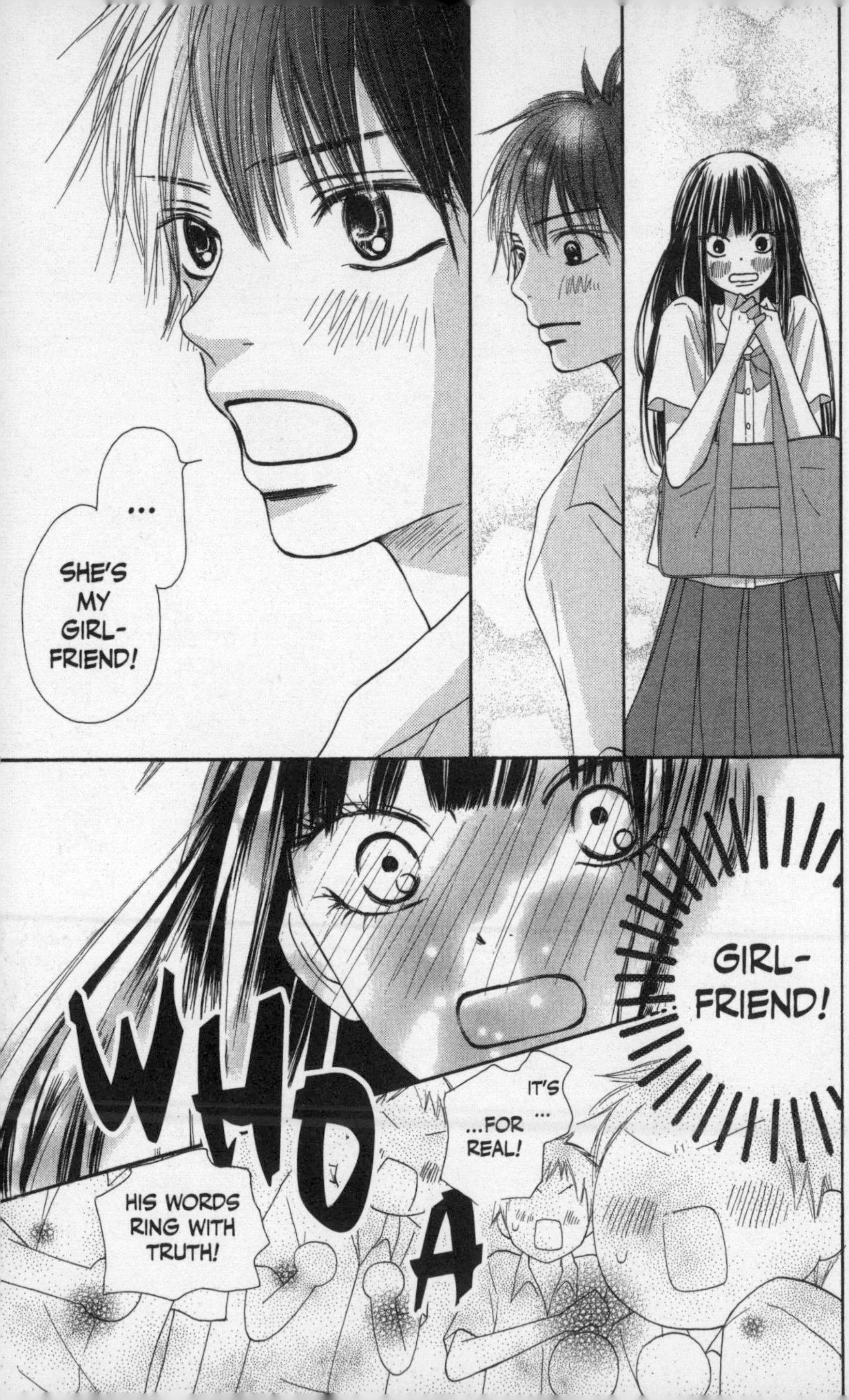
...
SHE'S MY GIRL-FRIEND!
GIRL-FRIEND!
WHOA
IT'S ...
...FOR REAL!
HIS WORDS RING WITH TRUTH!

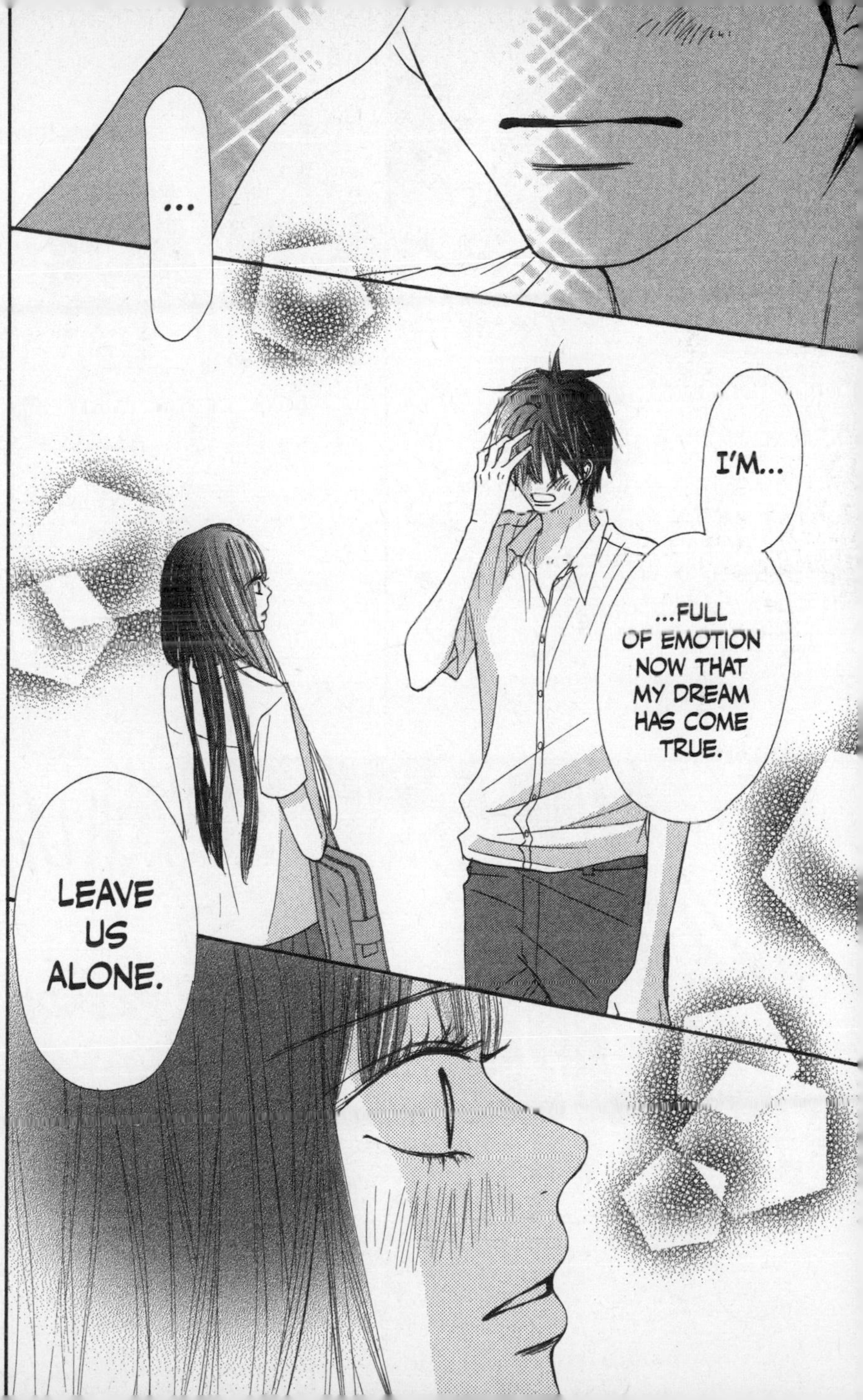
...
I'M...
...FULL OF EMOTION NOW THAT MY DREAM HAS COME TRUE.
LEAVE US ALONE.

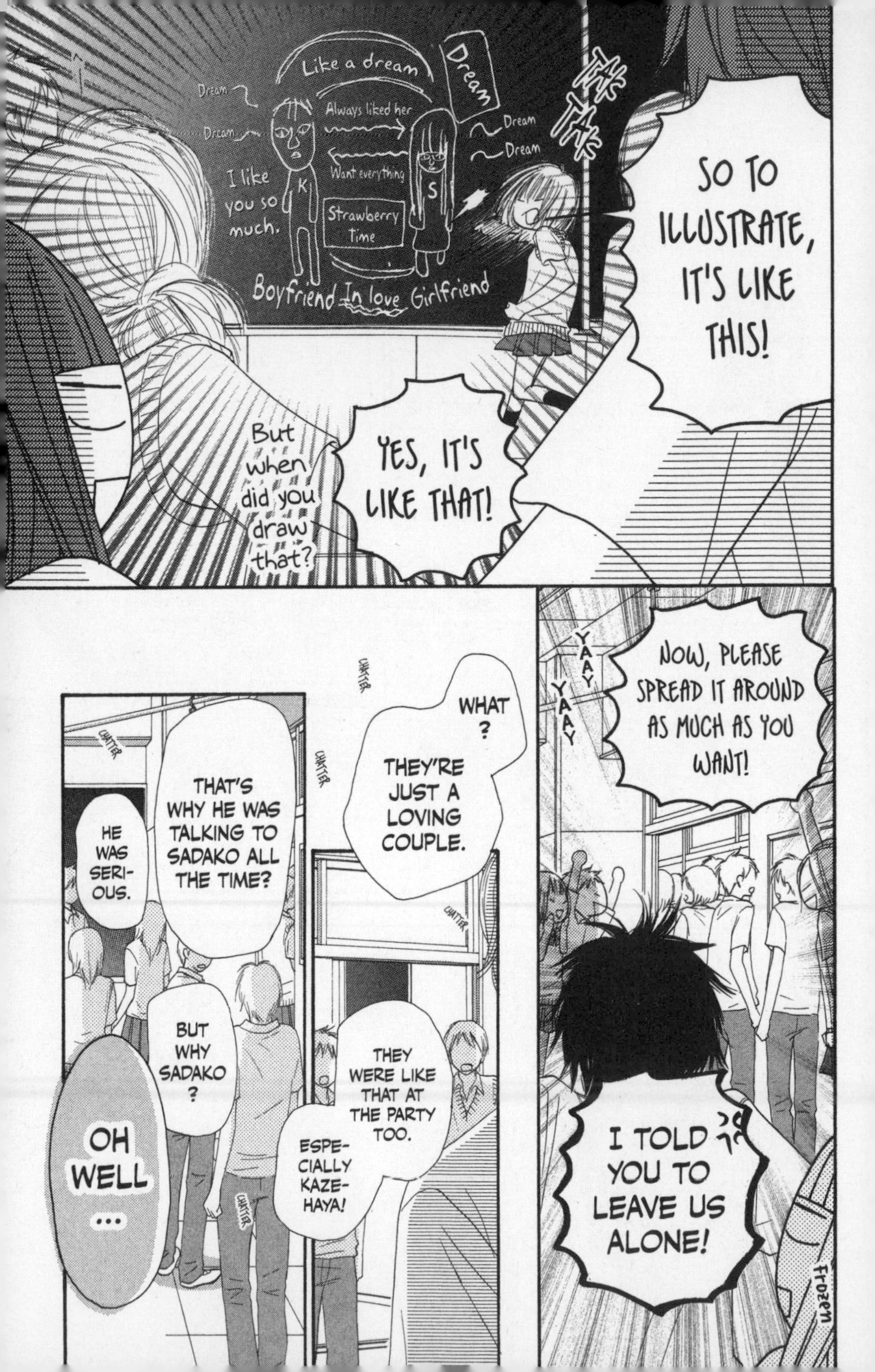
TAK TAK
SO TO ILLUSTRATE, IT'S LIKE THIS!
Dream
Like a dream
Dream
Dream
Always liked her
Dream
Dream
I like you so much.
K
Want everything
S
Strawberry Time
Boyfriend In love Girlfriend
YES, IT'S LIKE THAT!
But when did you draw that?
YAAY YAAY
NOW, PLEASE SPREAD IT AROUND AS MUCH AS YOU WANT!
I TOLD YOU TO LEAVE US ALONE!
Frozen
CHATTER
WHAT?
THEY'RE JUST A LOVING COUPLE.
CHATTER
THAT'S WHY HE WAS TALKING TO SADAKO ALL THE TIME?
CHATTER
HE WAS SERIOUS.
CHATTER
THEY WERE LIKE THAT AT THE PARTY TOO.
ESPECIALLY KAZEHAYA!
BUT WHY SADAKO?
CHATTER
OH WELL...

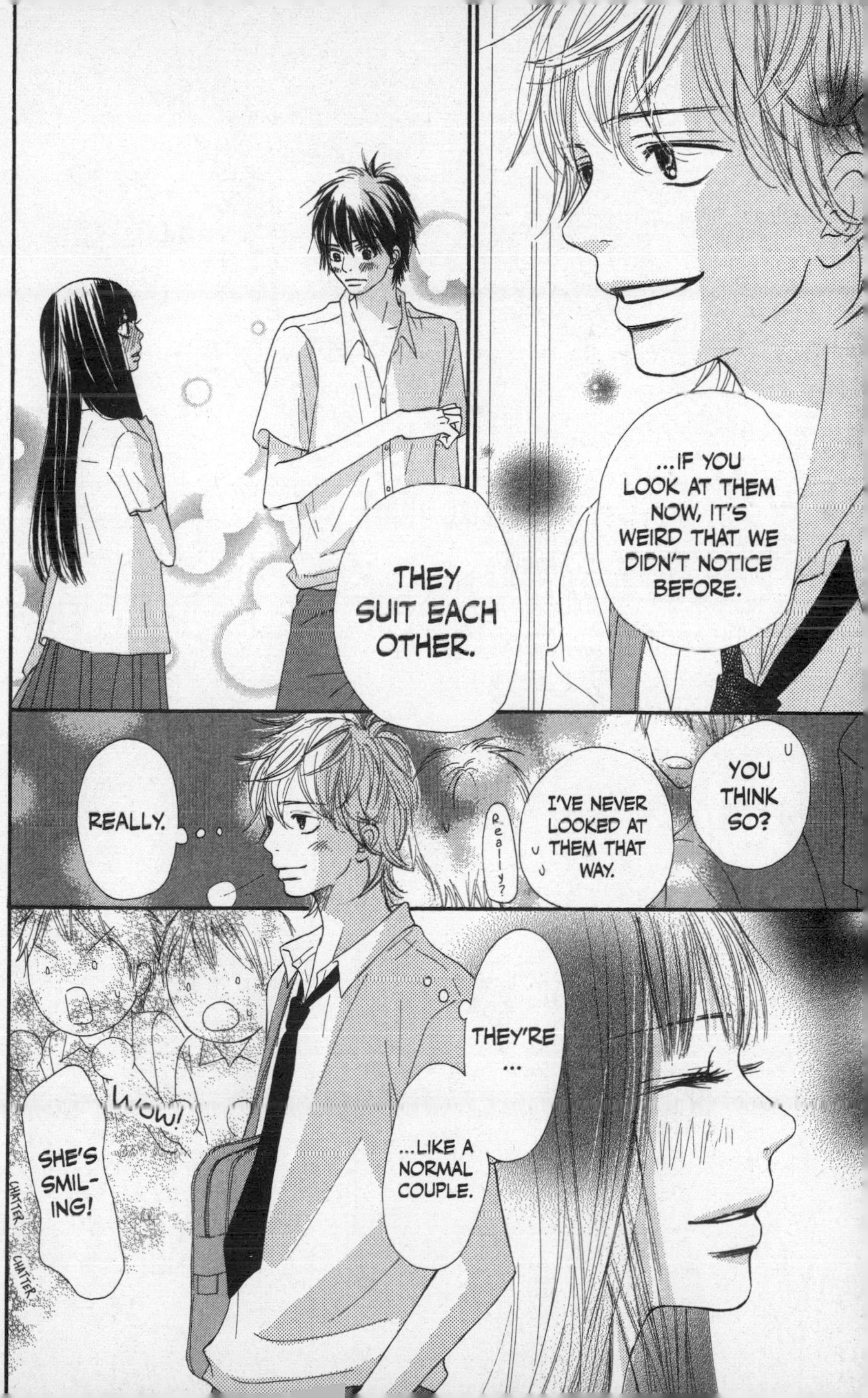
...IF YOU LOOK AT THEM NOW, IT'S WEIRD THAT WE DIDN'T NOTICE BEFORE.
THEY SUIT EACH OTHER.
YOU THINK SO?
I'VE NEVER LOOKED AT THEM THAT WAY.
Really?
REALLY.
THEY'RE ...
...LIKE A NORMAL COUPLE.
WOW!
SHE'S SMIL-ING!
CHATTER CHATTER

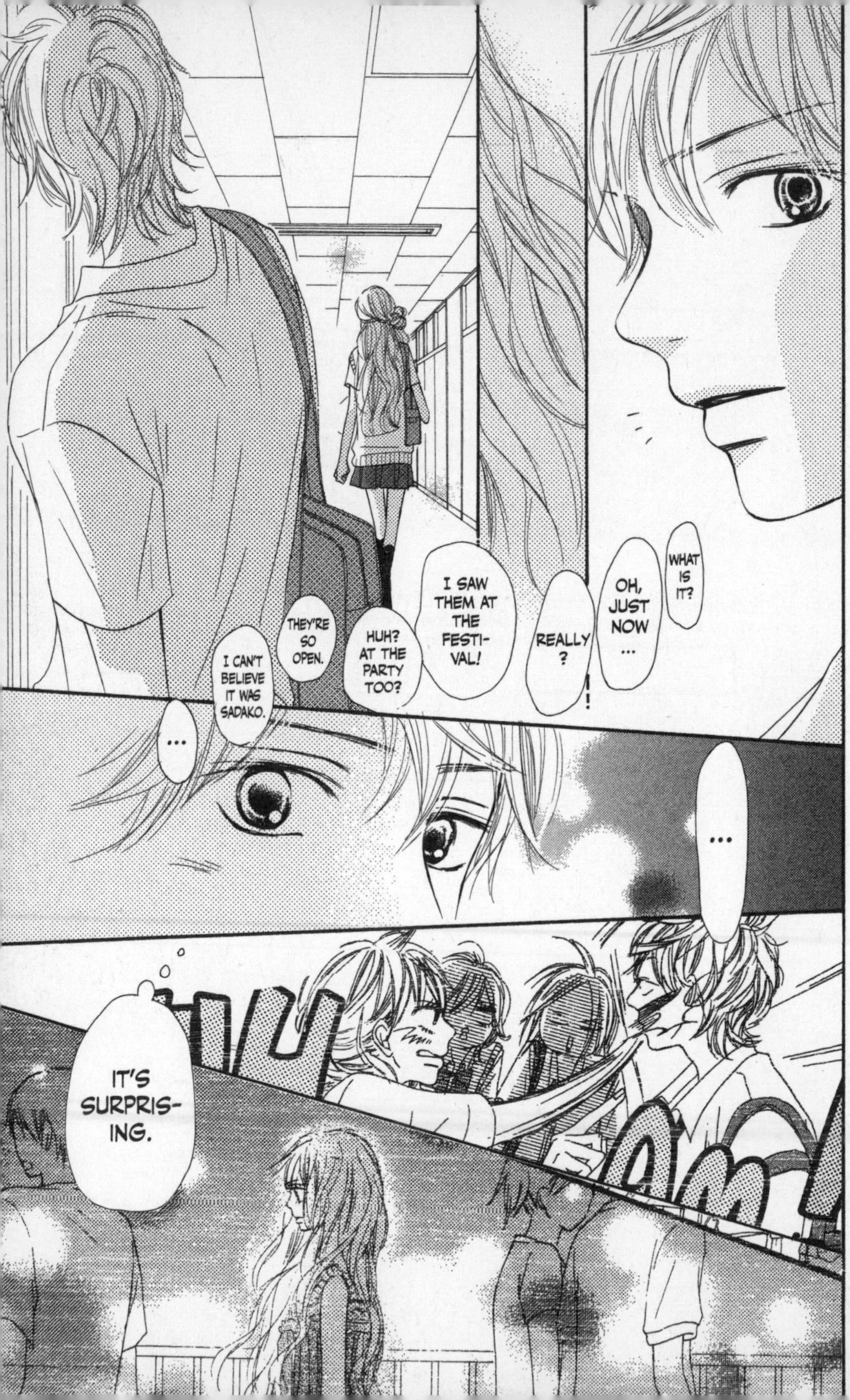
WHAT IS IT?
OH, JUST NOW ...
REALLY?
I SAW THEM AT THE FESTIVAL!
HUH? AT THE PARTY TOO?
THEY'RE SO OPEN.
I CAN'T BELIEVE IT WAS SADAKO.
...
...
IT'S SURPRISING.

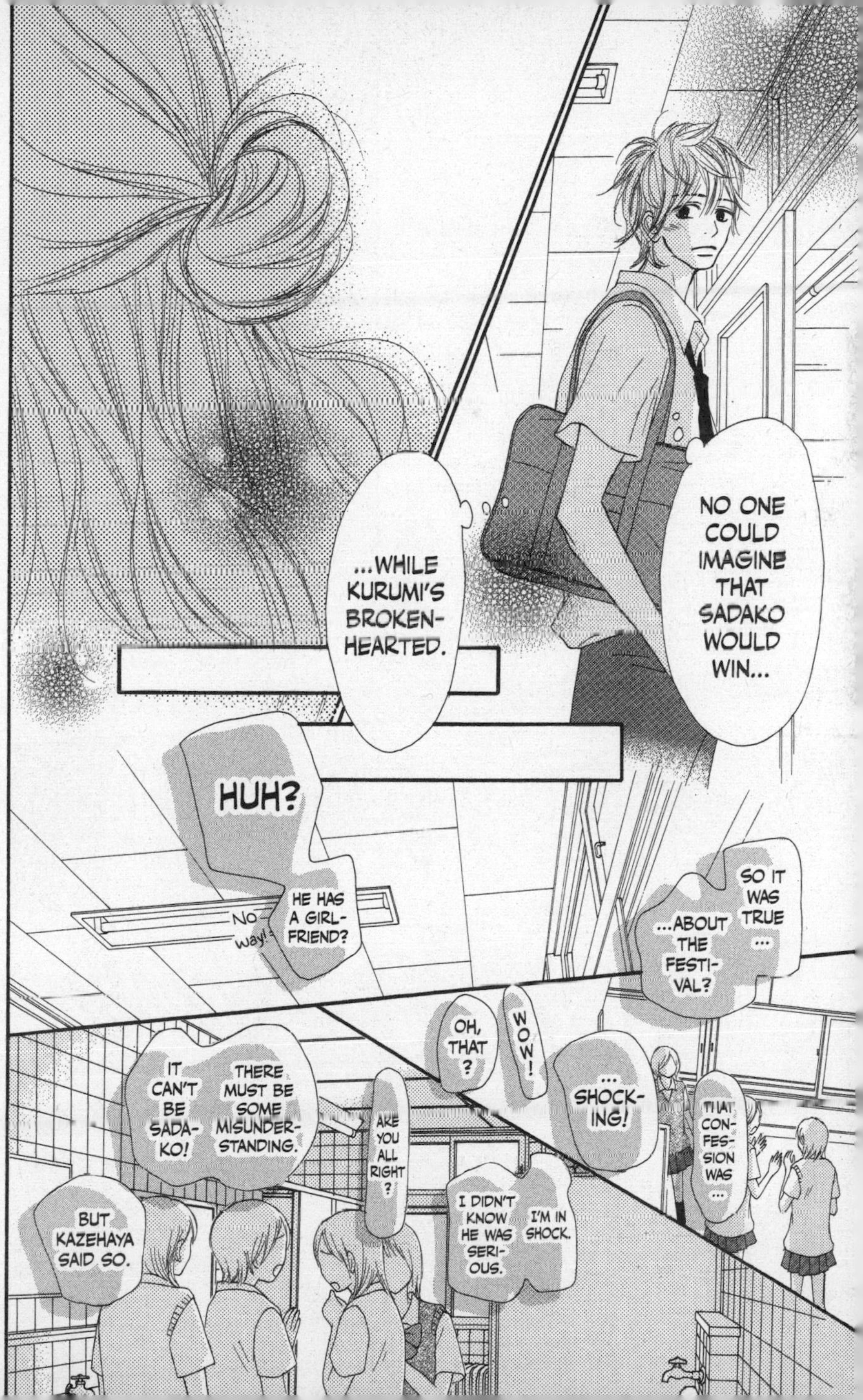
NO ONE COULD IMAGINE THAT SADAKO WOULD WIN...
...WHILE KURUMI'S BROKEN-HEARTED.
SO IT WAS TRUE...
...ABOUT THE FESTIVAL?
HUH?
HE HAS A GIRLFRIEND?
No way!
THAT CONFESSION WAS...
...SHOCKING!
WOW!
OH, THAT?
I'M IN SHOCK.
I DIDN'T KNOW HE WAS SERIOUS.
ARE YOU ALL RIGHT?
THERE MUST BE SOME MISUNDERSTANDING.
IT CAN'T BE SADAKO!
BUT KAZEHAYA SAID SO.

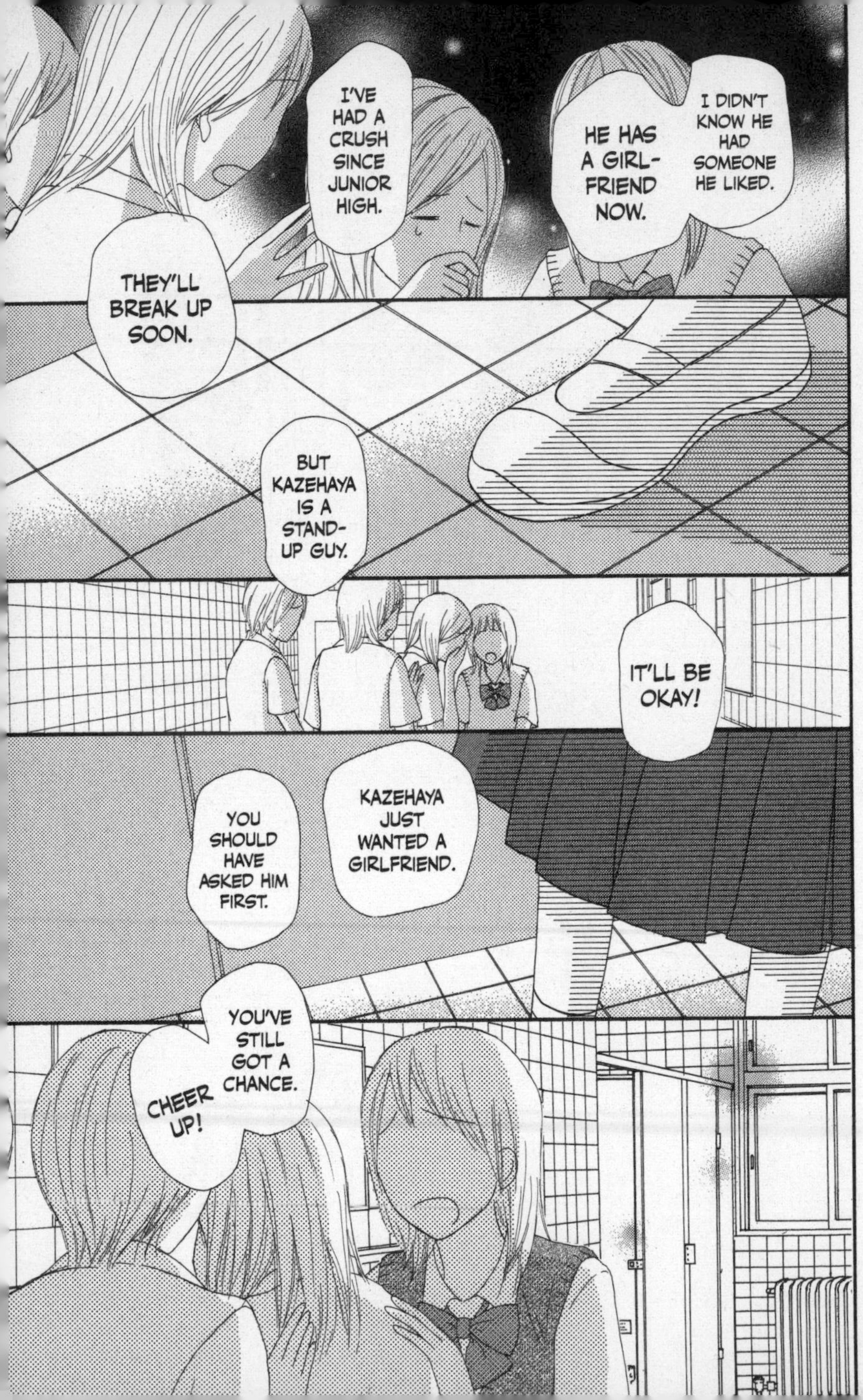
I DIDN'T KNOW HE HAD SOMEONE HE LIKED.
HE HAS A GIRL-FRIEND NOW.
I'VE HAD A CRUSH SINCE JUNIOR HIGH.
THEY'LL BREAK UP SOON.
BUT KAZEHAYA IS A STAND-UP GUY.
IT'LL BE OKAY!
KAZEHAYA JUST WANTED A GIRLFRIEND.
YOU SHOULD HAVE ASKED HIM FIRST.
YOU'VE STILL GOT A CHANCE.
CHEER UP!

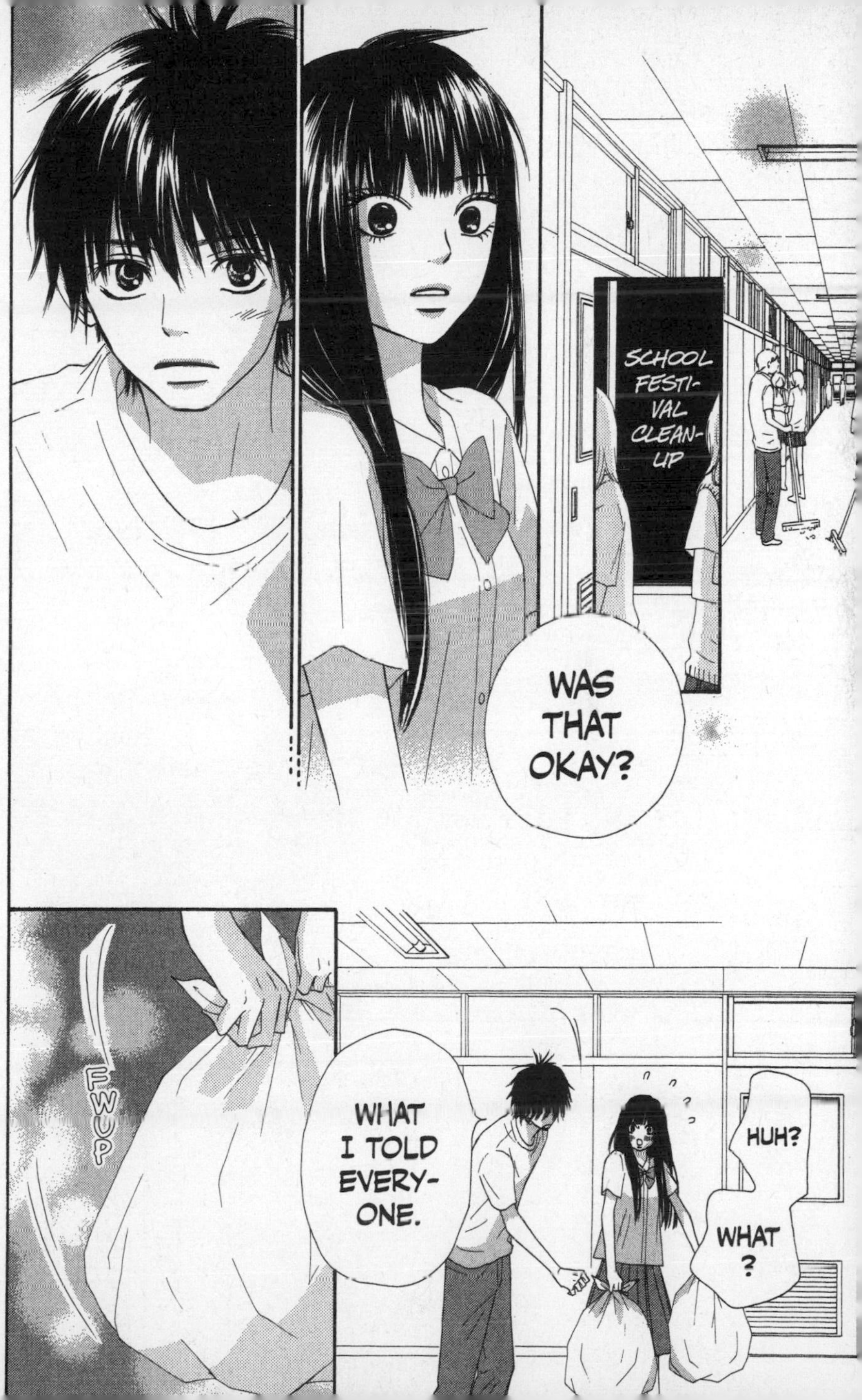
SCHOOL FESTIVAL CLEAN-UP
WAS THAT OKAY?
HUH?
WHAT?
WHAT I TOLD EVERYONE.
FWUP

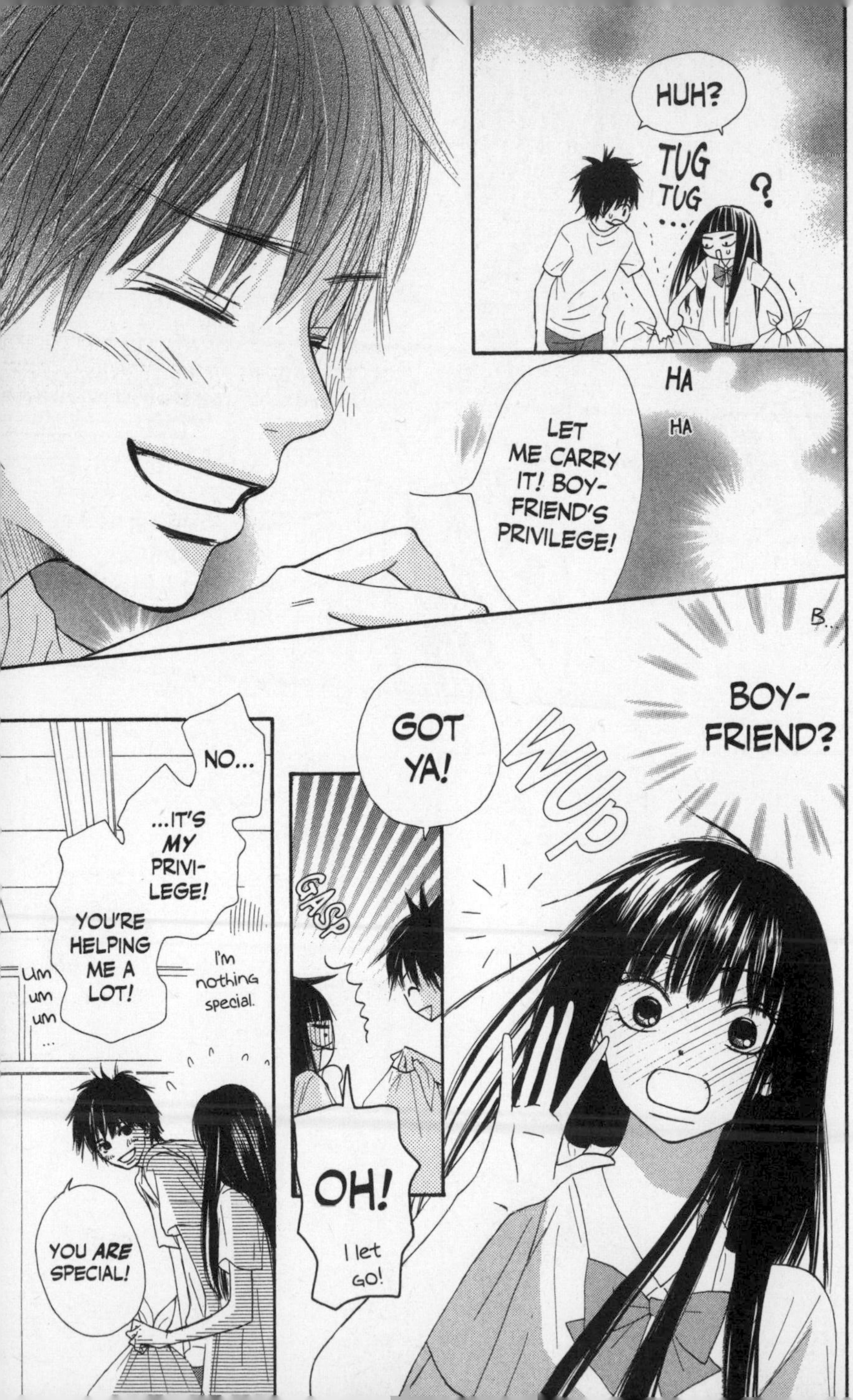
HUH?
TUG
TUG
...
?
HA
HA
LET ME CARRY IT! BOY-FRIEND'S PRIVILEGE!
B..
BOY-FRIEND?
WUP
GOT YA!
GASP
OH!
I let GO!
NO...
...IT'S MY PRIVI-LEGE!
YOU'RE HELPING ME A LOT!
I'm nothing special.
Um um um ...
YOU ARE SPECIAL!

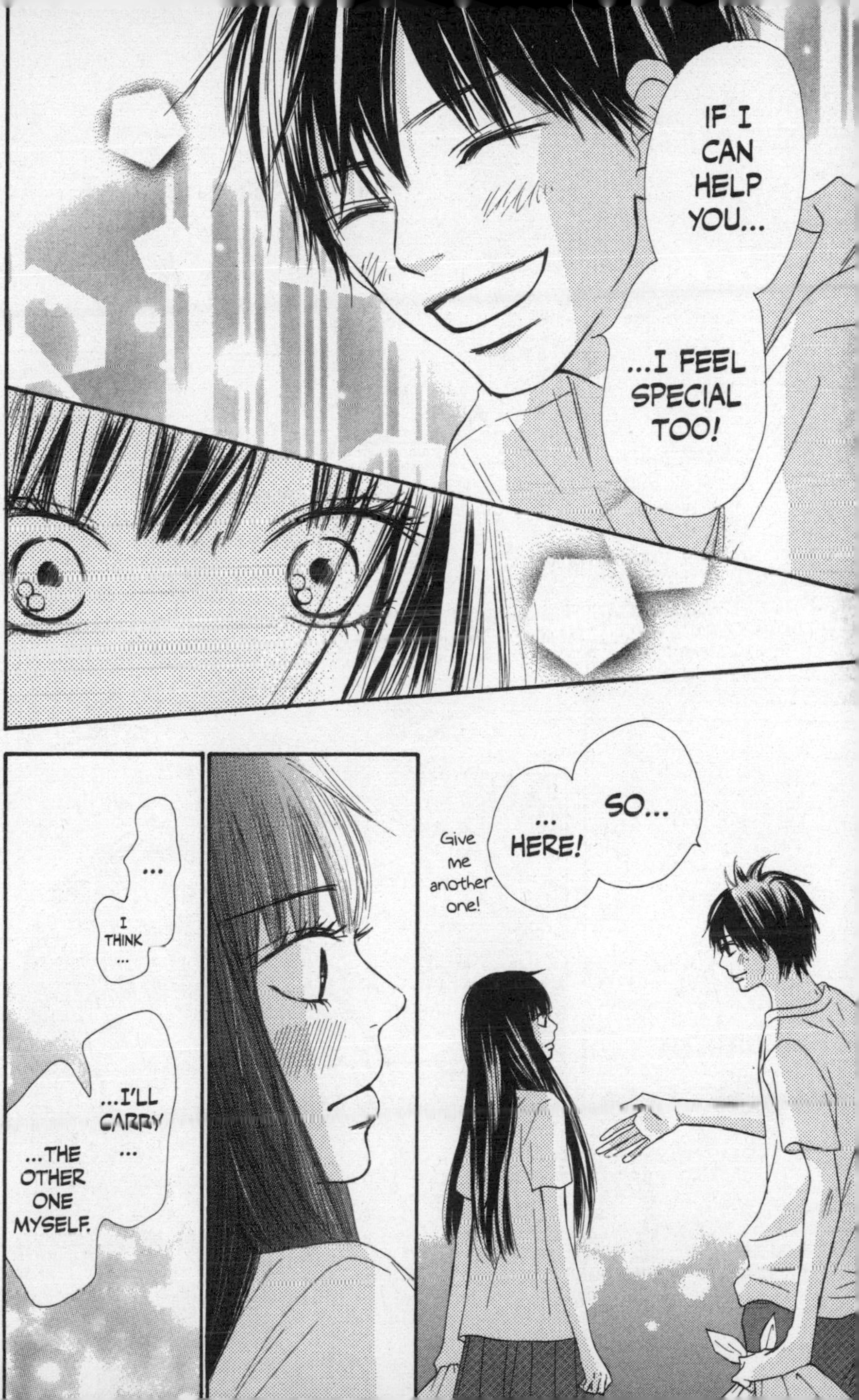
IF I CAN HELP YOU...
...I FEEL SPECIAL TOO!
SO... ...HERE!
Give me another one!
... I THINK ...
...I'LL CARRY ...
...THE OTHER ONE MYSELF.

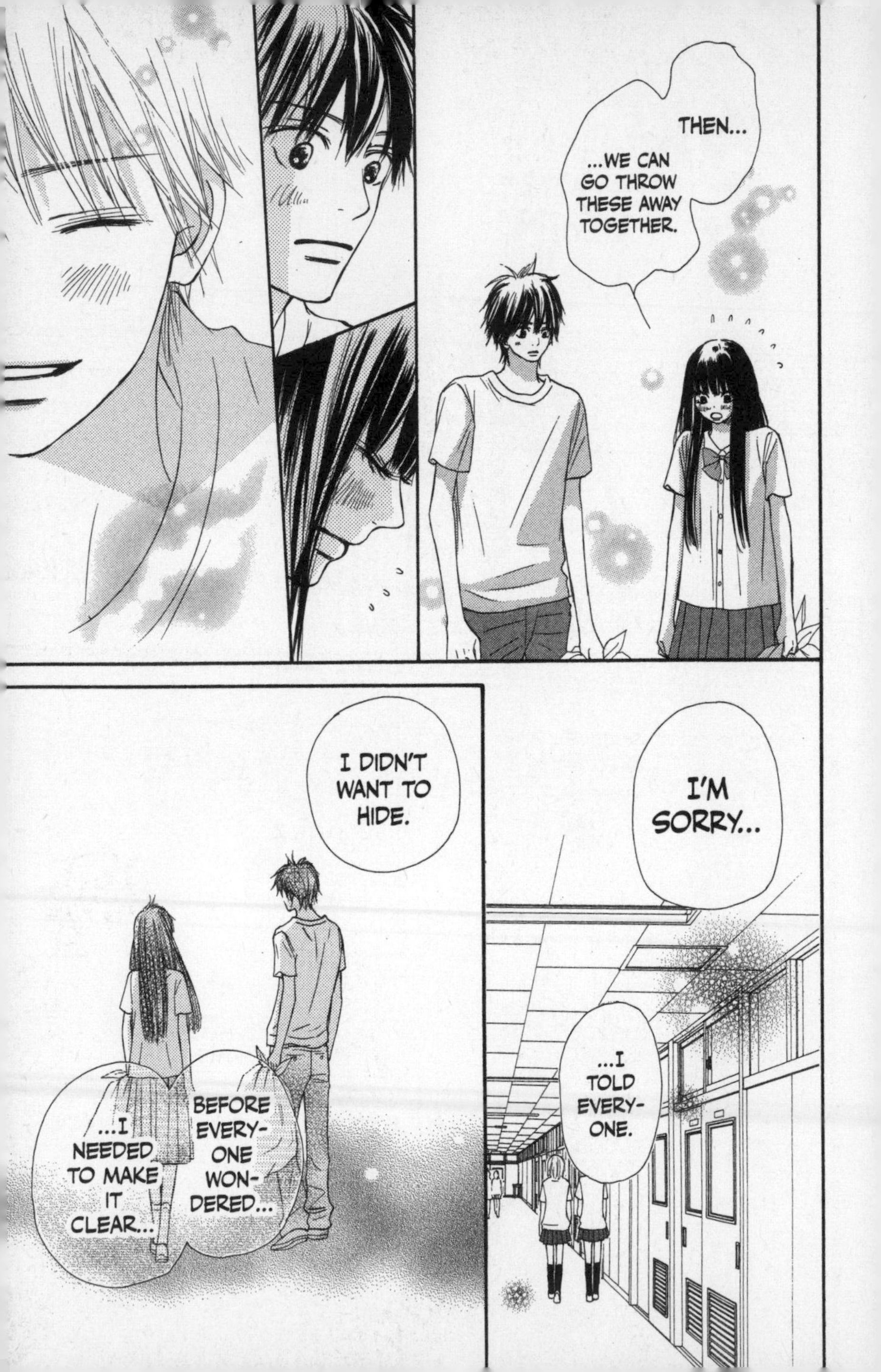
THEN...
...WE CAN GO THROW THESE AWAY TOGETHER.
I'M SORRY...
...I TOLD EVERY-ONE.
I DIDN'T WANT TO HIDE.
BEFORE EVERY-ONE WON-DERED...
...I NEEDED TO MAKE IT CLEAR...

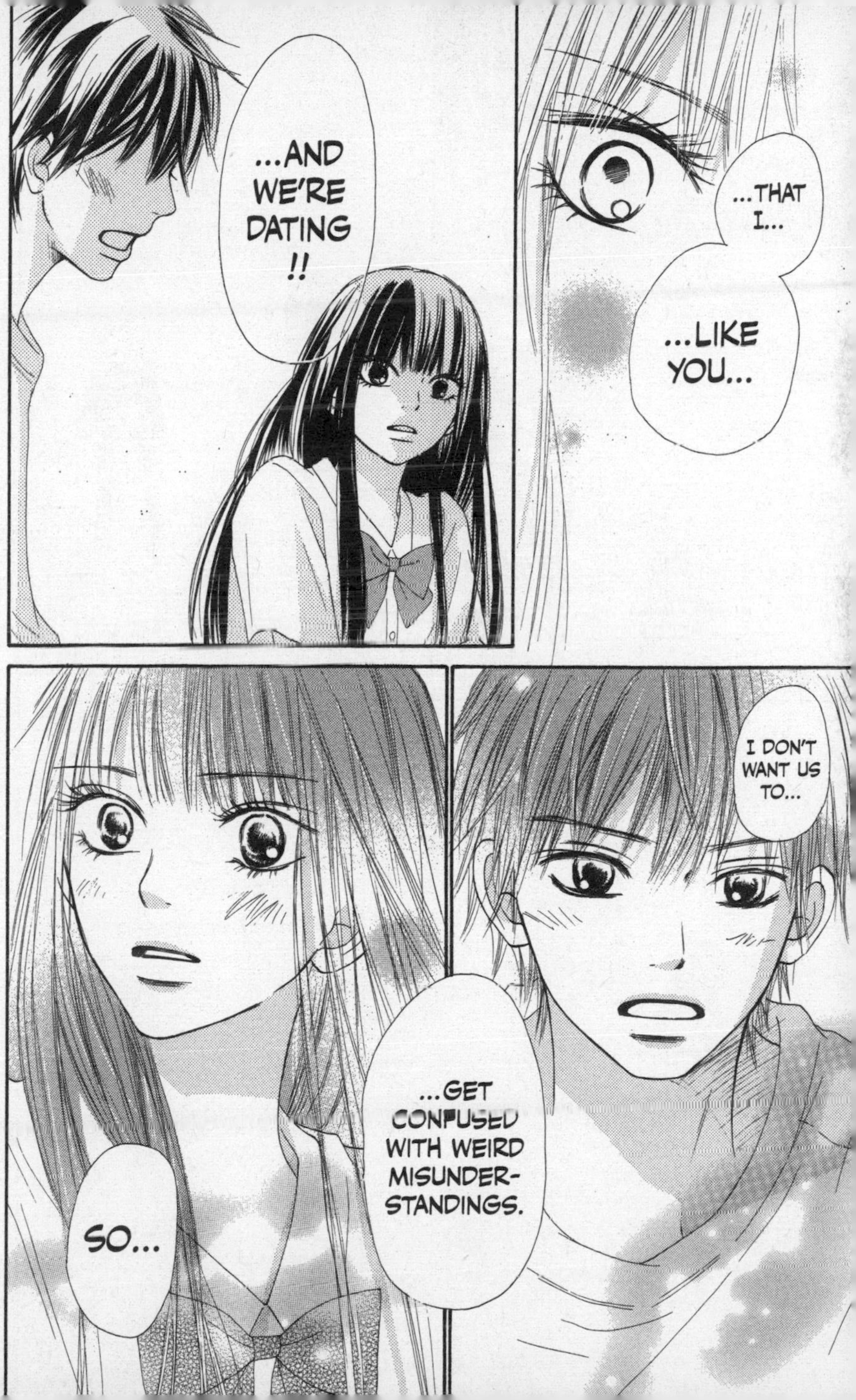
...THAT I...
...LIKE YOU...
...AND WE'RE DATING !!
I DON'T WANT US TO...
...GET CONFUSED WITH WEIRD MISUNDER-STANDINGS.
SO...

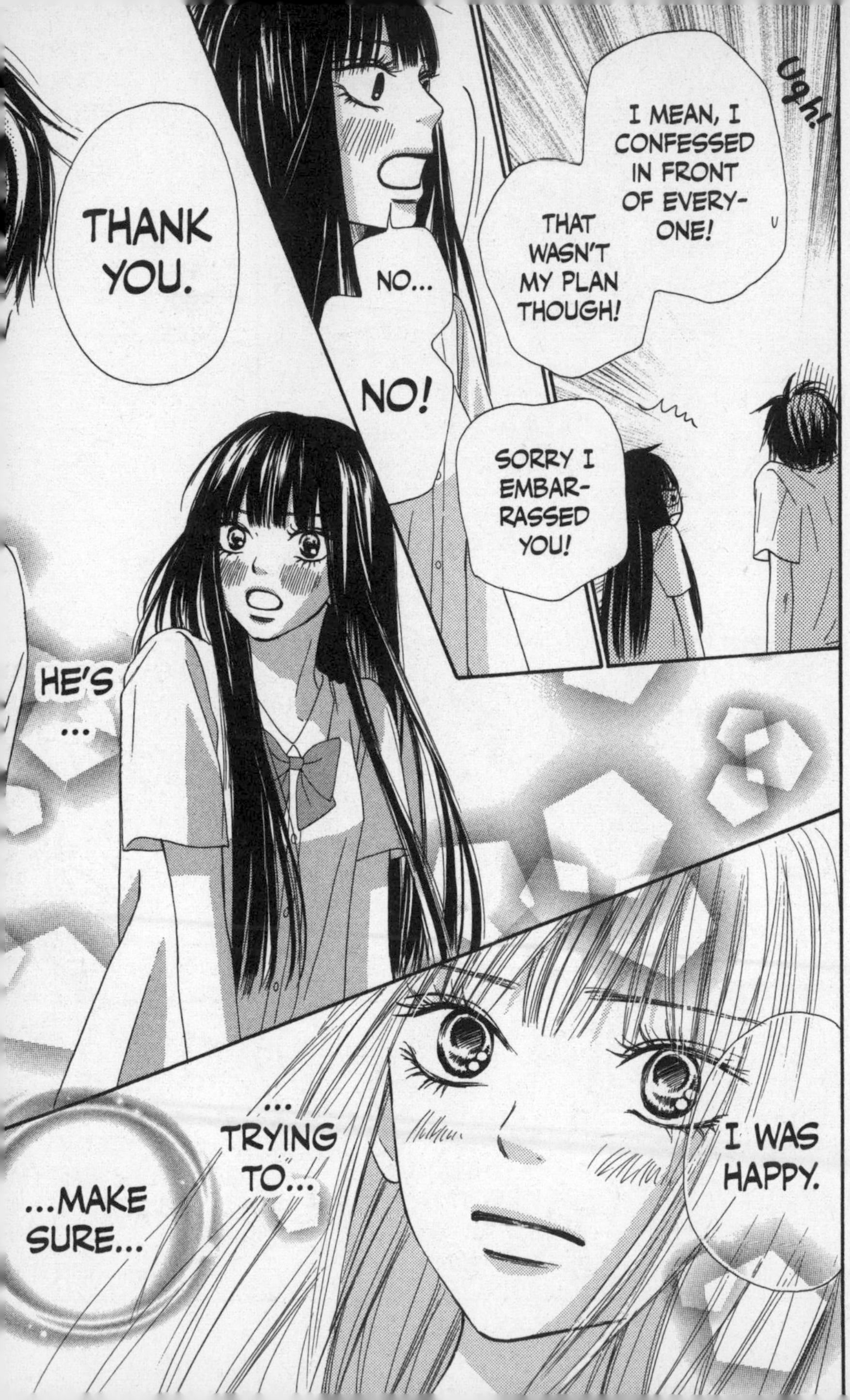
Ugh!
I MEAN, I CONFESSED IN FRONT OF EVERY-ONE!
THAT WASN'T MY PLAN THOUGH!
SORRY I EMBAR-RASSED YOU!
NO...
NO!
THANK YOU.
HE'S ...
I WAS HAPPY.
... TRYING TO...
...MAKE SURE...

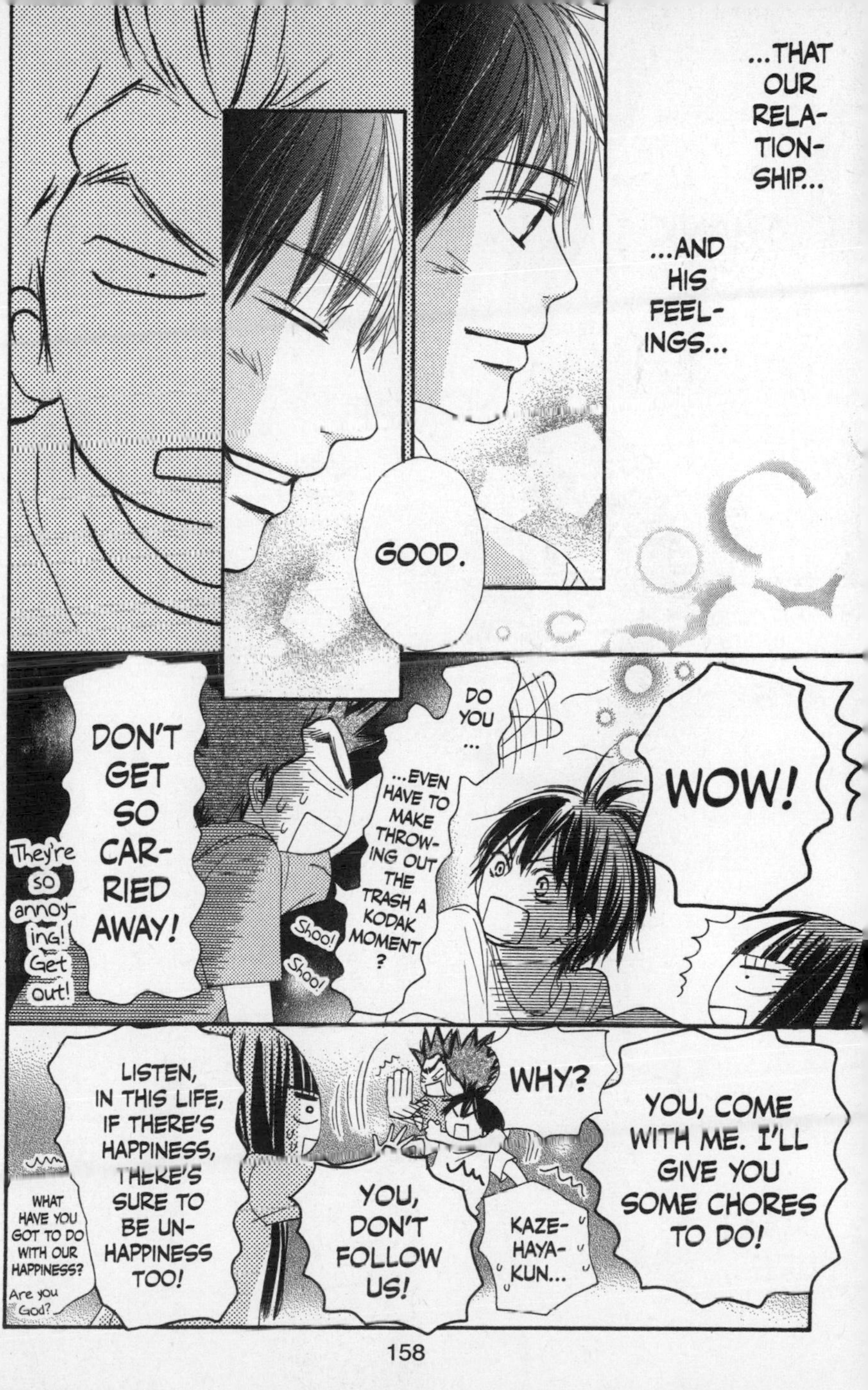
...THAT OUR RELATIONSHIP...
...AND HIS FEELINGS...
GOOD.
WOW!
DO YOU ...
...EVEN HAVE TO MAKE THROWING OUT THE TRASH A KODAK MOMENT?
Shoo! Shoo!
DON'T GET SO CARRIED AWAY!
They're so annoying! Get out!
YOU, COME WITH ME. I'LL GIVE YOU SOME CHORES TO DO!
WHY?
KAZEHAYA-KUN...
YOU, DON'T FOLLOW US!
LISTEN, IN THIS LIFE, IF THERE'S HAPPINESS, THERE'S SURE TO BE UNHAPPINESS TOO!
WHAT HAVE YOU GOT TO DO WITH OUR HAPPINESS?
Are you God?

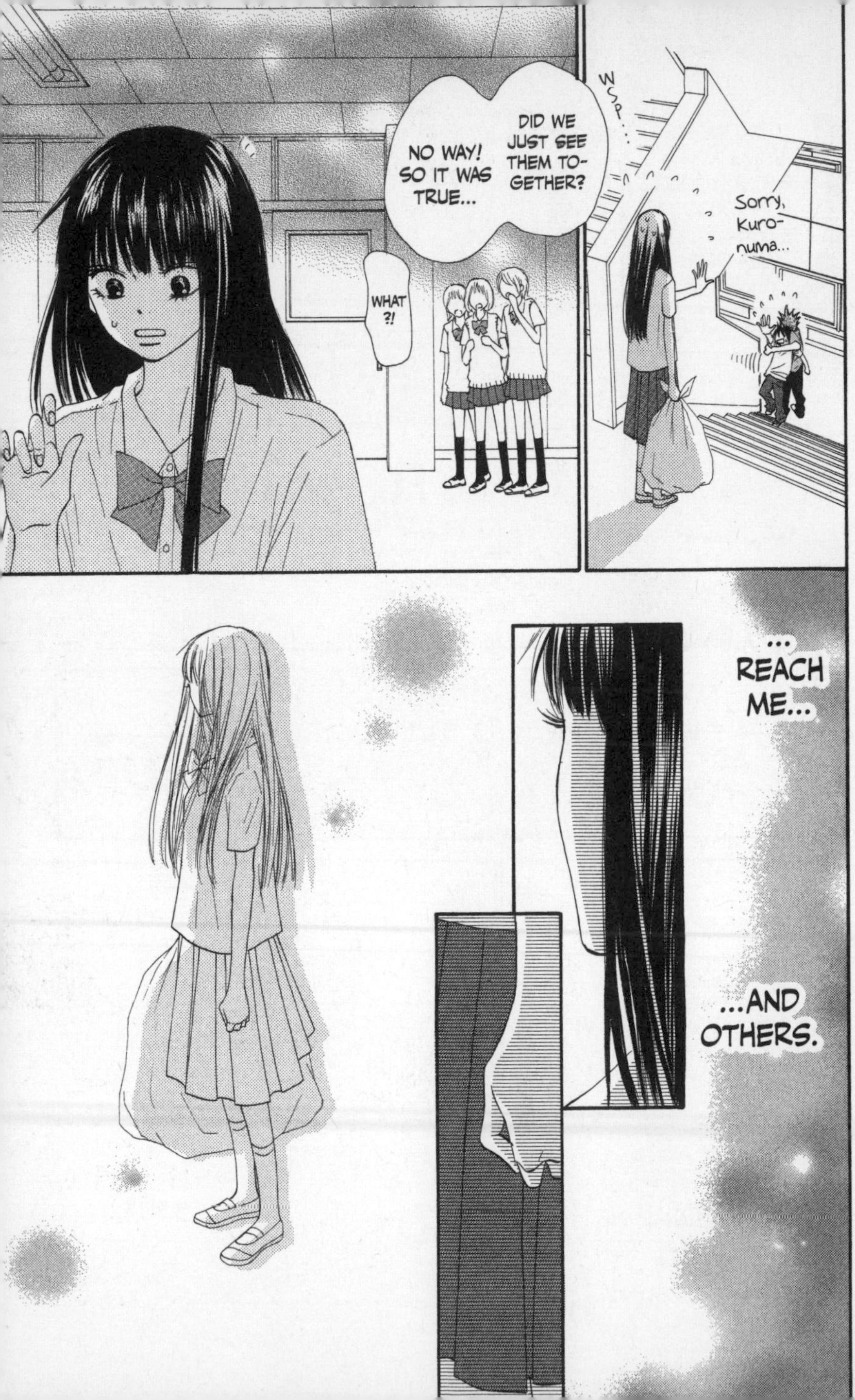
WSP...
Sorry, Kuro-numa...
DID WE JUST SEE THEM TO-GETHER?
NO WAY! SO IT WAS TRUE...
WHAT ?!
... REACH ME...
...AND OTHERS.

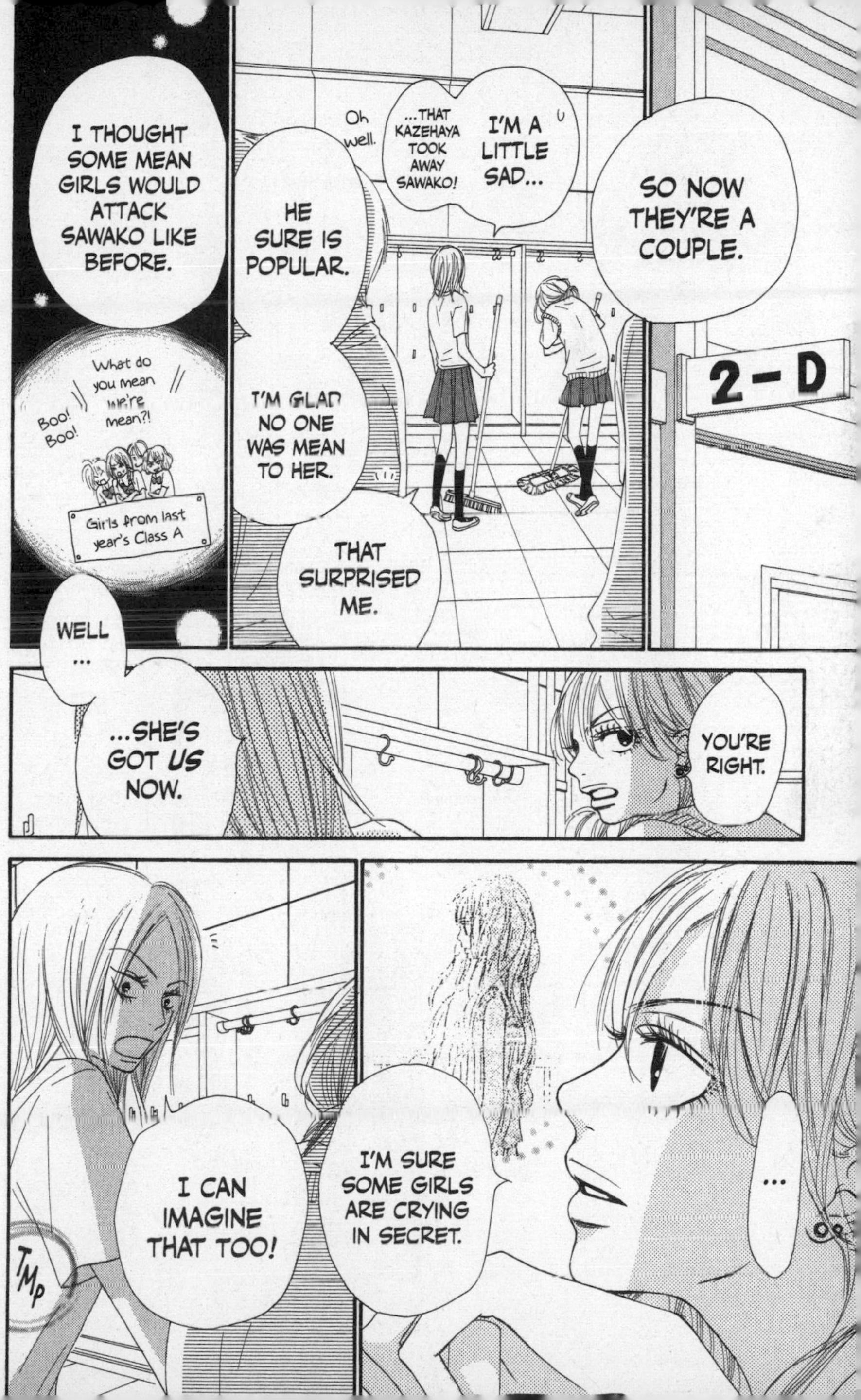
2-D
SO NOW THEY'RE A COUPLE.
I'M A LITTLE SAD...
...THAT KAZEHAYA TOOK AWAY SAWAKO!
Oh well.
HE SURE IS POPULAR.
I'M GLAD NO ONE WAS MEAN TO HER.
THAT SURPRISED ME.
I THOUGHT SOME MEAN GIRLS WOULD ATTACK SAWAKO LIKE BEFORE.
What do you mean we're mean?!
Boo! Boo!
Girls from last year's Class A
WELL ...
...SHE'S GOT US NOW.
YOU'RE RIGHT.
...
I'M SURE SOME GIRLS ARE CRYING IN SECRET.
I CAN IMAGINE THAT TOO!
TMP

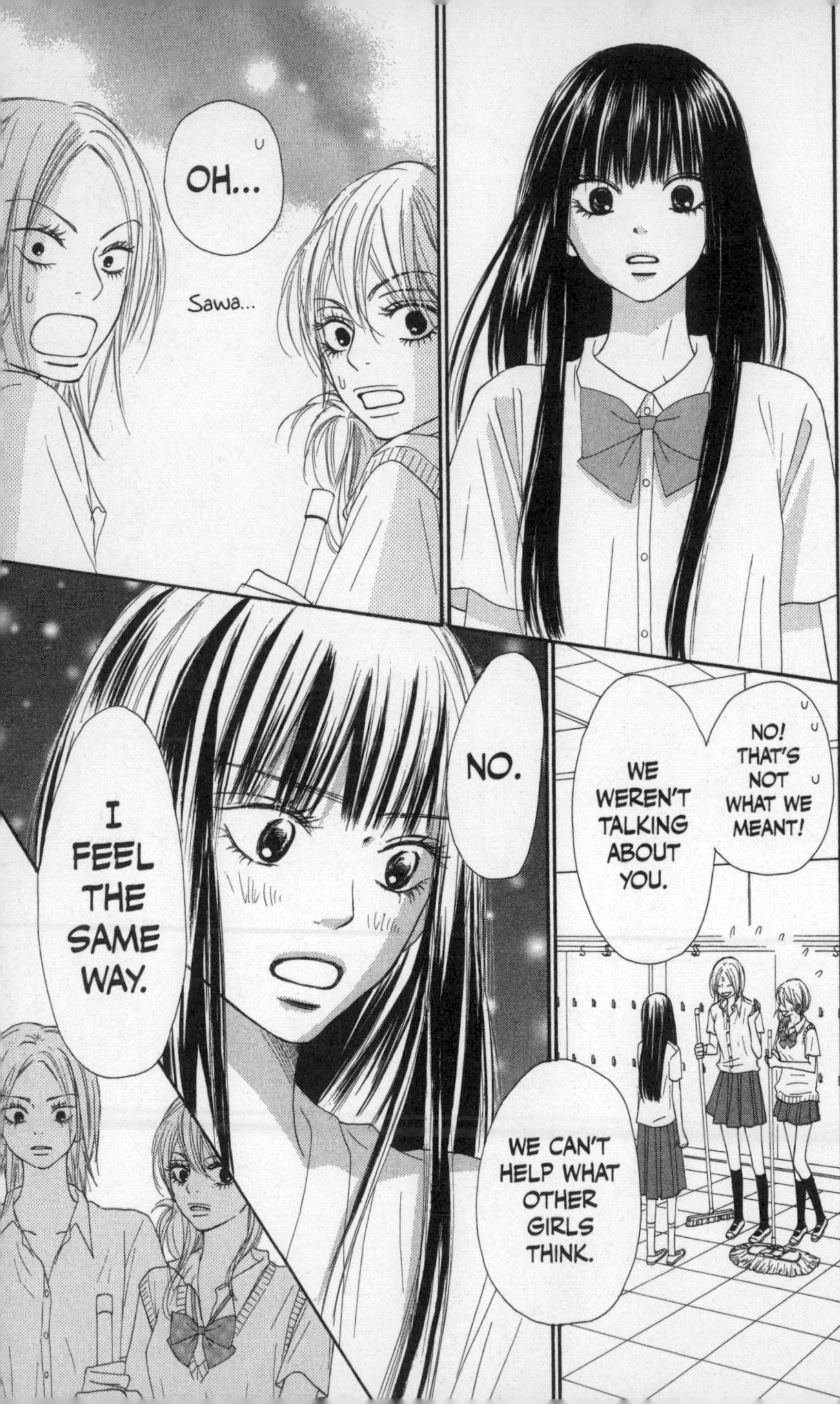
OH...
Sawa...
NO! THAT'S NOT WHAT WE MEANT!
WE WEREN'T TALKING ABOUT YOU.
WE CAN'T HELP WHAT OTHER GIRLS THINK.
NO.
I FEEL THE SAME WAY.

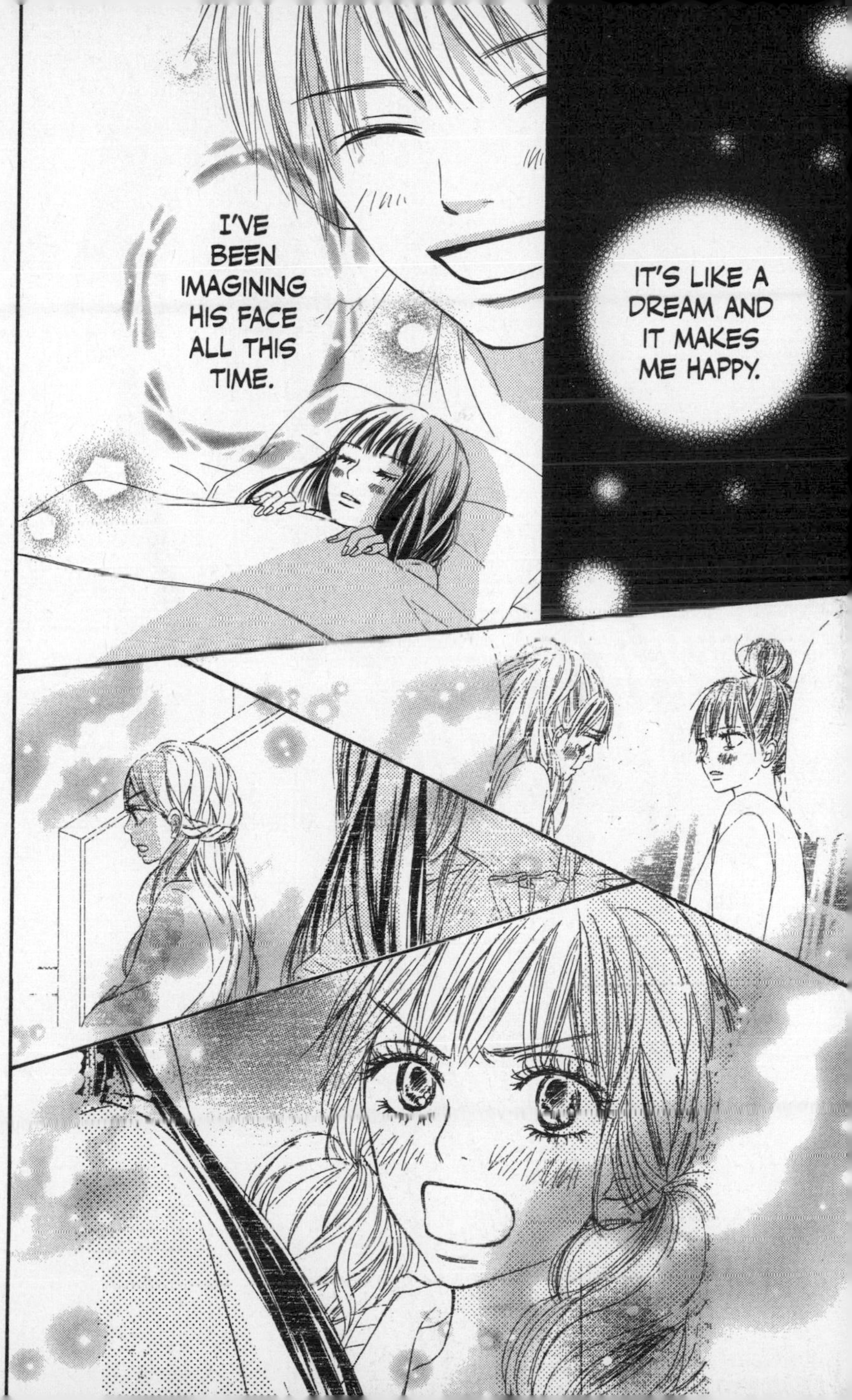
IT'S LIKE A DREAM AND IT MAKES ME HAPPY.
I'VE BEEN IMAGINING HIS FACE ALL THIS TIME.

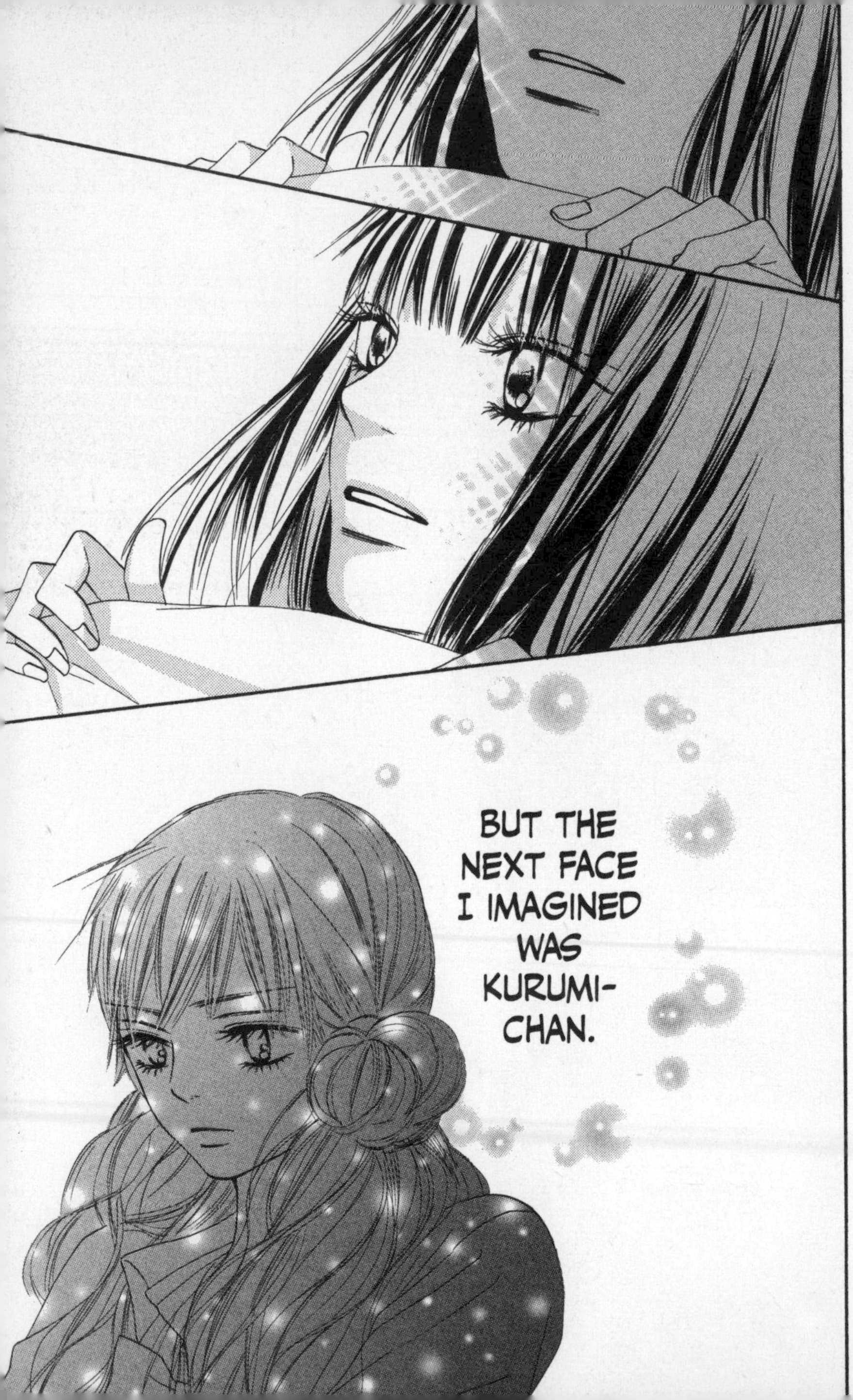
BUT THE NEXT FACE I IMAGINED WAS KURUMI-CHAN.

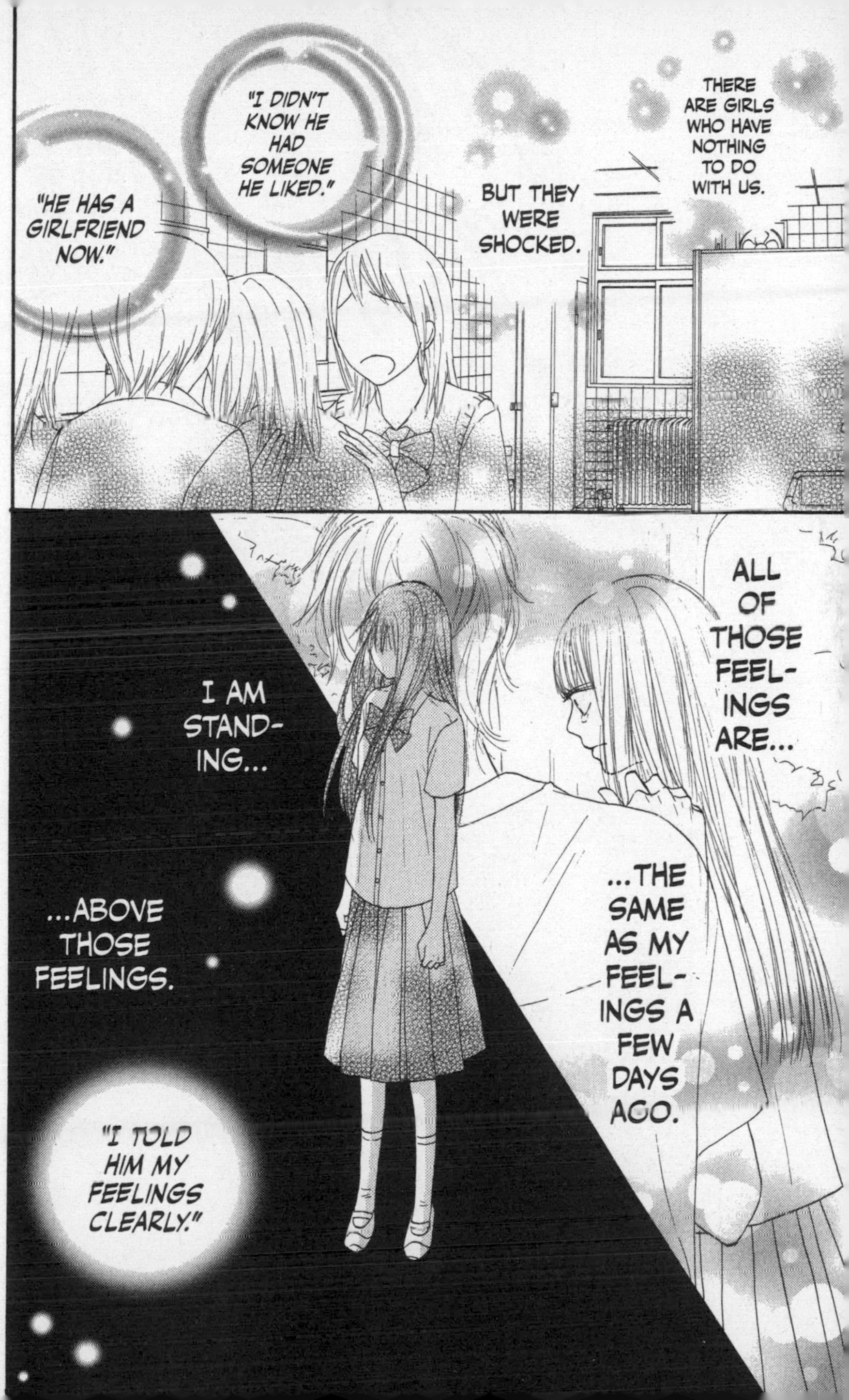
THERE ARE GIRLS WHO HAVE NOTHING TO DO WITH US.
BUT THEY WERE SHOCKED.
"I DIDN'T KNOW HE HAD SOMEONE HE LIKED."
"HE HAS A GIRLFRIEND NOW."
ALL OF THOSE FEEL-INGS ARE...
...THE SAME AS MY FEEL-INGS A FEW DAYS AGO.
I AM STAND-ING...
...ABOVE THOSE FEELINGS.
"I TOLD HIM MY FEELINGS CLEARLY."

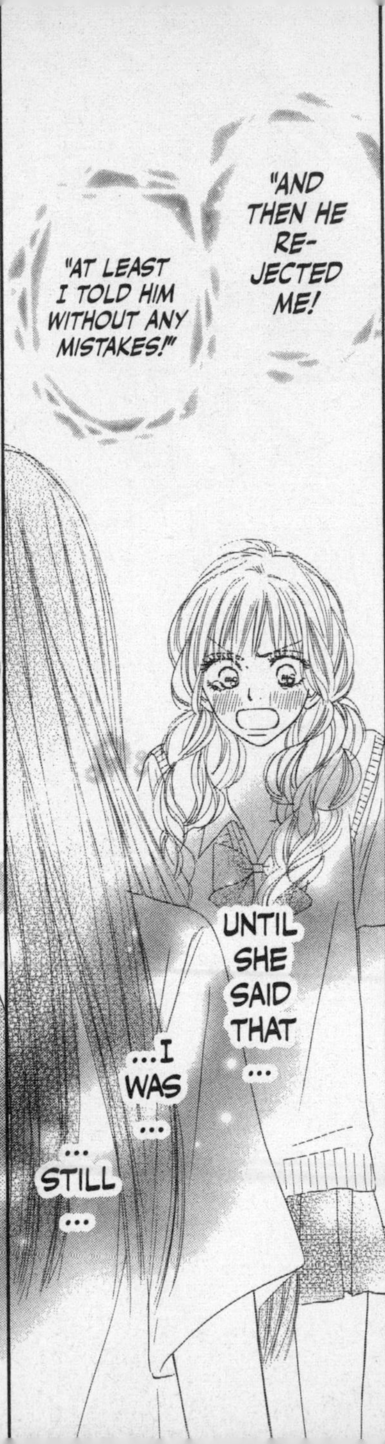
"AND THEN HE RE-JECTED ME!
"AT LEAST I TOLD HIM WITHOUT ANY MISTAKES!"
UNTIL SHE SAID THAT...
...I WAS...
...STILL...
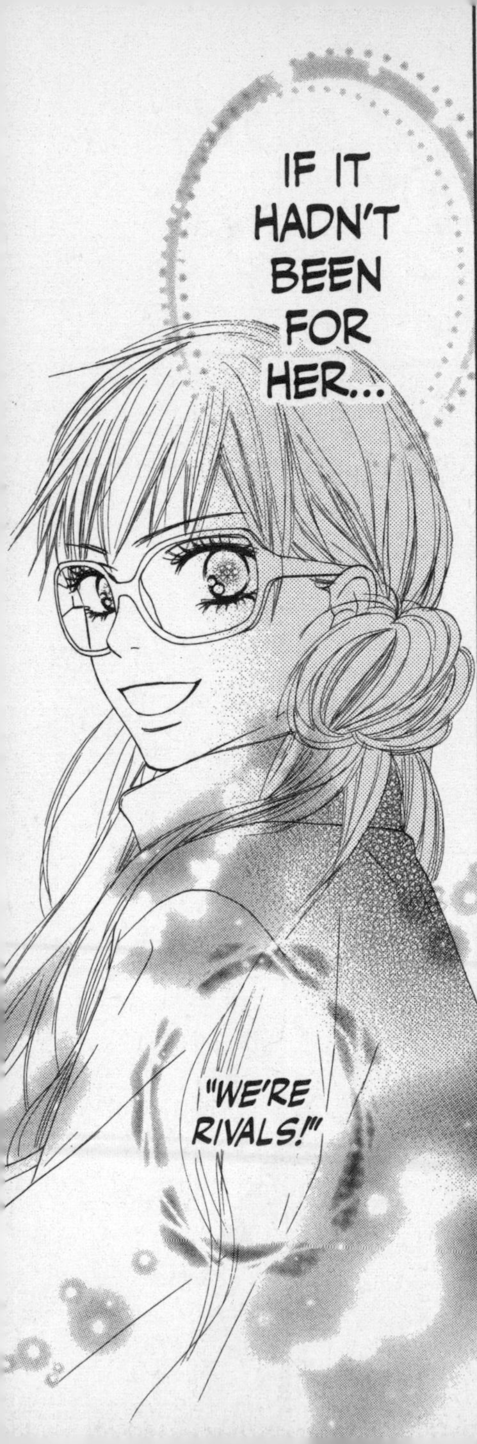
IF IT HADN'T BEEN FOR HER...
"WE'RE RIVALS!"

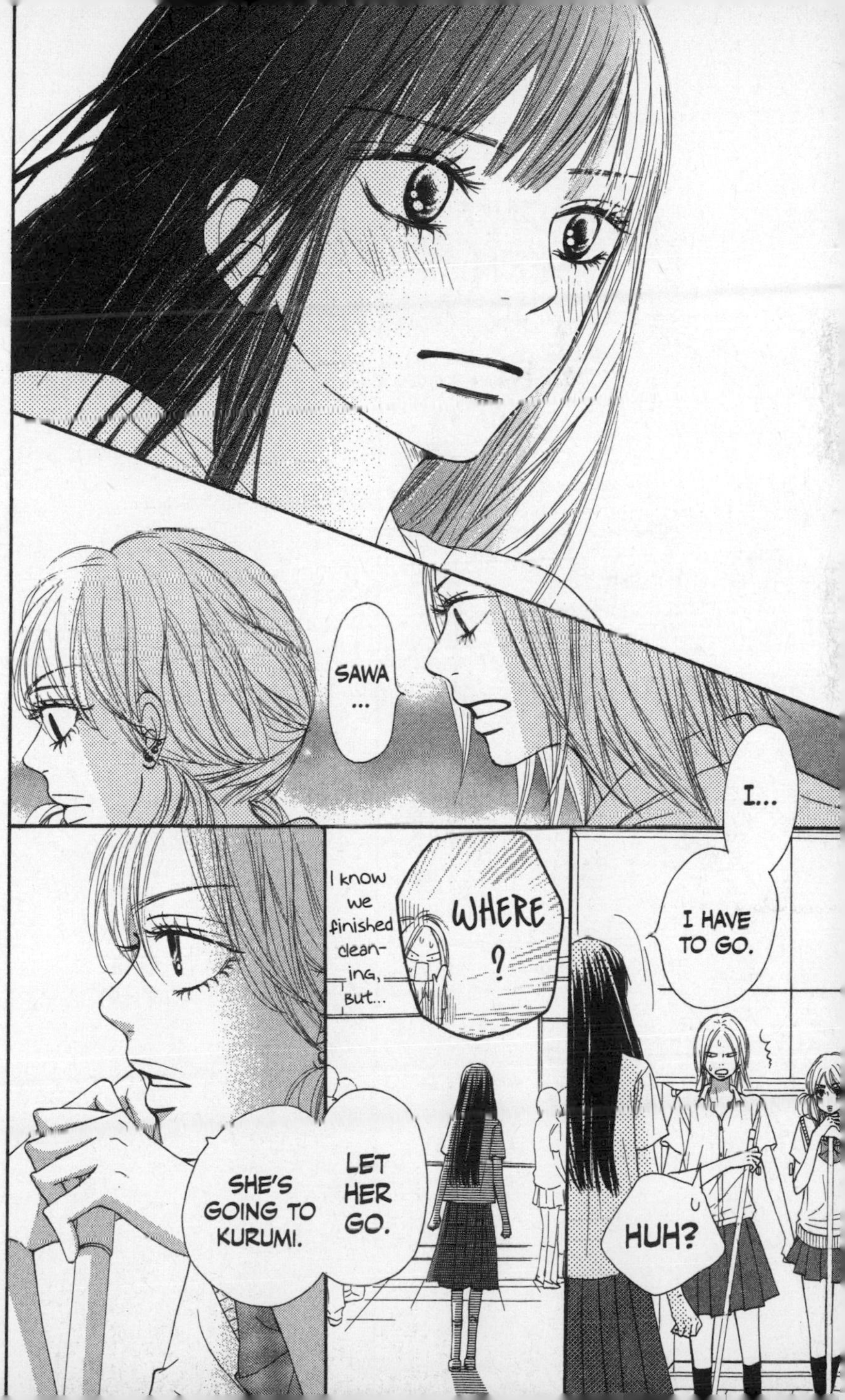
SAWA ...
I...
I HAVE TO GO.
HUH?
WHERE ?
I know we finished clean-ing, but...
LET HER GO.
SHE'S GOING TO KURUMI.

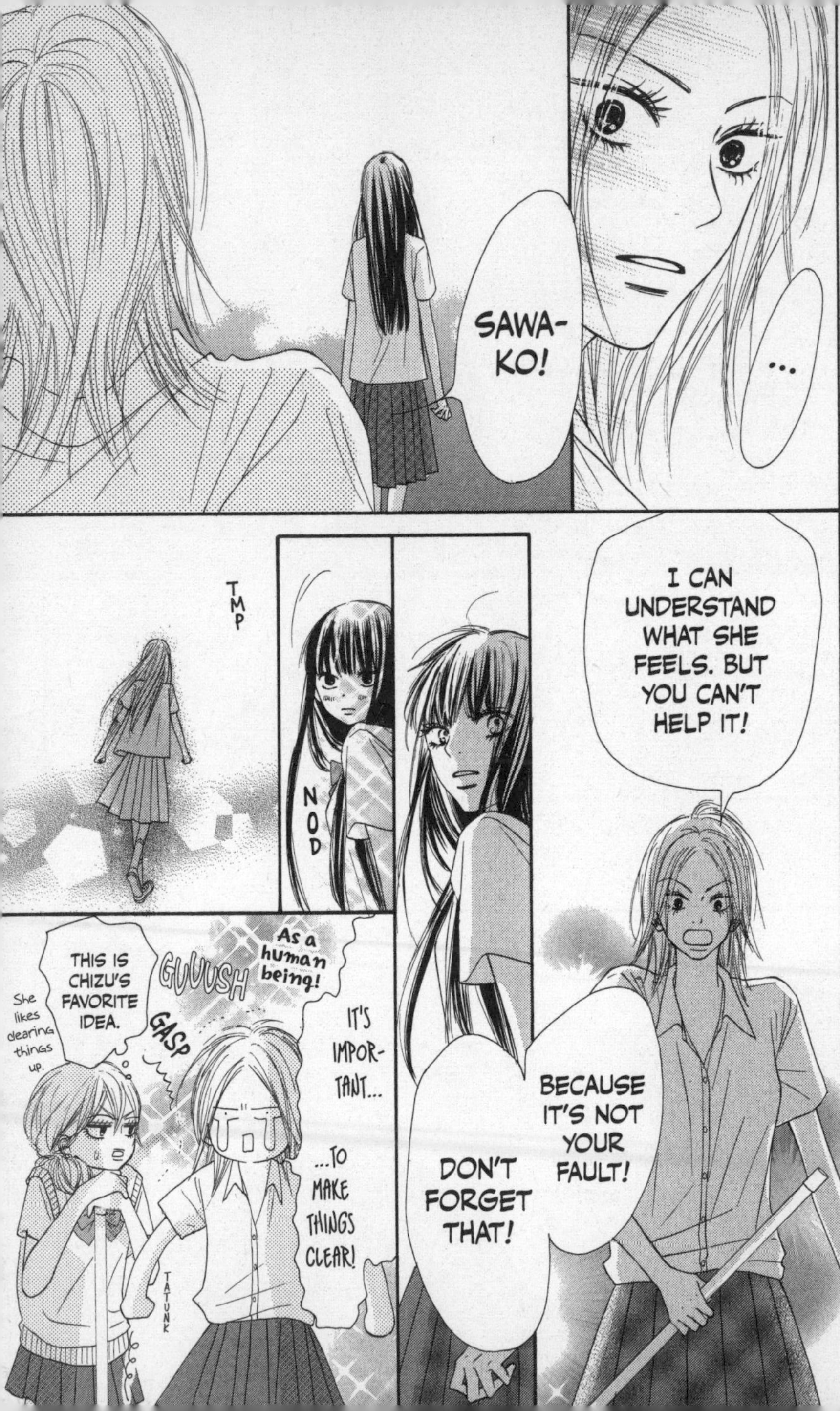
...
SAWA-KO!
I CAN UNDERSTAND WHAT SHE FEELS. BUT YOU CAN'T HELP IT!
BECAUSE IT'S NOT YOUR FAULT!
DON'T FORGET THAT!
NOD
TMP
As a human being!
GUUUSH
GASP
IT'S IMPOR-TANT...
...TO MAKE THINGS CLEAR!
THIS IS CHIZU'S FAVORITE IDEA.
She likes clearing things up.
TATUNK

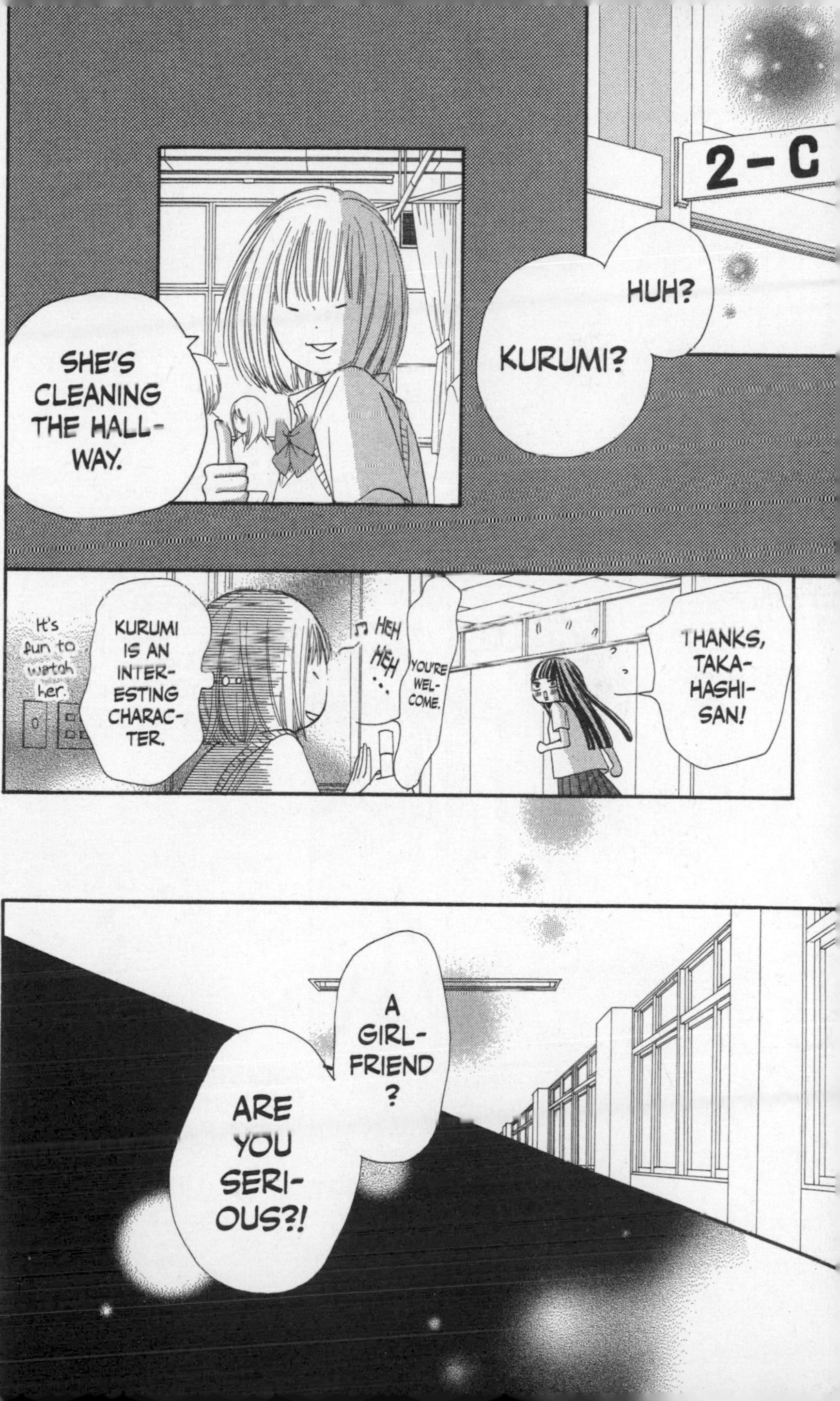
2-C
HUH?
KURUMI?
SHE'S CLEANING THE HALL-WAY.
THANKS, TAKA-HASHI-SAN!
YOU'RE WEL-COME.
HEH HEH...
KURUMI IS AN INTER-ESTING CHARAC-TER.
It's fun to watch her.
A GIRL-FRIEND?
ARE YOU SERI-OUS?!

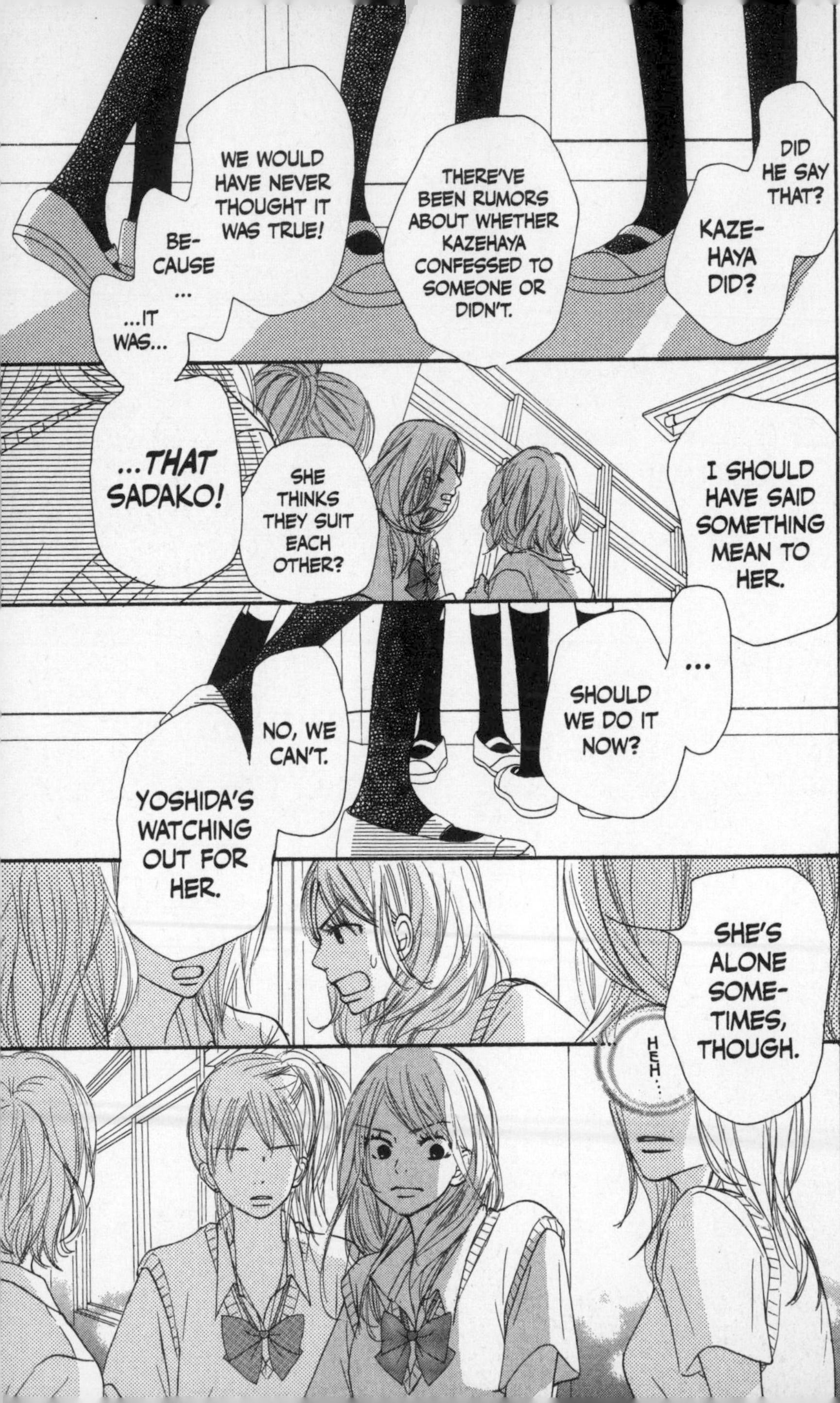
DID HE SAY THAT?
KAZE-HAYA DID?
THERE'VE BEEN RUMORS ABOUT WHETHER KAZEHAYA CONFESSED TO SOMEONE OR DIDN'T.
WE WOULD HAVE NEVER THOUGHT IT WAS TRUE!
BE-CAUSE ...
...IT WAS...
...*THAT* SADAKO!
I SHOULD HAVE SAID SOMETHING MEAN TO HER.
SHE THINKS THEY SUIT EACH OTHER?
...
SHOULD WE DO IT NOW?
NO, WE CAN'T.
YOSHIDA'S WATCHING OUT FOR HER.
SHE'S ALONE SOME-TIMES, THOUGH.
HEH...

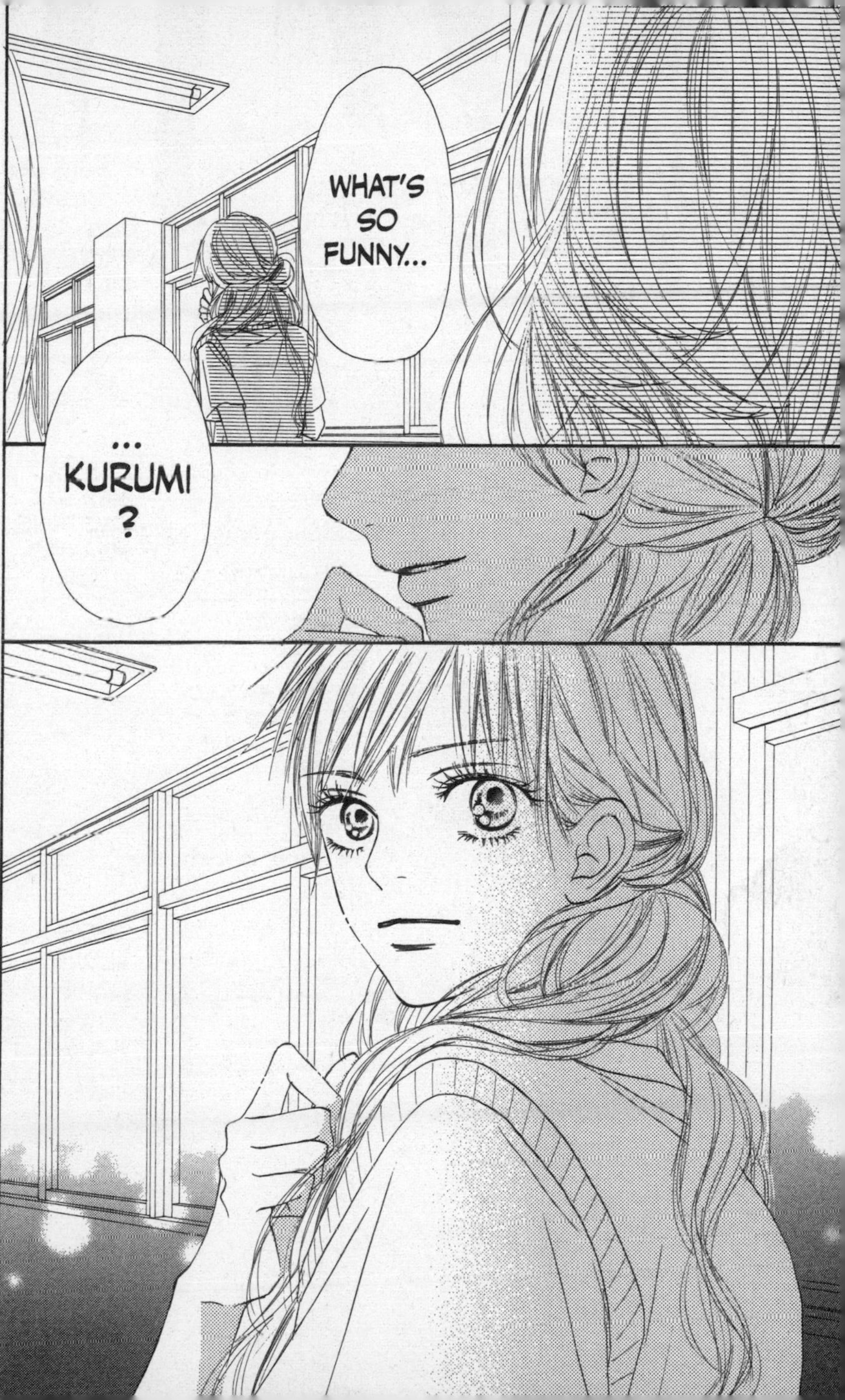
WHAT'S SO FUNNY...
... KURUMI ?

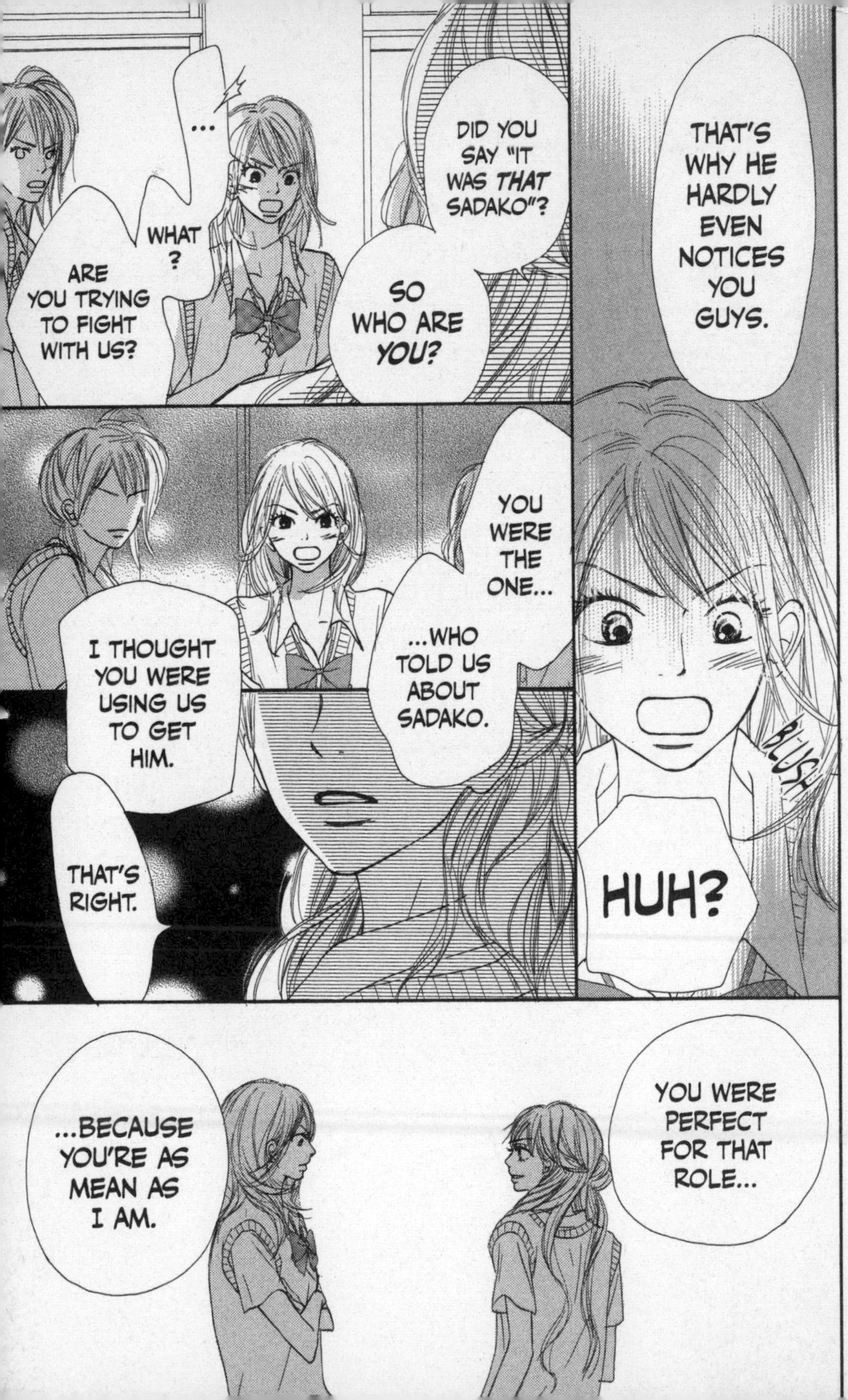
THAT'S WHY HE HARDLY EVEN NOTICES YOU GUYS.
BLUSH
HUH?
DID YOU SAY "IT WAS *THAT* SADAKO"?
SO WHO ARE *YOU*?
...
WHAT?
ARE YOU TRYING TO FIGHT WITH US?
YOU WERE THE ONE...
...WHO TOLD US ABOUT SADAKO.
I THOUGHT YOU WERE USING US TO GET HIM.
THAT'S RIGHT.
YOU WERE PERFECT FOR THAT ROLE...
...BECAUSE YOU'RE AS MEAN AS I AM.

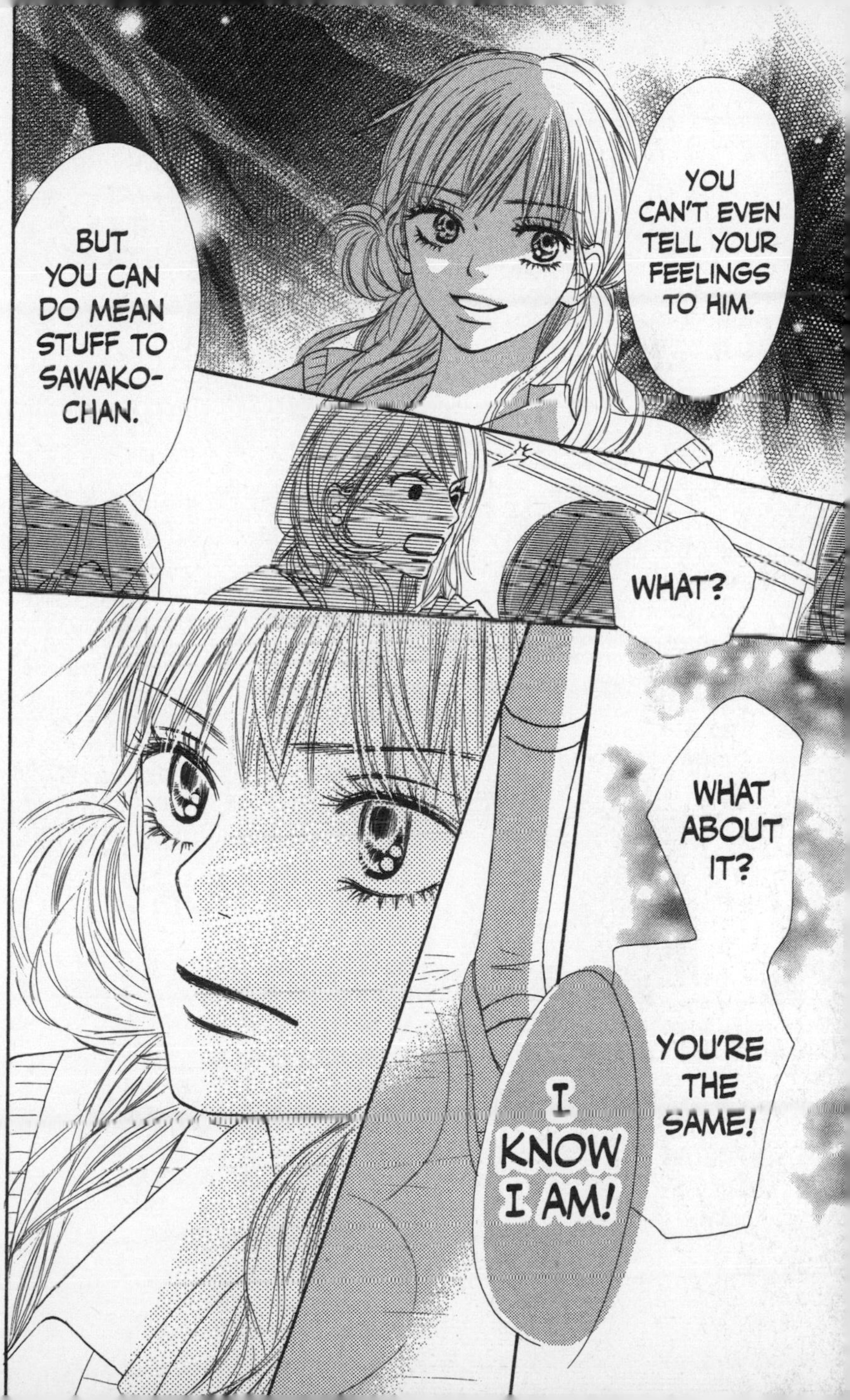
YOU CAN'T EVEN TELL YOUR FEELINGS TO HIM.
BUT YOU CAN DO MEAN STUFF TO SAWAKO-CHAN.
WHAT?
WHAT ABOUT IT?
YOU'RE THE SAME!
I KNOW I AM!

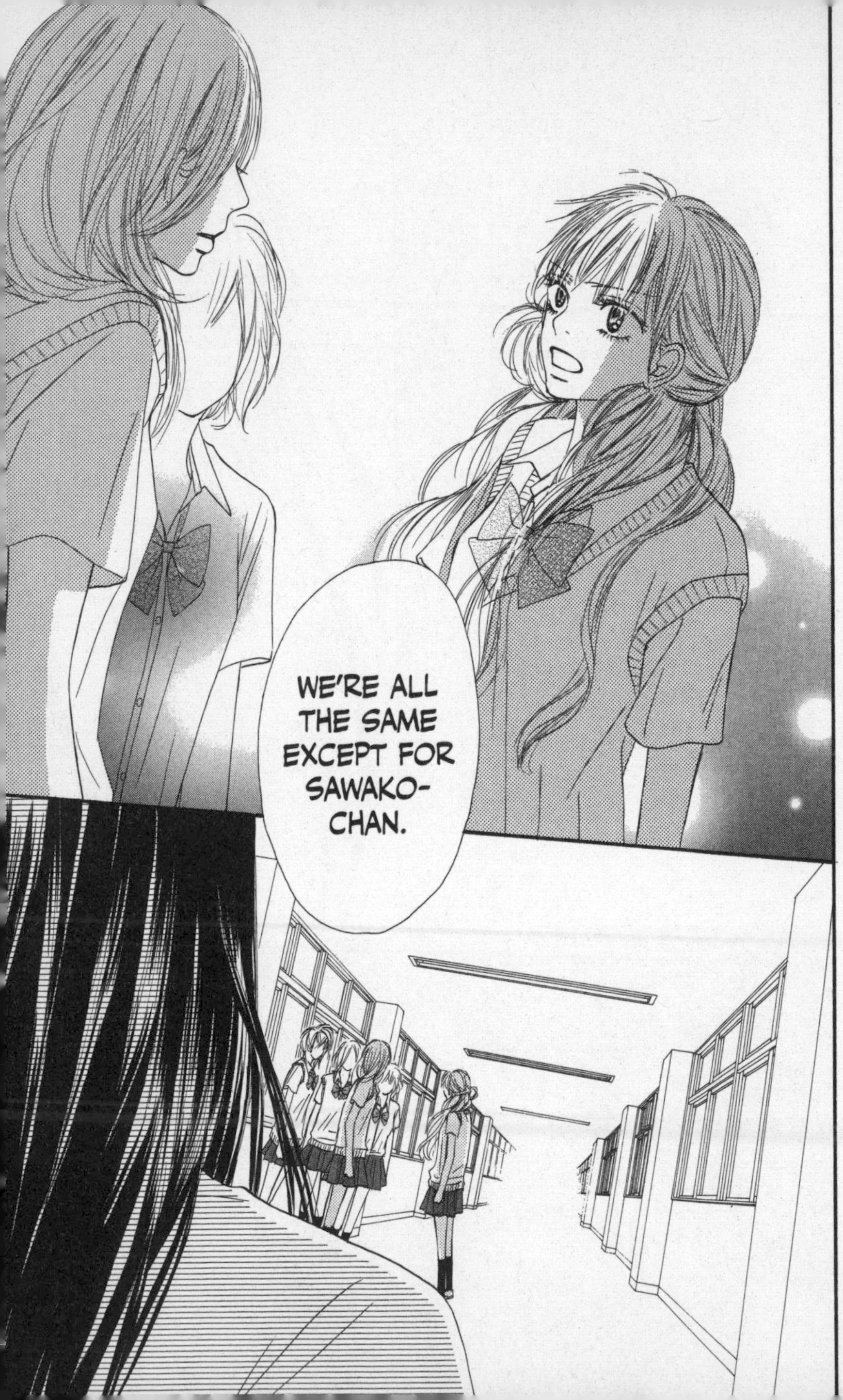
WE'RE ALL THE SAME EXCEPT FOR SAWAKO-CHAN.

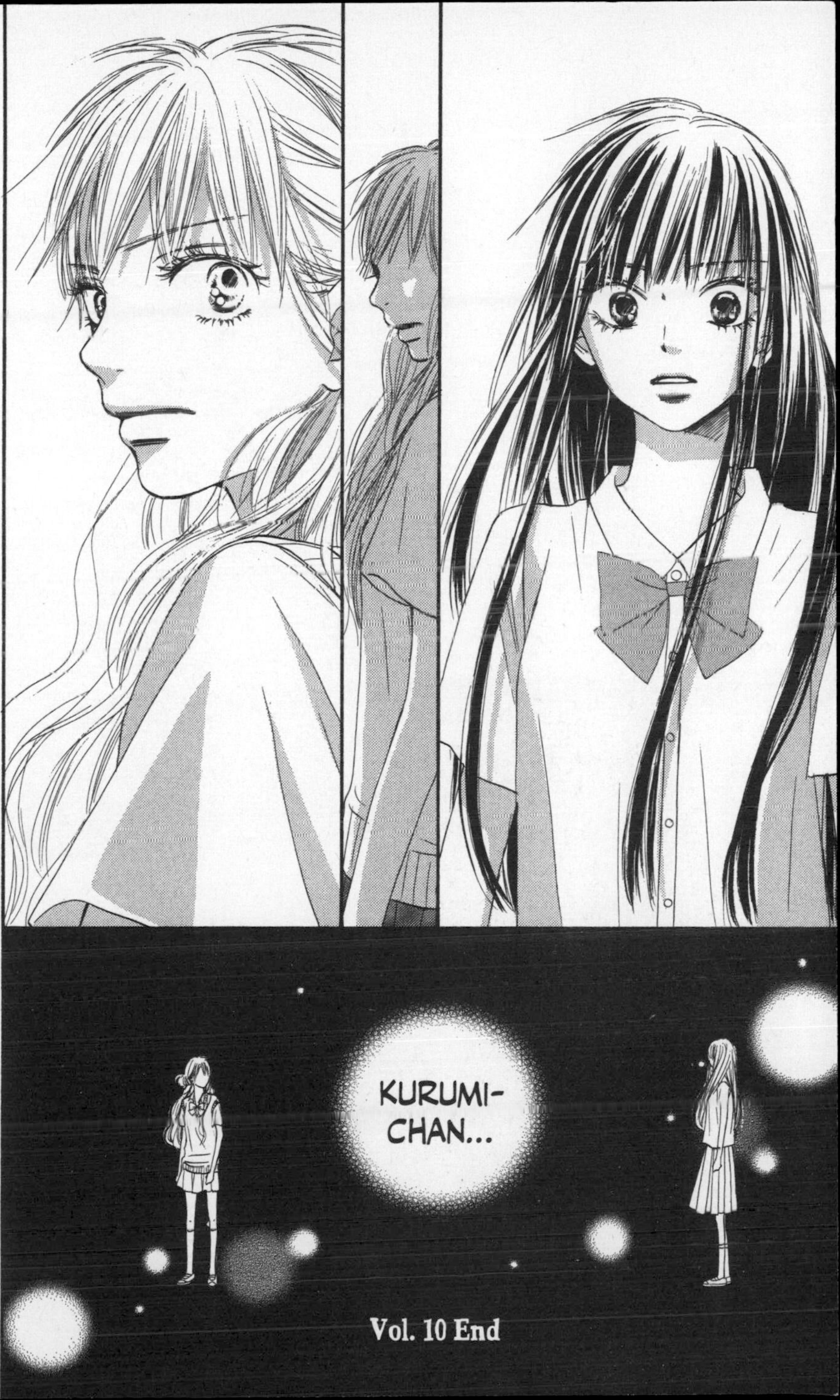
KURUMI-
CHAN...
Vol. 10 End

From me (the editor) to you (the reader).

Here are some Japanese culture explanations that will help you better understand the references in the *Kimi ni Todoke* world.

Honorifics:
When saying someone's name in Japanese, a suffix is often attached to indicate how familiar the speaker is with the person. Some are more polite and respectful, while others are endearing. Calling someone by just their first name is the most informal.
-*kun* is used for young men or boys, usually someone you are familiar with.
-*chan* is used for young women, girls or young children and can be used as a term of endearment.
-*san* is used for someone you respect or are not close to, or to be polite.

Page 43, Igoyoshinani, Persona, Velvet Room:
The Velvet Room and "igoyoshinani" are from the anime *Persona*. One of the characters often says, "igoyoshinani," which roughly means, "Please regard me faithfully from now on."

Page 43, Tokuho logo:
In Japan medicinal foods go through an approval process and are marked with the logo for Tokuho (Tokutei Hokenyo Shokuhin / Foods for Specified Health Use). The logo features a jumping stick figure.

Page 62, Okiku in *Sarayashiki*:
A popular Japanese ghost story, *Bancho Sarayashiki* is about a servant named Okiku who is killed, but because of a grudge comes back to haunt her former employer.

Page 63, Talisman:
Joe is dressed as an *ofuda*, a type of talisman issued by temples and shrines. In Japanese, his costume reads "Namu Amida Butsu," which is a prayer that means to "Hail to Amitābha Buddha."

Page 105, Harajuku Jack:
The author is referring to an event in the Harajuku section of Tokyo that commemorated the premiere of the *Kimi ni Todoke* anime. The "hijacking" included a café, a stamp rally for participants to visit booths and collect stamps in a booklet, and a gallery dedicated to *Kimi ni Todoke*.

Page 105, Chara-san:
Chara is the artist who sings the *Kimi ni Todoke* anime ending theme, "Kataomoi."

Page 110, Ginkoi:
"Ginkoi" is short for "Ginza no Koi no Monogatari," a duet sung by Yujiro Ishihara and Junko Makimura. The song's name means "A Story of Love in Ginza."

Page 111, Izakaya:
"Izakaya" is an enka duet sung by Hiroshi Itsuki and Nana Kinomi. An *izakaya* is a Japanese-style pub.

It's already volume 10! What a nice round number! And part of the story itself is settling down! While I was working on volume 10, a lot happened in both my professional and personal life. So much happened that it doesn't even seem real. My editor and I often talk about what has happened, saying, "It doesn't seem real..." and "No, it doesn't seem real..." Was it real? No, it wasn't. Or... was it? No, it wasn't.

--Karuho Shiina

Karuho Shiina was born and raised in Hokkaido, Japan. Though *Kimi ni Todoke* is only her second series following many one-shot stories, it has already racked up accolades from various "Best Manga of the Year" lists. Winner of the 2008 Kodansha Manga Award for the shojo category, *Kimi ni Todoke* also placed fifth in the first-ever Manga Taisho (Cartoon Grand Prize) contest in 2008. In Japan, an animated TV series debuted in October 2009, and a live-action film was released in 2010.

Kimi ni Todoke
VOL. 10

Shojo Beat Edition

STORY AND ART BY
KARUHO SHIINA

Translation/Ari Yasuda, HC Language Solutions, Inc.
Touch-up Art & Lettering/Vanessa Satone
Design/Nozomi Akashi
Editor/Carrie Shepherd

KIMI NI TODOKE © 2005 by Karuho Shiina
All rights reserved. First published in Japan in 2005 by SHUEISHA Inc.,
Tokyo. English translation rights arranged by SHUEISHA Inc.

The stories, characters and incidents mentioned
in this publication are entirely fictional.

Printed in the U.S.A.

Published by VIZ Media, LLC
P.O. Box 77010
San Francisco, CA 94107

10 9 8 7 6 5 4 3 2
First printing, September 2011
Second printing, November 2014

PARENTAL ADVISORY
KIMI NI TODOKE is rated T for
Teen and is recommended
for ages 13 and up.
ratings.viz.com

www.viz.com

www.shojobeat.com